Remedial Reading

TEACHING AND TREATMENT

REMEDIAL READING

Teaching and Treatment

MAURICE D. WOOLF, Ed.D.

Professor of Education, Kansas State College

JEANNE A. WOOLF, M.A.

McGRAW-HILL BOOK COMPANY, INC.

New York   Toronto   London

1957

REMEDIAL READING: TEACHING AND TREATMENT

Library of Congress Catalog Card Number 57-6413

6 7 8 9 10 11 12 - MP - 9 8 7 6

71885

THE MAPLE PRESS COMPANY, YORK, PA.

Preface

This book presents to the reader the philosophy and theory behind the program of remedial reading. It tries to assemble a body of psychological fact in such a way as to seem meaningful to those engaged in work with students. The techniques described are those that have been found useful in the authors' classes and clinical work. Considerable emphasis is put on the role of emotion in the reading process. The techniques used to help resolve the emotional problem are explored and illustrated through case study. The system of motivation is brought to bear on the student through class routine, counseling, group techniques, and group therapy. The outcomes of this approach to remedial reading are shown by the authors' research in many instances.

This book can be used as a text in such courses as Diagnostic and Remedial Techniques in Reading, The Psychology of Reading, Developmental Reading, Motivation and Reading, and as a supplemental text in other teaching of reading courses. English teachers in Kansas have shown a marked pre-publication interest in this book, both in their state teachers' meetings and workshops. It would be useful as a reference in the standard course in the teaching of English in the secondary school. In many instances the English Department takes the responsibility for improving the reading skills of students in the secondary school. Psychological and educational reading clinics would find it quite helpful.

MAURICE D. WOOLF
JEANNE A. WOOLF

Contents

CHAPTER 1

Nature and Scope of Reading Problems

"Viewing with alarm" the deficiencies of today's readers is a popular pastime. Some of the popular magazine articles leave mistaken impressions about the nature of our educational problems, and some include misstatements of fact. In spite of perennial attacks upon the public schools, there is mounting evidence that they have made notable progress in the past 10 or 15 years.[1] To be perfectly honest, however, we must agree that there is still room for improvement.

Erroneous conclusions can also be drawn from professional works on the teaching of reading. For example, the retarded reader is often described as any student whose scores on standardized reading tests rank him one or more years below the national average for his age and grade. This definition of reading disability fails to distinguish between the individual who is reading about as well as his ability will permit and the student whose reading skills are decidedly inferior to his level of general ability.

Some writers concentrate on a single causal factor: a physical disability, eye span, eye fixations, lack of training in phonics. Some present a single technique with the result that their followers are inclined to interpret it as a cure-all. The teaching of reading is frequently treated as if it were an operation which can be separated from psychological principles and from the teaching of other verbal skills.

This book will be principally concerned with a reading program designed for elementary-school, high-school, and college students whose reading skills rank appreciably below the level of their scholastic aptitude. Methods and techniques will be offered in terms of multicausal factors and psychological principles. Because the laws of learning apply

[1] Bloom, B. S., "The Normative Study of the Test of General Educational Development," *School Rev.*, March, 1956, pp. 110–124.

1

to the learning of reading skills, some attention will be given to the learning process. Reading is a function of the whole personality. Therefore, a section of the book will be devoted to the interrelationships between reading performance and personal development. Reading ability will be discussed as one of a constellation of related communicative skills, including speaking, writing, spelling, etc. Experimental evidence will be offered in support of teaching methods described. Reading materials, equipment, teaching aids, and evaluative techniques will be cited. Hints for in-service training of teachers will be given. Sample case studies will illustrate the processes of diagnosis, treatment, and evaluation of progress, as well as changes in personal adjustment which accompany improvement in reading skills. Classroom discussion and leadership techniques will be presented in relation to reading for meaning and for critical analysis. Much of the material included regarding personality dynamics and methods of teaching apply to the learning situation in any classroom.

The techniques of developing sight vocabulary, word-attack skills, facility with phonics, and the like will not be discussed in detail. A work of encyclopedic proportions would be required to cover previous studies and volumes on the techniques of teaching beginning reading. It is necessary to assume that teachers are already familiar with classroom procedures presented by such writers as Gray, Gates, Adams, Bond, and others, or that they will acquaint themselves with these contributions if they feel the need to do so. The emphasis in this book will be upon newer techniques and upon reading as a facet of human development.

We shall attempt to treat the subject of developmental reading in the context of the total school program and in the larger context of a democratic society which demands literacy. Reading proficiency is virtually a requirement for participation in government, for vocational success, and for social acceptability.

Before taking a look at the national educational scene, would you like to meet some students with a reading problem? Bob had little trouble with high-school classes, and it was the surprise of his life when he found he could not complete required reading for college classes. Entrance test results ranked him in the upper 25 per cent of his class in scholastic ability, but closer examination of his scores revealed that his tested quantitative ability exceeded linguistic ability by 23 percentile points, and his scores in the reading test placed him in the lower 10 per cent of his class. With an alert mind and a charming smile, he had coasted along easily in his small high school, but college classwork is another story.

Stanley, on the other hand, felt worthless and depressed, convinced of his inadequacy for competition in college work. Even his teachers did not suspect that he ranked better than 78 per cent of his classmates in quantitative ability. His reading scores fell in the lower 15 per cent of his class.

By their scores on general scholastic-aptitude tests, these students demonstrate a potential for improvement. Their problems are not isolated. More than 300 college freshman, or about one-fourth of their class, manifested similar problems. This number was in addition to the usual proportion of students whose low reading scores were consistent with inferior scholastic ability. Such data give some idea of the extent of reading problems. Previous writers have made mention of the percentage of public-school pupils who ranked beneath their age-grade level in reading skill, but often failed to take notice of those whose reading performance lags behind general ability. The movement toward "developmental reading," led by William Gray, involves adequate provision for reading growth of all pupils consistent with their academic potentials, extending instruction into the upper grades, high school, and college. Rather than lumping all poor readers together, regardless of potential, the trend is toward careful study of individual strengths, weaknesses, and possibilities for improvement.

Public concern over the teaching of reading has mounted in response to inflammatory articles in popular magazines. Educators, however, have long been aware of many of the problems now being aired. From 8 to 25 per cent of the children enrolled in public schools were reported in 1936 to have difficulty in learning to read.[2] "In most schools," according to Traxler, "from 10 to 25 per cent of the children are two or more grades retarded in reading achievement, as measured by standard tests, by the end of the elementary school."[3] The impetus for innovations introduced during the past 25 years came, in part, from the first report in 1925 of the Committee on Reading.[4] More research probably has been devoted to reading than any other aspect of the schools program.[5] Gray counted 2,700 studies between the years 1881 and 1948.

Many of these studies emphasized the relative importance of reading as an avenue to learning. As might be expected, relationships were found

[2] Betts, Emmett A., *The Prevention and Correction of Reading Difficulties*, Row, Peterson & Company, Evanston, Ill., 1936, p. 299.

[3] Traxler, Arthur E., "Research in Reading in the United States," *J. Educ. Res.*, vol. 42, no. 7, March, 1949, p. 496.

[4] National Committee on Reading, *Twenty-Fourth Yearbook of the National Society for the Study of Education*, Public School Publishing Company, Bloomington, Ill., 1925, pp. 4–8.

[5] Editor's note, *J. Educ. Res.*, vol. 42, no. 7, March, 1949, p. 481.

between reading proficiency and achievement in literature,[6] law,[7] history, government, psychology, sociology,[8] and language arts.[9] Somewhat more surprising is the influence of linguistic ability upon achievement in scientific-technical curricula. Students with poor linguistic ability tended to be eliminated from college before completion of four years in engineering and other scientific technical curricula. Those remaining for four years tended to demonstrate linguistic ability equal to quantitative ability.[10]

A later study (unpublished) reveals that students with high "Q" (quantitative ability) and low "L" (linguistic ability) drop out of college, on the average, about one semester earlier than students with even "Q" and "L" and students with higher "L" than "Q," as measured by the American Council on Education Psychological Examination. Characteristic of research findings is the report of Percival[11] that reading disability is "the most frequent cause of school failure."

FACTORS IN READING RETARDATION

Multicausal factors in reading difficulties are receiving increasing attention. Investigations have brought to light various related problems such as visual anomalies, hearing defects, limitations in eye span, impoverished vocabularly, irregularities in eye fixations, phonetic weaknesses, and a host of others. Each of a succession of techniques for diagnosis and treatment enjoyed the limelight for a time as teachers tried out the phonetic approach, word analysis, word synthesis, flash cards, and occasionally the tachistoscope, metronoscope, ophthalmograph, films, and others. Each has its usefulness, but each has its limitations. Some of the intriguing "tricks of the trade" have emphasized the mechanics of reading to the point of ignoring getting meaning. In his discussion of devices for training eye movements, Traxler remarks,[12] " . . . the weight

[6] Bond, Eva, "Reading and Ninth Grade Achievement," Teachers College, Columbia University, New York, 1938, p. 34.

[7] Havens, Virginia, "A Prediction of Law School Achievement from High-School Rank, Reading Test Scores, Psychological Test Scores, and Average Grades in Prelaw Courses," *J. Educ. Psychol.*, vol. 34, April, 1948, pp. 237–242.

[8] Shaffer, R. H., "English Deficiency and Social Adjustment," *J. Higher Educ.*, vol. 20, October, 1949, p. 373.

[9] Hildreth, Gertrude, "Interrelationships among the Language Arts," *Elem. Sch. J.*, vol. 47, June, 1948, pp. 538–549.

[10] Woolf, Maurice D., and Jeanne A. Woolf, *The Student Personnel Program*, McGraw-Hill Book Company, Inc., New York, 1953, pp. 233ff.

[11] Percival, W. P., "A Study of the Courses and Subjects of School Failure," doctor's dissertation, Teachers College, Columbia University, New York, 1926.

[12] Traxler, Arthur E., "Research in Reading in the United States," *J. Educ. Res.*, vol. 42, no. 7, March, 1949, p. 494.

of both experimental evidence and expert opinion is on the side of emphasizing comprehension with the expectation that improved comprehension will result in greater maturity of eye-movements during the reading process."

Physical causes for reading disability should, of course, be diagnosed and corrected when possible. Such handicaps as lack of acquaintance with sounds, word structure, letters, and the like should also be attacked. Even when these conditions can be corrected, the over-all view must still include questions of motivation, of emotional involvement, of making symbols meaningful to the reader, and of the improvement of reading skills as a function of the individual's whole personality. Let us inform ourselves about the nature of physical handicaps and the kinds of professional help available for diagnosis and correction, but let us avoid the mistaken assumption that these measures will solve all reading difficulties.

PHYSICAL HANDICAPS

Eames and others have found that malnutrition, infections, and glandular disorders occur more frequently among poor readers.[13] Thyroid imbalance is believed a factor in some cases.[14] General ill health, low level of energy, any physical disability or disease might conceivably interfere with reading progress or delay the child to such an extent that he becomes discouraged and loses interest.

Loss of hearing can be a handicap since the child may not be able to discern correct pronunciation or reproduce sounds faithfully. Instructions may be misunderstood; the child may be made to feel stupid or unacceptable to teacher, parents, or group, and thus suffer damage to motivation and self-confidence.

Physical examinations were given 20 college students who had requested help in reading or had been assigned to reading class because of low reading-test scores. Physical handicaps were reported as follows: impaired visual acuity, 3; faulty binocular vision, 4; hearing loss, 3; nutritional and digestive problems, 6; respiratory and heart disorders, 5; glandular imbalance, 2; nervous disorders, 2.[15]

[13] Eames, Thomas H., "A Frequency Study of Physical Handicaps in Reading Disability and Unselected Groups," *J. Educ. Res.*, vol. 4, April, 1930, pp. 98–101.

[14] Cavanaugh, Lyman A., "Reading Behavior with Regard for Thyroid Imbalance," *Claremont College Reading Conference Thirteenth Yearbook*, 1948, pp. 98, 100.

[15] Watts, Phyllis, "Application of Clinical Diagnostic Techniques in the Classroom Situation for the Improvement of Reading at the College Level," *J. Educ. Res.*, vol. 42, no. 7, March, 1949, pp. 513–524.

Among our own students have been many who reported physical ailments and a considerable number whose gains in reading were accompanied with a decline in physical symptoms. One student, for example, was afflicted with boils which disappeared as he solved emotional and educational problems. "I don't have headaches any more," declare numerous students showing improvement in other areas. One student leaped from marginal achievement to A and B grades after taking thyroid extract prescribed for him by a physician. Occasionally, treating a physical disability is all that is required to bring about improvement. More often, a thorough diagnosis reveals a complicated pattern of interrelated conditions.

VISUAL ANOMALIES

Although research on the relationship between vision and reading proficiency produces conflicting evidence, there is some support for the belief that poor vision is a handicap. One hundred children, either nearsighted or farsighted, were fitted with glasses and then tested tachistoscopically with and without lenses. In most cases, speed of perception was increased by correction with lenses. The higher the refractive error, the more frequently an increment in speed followed correction. Word perception tended to be more improved than did object perception. In cases with small error, glasses sometimes retarded the speed of perception.[16]

Case studies reported by Berens and Enos[17] support the view that motor anomalies are associated with reading disability. They emphasize that convergence inefficiency is the most common of these motor difficulties. Individuals thus handicapped complain of discomfort, pain, and headaches after a short period of reading. Similar findings are reported by Park.[18] An exhaustive study made at Dartmouth College shows that 36 per cent of the entering freshmen class for one year had not had adequate ocular medical attention.[19] According to this and other studies,

[16] Eames, Thomas H., "The Effect of Glasses for the Correction of Hypermetropia and Myopia on the Speed of Visual Perception of Objects and Words," *J. Educ. Res.*, vol. 42, no. 7, March, 1949.

[17] Berens, Conrad, and Marjorie Enos, "Ocular Factors in Reading Disabilities," *Amer. J. of Orthopsychiat.*, vol. 17, July, 1947, pp. 397–403.

[18] Park, George E., "Reading Difficulty (Dyslexia) from the Ophthalmic Point of View," *Amer. J. of Ophthal.*, vol. 31, January, 1948, pp. 28–34.

[19] Bear, Robert M., "The Dartmouth Program for Diagnostic and Remedial Reading with Special Reference to Visual Factors," *Educ. Rec. Suppl.*, vol. 20, suppl. 12, January, 1939, p. 76.

the conditions that most often interfere with reading are imbalance of ocular muscles and inability to achieve full-time binocular vision, although debate goes on as to whether these are actually the basic causes or merely symptoms of other problems. Technical names for these defects are esophoria, exophoria, vertical phoria, poor fusion, delay fusion, aniseikonia, aniseimetropia, or any incoordination of the eyes.

Many eye-muscular conditions "hide" themselves in the doctor's office only to reveal themselves a few hours later, according to Clark.[20] Some children with 20/20 vision in either eye cannot achieve binocular vision. Some who fuse at the far point cannot fuse at the near point. Dr. Walter H. Fink of Minneapolis, speaking before the sight-saving conference of the National Safety Society for the Prevention of Blindness, stated that on the basis of recent surveys, from 20 to 25 per cent of school children have eye defects. He warned that visual problems are not always detected by simple chart tests and that 20/20 vision does not insure the absence of eye defects.[21] Gray[22] takes the sensible stand that children with visual defects who read well might read even better or with less discomfort if such conditions were corrected or eliminated. When both eyes cannot work together, Morrison[23] says, abnormal effort is required for fixation upon an object so it may be seen singly. The effort of the individual is put upon seeing instead of on getting meaning.

The visual condition known as aniseikonia may interfere with the peripheral view of a line of print. The incongruent images may thus present different space cues for the movements of the eyes as they proceed from one fixation to the next. Frustration and conflict, as a result, would seem to lead inevitably to a dislike for reading.[24]

Traxler[25] concedes that aniseikonia appears to influence reading achievement significantly. This condition produces the effect of a double exposure with one picture larger than the other. Aniseimetropia gives a similar effect with portions of the two pictures out of proportion. The edges of images are apparently vague and fuzzy. Associated symptoms are headaches, nausea, car-sickness, and nervousness.

[20] Clark, B., "Binocular Anomalies and Reading Ability," *Amer. J. Ophthal.*, vol. 23, 1950, pp. 885–892.

[21] Reported in *Science News Letter*, March 27, 1954, p. 203.

[22] Gray, William S., et al, "Reading," *Rev. Educ. Res.*, vol. 7, December, 1937, p. 505.

[23] Morrison, Donald, "Visual Skills and Visual Training," *Claremont College Reading Conference Thirteenth Yearbook*, 1948, p. 62.

[24] Carmichael, Leonard, and Walter Dearborn, *Reading and Visual Fatigue*, Houghton Mifflin Company, Boston, 1947, p. 39.

[25] Traxler, Arthur E., "Research in Reading," *J. Educ. Res.*, May, 1949, vol. 42, no. 7, p. 479.

Reviewing previous studies, Joslin[26] concludes that the visual difficulties most frequently linked with reading disability and in need of
more careful investigation are hyperphoria, astigmatism, binocular incoordination, unstable visual fields, and aniseikonia. On this subject,
Romaine[27] says:

In my opinion, muscular imbalances themselves, more definitely than any
other ocular defect, are factors in poor reading. It may seem odd that patients
with severe defects of muscular imbalances are actually better off than those
with minor defects. Experiments at the Harvard laboratories have indicated
that monocular reading more often than not surpasses binocular reading.

While the monocular reader cannot achieve depth perception, he is
spared the effect used by the partially binocular to maintain continuous
balance between his eyes.

Dr. Romaine states further that sensitivity of individuals varies tre-
mendously; thus a small defect may be of little hindrance to one person,
but another person may be completely blocked in his work by the same
defect. He reported that small degrees of fusional disorder respond
readily to various forms of orthoptic training and that improvement is
frequently accompanied by gains in reading ability.

Five case studies, presented in capsule form by Lyons and Lyons,[28]
reveal startling gains in both verbal and non-verbal ability as measured
by the Thurstone Primary Mental Abilities tests, given before and after
visual training. The authors regard vision as a function of the total
organism, combining the intake of all sense organs, memories of past
experiences, and the use of innate abilities. The reading process is defined
in similar terms by Malcolm MacLean[29] who describes how taste, smell,
values, memories, and emotions give meaning to the printed or spoken
word.

The possibility of psychosomatic or simulated ocular disease is discussed by Dr. Birge.[30] Some symptoms are severe headaches, ocular
pains, burning and twitching of the lids, and visual loss varying from

[26] Joslin, Ethel S., "Physical Factors in Reading," *Columbia Optometrist*, vol. 22,
December, 1949, pp. 6–7, February, 1950, pp. 5–6.
[27] Romaine, Dr. Hunter, "Reading Difficulties and Eye Defects," *Sight Saving Rev.*,
vol. 19, no. 2, pp. 98ff.
[28] Lyons, C. V., and Emily Bradley Lyons, "The Power of Visual Training," *J.
Amer. Optometric Ass.*, December, 1954, pp. 256–262.
[29] MacLean, Malcolm, "A Multi-sensory Approach to Reading," *Claremont College
Reading Conference Thirteenth Yearbook*, 1948, pp. 103–111.
[30] Birge, Henry L., M. D., "Psychosomatic Ophthalmology," *Sight Saving Rev.*, vol.
19, no. 4, Winter, 1949, pp. 202ff.

complete blackouts to spots before the eyes. These conditions are sometimes present even though no pathology can be discerned and may be associated with personality problems.

The effect of poor vision upon personality development is suggested by English.[31] It restricts play in which children acquire status with their peers and learn ease and grace. It is difficult for a person with poor sight to notice and respond to facial expressions, gestures, social cues, etc.

Depth perception is impaired in people who cannot achieve binocularity. They have difficulty in judging how far to step up on a curb or where to reach for a handshake. Some cannot see a ball coming toward them. Sometimes focusing on an object takes place slowly so that a child appears dull in comparison with those whose vision is normal. Such handicaps often arouse embarrassment which inhibits communication and performance.

In view of the foregoing evidence, we can assume that there is some agreement among physicians, optometrists, and educators regarding the kinds of visual problems most frequently found among retarded readers. We cannot assume that all people thus handicapped will be poor readers, or that all poor readers have visual handicaps, or that all people with good vision will be good readers, or that all poor readers have any kind of physical disability. We can, however, be alert to the possibility and recommend examination by qualified specialists.

The debate over cause and effect in the case of visual error is somewhat more involved than the historic one over the chicken and the egg. "Which came first?" Some contend that individuals are born with varying qualities of muscle fiber and membranous tissue and with different kinds of eye structure. Others heartily defend the view that vision is learned, that "function alters structure more than structure alters function," and that unsatisfactory habits of vision can be unlearned and satisfactory habits learned. Some attribute visual handicaps to lack of experience in coping with space and using both arms and both legs equally or to habits established in infancy of lying for long periods of time in one position. Some believe that personality characteristics are reflected in the kind of error which develops, that nearsightedness more often develops among people who tend to be withdrawing, retiring, and introverted, hesitant to venture far in space. Merit can be claimed for each point of view.

If a person is born with inferior eye tissues or structure, he might conceivably develop more fears, meet with more frustrations and failures, and hence suffer more emotional disturbances than people with normal

[31] English, Horace, *Child Psychology*, Henry Holt and Company, Inc., New York, 1951, pp. 273ff.

equipment and be less proficient in communicating with other people. On the other hand, with the help of understanding parents and teachers, he may compensate sufficiently to avoid maladjustment, and even to use effectively the physical equipment with which he is endowed.

We might also speculate that if the child lives in a climate of rejection, fear, criticism, ridicule, neglect, or otherwise unfavorable surroundings, he may wish to shut out part of the perceptual field and reflect his desire in the way in which he uses his eyes. This tendency might be more pronounced if a physical weakness were present.

The results of a series of experiments in which students were deliberately frustrated suggest that frustration does distort perception, lead to primitivation of response, and interfere with improvement in the recognition of tachistoscopically presented sentences.[32]

Skeffington[33] describes the motion of the eyes recorded by the Book-Retinascope as individuals react to reading materials of varying difficulty. When the materials are too difficult, the Book-Retinascope records an "against" motion. When the materials are within or below the individual's level of ability, the instrument records a "with" motion. A free, flexible motion reflects the individual's feeling that he can cope with the situation. The against motion is given by preschool children when a complex picture is presented. These reactions lead us to believe that the so-called physical function of the eyes is affected by psychological reactions.

A college professor tells us that when he is obliged to read materials that demand intense concentration, his eyes burn and water. He becomes more and more uncomfortable as he yawns, rubs his eyes, and wipes away the tears. If he puts aside the difficult text for a sports magazine, he notices that these unpleasant symptoms disappear.

Visual problems apparently may stem from a physical weakness, lack of experience, or unsatisfied psychological needs. In many cases, these factors must be interrelated, each aggravating the other. Errors in visual performance can be present even though there is no organic involvement, in which case we must look further than eyes to find the source of the trouble.

Vision is an act of perception. Whatever interferes with perception may also interfere with vision. Actually no two people see the same scene exactly in the same way. Some see details. Others see wholes. Each adds or deletes or emphasizes according to his native ability, his past experi-

[32] Korchin, S. J., J. L. Singer, and R. G. Ballard, "The Influence of Frustration on the Reproduction of Visually Perceived Forms," *Personality*, vol. 1, no. 1, January, 1951, pp. 54ff.

[33] Skeffington, Dr. A. M., Seminar of the Optometric Extension Program, Tokepa, Kans., March 17, 1954.

ences, desires, successes, and failures. We shall dwell more on this subject in the discussion of perception as it relates to reading.

POOR TEACHING

The commonest explanation for reading problems is "poor teaching." While there is some justification for this charge, most popular writers and parents reveal in their criticism lack of information and understanding regarding many factors involved in teaching and learning. Before exploring the validity of specific criticisms, we should like to offer two comments on this subject:

1. There is danger in becoming wedded to any one method. All known methods and techniques, including word recognition, phonics, kinesthetic approach, word analysis, word synthesis, vocabulary study, alphabet study, context cues, and work experience, have value for all children. Some pupils respond best to one technique and some to another. Good teachers use all of these and others.

2. One of the most important factors involved in reading disability is the failure of teachers to understand the learning process and personality dynamics involved or to apply their understanding to the teaching of reading. Most teachers can glibly parrot the phrase, "Learning (or reading) is a function of the whole child." Or this, "Reading is a complex act of perception." Evidence is lacking that teachers apply these concepts to teaching. More often, they rely on a formula, or conceive of reading as something one does with his eyes. Reading is one of the communicative skills. The writer communicates something to the reader.

If teacher and pupil are to communicate satisfactorily with each other, each must have some idea of how each reading situation appears to the other. The pupil with less experience and less maturity cannot comprehend exactly how the teacher perceives, so it is the responsibility of the teacher to try to understand as nearly as possible how the pupil perceives a situation, a story, a phrase, a word, an experience, an idea. If learning is really a function of the whole personality, the child puts into a given act of learning his interpretations of physical sensations, memories, and feelings. He may see threats or rewards not clearly visible to the teacher. In a later chapter, we shall expand on the application of the reinforcement principle, theories of self-concept and frustration, and personality dynamics as they relate to perception and the learning process. Relatively few teachers take note of emotional involvement in reading disability.

There isn't any doubt that some poor readers are victims of poor teaching. Other factors, not directly the fault of teachers, cause or aggravate reading problems. Overcrowded classrooms, especially in the early grades, are responsible for many failures. Expert remedial services which could reclaim many, especially in the early grades, are not made available in most schools for financial reasons. Some administrators make a practice of placing the weakest teacher in the second grade where a resourceful teacher could help the laggards over the worst humps. First-grade teachers are reluctant to "flunk" any child and pass along many who would benefit by another year of beginning reading. Some teachers rely so heavily on workbooks that pupils arrive at college having had little linguistic experience beyond placing a cross in the proper box.

Some teachers in the elementary school have had only the scantiest preparation for teaching reading. Because of bulging enrollments, school boards are glad to get them. In many schools, little attention is given to the teaching of reading beyond the fourth grade. Although reading books are provided and assignments are made, pupils are largely on their own as far as getting meaning is concerned. The terrific range of reading ability by this time accordingly demands a range of materials suitable for different levels of competency. Interests of pupils at this age also vary greatly. Many pupils who read only what is absolutely necessary would respond to materials which appeal to their interests. Group discussion, using some of the newer techniques of leadership, would help to maintain interest and add meaning to the reading.

Popular writers clamor for more phonics, more alphabet study, more spelling, and less word recognition. Most of them reveal little or no understanding of teaching methods or the learning process. They draw conclusions from isolated examples, report gripes and prejudices, and frequently focus their attacks on the very techniques which if properly used could solve many of our problems.

Distortions and misinterpretations of facts are common. The word and sentence methods of teaching reading are often presented as newborn fads. One widely read "slick magazine" writer reported that the word-recognition method sprang from the gestalt theory of psychology which emerged about 1912. The word-recognition method was recommended by Comenius in 1657, was introduced into this country as early as 1828, probably by the Worchester Primer, and was advocated by the revered educator, Horace Mann, in pre-Civil War days. It was well on the way toward general usage by 1870. Historically, it is probably the oldest method in existence, since it was widely used in the Orient before the time of Comenius. It has been amended and modified through the study and research of able and conscientious educators.

Although training in phonics has its uses, there is little evidence to support the view that it offers a cure for the ills of the retarded reader.

"It appears that teachers have no basis for replying exclusively on or overemphasizing the phonetic or 'sounding' methods in teaching reading," remarks Ewers[34] after a careful study of the skills of 140 students in grades 9 to 12. She studied the relationships between their scores on two standardized reading tests and facility with vowels, consonants, initial letter sounds, accent, and syllabication. Low or negative correlations were found between reading proficiency and these skills. Reversals, such as "was" for "saw," apparently had little effect upon reading skill as measured by the Iowa Silent Reading Test. As Ewers emphasizes, more study is needed regarding the relative significance of this and six other methods of word attack.

Wheeler and Wheeler[35] found little evidence that discrimination between sounds is related to reading skill. In grades 4, 5, and 6, 629 children were given tests to determine ability to distinguish sounds in auditory language situations, facility with sight vocabulary, and skill in silent-reading comprehension. The mean IQ of the group was 105.61, with a range from 76 to 139. Auditory discrimination was measured by a test of 100 items in four parts. Part I is composed of 25 pairs of words to be marked same or different, some identical like spangle-spangle, and other pairs with similar sound elements like never-ever. Part II uses pairs of sounds like *ur-or*. Part III requires the pupil to choose one of four words which does not rhyme with the other three, as hat, see, rat, fat. Each item in part IV includes a word followed by four sounds, one of which is contained in the word. Product-moment correlation coefficients computed between scores on the test of auditory discrimination and reading skills as measured by Metropolitan Achievement Tests suggest little relationship between the two.

In our experience, pupils taught by methods which emphasize phonics fail to look for meaning in the printed page. In a large school system where the phonetic method was popular, reading disability was a common problem. Non-readers could be found in every grade. Some at age 14 or above could not recognize the simplest words at pre-primer level. Tested mental ability among 90 non-readers ranged from dull-normal to "gifted." Only when they found reading satisfying and meaningful did they begin to improve.

Word and sentence methods are described by critics as memory meth-

---

[34] Ewers, Dorothea, W. F., "Relations between Auditory Abilities and Reading Abilities: A Problem in Psychometrics," *J. exp. Educ.*, vol. 18, March, 1950, pp. 239–263.

[35] Wheeler, Lester R., and Viola D. Wheeler, "A Study of the Relationship of Auditory Discrimination to Silent Reading Abilities," *J. Educ. Res.*, vol. 47, no. 2, October, 1954, pp. 103ff.

ods. Common sense suggests that phonics require much more memory work. Often ignoring the meaning of a word, the child learns to sound out the vowels and consonants and to apply the rules. He is supposed to remember that *s* is the sound made by a teakettle and that "the lazy little 'e' on the end of a word makes the vowel say its name." By word and sentence methods, the child dictates and then reads, "We saw the monkeys. The monkeys ate bananas." In time, he learns to write the story he has told. Why should a defenseless six-year-old be expected to learn to recognize the word "saw" by a devious route around a teakettle? He actually saw something interesting. He saw the monkeys do something interesting. They *ate* bananas. After he goes through the exciting experience of discovering that these words actually say "saw" and "ate," he is ready to take them apart and discover that "saw" is something like "sat," but not exactly, and so on into the intricacies of word analysis, word synthesis, phonics, alphabet study, and spelling. "What should be taught" is the natural concern of parents. "How it should be taught" is best left to educators who have spent a lifetime studying this question.

It is fallacious to assume that the word-recognition or sentence methods of teaching reading are universally taught or that they are well taught. Any method can fail because it is not properly used. Lacking sufficient time or understanding, some teachers fail to introduce alphabet study, phonics, or other methods of word study at the time when they can best be used, in late first grade or at the second- or third-grade level. Spelling and writing in connection with learning words are sometimes neglected, but not so often as critics claim. Much more use could be made of "work experience" which encourages the pupils to compose stories or report interesting experiences and permits them to see their own thoughts in print upon the blackboard. This technique can be used profitably in the intermediate and upper grades as well as among primary pupils. Proper use of the word and sentence method includes many other techniques, introduced when needed.

The reading-readiness program is also under attack. Although it is not always carried out effectively, it is based on the indisputable fact that children mature at different rates. All children who arrive at the chronological age of six years are obviously not uniform in weight, height, bone structure, nutrition, mental age, emotional stability, or reading readiness. Betts[36] reports a six-year range of maturity level among school beginners. Evidence that reading-readiness training helps to pre-

[36] Betts, Emmett Albert, paper reported in *Science News Letter*, March 6, 1954, p. 152.

vent reading disability is given by Scott[37] and others. Comparing the school achievement of three groups of children, she found those with reading-readiness training superior to those with only kindergarten training and to those with no training. We suggest that development of reading skill is arrested in some pupils, not because of the reading-readiness program, but because it is not properly applied.

The most pervasive concept in psychology is maturation. If teachers and administrators are acquainted with professional literature on this subject, they are able to choose the most suitable time to introduce new facts and skills. For example, certain studies indicate that the effectiveness of teaching numbers in the first or second grade is debatable. Third-grade children can learn in a few weeks what younger children require two years to learn.

Maturation means that children are able to do at certain stages of development, certain tasks that they could not do previously. Abilities are manifested at various stages which are not a result of learning, but which facilitate learning.

When the teaching of reading is imposed upon a child who is not "ready" (appropriately mature), we are doing him a disservice. Under such circumstances, he may learn something, perhaps negative attitudes, but not the skills we think we are teaching. We oblige him to put forth several times as much the effort than is required if we wait for maturity. While waiting, he would be better occupied with tasks of a suitable level of difficulty.

A suitable application of the reading-readiness principle would also include provision for the child who is "ready" at the age of six or younger. We were once introduced to a five-year-old who read quite easily a selection from the Stanford-Binet Intelligence Scale at the sixth-grade level. When offered some publishers' copies of story books not yet available in stores and libraries, she was able to read them with ease and enjoyment. Obviously, a child with this ability will be bored with reading-readiness training.

The charge "poor teaching" is often made without consideration for the obstacles to teaching. Tested reading ability in a typical fifth grade is reported to have varied from grade 2 to grade 8.9.[38] In the upper grades, the range can be, and often is, from zero to the adult level. One junior-high-school teacher who was trying to combine reading instruction with grammar found herself with a total of 350 pupils, ranging from one

[37] Scott, Carrie M., "An Evaluation of Training in Readiness Classes," *Elem. Sch. J.*, vol. 48, September, 1947, pp. 26–32.

[38] Tiegs, E. W., "Educational Diagnosis," California Test Bureau, 1951, p. 5.

extreme to the other. Consider the demands made on the teacher of so many pupils with such a variety of needs and abilities. Smaller classes would permit teachers to give more individual attention. Remedial services by reading specialists would cut down the academic mortality.

Grouping together pupils of similar needs and abilities has proven successful in the treatment of reading disability. Two studies, chosen from a number on this subject, report convincing evidence of the value of this plan. Dellone[39] reports gratifying gains among pupils from grades 4, 5, and 6 who were grouped according to their needs and reading levels without regard to grade classification. A similar plan for reading instruction was described by Jones.[40]

In the light of these brief remarks, we find no justification for placing the entire blame for reading disability on elementary-school teachers. It must be shared by school administrators, curriculum planners, supervisors, teacher-trainers, parents, and ultimately by the public to whom, in the last analysis, the schools belong.

Positive measures are being taken by some schools. The St. Louis school system has reduced the size of the third-grade classroom to 20 pupils in an attempt to identify and correct reading problems before they become acute.[41] Another large school system provides counselors to work with retarded readers and their teachers in the elementary schools. Each school has the services of a counselor about every tenth day. The increase of college reading clinics throughout the country is reported by Ullman.[42] A reading conference in Wisconsin, planned for 24 teachers, attracted 240 interested participants. High-school administrators are exploring the values of homogeneous grouping, reading instruction in freshman English classes, and the use of films, slides, and other drills. Teachers' workshops and in-service-training programs on this subject are on the increase.

New York City's Board of Education has ordered that pupils who do not meet standards in reading be kept in the same grade. The action is a direct result of a finding that there probably is a direct connection between retardation in reading and juvenile delinquency. Investigation had shown there were 20,000 New York children from the fourth to the sixth grades who were retarded two years or more in reading.[43] The situation

[39] Dellone, Augusta, "Individualized Instruction in Reading," *Baltimore Bulletin*, vol. 25, October–November, 1947, pp. 94–99.

[40] Jones, Daisy Marvel, "An Experiment in Adaptation to Individual Differences," *J. Educ. Psychol.*, vol. 34, May, 1948, pp. 257–272.

[41] *St. Louis Post Dispatch*, October 25, 1954.

[42] Ullman, Shirley, "A Comparative Study of Reading Rate Controller Technique versus the Speeded Book Reading Technique for Reading Improvement on the College Level," dissertation, New York University, Publication no. 2515, 1950, p. 35.

[43] *Kansas City Times*, June 3, 1955.

is certainly serious enough to demand action, but retardation is a debatable solution unless counseling and remediation are provided to supplement the efforts of the average classroom teacher.

Perhaps it is true, as many educators claim, that more people read better than ever before. It is also true that many people could read better than they do. Improvement will require the cooperation of all involved: teachers, administrators, curriculum experts, teacher-trainers, educational researchers, psychologists, student personnel workers, state and national legislative bodies, and an interested public. Educational research, needed to validate and justify present methods and to explore other methods, is held down to a minimum for financial reasons. Only 2 per cent of federal appropriation for research is given to all social studies, including education. The same proportion can probably be found in universities, where it is easier to get money for technical and scientific investigations than for exploring the effectiveness of educational methods. As a nation, for one year while spending more than 40 billion dollars for defense and past wars, we spent about 13 billion for education, both public and private, kindergarten through college. An important factor in the over-all problem is obviously inadequate financing.

Steps toward improving reading skills would include the following: adequate salaries to attract highly trained teachers in the elementary schools, particularly in the first three grades; smaller classes in the grades, particularly the first three; teacher-trainers who have had successful experience in the elementary schools and in the teaching of reading; scholarships to attract able people into teacher training; much more emphasis on how the laws of learning and personality dynamics apply to the teaching of reading; more emphasis on reading instruction in the intermediate and upper grades; much wider range of reading materials for a variety of interests and ability levels in each grade; diagnosis of each retarded reader's problems and the application of appropriate techniques and methods; counseling services for the emotionally disturbed; much more attention to classroom discussion which would help pupils to think about what they are reading and would stimulate their interest in more reading; provision for students with reading disability all along the way; many more opportunities for pupils of all ages to say and write thoughts they really want to express.

To the foregoing named improvements we should like to add the suggestion that organizing the three primary grades as a unit might make it possible to avoid the stigma of failure for the slow reader while he actually remains in the first grade for further help.

Also complicating the present problems is the furor raised by attacks on the public schools. Possibly, they have served a worthy purpose if the public has been stimulated to take an interest in more adequate financing and better standards for schools. On the other hand, uncritical insistence on eliminating valuable services or prescribing outmoded practices could do incalculable damage. Furthermore, teachers and school administrators, placed in the position of having to defend themselves, are possibly less than receptive to suggestions of the public. It is a wholesome state of affairs when patrons of the school take an interest in learning more about its operation and its needs. It is not wholesome when criticism is entirely destructive and when the critics take no responsibility for improving the situation. An imaginative effort among the teaching profession to improve communication between parents and teachers might turn this tide of criticism to the advantage of the schools.

Tied in with the reading problem is the over-all school picture. Teachers would have more time for individual instruction, for study of materials and techniques, and for classroom preparation if they could be relieved of their clerical duties, some of which are utter nonsense. (For example, all rural teachers in one county are required to record health information, height, weight, disease record, preventive shots, etc., on seven different forms.) Teachers would have more incentive for improving their methods if some effective system of evaluating teaching could be worked out, along with a suitable system of rewards.

Placing the blame for reading problems proceeds in this fashion. The college teacher blames the high-school teacher; the high-school teacher, the elementary teacher. The elementary-school teacher blames the mother, and the mother says, "He takes after his father." Somewhere in the process, the teacher who teaches the teachers gets his share of blame. Legislators and their constituencies should also come in for a liberal helping. Fixing the blame is not so important as considering how to correct the lamentable situation.

IMPOVERISHED EXPERIENTIAL BACKGROUND

Many linguistically handicapped students reveal a lack of meaningful experiences. They recall few successes, few trips or parties, and a sparse assortment of pleasant memories. Many of them say that they remember very little about their childhood. They laboriously dredge up a few fragments of information, often expressed in stereotyped or very general items, "My family was wonderful. I just love all my family." Some make vague references to work and to church activities. Typical of another kind of response is the remark of one girl, "All I remember about my childhood is sitting on a chair and how I hated it."

When asked to draw a tree, a large proportion of these students draw bare branches, said to represent a barren childhood. When they draw houses, they seldom add shrubs, flowers, or other ornamentation.

Among 90 retarded readers in a large school system, few had had opportunities to visit spots of interest afforded by the city: museums, art galleries, libraries, monuments, parks, lakes, industries, etc.

The reader enriches words and sentences through the application of his past experiences. If they are scanty, he is limited in getting meaning.

The influence of early experiences upon reading is disclosed by the remarks of a grown woman who discovered that she was trying to fit every story she read into a setting remembered from childhood. Whether the story was a Sherlock Holmes mystery or *Hamlet*, this reader contrived to place it in the same house with a small front parlor, narrow hall with antique rose-colored chandelier, and the dining room crowded with a fold-away bed. Even after becoming aware of this limiting trick of the unconscious, the memory trace intruded, obliging Anna Karenina, Scarlett O'Hara, and Kirsten Lavransdätter to adjust themselves to the unsuitable surroundings.

This kind of limitation upon understanding is seen in children's interpretations of hymns, prayers, and Biblical quotations. Sylvia Wright recorded these gems in *Harper's Magazine,* "Our Father who art in heaven, Harold be Thy Name. Surely good Mrs. Murphy shall follow me all the days of my life. Lead us not into Penn Station." Letters to the editor which followed her delightful article called up visions of the innocents singing at the tops of their voices, "Fight in the corner where you are. . . . While shepherds washed their socks by night."

The effect of experience upon language-conceptual growth is dramatically illustrated by an experiment reported by Helen Dawe.[44] Two groups of preschool and kindergarten children from an orphanage were matched for chronological age, mental age, IQ, vocabulary score, general-science score, and organization score. The control group was given regular fare in preschool and kindergarten. The experimental group was given training in the understanding of words and concepts and experience in looking at and discussing pictures, listening to poems and stories, and going on short excursions. New words and phrases were introduced and explained. The experimenter attempted to stimulate curiosity and encourage critical thinking. The aim was to promote real comprehension of words and concepts. Retests at the close of the training period revealed that the experimental group had gained significantly in

[44] Dawe, Helen C., "Environmental Influences on Language Growth," in *Psychological Studies of Human Development,* edited by Raymond G. Kuhlen and George E. Thompson, Century Psychology Series, Appleton-Century-Crofts, Inc., New York, 1952, pp. 239–244.

IQ while the mean change for the control group was a loss of two IQ points. The experimental group had made significantly greater gains than the control group in vocabulary, home-living information, and science information and were significantly superior on a test of reading readiness.

Illustrating the process by which the reader puts something of himself and his past into the act of reading, Dr. A. M. Skeffington, optometrist, shows his audiences a comic strip. The artist pictures the thoughts of a little boy as he listens to a fairy story. "Two pages held up the bride's train," says the storyteller. Timmy sees two book pages holding up a railway train. As Timmy hears that the heroine is imprisoned in a tower, he thinks of a water tower. Skeffington believes that a similar process takes place during the act of seeing, as the individual automatically selects objects that are important, meaningful, or threatening to him and adds his own interpretation to what he sees. You have doubtless had experiences similar to this one. Three people driving past a park reported what they saw. One noticed the flower garden. An expert swimmer saw the boys on the diving board. A girl whose pleasantest memories were her successes as a baseball pitcher saw the baseball game.

College students in developmental-reading classes reveal scant opportunities to say or write things they really wanted to say and write. They have seldom, if ever, been asked to tell how they feel about any issue, state likes and dislikes, express opinions, or evaluate evidence. Apparently they lack experience in communicating with people as well as other meaningful experiences.

INTELLECTUAL DEFICIENCIES

Too many retarded readers are written off as hopeless cases because of the ready assumption that they lack ability. As mentioned before, one-third of a large class of college freshmen demonstrated by standardized test results that their scores in linguistic ability and reading ability fell appreciably below their tested quantitative ability. All of these students ranked above the 35th percentile in scholastic aptitude, according to their scores on the American Council on Education Psychological Examination. By oral tests of intelligence, some non-readers fall in the category of gifted children. Among several hundred retarded readers in one school system, tested mental ability ranged from dull normal to gifted. Stanford-Binet scores of four third- and fourth-grade retarded readers from the same school yielded IQs of 128, 130, 135, and 140.

Children tested before and after a reading-improvement program are reported to have gained in scholastic aptitude.[45] Fifteen college students

[45] Abbott, E. Carleton, "Relationship between Variation in Silent Reading Ability and Mental Ability," dissertation, University of Pennsylvania, Philadelphia, p. 92.

in a class of 35 made gains of from 9 to 39 percentile points in total score, according to retest with the American Council on Education Psychological Examination.[46] It is possible that the second testing, in each of these cases, gave a more accurate estimate of the ability of these groups. It is also possible that improvement in reading with accompanying confidence in his own abilities places an individual in a position to make more effective use of his innate abilities than he was formerly able to do.

A second-grade teacher was dismayed to find that one of her pupils had an IQ of 83. When she looked up the results of the child's first intelligence test, taken two years earlier, she found a recorded IQ of 130. A reading problem was the explanation.

Pencil and paper tests of intelligence place the retarded reader at a disadvantage and fail to give an accurate measure of his potential. In cases of reading disability, careful consideration should be given to the results of non-verbal subtests and oral tests of intelligence.

Even students of low-average ability can make improvement. A group of 60 college freshmen ranking in the lower 25 per cent of their group in tested scholastic aptitude made gains in reading speed and comprehension during one semester of training. A comparison of mean raw scores from standardized pretest and retest showed differences statistically reliable at the 1 per cent level of confidence or beyond the probability of chance.[47]

Let us avoid leaping to the conclusion that every poor reader is inferior in mental ability. Let us not overlook the possibility that the poor reader of average scholastic ability may be able to improve his skills. Some estimate of the student's potential for improvement may be obtained by comparing his reading test results with results of non-verbal tests of mental ability. If the resources of the school are limited, then the decision must be made as to where to apply remediation to yield the most increment.

EMOTIONAL AND PERSONAL PROBLEMS

The question of which came first, reading disability or emotional problems, is often raised. Apparently, either sequence of events is possible. An emotional or perceptual block may interfere with learning to read. Anxiety intereferes with the concentration of the reader and inhibits performance. Depression decreases memory span and involves feelings of worthlessness and hopelessness. On the other hand, the child

[46] Woolf, Maurice D., unpublished report, Kansas State College, 1954.
[47] Woolf, Maurice D., "Annual Report on the Developmental Reading Program at Kansas State College, 1953," unpublished.

who fails to keep up with his fellows is daily subjected to embarrassment, humiliation, and frustration. He could easily develop emotional problems which are further obstacles to learning. If the retarded reader attends a small school where the achievement level is not too much higher than his own, or if he finds other means of achieving emotional satisfactions and self-esteem, his handicap may not lead to emotional problems.

We certainly cannot assume that every retarded reader has emotional problems or that every disturbed person will be a poor reader. We can however say with confidence that a very large proportion of retarded readers show symptoms of maladjustment. Evidence of this involvement is not lacking in the writings of educators, psychologists, and physicians.

Fifty per cent of seriously retarded readers are characterized by fears and anxieties which require a program of reeducation aimed at the re-establishment of self-confidence and removal of anxieties, according to Witty and Kopel.[48]

Forty per cent of the retarded readers studied by Jensen[49] were judged neurotic and a large proportion of them demonstrated problems of home adjustment.

Children with reading difficulties lack persistence and ability to concentrate, tend to withdraw from social contacts, and often show a lack of normal aggressiveness, according to Gates,[50] a well-known reading specialist. Daydreaming and marked sensitivity are other symptoms noted by Gates. Tiegs[51] advises teachers to watch for bashfulness, extreme fear or anger, embarrassment, timidity, stubbornness, tantrums, braggadocio, crying, unusual lack of poise, inability to get along with other children. Symptoms reported by Bennett[52] are lack of persistence and attention, preference for solitary and inactive life, fears, indecision, loneliness, and crying spells. Timidity and inferiority are mentioned by Hardwick[53] as traits of retarded readers.

Mental illness is closely associated with disturbances in communica-

[48] Witty, P., and D. Kopel, *Reading and the Educative Process*, Ginn & Company, Boston, 1939, p. 231.

[49] Jensen, M. B., "Reading Deficiency as Related to Cerebral Injury and to Neurotic Behavior," *J. appl. Psychol.*, vol. 27, December, 1943, pp. 535ff.

[50] Gates A. I., "Failure in Reading and Social Maladjustment," *J. of Ntl. Educ. Ass.*, vol. 25, 1936.

[51] Tiegs, Ernest W., "Diagnosis in the Reading Program," California Test Bureau Educational Bulletin, no. 10, 1951, p. 6.

[52] Bennett, C. C., "An Inquiry into the Genesis of Poor Readers," Teachers College Contributions to Education, no. 755, Columbia University, New York, 1935.

[53] Hardwick, R. S., "Types of Reading Disability," *Childhood Education*, vol. 8, 1932, p. 425.

tion, Dr. Jurgen Ruesch, psychiatrist of the University of California School of Medicine, told a workshop audience.[54] Patients were apparently hampered in their development by parents' lack of responsiveness to their earliest attempts to communicate.

Apparently extremes in behavior may be expected from retarded readers. Both extreme aggressiveness and lack of overt aggressiveness are reported as characteristics of retarded readers by qualified observers. Also mentioned is concealed aggressiveness. Klein[55] believes that neurotic conflict which is largely concerned with trying to repress aggressive drives will be reflected in the individual's response to reading and learning. This view is supported by Vorhaus.[56] On this subject, Strachey[57] says that if oral drives are unstable or completely repressed, reading skill breaks down. Undesirable behavior patterns or personality maladjustment may be traced to reading disability, according to Tulchin.[58]

In an unpublished study, a group of 35 reading students with high "Q" and low "L" yielded a score on the "K" scale of the Minnesota Multiphasic Personality Inventory which deviated appreciably from the norm. A high K score is said to represent defensiveness against revealing psychological weakness and may border on distortion in the direction of making a normal appearance.

The Rorschach test was administered to 20 college freshmen who had "A" or "B plus" patterns on the Strong Vocational Interest Blank (SVIB) scales most heavily loaded with the verbal factor and to 20 matched freshmen (according to American Council on Education Psychological Examination) who had "A" or "B plus" patterns of interests on SVIB scales most heavily loaded with non-verbal factors. Students in each group were equally distributed in each quarter on the ACE. Individuals in the non-verbal group were found to reveal less emotional flexibility and less interest in people, and to expend more effort in emotional control.[59] Testing 143 college students with the SVIB and the Szondi Experimentelle Treibdiagnostik led to the tentative conclusion that people

[54] Reported in *Science New Letter*, April 2, 1955, p. 213.

[55] Klein, M., "A Contribution to the Theory of Intellectual Inhibition," *Intern. J. Psychoanal.*, vol. 12, 1931.

[56] Vorhaus, P. G., "Non-reading as an Expression of Resistance," *Rorschach Research Exchange*, 10, 1946, pp. 60–69.

[57] Strachey, J., "Some Unconscious Factors in Reading," *Intern. J. Psychoanal.*, vol 11, 1930.

[58] Tulchin, S. H., "Emotional Factors in Reading Disabilities in School Children," *J. Educ. Psych.*, vol, 26, 1935, p. 444.

[59] Torrance, Paul, "Summary of Counseling Bureau Studies Completed between September, 1950 and June 1, 1951," Kansas State College, pp. 23–24, unpublished.

interested in the non-verbal occupations expended more effort in emotional control than did people interested in the verbal occupations.[60]

Excessive control is suspected to be related to uneven intellectual development and to a linguistic lag. A person who habitually exercises denial and avoidance of any situation which might stir up unacceptable impulses or painful memories is hampered in the development of curiosity, free play of imagination, forceful exploration of new modes of self-realization.[61]

The effect of attitude upon reading is similar to the effect of mental set upon the interpretation of any situation. If the attitudes of the reader differ markedly from those of his teacher or of other members of his group, he will not find the same meaning in a given paragraph. McKillop[62] notes the tendency of students to label "false" or "stupid" passages which do not fit with their attitudes and to interpret what they read in the light of their own values and needs. Such students might be expected to give unsatisfactory answers to questions intended to test comprehension and perhaps fail to find satisfaction in reading and discussing.

Changes in attitude toward reading are reflected in critiques of reading students who have made improvement: "I used to think reading was a waste of time. As I discovered what this class could do for me I have a changed mind." A change in attitudes toward other kinds of communication is apparent in such statements as these made at the beginning and at the close of a semester of reading instruction: "February: Talking to people is hard. May: Talking to people is fun." Problems of retarded readers relating to interest, motivation, and lack of success are recognized by Boney,[63] Meek,[64] and Schlesser and Young.[65]

Negativism, antagonism, and resistance toward learning to read are reported by various writers[66,67,68] to be common among poor readers.

[60] *Ibid.*, pp. 24–28.

[61] Anderson, Harold and Gladys Anderson (eds.), *Introduction to Projective Techniques,* Prentice-Hall, Inc., Englewood Cliffs, N. J., 1951, p. 546.

[62] McKillop, Anne Seely, "The Relationship between the Reader's Attitudes and Certain Types of Reading Response," doctoral dissertation, University of Michigan microfilm, Ann Arbor, Mich., Publication no. 2543, 1951, pp. 5, 109.

[63] Boney, C. D., "Reading—Go Slow," *School Executive,* vol. 65, September, 1945, pp. 56ff.

[64] Meek, L. H., "Behavior Problems in the School," *Teachers College Record,* vol. 37, January, 1936, p. 300.

[65] Schlesser, G. E., and C. W. Young, "Study and Work Habits," *School Rev.,* vol. 53, February, 1945, pp. 85ff.

[66] Ephron, Beulah Cantor, *Emotional Difficulties in Learning,* Julian Press, New York, 1953, p. 13.

[67] Dolch, Edward W., *The Psychology and Teaching of Reading,* Ginn & Company,

Frustration as a factor in reading disability is discussed by Robinson,[69] and by Korchin, Singer, and Ballard.[70]

Evidence that adjustment problems are related to reading disability can be found in studies of the effect of counseling and psychotherapy upon improvement. Significant changes in reading ability in a class of third-graders occurred during a series of play-therapy sessions, according to Bills.[71] A group of 12 delinquent boys were given group therapy in addition to remedial-reading instruction. Another group, matched with the experimental group for age, IQ, reading ability, and degree of retardation, was given only the remedial instruction. The experimental group gained 39.4 per cent more than the non-therapy group.[72] Support for these views is given by Axline[73] and Bixler.[74]

Social adjustment as a factor in reading is suggested by the fact that a college class of retarded readers made significant gains in social adjustment, as shown by retest with the Minnesota Personality Scale.[75] Items frequently marked by college students in reading classes as being of concern to them include the following: lack self-confidence, feel inferior, have trouble talking in company, too few social contacts, have troublemaking friends.

Clues to personal-adjustment problems of retarded readers can be found in their responses to such projective measures as the Bender Visual Motor Gestalt and the House-Tree-Person Test. Although these instruments do not lend themselves to standardization, they can give the clinician valuable hints about the way in which the individual sees himself and others and the kinds of situations which appear to him to be threatening. In our experience, results of testing with projective tech-

Boston, 1931, p. 241.

[68] Leichty, Dr. Mary M., report to Midwestern Psychological Ass., reviewed in *Science News Letter*, May 8, 1954, p. 292.

[69] Robinson, Helen M., *Why Pupils Fail in Reading*, University of Chicago Press, Chicago, 1946, p. 82.

[70] Korchin, Sheldon J., Jerome Singer, and Robert Ballard, "The Influence of Frustration on the Reproduction of Visually Perceived Forms," *Personality*, vol. 1, no. 1, January, 1951, p. 54.

[71] Bills, R. E., "Non-directive Play Therapy with Retarded Readers," *J. consult. Psychol.*, vol. 2, 1950, pp. 140–149.

[72] Fisher, Bernard, "Group Therapy with Retarded Readers," *J. Educ. Psychol.*, vol. 44, no. 6, October, 1953, p. 354.

[73] Axline, V. M., "Non-directive Therapy for Poor Readers," *J. consult. Psychol.*, vol. 2, 1947, pp. 61–69.

[74] Bixler, Ray. H., "Treatment of a Reading Problem through Non-directive Play Therapy," *J. Consult. Psychol.*, vol. 9, no. 2, March-April, 1945, pp. 105–118.

[75] Woolf, Maurice D., and Jeanne A. Woolf, *The Student-Personnel Program*, McGraw-Hill Book Company, Inc., New York, 1953, p. 209.

niques tend to support the evidence gathered by means of standardized personality tests, interviews, observations, and other means.

Reading students commonly draw the human figure as very small, indicating a feeling of personal insignificance. Figures of the Bender Visual Motor Gestalt are almost invariably reproduced in minute, constricted form, usually crowded into the upper left of a page. Erasures, retracing, and faint, hesitant lines are common. The average amount of space used for the Bender is about a page and a half. Reading students usually use about one-third of one page. These characteristics are believed to indicate feelings of insignificance, inadequacy, and insecurity. Difficulties in drawing eyes and hands, said to be related to barriers to communication and to acceptance of perceived environment, are manifested by these students.[76]

Immaturity is strongly suggested by test results and behavior of retarded readers of college age. A group of 119 college students of inferior reading ability was chosen for study from among 1,231 entering freshmen in a scientific-technical college in 1949. Each of this group produced a rank in quantitative ability 20 or more percentile points greater than his rank in linguistic ability, according to the results of the American Council on Education Psychological Examination. This group, called the A group, was compared with two other groups of approximately the same size and same percentile rank in quantitative ability. The B group had even scores on the ACE in quantitative and linguistic abilities. The scores of the C group in linguistic ability exceeded their scores in quantitative ability by 20 or more percentile points. The A group with inferior linguistic ability and reading skills was also inferior in interest-maturity, as measured by the SVIB, by a statistically reliable margin. Their scores on the interest-maturity scale suggested that their interests were more nearly like those of 15-year-old boys than those of men in general of 25 years of age. Since the major changes in interest occur before the age of 18.5, these students appear to be retarded in development along these lines.

A low score in interest-maturity is interpreted to mean these characteristics as compared with 18-year-old men in general:

1. Less interest in people and less tolerance for all kinds of people than is common among people of their age

2. Less interest in reading, speaking, cultural activities, and group discussions

3. Fewer likes and more dislikes as indicated on SVIB items, particularly those relating to educational and occupational interests

[76] Woolf, Maurice D., and Jeanne A. Woolf, "The Case of the Tired Readers," *Personnel and Guidance J.*, vol. 33, January, 1955, pp. 294–296.

4. Greater interest in amusements such as movies, picnics, etc.

5. Greater interest in feats of physical skill and daring and in mechanical, scientific, exploratory, and outdoor activities

Students in the high "Q" and low "L" group showed significantly less interest in social-welfare occupations than did students with even scores in "Q" and "L." The relationship between interest-maturity and the social-welfare pattern of interests is reported by Darley.[77]

Based on his research on the SVIB scores of 1,000 college students, Darley offers this definition,[78] "Interest-maturity, redefined as a phase of personality, might characterize the well-organized, socially sensitive, generally mature, tolerant, insightful individual." Thus, students whose linguistic and reading skills fail to equal their quantitative skills appear to lag in the development of acceptable social attitudes and social skills.

Students who improve reading skills apparently make growth in favorable attitudes toward people, judging from statements made before and after reading instruction. Characteristic first statements are: "I hardly ever trust anybody. When other people are around, some people always have to show off." Characteristic final statements are: "Most people are easy to get along with. When other people are around, time goes faster. I hardly ever have a fight any more. I used to think Negroes were bad. I used to think grownups were stupid. My father is becoming a person I can understand."[79]

Lack of vocational objective may be related to immaturity. Among the items most often checked by reading students on personal-data questionnaires is this: "I do not know what occupation would be best for me." Responses to an incomplete sentence test often reveal the same problem, "I do not know what I should do when I am out of college." In the latter questionnaire, there was no reference to vocational choice. When the problem was indicated, it was entirely the student's idea.

More definite ideas about life purpose are expressed in final statements of students who make improvement in reading skills. Statements made early in the semester tend to be vague and general: "My purpose in life is to get an education. My purpose in life is to live a good life. My purpose in life is to be a good citizen." Final statements tend to be more decisive: "My purpose in life is to be a good farmer (or school teacher, or engineer, etc.)."

Immaturity is also suggested by the tendency among reading students to draw only the head when asked to draw a person. Heads are featured

[77] Darley, John G., *Clinical Aspects and Interpretation of the Strong Vocational Interest Blank*, Psychological Corporation, New York, 1941, p. 61–64.

[78] *Ibid.*, p. 60.

[79] Woolf, Maurice D., unpublished study, Kansas State College, 1955.

in the drawings of young children. The figures of the Bender Visual Motor Gestalt are often reproduced carelessly or incompletely, reflecting a lack of incentive to do a thing thoroughly and completely.

Boy-girl relationships, observed in reading classes, are similar to those of the early adolescent level. Difficulties in this area are expressed both verbally and in response to personal-adjustment questionnaires: "I would like to ask a girl for a date, but I don't know how to go about it. I don't know what to do when a movie is over. I am afraid I will run out of talk on the way to a show. I hardly ever have any dates. What do people talk about on a date?"

Reading students frequently express confusion concerning their appropriate sex roles. When drawing the human figure, they portray the opposite sex as often as their own. (The first figure offered in response to the request to draw a person is believed related to the self-portrait.) Thirty-five retarded readers (with high "Q" and low "L") tested with the Minnesota Multiphasic Personality Inventory deviated significantly from the norm on the masculinity-femininity scale. Another group of 41 reading students (with high "Q" and low "L") who made tested improvement in reading skills also demonstrated a statistically significant change toward the norm on the Mf scale of the MMPI. As a group, they did not deviate sufficiently from the norm to indicate identification with the opposite sex, but rather their scores appeared to reflect a lack of self-understanding and a delay in identification with adults of the same sex. Identification with the same-sex parent usually begins in infancy. By college age, it is fairly well established as a part of the personality.

Hostility between sexes, either overt or veiled, is often expressed: "You gotta look out for women or they'll take advantage of you." When dividing up the work of the class, the boys may take sides against the girls, attempting to saddle them with duties they consider least agreeable. Hostility toward women can be seen in their remarks and writings, as in the case of the boy who offered this sentence in a vocabulary exercise: "Primitive men carried a club to hit people and girls over the head with." Retesting with the House-Tree-Person Test reveals a tendency among reading students to make a change in drawings from opposite-sex figures to same-sex figures. For example, a male student first offered the head and shoulders of a girl above a board fence. At the close of the semester, he pictured a masculine figure with hair on the chest. Another boy who made a change from a feminine figure to one more masculine in appearance eventually portrayed either a girl in slacks or a rather effeminate-looking boy. Women are seen as mothers, but otherwise they are unknown quantities or perhaps objects of suspicion.

Women reading students commonly show a preference for sports, outdoor activities, and farm work. Their conversations reveal experiences which have been meaningful to them and their picture of normal, everyday living. They like to remember when they played shortstop on the boys' baseball team and competed successfully with their brothers in swimming and foot races. A typical comment offered by a husky girl tells a good deal about how she regards herself and her role in the family and the community, "I write with my left hand, but when I scoop . . . when I scoop wheat, I scoop right-handed and when I chop wood, I chop right-handed." Various kinds of evidence drawn from standardized tests, performance on projective measures, and verbalizations over a period of three years support the belief that these young people are still in early stages of trying to determine what kind of people they are and that they have little information about the roles of men and women as commonly defined in western society. Their naïveté in these areas leads us to suspect that the taboos regarding sex have been so strong as to stifle normal curiosity and delay the process of identification. The development of a wholesome interest in the opposite sex is reflected in responses to the incomplete sentence test and other instruments used in retest.

Fully one-third of the preadolescent youngsters with police records have had difficulty deciding whether they want to play the man's or woman's role in life, according to Miss Lillian Johnson of the Ryther Child Center of Seattle.[80] Youngsters approaching adolescence often get caught in some situation at home or in social life which prevents them from developing naturally, she explained. A girl may become boyish and aggressive because she sees men as dominant and she wants to be on the winning side. A boy may turn effeminate to please a parent who wanted a daughter instead of a son, especially when he can get concessions or pleasure by doing so. Retarded readers in our experience have been less inclined toward delinquency than toward over-conformity. However, the foregoing illustration calls attention to the seriousness of such a problem.

Our reading students commonly display stereotypy, over-conformity, and exaggerated dependency upon the opinions or directions of adults. Opinions are seldom offered. These students shy away from taking a stand on any issue, whether it is on the subject of bobby socks or atomic energy. The popular attitude appears to be, "I'll wait and see what the gang thinks (or does)." Standards of the group to which the retarded reader wants most to belong are strictly observed. Whether the admired clique is religious, social, or political in nature, the individual seeks security by patterning his talk, clothes, and habits according to their dictates. Conversation is sprinkled liberally with clichés: "Be a friend

[80] *Kansas City Times,* June 3, 1955.

and you'll have a friend." "Do right and you will succeed." There is a somewhat punitive flavor to many of their comments: "If a person doesn't get along, it's his own fault." They are inclined to have a naïve, if vague, belief that "Anybody can do anything if he puts his mind to it." If he doesn't, he deserved his ignominious fate. Quoting parents, teachers, political leaders, and ministers is a favorite method of settling matters. One can note reluctance to take responsibility and a decided tendency to demand detailed instructions about study from teachers. "Why don't you just tell us exactly what to do and *make* us do it?"

In foregoing paragraphs are a number of references to projective techniques, such as the House-Tree-Person Test and the Bender Visual Motor Gestalt, instruments which do not command as much respect as some other measures of personality. One regards them with more confidence when he discovers that reading classes repeatedly make improvements in their drawings concurrently with gains in reading speed and comprehension. In the fall semester of 1954, 25 of 41 college students pretested and retested with these two tests noticeably increased their use of space. Some doubled, tripled, or quadrupled the amount of space used. The human figure was drawn more completely. Drawings were moved from the upper left or the extreme edge of the page to the center; crowding was less noticeable. Bender figures were reproduced more accurately and completely. Erasures and retracings were reduced; faint, hesitant lines gave way to firm, even strokes. More same-sex figures were offered. Progress in reading skills was indicated by test and retest with standardized instruments. A total of 37 from this group made progress toward self-confidence and sense of personal worth, as indicated by changes in drawings.

Evidence of personal problems is found in the results of the incomplete sentence test which offers items such as this: "My father _____ When I was little _____ I hardly ever _____ Grown-ups think _____." Students' attitudes and problems are reflected in the following answers: "I am afraid of being wrong all of the time. When others are around I don't feel right. When I was little I worried a lot. Brothers and sisters are a bother." Resentment, otherwise concealed, can often be expressed in the third person, as: "Grown-ups think children are mean; they know best; children should be punished; young people do foolish things; children never grow up."

Progress toward personal adjustment can be noted in the second testing with the incomplete sentence test. Changes in adjustment among 75 reading students as shown by test and retest with the incomplete-sentence test included the following: more favorable attitudes toward brothers and sisters and grown-ups; more interest in world affairs; more meaningful statements; better sentence structure; better spelling; more complete statements; less dependency on parents; more interest and trust in other people; more self-confidence; more specific goals. Representative of statements indicating change is this one, "I used to hate people who thought they were better than me." A new feeling of responsibility seems apparent in the student who made this change. February: "If you want to belong to an organization just join." May: "If you want to belong to an organization, work in it and take part."

Younger pupils with reading problems do not escape disabling emotional involvements. Temper tantrums, hyperactivity, violations of rules are common. On the other hand, some retarded readers are observed to be very quiet, retiring, withdrawn, and over-conformative. One fourth-grade boy of superior scholastic ability was a constant troublemaker in the schoolroom, noisy, belligerent, insolent to his teacher. He was the victim of a broken home, followed by his father's second marriage and the birth of a younger brother. A hyperactive second-grade boy stuttered, was subject to nightmares, and had nervous mannerisms. Robbie's third-grade teacher reported her only objection to him was that he didn't pay any attention to anything she said. He found his daydreams and fantasies so much more satisfying than real-life experiences that he had almost lost touch with reality. (This kind of defense mechanism was observed in a college girl who said, "You know how reading seems to me? It's like something a way off.")

Second- and third-graders who made tested improvement in reading skills were observed to make changes in drawings and verbal expressions similar to those made by college students. Statements made by an apathetic third-grade boy early in the school year were almost entirely negative: "I don't like it if we have even a day of school. I hardly ever get to do anything I like to do. My home is not very clean. My brothers tore my book." His first drawing showed a long passageway with a small window at the far end, as if he could see only a glimmer of hope in a barren existence. As he improved in reading skill, his stories became increasingly happier in tone, containing expressions of positive emotions: "I liked the song. I liked the picture. The story I liked best was . . . . You can have fun on a farm." Later pictures showed fewer barriers, more sunlight, expanding horizons. Improvements were also noted in his posture, physical energy, cleanliness, social participation, and imagination. During the six months while these changes in personal adjustment took place, he gained a year and a half in reading skills, according to standardized tests, and greatly increased the volume of voluntary reading.

Hostility was violently expressed by a retarded reader in the second grade. Early pictures of houses were complicated mazes, surrounded by blazing guns. Some buildings were portrayed as sending off lethal rays. These gave way to more attractive, conventional dwellings. His drawings of the human figure changed from frowning profiles to smiling full-face figures. Early stories included expressions of discontent, "I hate the farm, the sunshine, the hard work, the dark, old house." Later writings were more positive in tone, "I like Tommy. I like Joan. I like Sam." His reading skills improved from below average for his grade to better than average.

MMPI text results suggest that reading disability is often associated with frustration. Among 41 college students with the characteristic high "Q" and low "L" ability pattern, 17 yielded scores in various scales approaching or exceeding two standard deviations from the mean, and 16 additional students showed moderate deviations from the mean. The modes of behavior which these students have developed as a result of frustration can be illustrated by a brief discussion of their scores. Standard scores of five students, ranging from 66 to 93 on the manic scale, suggest hyperactivity, impatience, and a tendency to start many projects and complete few, if any. People with these tendencies commonly pay considerable attention to prestige and financial gain. They know the rules and the laws, but they look for loopholes. They enjoy taking a calculated risk. They may be observed to cultivate people who appear able to do them favors.

Five of the 17 reading students whose MMPI test results suggest more serious problems yielded standard scores of 67 to 92 on the depression scale. Characteristics suggested by these scores are low morale, lack of self-confidence, feelings of worthlessness, worry, narrowness of interests, introversion, and little hope for the future.

Three people, with standard scores from 66 to 103, appear inclined toward hypochondriasis, or over-concern with bodily ills. Other problems suggested by MMPI scores are social introversion, extreme anxiety, hysteria, and rigidity combined with supersensitivity.

Adding weight to the belief that these problems are associated with reading disability is evidence that many of these scores were reduced as reading skills improved. Five students who reduced their manic scores made an average gain in reading speed of 38 percentile points and three made considerable gain in comprehension during one semester of reading instruction plus professional counseling. Nine who reduced moderate-to-serious anxiety made an average gain in speed of 43.8 percentile points, and five made substantial gains in comprehension. An average gain in speed of 68 percentile points was made by six students who reduced social-introversion scores, and five of these made gains in comprehension. Hypochondriasis scores came down for five students who made an average gain in speed of 57 percentile points. Five people manifesting rigidity and hypersensitivity made improvement in adjustment and an average gain in speed of 56.6 percentile points. Measurable improvement in both reading speed and personal adjustment was noted in the case of three depressives, three hysterics, two with a naïve disregard for conventions, and three with tendencies to withdraw from reality.

Dramatic improvements among individuals are often concealed in reports of group progress. For example, one student reduced his social introversion score from 66 to 54 while making tested gains in reading skills as follows: from the 9th to the 95th percentile in speed, 11th to 66th percentile in vocabulary, and 12th to 24th percentile in comprehension. Reductions were made in five other MMPI scores by this student.

A freshman girl who gained 50 percentile points in comprehension and doubled her speed also showed reductions in depression from 73 to 69, in anxiety from 68 to 53, and toward feminine identification from 66 to 62. Her H-T-P and Bender drawings also suggested progress toward femininity and reduction of anxiety. The first drawing of the human figure was a man and the second, offered at the end of the semester, was a woman. Second drawings of the Bender figures were larger and distributed over the page instead of crowded into the upper left.

The dismal test pattern of one boy at the onset of the semester pictured him in the lower 5 per cent of his class in reading speed, in the lower 9 per cent in comprehension, and two standard deviations above the mean as per the MMPI in depression. Two other deviate scores on MMPI scales suggested decided tendencies toward social introversion and hysteria. At the close of the semester, his tested speed ranked in the upper 33 per cent of his class; his tested comprehension had more than doubled; depression score was reduced to the 48th percentile; and both of his other two deviate scores were appreciably reduced. Increased personal security was suggested by his reproductions of the Bender Visual Motor Gestaldt, depicted at the time of second testing with fewer retracings and erasures, firmer and more consistent pencil stroke, and rearrangement of the figures away from the edge of the page. His drawings of the human figure showed changes from profile (believed to reflect evasion) to full face and from a frown to a smile.

Gains of one girl from the 21st to the 93d percentile in speed and from the 5th to the 75th percentile in comprehension were accompanied by a reduction of tension in five areas as measured by retest with the MMPI. Her standard score on the anxiety scale was reduced from 73 to 55.

These illustrations of students who made progress toward a wholesome personal adjustment suggest that reading students have frequently found themselves in situations with which they could not cope. We might assume that the modes of behavior represented by their scores on the MMPI were developed in response to frustration which became intolerable. They could not meet the demands of these situations and sought to relieve their tensions by whatever responses were available to them, worry, excessive activity, preoccupation with physical health, etc. More attention will be paid to this subject in later chapters. Explanations of such terms as "percentile rank" will be given in the chapter on diagnosis.

SUMMARY

Developmental reading is designed for students who fail to read as well as tests of general ability indicate they are able. Evidence is offered in support of the statement that reading disability is a widespread educational problem, extending from the early grades to the adult level. The scope of the problem is further explored in a discussion of multi-causal factors. Physical handicaps, visual anomalies, poor teaching, although they cannot be ignored, are no more important factors in reading than emotions and personal adjustment. All retarded readers do not manifest emotional problems. Neither are all maladjusted people poor readers. However, there is considerable evidence that reading is a function of the whole personality, and that improvement in reading skills is often concurrent with improvement in personal adjustment.

These insights into the nature and scope of the problem should be kept in mind while choosing methods and techniques of teaching and instruments for diagnosis and evaluation. Objectives of reading classes should be stated in terms of total growth of individuals and groups, as well as improving reading skills.

CHAPTER 2

The Application of Psychological
Concepts to the Reading Program

Among the many psychological principles which might be associated with the teaching of developmental reading, we have selected for discussion a few that appear to be most pertinent and some which might be forgotten or overlooked by teachers. Although most or perhaps all of these findings are doubtless covered in psychology classes for teachers, their application to teaching is less well explored. Most teachers are familiar with the phrases "teaching the whole child" and "meeting the psychological needs of the individual" but putting them into practice in the classroom is a complicated and difficult task.

It would be impossible for a training program to anticipate and cover thoroughly every classroom problem. If the teacher has adopted a theory or philosophy or set of principles, he then has a flexible frame of reference which can be applied to specific problems and which lends consistency to practice. As he applies techniques consistent with his philosophy and sees them work, he expands and modifies the theory and it becomes more meaningful to him.

Some of the most useful psychological concepts are these. Every individual has certain psychological needs. If the school and the class meet some of these needs or help to meet them, learning is facilitated. Facts, skills, and attitudes related to psychological needs are more easily learned than those which are not related. If psychological needs are not met, learning is retarded.

Beginning in infancy, each individual builds a self-concept. If he can like and respect himself, he is better able to learn than if he feels himself unworthy, guilty, incompetent, or inadequate. His self-concept is greatly influenced by the way in which he is treated by parents, siblings, classmates, teachers, and all people with whom he is associated. The kinds and amounts of learning are governed by his self-concept. If he regards himself as a person who cannot learn reading or verbal skills, he will resist learning them.

No two people see reality in exactly the same way. The child's picture of reality is not the same as the teacher's view. In order for them to communicate with each other, the teacher must be able to see into the child's "field!" The process of perception can be modified and impaired by excessive pressures on the child or his need to blot out painful or disagreeable portions of his perceptual field. If the perceptual field is markedly distorted or restricted, communicative skills, including reading, are impaired. Remediation may involve changing the perceptual field as well as practice in skills.

When learning takes place, the individual feels a confirming or reinforcing reaction, not necessarily verbalized, but as if he were saying to himself, "I can use this; this is satisfying;" or "This fits; this confirms my perceptions;" or "This is a new and important discovery. I see a new relationship." If the individual discovers for himself the correct response or shares in its discovery, the confirming reaction is more intensely experienced and the learning is more profound and permanent than if a new fact or the solution to a problem is given to him by someone else. Some guidance aids learning, but too much is detrimental.

In the case of retarded readers, learning has somehow "gone wrong." They have had experiences which might be termed "unnegotiable," or they lack meaningful experience associated with skill in communication. They have learned not to communicate. The reading teacher's job is to help them unlearn and relearn as well as learn.

SOURCES OF MOTIVATION

Aside from basic physical necessities, a number of other needs are acknowledged to be related to wholesome development. Among them are love, respect, sociality, self-esteem, adequacy. Maslow[1] emphasizes the need to love as well as to be loved. Also discussed by Maslow is the desire for self-actualization or self-fulfillment. Some say that all psychological needs stem from the drive for self-enhancement. For optimum development, these needs must be satisfied all along the way, in school and elsewhere. It is not enough to present facts and skills that would be useful in the future. The present, immediate needs of pupils are much more real and pressing to them than are the problems they will be called upon to meet in the future.

Although the desire for approval and affection is conceded to be a

[1] Maslow, A. H., *Motivation and Personality*, Harper & Brothers, New York, 1954, pp. 90, 91.

source of motivation, its place in the schoolroom is debated pro and con by popular writers and some psychologists. Starch's[2] pooled ratings of 44 biological and social drives give hunger first place and love of offspring second. Love and related emotions are given fifth, tenth, and eleventh places. Evidence is accumulating to suggest that the need for love is as strong as, if not stronger than, the need for food.[3,4,5] If not satisfied, this need appears to have an adverse effect upon appetite, nutrition, and physical development as well as upon personality. It is believed to be an important factor in infant mortality. Denying a child love virtually ensures that he will spend his life continually seeking and craving affection.[6] The child who is fortified by love ultimately becomes able to love others.

Hunger, as a basic drive, we can use but little in the classroom, although some attention is paid to the desire for possessions and status. Use can be made of psychological motivations. Perhaps love is not the most appropriate term to express a desirable relationship between teacher and pupil. The desired relationship is warm and positive, inclusive of mutual respect, sociality, responsiveness, permissiveness, acceptance, and understanding. Optimum development demands this kind of relationship between parent and child, among siblings and classmates, and between teacher and pupil. If primary psychological needs are relatively well satisfied, the child is free to give his attention to the learning of facts and skills and to the needs of other people.

This concept of classroom climate is sometimes associated with the progressive-education movement. Actually it is not that new. John Gerson, Chancellor of the University of Paris in the fifteenth century, made this statement, "Where there is no love, what good is instruction, as one neither likes to listen to it nor properly believes in the words heard nor follows the commandments."

The need of all for self-esteem, recognition, and approval is emphasized by Gardner Murphy[7] throughout his book on personality. He summarizes a passage on this subject by remarking that, " . . . one of the

[2] Starch, D., *Principles of Advertising*, A. W. Shaw Company, Chicago and New York, 1923.

[3] Ribble, Margaret, *The Rights of Infants*, Columbia University Press, New York, 1934.

[4] Ruch, F. L., *Psychology and Life*, Scott-Foresman and Company, Chicago, 1948, pp. 444–445.

[5] Weininger, Dr. Otto, address at a meeting of the American Association for the Advancement of Science, reported in *Science News Letter*, January 2, 1954.

[6] Levy, D. M., "Primary Affect Hunger," *Amer. J. Psychiat.*, 1937, vol. 94, pp. 643–652.

[7] Murphy, Gardner, *Personality: A Biosocial Approach to Origins and Structure*, Harper & Brothers, New York, 1947, p. 513.

chief aims of the young adult is status, and his picture of himself as the recipient of a certain kind and degree of status is so clearly drawn that almost every aspect of it gives a fair clue to all the rest." The studies of Greenberg[8] and Leuba[9] present convincing evidence that competition among children for objects is actually competition for status. English[10] lists the need for approval and the need to belong as primary social motivations.

Critical attitudes toward the drive for status or self-enhancement may be a result of the Puritan influence in our country. We are admonished that: "Pride goeth before a fall." Parents and teachers sometimes fail to recognize the child's successes for fear "he will get too big for his britches." Experimental data indicate that if children think well of themselves, believe themselves competent, successful, and acceptable, they will undertake more tasks and persist longer against difficulties than those who regard themselves incompetent and unsuccessful.[11,12] A child's strengths sometimes remain unrewarded because his teacher focuses her attention on helping him overcome his weaknesses. However, a feeling of success in one task may produce a spread of effect which extends to motivation to perform another task. A shift in the level of performance in one task may cause a shift in the general level of aspiration.[13] Rather passive children can be moved by success to more active behavior, and active children tend to become more passive as a result of failure.[14] These studies lend support to Rogers' view that, "Every individual exists in a continually changing world of experience of which he is the center."[15]

If teachers are aware of the normal and continuous need for love, status, and self-esteem, they might then seek methods, techniques, and materials which fit the situation. These sources of motivation should not

[8] Greenberg, P. J., "Competition in Children: An Experimental Study," *Amer. J. Psychol.*, 1932, vol. 44, pp. 221–248.

[9] Leuba, C. J., "An Experimental Study of Rivalry in Young Children," *J. comp. Psychol.*, 1933, vol. 16, pp. 367–378.

[10] English, Horace, *Child Psychology*, Henry Holt and Company, Inc., New York, 1951, p. 225.

[11] Keister, M. E., "The Behavior of Young Children in Failure," *University of Iowa Studies in Child Welfare*, vol. 14, 1938, pp. 27–82.

[12] Keister, M. E., and R. Updegraf, "A Study of Children's Reactions to Failure and an Experimental Attempt to Modify Them," *Child Development Monograph*, vol. 8, 1937, pp. 241–248.

[13] Lewin, Kurt, *A Dynamic Theory of Personality*, McGraw-Hill Book Company, Inc., New York, 1935, pp. 252ff (quoting studies by Frank).

[14] *Ibid.*, pp. 252ff.

[15] Rogers, Carl, *Client-Centered Therapy*, Houghton Mifflin Company, Boston, 1951, p. 483.

be ignored, first, because the development of wholesome and acceptable behavior patterns demands their recognition, and second, because the learning of facts and skills can be greatly enhanced through their use. We learn about human needs from psychology books and lectures, but some classroom techniques and practices deny their existence and interfere with normal satisfactions. The test results, remarks, and behavior of many retarded readers strongly suggest that their basic psychological needs have not been and are not being adequately met. A part of the reading teacher's job is to promote and bring about within students self-esteem, self-respect, and a sense of personal worth. On this subject, Harris[16] asserts that the motivation of the poor reader is of vital importance and the teacher must convey to the learner the feeling that he is accepted, liked, and understood. Status, recognition, security, and belongingness are among the needs said to affect the motivation of the learner.[17]

The basic psychological needs, love, approval, status, are social needs. Even adequacy and self-esteem are partially realized through contacts with other people. Thus classroom climate and opportunities for participation and social interchange with peers are related to the degree to which basic needs can be met. The nature of the classroom atmosphere, Lifton[18] reminds us, "is basic to how people develop their security patterns."

Communication is social behavior. Reading, as one of the communicative skills, requires a response by the reader. When efficient reading skills are firmly established, the communication goes on between the writer and the reader without an oral response, but for one who is trying to overcome communicative and reading handicaps, talking with others about reading adds meaning to the reading.

FRUSTRATION

When a person finds obstacles in the way of reaching a goal which he regards as important, he experiences frustration. It is especially intense when a fundamental need remains unsatisfied. It is felt acutely when one finds himself repeatedly confronted with a problem with which he feels he cannot cope. Frustration is not keenly experienced unless the goal is regarded as important.

[16] Harris, Albert J., "Motivating the Poor Reader," *Education*, vol. 73, May, 1953, pp. 566–574.

[17] Hoffman, Rosella E., "How Motivation Influences Student Learning," *USAF, ATC Instructors J.*, vol. 5, 1954, pp. 64–68.

[18] Lifton, Walter M., "The Teacher's Role in Mental Hygiene, Therapy and Social Reconstruction," *Progressive Educ.*, May, 1955, p. 67.

Frustration is linked with repeated failure. The unwholesome effects of repeated failure are emphasized in the findings of Pauline Sears.[19] Toleration of failure is learned only when it is temporary and is linked with the expectation of ultimate success.[20] Retarded readers have commonly experienced many failures and associate failure with verbal activities.

Another study suggests that the further one is from a goal, the fewer trials he will make when frustrated.[21] Retarded readers might be expected to regard their scholastic goals from a greater distance than would able readers and thus be more susceptible to frustration. These studies point up the importance of helping them to set goals which appear within their reach and of alleviating or minimizing frustration whenever possible.

Jones[22] produced frustration in 144 subjects and noted an immediate increase in time needed for learning and increased stereotypy of response. Vacillation of response increased when frustration was expected to be at its peak. Stereotypy as observed in reading students may be caused by past frustrations. If original and critical thinking is to be encouraged, it appears that teachers must take steps to repair the damage and to avoid, if possible, increasing frustration in the reading class.

All people experience some frustration. Some possess a higher threshold of tolerance than others. If the threshold of tolerance is exceeded, behavior is adversely affected. The responses of the frustrated individual deteriorate in quality.[23],[24] Rational thinking is less apparent, and the individual resorts to simple and primitive responses. The characteristic response of an individual may become fixated and elicited at unexpected and inappropriate times.[25] Some respond to excessive frustration with rebellion, some with submission, and others with other modes of behavior.

[19] Sears, Pauline S., "Levels of Aspiration in Academically Successful and Unsuccessful Children," *J. abnorm. soc. Psychol.*, 1940, vol. 35, pp. 498–536.

[20] Keister, Mary E., "The Behavior of Young Children in Failure," *University of Iowa Studies in Child Welfare*, vol. 14, 1938, pp. 27–82.

[21] Adelman, Harvey M., and Gerald Rosenbaum, "Extinction of Instrumental Behavior as a Function of Frustration at Various Distances from the Goal," *J. exp. Psychol.*, vol. 47, 1954, pp. 429–432.

[22] Jones, Leonard, "Frustration and Stereotyped Behavior in Human Subjects," *Quart. J. exp. Psychol.*, vol. 6, 1954, pp. 12–20.

[23] Barker, R. G., T. Dembo, and K. Lewin, "Frustration and Regression, an Experiment with Young Children," *University of Iowa Studies: Studies of Child Welfare*, 1941, vol. 18, no. 1.

[24] Korchin, S. J., J. L. Singer, and R. G. Ballard, "The Influence of Frustration on Visually-Perceived Forms," *Personality*, vol. 1, no. 1, January, 1951, pp. 54ff.

[25] Maier, Norman, *Frustration*, McGraw-Hill Book Company, Inc., New York, 1949, pp. 82, 87, 119.

Whatever the pattern, when the threshold of tolerance is exceeded, the individual tends to become inflexible and rigid, losing his ability to respond rationally and appropriately to the demands of a situation. Under these conditions, resistance to learning mounts.[26,27] Repeated frustration is believed to lower the threshold of tolerance.

The response of individuals to environmental press is described by Anderson and Anderson[28] in terms of six levels of behavior. The optimum level is (1) minimum press. Spontaneity, productivity, and creativity are maintained. The individual knows that all people cause some inconvenience to others and expects some. As the scale descends, spontaneity, productivity, and creativity decrease. Remaining levels in descending order are: (2) avoidance of press; (3) resistance or rebellion; (4) vacillation between rebellion and submission; (5) submission to domination; and (6) personality disintegration. The reader will notice that resistance is regarded as a higher-level adjustment to environmental press than is submission. The submissive person has fewer resources and has further to go toward rehabilitation. Submissive pupils give the teacher less trouble than rebellious ones, and their problems are often overlooked. Our observations suggest that an individual suffering from excessive press of environment may go through a stage of rebellion before arriving at submission. Perhaps the overly submissive individual must go through a stage of rebellion on the road to rehabilitation. As the scale descends, the individual at each successive level has less energy available for productivity. Energy is wasted in rebellion, anxiety, or excessive self-control. Energies become less goal-directed, except as they are directed toward relieving tensions or avoiding tension-producing situations. At the final point of personality disintegration, environmental press is unbearable, and energy is aimlessly expended.

Vacillation between aggression and submission is associated with anxiety, although it is not the only source. In the opinion of one author, anxiety neuroses, obsessions, and compulsions develop as a result of early damage to one's aggressiveness and self assertion.[29] Penalties on aggressiveness have led to guilt feelings and fear of freedom. Anxiety is not a successful solution and recurs. The behavior and related past experiences of retarded readers lead one to suspect that aggressiveness has been

[26] *Ibid.*, pp., 18, 72, 75ff.

[27] Patrick, J. K., "Studies in Rational Behavior and Emotional Excitement: II The Effect of Emotional Excitement on Rational Behavior and Human Subjects," *J. comp. Psychol.*, 1934, vol. 18, pp. 153–195.

[28] Anderson, H., and G. Anderson (eds.), *Introduction to Projective Techniques*, Prentice-Hall, Inc., Englewood Cliffs, N. J., 1951, Chap. II.

[29] Muller-Eckhard, Hans, "Contribution to the Pheno-Analysis of the Obsessive-Compulsive Neurosis," *Psyche. Heidel.*, vol. 8, 1954, pp. 143–160.

punished, in one way or another, in some cases by the withholding of approval and affection. Anxiety may be the result of the need for self-assertion, conflicting with the fear of its results. Fear of freedom to express and assert oneself is noted among retarded readers, many of whom imply that early attempts at conversation were ignored, discouraged, criticized, or penalized. Symptoms of retarded readers are not usually sufficiently alarming as to suggest mental illness, but they are often present to a degree which interferes with productivity and normal satisfactions.

Schwidder[30] finds that stringent and cold parental treatment of children results in damage to normal aggressiveness and the appearance of strong guilt, leading in numerous cases to obsessive-compulsive neuroses. Vigorous outbursts of hostile and aggressive feelings may occur preceding a successful conclusion to therapy.

A comment by Vorhaus[31] suggests the relationship between the press of environment and reading retardation. She believes that in students of normal intelligence, reading disability represents indirect or unconscious resistance to environmental pressure.

The characteristics of responses to excessive frustration have been described: primitivation, fixation, and resistance to learning. Some specific responses to excessive frustration can also be identified. They may be made by normal people, but carried to extremes, they become mental illness.

Some modes of behavior developed in response to frustration are described in Chapters 3 and 4 in connection with the discussion of the Minnesota Multiphasic Personality Inventory. Among them are imagined illnesses, converting emotional problems into physical symptoms, anxiety, depression, rationalizations, suspiciousness, hypersensitivity, blaming others, retreat into fantasy, social introversion, flattening of feeling, inability to distinguish right from wrong, excessive respect for status and financial gain, and hyperactivity. Other responses to frustration are obsessions, compulsions, scapegoating, drug addiction, alcoholism, nomadism, over-conformity.

One of the most serious responses to frustration is resignation, a state in which the individual strives for nothing, makes no decisions, and simply waits for things to happen to him. Probably he does not even desire that which he no longer hopes to achieve. He may not have passed through stages of rebellion, anxiety, and submisson and finally arrived

[30] Schwidder, Werner, "Symptom Picture, Basic Structure and Therapy of the Obsessive-Compulsive Neurosis," *Psyche. Heidel.*, vol. 8, 1954, pp. 126–142.

[31] Vorhaus, Pauline G., "Rorschach Configurations Associated with Reading Disability," *J. proj. Tech.*, vol. 16, 1952, pp. 3–19.

at complete apathy. Maier[32] suggests that resignation may be the final stage of frustration. This mode of behavior is not found in combination with other kinds of adjustment.

As the reader will observe, these various modes of behavior (with the exception of resignation) are not mutually exclusive. Various combination adjustments will be found: anxiety with repression, aggression with fixed ideas, etc. All people who resort to these defenses are seeking security or satisfactions which they have not been able to find through acceptable modes of behavior. Their normal needs for self-esteem, love, and adequacy have not been met. Their behavior patterns have developed according to the satisfactions available to them. These adjustments reduce productivity and hamper the full use of the individual's potentials.

The discovery of such a problem is not an occasion for moralizing, but for an exploration of the child's resources and resources of the school and community. If the source of the trouble is understood, the teacher or counselor will realize that entirely rational behavior cannot be expected and will try to handle the situation so as not to increase frustration or the press of environment. Obviously, a display of force will contribute little to a long-term solution. The aggressive child will respond with increased aggression or ultimately move in the other direction toward anxiety and submission. Whatever response is made to frustration, force, criticism, or punishment will tend to fixate it or to drive the individual further from a wholesome adjustment.[33] Obviously, threats, admonitions, embarrassment, or punishment will not solve the problem of people who already feel uncertain of their own worth. As teachers and counselors, we need to explore teaching methods and techniques of interpersonal relationship which make use of the needs, motivations, and sources of wholesome satisfactions of human beings.

We need also to recognize when our own behavior is influenced by frustration. Frustration is demonstrated on both sides in this classroom incident. During education week, the class was visited by numerous parents. Both teacher and pupils were tired and nervous by the time it was over. When a timid child opened her report with a rather obvious statement, a classmate remarked derisively, "Not really!" The harassed teacher told the student to lie on the floor with his feet on a chair, and she kept him there so long that he had an embarrassing accident. Because the class laughed at him, they were denied recess for a week. It seems

[32] Maier, Norman R. F., *Frustration*, McGraw-Hill Book Company, Inc., New York, 1949, p. 114.

[33] Merrill, M. A., *Problems of Child Delinquency*, Houghton Mifflin Company, Boston, 1947.

highly improbable that this humiliating experience could have a salutary effect either on the unfortunate pupil or his classmates. All were apparently seeking some release from tension which had been building up for a week. How much better it would have been if the teacher could have said, "We are all tired and a little upset. What would you like to do for 10 minutes?" She might have asked if they would care to talk about the visits of the past week before beginning the work of the school day. Actually, she was aiming at submissive behavior, without contemplating its side-effects. She apparently did not understand the source of the children's behavior or her own.

From popular magazine articles on the subject of discipline, one gathers the impression that the teacher must choose between bedlam in the classroom or strict authoritarian rule. There are other choices which will be described in chapters to follow.

WHOLESOME RESPONSES TO FRUSTRATION

There are some wholesome responses to frustration. One of them is hard work. This solution is attemped only if the individual believes it is possible to reach a goal or overcome an obstacle in the path toward a goal. If he is unable to conceive of its being possible, he cannot spur himself to the necessary effort.

Another acceptable solution is detour. Linda has her heart set on being a concert singer. She snatched Sally's songbook and tore it up when Sally won the coveted solo part in the Christmas program. Linda can't carry a tune, but she dances beautifully and speaks well. With counseling perhaps she can find satisfaction in a role she can perform competently. Actually her goal is self-esteem and status which can be attained by a detour route.

Compensation can be an acceptable response if it is not overdone. The struggles of Lord Byron and Theodore Roosevelt to overcome physical weakness are often cited as examples of successful compensation. A novel by Aldous Huxley describes the financial success of an intellectually mediocre man. Compensation occurs when the blind develop acute sense of hearing or touch or when the loss of hands is followed by extraordinary dexterity in using the feet. If compensation is not rewarded by status, self-esteem, affection, and security, the individual again finds himself in a situation where he cannot succeed. If his goal cannot be reached, the ultimate result may be physical and mental collapse.

The role of the school is to help students find wholesome responses to frustration and to avoid, if possible, adding to excessive press of environment. Positively stated, the school can help pupils to reach goals which are important to them and to satisfy the fundamental, universal need for self-enhancement.

DISTORTION AND SELECTION IN PERCEPTION

When considering the unacceptable modes of adjustment to frustration, we observe that the maladjusted individuals perceive their environment as markedly different from that perceived by so-called normal associates. More threats are seen, and fewer satisfactions appear to them to be available. New facts and skills will not appear to these people in the same context as to people in harmony with environment.

The individual's perception of self and environment may be distorted by feelings of guilt and unworthiness. Acceptable behavior seldom if ever results from a disproportionate sense of guilt or shame. In some cases, such a generalized and disabling emotional state develops from our unrealistic conception of human nature. Standards for the behavior of children are often unrealistic, in view of perfectly normal needs and tendencies. In spite of much ado about the lax discipline of today, there are still many who make children feel guilty if they do not sit still, play quietly, share their toys, keep clean, work hard, etc. Some children are actually made to feel guilty because they are "in the way," because their existence reduces the supply of comforts and luxuries for other members of the family. Children are taught that "good people" always tell the truth, help one another, are kind to animals, etc. The natural curiosity of the child about his own body is often viewed as reprehensible by parents and teachers.

If standards for behavior are so high they cannot be reached, the child grows up with a feeling of guilt because he is not perfect. If he acknowledges the perfection of man, he must repress the memories of his little digressions and pretend that he is better than he really is, or he must confess to his failure to reach the desired state of perfection. Either course leads to a distorted picture of reality. If he finds that people are not as good as he has been taught, he must question the veracity of parents and teachers. This conclusion upsets his system of values and leads him to doubt his own perceptions.

If his conflict is acute, portions of environment and self are blotted out of the picture, and new learning relating to these areas cannot be fully admitted. Information which threatens to disturb the picture is unwelcome.

The person so conditioned builds a defense between himself and others. He must never reveal that he is not as good as he is supposed to be. In conversation and relations with others, he must always be on guard, lest someone discover the horrible truth. Thus, he cuts himself off from developing and expressing his own convictions and from social and intellectual interchange. Spontaneity is restricted, and some areas of learning are barred to him. Probably, his resistance is raised to learning and using and reading certain words, phrases, and meanings related to these repressed materials.

Such conditioning may result in uneven intellectual development.[34] For example, wealth and precision of vocabulary is believed to depend partly upon the individual's emotional receptivity to necessary experiences. If emotional development sets restrictions on those aspects of thought functioning that underlie the development of vocabulary, it will interfere with the acquisition of a wide range of words.[35] As a result of undue controls, uneven development might be expected in verbal, quantitative, and motor functioning and abstract reasoning ability. Interpersonal relations will also be affected as the over-controlled person struggles to maintain his defenses.

Slow readers appear to be inferior to fast readers in speed and accuracy of perception, according to a study reported by Thurstone.[36] Fast readers were quicker in identifying dotted outlines, had a higher flicker-fusion rate, were more likely to perceive the whole picture, made more rapid decisions in color-form sorting, were better in object judgments, and were superior in verbal factor, number factor, word fluency, and reasoning. He used 74 tests in an extensive factorial study of perception.

Recent psychological experiments suggest that a person sees the world around him, including what he reads, in terms of his own needs, those which have been satisfied, those which remain unsatisfied, and modes of behavior which are attempts to satisfy needs. If the individual perceives something which promises to satisfy a pressing need, this desired experience or object or person (whatever it is) appears to him magnified and it may shut out a portion of the environment so that he does not see the environmental field as it appears to others. Thus, reading may appear to this individual to be of little importance, or if he does read, certain words or passages may be meaningless to him. Communication with others is difficult for him, because their perceptions and his are not in agreement.

Studies of Bruner and Postman[37] shed some light on this subject. What

[34] Anderson, Harold, and Gladys L. Anderson, (eds.), *Introduction to Projective Techniques,* Prentice-Hall, Inc., Englewood Cliffs, N. J., 1951, p. 546 (Chap. 19 by Martin Mayman, Roy Schafer, and David Rapaport).

[35] *Ibid.,* p. 551.

[36] Thurstone, L. L., *A Factorial Study of Perception,* University of Chicago Press, Chicago, 1944, pp. 125–130.

[37] Bruner, Jerome, and Postman, Leo, "Symbolic Value as an Organizing Factor in Perception," *J. soc. Psychol.,* vol. 27, second half, May, 1948, pp. 203–208.

is important to the subject apparently looms larger in perception. That which is desired or which fulfills a need tends to be emphasized in perception through magnification. They report an experiment in which small children were given three-inch toys to play with. When asked to guess the size of the figures, they guessed the toys they liked best as larger than the others. After the toys were withheld, the desirable toys appeared still larger to the children. In other words, desirability made the figures seem larger than they really were, and desirability plus unavailability further increased their imagined size.[38] A similar study is reported by Beams.[39] If this finding can be applied to reading problems, the person who sees something which he believes could satisfy an important and pressing need might not be able to concentrate on reading unless it is related to the "something" which he wants so much. That blonde with the Coke-bottle figure may loom so large that she eclipses verbs, nouns, and punctuation marks. If getting a date or success on a date is exceedingly important to the high-school or college student, improving reading skills may seem relatively unimportant by contrast. In a later chapter, role-playing of such experiences is related to reading.

When a person is presented with a story, picture, or idea which appears to him to be threatening, that is, to call up painful, disagreeable, or disturbing thoughts or memories, he may fail to perceive anything at all, or may report jumbled or incomplete perception, or may report seeing material which is contradictory to the actual nature of what is presented. He may report things which are not there at all or which could not be interpreted from the material presented.[40] A person who wishes to forget earlier experiences or to conceal things about himself which he considers damaging might have trouble with reading if it threatens to call up thoughts or memories which he prefers to ignore.

It is possible that each person goes through a sort of screening process when he is offered a new bit of information. If the information appears threatening, it is rejected in a prerecognition period and does not become a part of the person. He can't use it. Past learning is not all equally available to an individual. If a skill or piece of information is associated with deprivation or punishment in the past, he cannot call it up readily when he needs it. This may also be true if it has not been used or if it has not been reinforced with success or pleasant associations.[41] This block

[38] Bruner, Jerome, and Leo Postman, "Perception, Cognition and Behavior," *J. Pers.*, vol. 18, no. 1, September, 1949, p. 20.

[39] Beams, Howard L., "Affectivity as a Factor in the Apparent Size of Pictured Food Objects," *J. exp. Psychol.*, vol. 47, 1954, pp. 197–200.

[40] Bruner and Postman, *op. cit.*, p. 25.

[41] *Ibid.*, p. 26.

in the way of using skills and information applies to reading as well as to other kinds of learning.

Frenkel-Brunswik[42] speaks of want, fear, insecurity, rigidity, prejudice, social influences, and conformity as they distort perception. She describes the reactions of two groups of children to a story. Each group was composed of children from grades 5, 7, and 8. According to test results and clinical judgment, the children in one of these groups might be described as stereotyped, rigid, and prejudiced. They were inclined to take an all-or-none attitude toward everything. Parents (or all people) were regarded as either all good or all bad. Parental standards for behavior had been rigid, and the children had conformed to them without understanding them. They made safe, stereotyped statements. The other group of children did not have these characteristics. When asked to reproduce the story in writing, the rigid group tended to inject materials which were not in the story and which could not possibly have been interpreted from it. They recalled more disagreeable than agreeable aspects and made other distortions. Over-emphasis on negative, hostile, and catastrophic features were also found in clinical data, interviews, and TAT (Thematic Apperception Test) stories of these children. The other group of children tended to follow the story more faithfully and to reproduce the undesirable and desirable features in the ratio in which they occurred in the story. Forty-three per cent of the children in the rigid group as contrasted with 8 per cent of the other group recalled exclusively the part of the story concerned with fighting. The difference is statistically significant at the 1 per cent level of confidence.[43]

Other experiments showed further differences between these two groups. They were shown a picture of a dog which was followed by transitional pictures, finally leading to a picture of a cat. The stereotyped group reported that they still saw a dog, while the other group reported the change. In other words the rigid group tended not to see what did not harmonize with the first mental set and to hold on to the first object. Once perseveration was broken, subjects in the rigid group tended toward haphazard guessing or blocking.

Resistance to change was further shown by the rigid group when the children were introduced to a progressive series of colors. The rigid group apparently tended to perseverate longer than the other group.

In another experiment, the rigid group was inferior in recognizing numbers emerging from indistinctness and numbers changing from other

[42] Frenkel-Brunswik, Else, "Intolerance of Ambiguity as an Emotional and Perceptual Personality Variable," *J. Pers.*, vol. 18, no. 1, September, 1949, pp. 109, 130–134.

[43] Frenkel-Brunswik, *op. cit.*, pp. 122–127.

numbers, and tended to cling to the first impression, though faulty. Differences between the two groups were statistically significant at the 1 per cent level of confidence.[44]

In another experiment, the subjects were first shown a long, complicated method of solving an arithmetic problem and then were shown a simpler method. The stereotyped group persisted longer in using the complicated method introduced first. A similar study employed a map on which a long, complicated route was first established. The rigid group resisted learning the shorter path. Thus rigidity scores derived from the simple arithmetic problem tend to correlate with over-all clinical ratings of children's rigidity, based on attitudes toward parents, sex roles, self, moral values, etc., revealed in interviews and personality test results.[45]

These six experiments suggest that stereotyped people actually perceive an incident, a story, a picture, or a scene as different from the way in which it is perceived by other people, and that they are inclined to resist new ideas or change. This handicap would interfere with improvement in reading skills as well as in other kinds of learning. The author presents evidence that stereotyped people feel very insecure. Their all-or-none attitude appears to offer them some security, and anything which threatens their prejudices cannot be learned. Insecurity seems related to failure to meet unreasonable or incomprehensible standards or demands, but in some cases it appears to be the result of other conditions, such as physical disability.

In view of the retarded reader's confusion about his own identity, this observation is interesting. Rigid people, says Frenkel-Brunswik, tend toward an underlying identification with and envy of the opposite sex and discontinuity between the sex roles. Also, like linguistically inferior people, the intolerant individual makes few spontaneous references to early childhood.[46]

Discussing factors contributing to rigidification of personality in children, Frenkel-Brunswik mentions parental emphasis on stereotyped behavior, expectancy of self-negating submission, and pressure to repress non-acceptable tendencies. The result is described as conflict and lack of communication within the person between layers of his personality.[47]

The effect of personal values upon learning is suggested by several recent studies. The Allport-Vernon Study of Values was given 22 male senior and graduate students. This instrument classifies people into six groups, according to values which are most important to them, e.g.,

[44] Frenkel-Brunswik, *op. cit.*, pp. 127–130.
[45] Frenkel-Brunswik, *ibid.*, p. 120.
[46] Frenkel-Brunswik, *op. cit.*, pp. 133, 134.
[47] *Ibid.*, p. 117.

artistic, religious, scientific, etc. Then the students were asked to listen to a recording of 36 words, each of which was repeated 10 times. Each word was first played very low and the volume increased during the 10 repetitions. The students were asked to indicate when they first recognized the words. They recognized those related to their most important values at an earlier point, that is at significantly lower intensity levels, than words related to lower values. All subjects were tested for hearing, and, as a group, hearing was essentially normal. One subject whose audiometric thresholds were among the poorest was among the best in recognizing words. The authors conclude,[48] " . . . some mechanism of perceptual sensitization operates to differentially raise or lower recognition thresholds." This study has significance for the teachers of reading, since it relates to verbal learning as well as to other kinds of learning.

McClelland and Liberman[49] studied the effect of need for achievement on the recognition of need-related words. A need for achievement score was calculated for 36 male undergraduates from the TAT and performance tests. Then they were asked to recognize 30 tachistoscopically presented words. The words were presented dimly and then with increasing illumination until recognized. Of these, 10 were neutral words, 10 were security related, and 10 were achievement related. Students with a high score in need for achievement recognized achievement-rated words with positive (success) connotations more readily than did students with low need for achievement scores. The group with low need for achievement was slow to recognize positive achievement-related words. The group with middle need for achievement was slow in recognizing negative-achievement words and might be said to be chiefly concerned in avoiding failure. The high-need group was also faster than other students to see positive security-related words. The results of this study suggest that the central motive state measured previously in imagination and performance influences the way in which a subject perceives his world and influences speed of recognition of certain need-related stimuli. An increase in achievement motivation leads first to a concern to avoid failure and then, as motivation grows more intense, to a greater concentration on success.

The effect of values on perception is further demonstrated by a study by McGinnies and Bowles.[50] Twenty-four undergraduate students, 12

[48] Vanderplan, James M., and Robert R. Blake, "Selective Sensitization in Auditory Perception," *J. Pers.*, vol. 18, no. 2, December, 1949, pp. 252–266.

[49] McClelland, David C., and Alvin M. Liberman, "The Effect of Need for Achievement on Recognition of Need Related Words," *J. Pers.*, vol. 18, no. 2, December, 1949, pp. 236–251.

[50] McGinnies, Elliott, and Warren Bowles, "Personal Values as Determinants of Perceptual Fixation," *J. Pers.*, vol. 18, no. 2, December, 1949, pp. 224–235.

males and 12 females, were given the Allport-Vernon Study of Values. Then they were shown 12 portraits of men (none sufficiently prominent to be identified). The portraits were presented tachistoscopically, and each was introduced by a statement, e.g., "This is a scientist." Two were called scientists, two artists, etc. When the series was shown again, the students in general were better able to identify the portraits associated with their highest values than those representing their lowest values. The authors conclude that " . . . in the absence of primary reward of differential frequency of experience, fixation will occur more readily for percepts having secondary reward value acquired through association with value-related activity." This study suggests that people learn more easily materials which they associate with their most important values. Might this apply to the learning of reading skills?

These findings regarding perception are significant in the light of Peter Fireman's[51] remark that " . . . all knowledge begins with accurate perception." Helping the reading student to perceive accurately is a complex task which goes beyond the presenting of materials and routine drills.

Several studies reported by Eriksen[52] relate anxiety to perceptual defense. Russell[53] reminds teachers that:

There is considerable research evidence that one's reading is not a purely intellectual response, but an activity influenced by emotional and attitudinal factors . . . attitudes have been shown to influence perception, learning, and recall, problem-solving and judgment, all of which may be involved in reading."

CURBS ON CREATIVITY

Mention has been made of the effect of environmental press upon creativity and of the restrictive influence of guilt. An important function of the school should be to preserve and encourage creativity, not only in art, writing, and music, but in mechanical inventiveness, creative thinking, and problem-solving. Not only the gifted, but also the average pupils are entitled to satisfactions and productivity accruing from the creativity with which they are endowed. Gardner Murphy[54] observes that the desire to create must be almost universal and that almost everyone has some measure of originality.

[51] Fireman, Peter, *Perceptualistic Theory of Knowledge*, Philosophical Library, Inc., New York, 1954.
[52] Eriksen, Charles W., "The Case for Perceptual Defense," *Psychol. Rev.*, vol. 61, 1954, pp. 175–182.
[53] Russell, David H., "Unsolved Problems in Reading, A Symposium," *Elementary English*, vol. 31, October-November, 1954, pp. 325–328, 416–430.
[54] Murphy, Gardner, *Personality, A Bio-Social Approach*, Harper & Brothers, New York, 1947, pp. 453ff.

In a culture where material rewards are greatly valued, creativity tends to decline. If great value is attached to conformity, less is given to spontaneity, new ideas, and freedom of response.

It is surprising how many teachers still insist that all their pupils should be doing exactly the same thing at the same time in the same way. In a class of 30 third graders, all were making daffodils, except one little boy. He was drawing a horse and stopped apologetically to explain, "No matter what I start out to draw, it always turns out to be a horse." It isn't too difficult to imagine a teacher saying to little Thomas Hart Benton, "But your man is all out of proportion," or to Grand Wood, "Hills are not so symmetrical," or to young Albert Einstein, "But you cannot split the atom!"

Dollard and Miller[55] discuss the effect of conformity upon creativity:

The training in social conformity that results in the fear of being different can also interfere with creative thinking, even in science. By its very nature, every truly original idea must be somewhat different from the previous conventional ones. Some otherwise highly intelligent people seem to be so afraid of original ideas that they cannot express them either to others or to themselves and therefore cannot be creative.

Attitudes toward authority appear related to original thinking, according to the results of a recent investigation by Siegel.[56] Students with high authoritarian tendencies tended toward stereotyping as well as "high status," seeking orientations and compulsions to identify in-group and out-group members. Siegel proposes that conflict, anxiety, and rejection of ambiguity foster the authoritarian mode of adjustment.

Fears and anxieties have an adverse effect upon creativeness. Resultant distractibility and indecisiveness interfere with problem-solving and constructive use of energies. People with anxiety often discover that they have lost the ability to carry a tune. Tensions prevent one from guiding the pencil or brush in the way he wants it to go.

Reading with understanding involves creative thinking. The effect of threat upon creative thinking is suggested by Beier.[57] After giving a test measuring abstract ability to two groups, he induced threat in the experimental group. Retests for abstract reasoning indicated that the experimental group had lost in powers of abstract thinking and increased

[55] Dollard, John, and Neal E. Miller, *Personality and Psychotherapy*, McGraw-Hill Book Company, Inc., New York, 1950, p. 122n.

[56] Siegel, Sidney, "Certain Determinants and Correlates of Authoritarianism," *Genet. Psychol. Monogr.*, vol. 49, 1954, pp. 187–229.

[57] Beier, Ernst B., "The Effect of Induced Anxiety upon Some Aspects of Intellectual Functioning," doctoral dissertation, Columbia University, New York, 1949.

in rigidity of thinking as compared to the control group. Some studies quoted in the discussion of punishment and reward also apply to this subject.

Creativity does survive in a few exceptional individuals in spite of restrictive environment, but the proportion of people able to retain spontaneity under such conditions is small. Creativity belongs to all of us and should be encouraged in all, including the potential geniuses.

REWARD AND PUNISHMENT

Teachers and counselors are generally familiar with the laws of learning. The famous law of effect (stated and restated by John Locke, Thorndike, and others) conveys the idea that if a response made to a situation is associated with satisfaction, the strength of the connection between the situation and the response is increased. A casual interpretation is that reward increases the desire of the person to repeat the rewarded response, or that reward helps to fixate the desired learning. However, the satisfaction which leads to learning is not necessarily reward in the form of a gold star, a dollar bill, or even praise, but a confirming or reinforcing reaction within the person. It might be conceived as a "yes" reaction, as if the person feels, "This fits. I can use this." As suggested in the opening remarks of this chapter, when a fundamental need is satisfied, the reinforcing reaction is undoubtedly strong. A superficial reward can be associated with a situation, but it is not necessarily associated.

The motive of the learner helps to determine whether the effect is interpreted as reward. If the child's motive is to gain the approval of peers, a good grade in arithmetic will not be interpreted as reward unless it is so regarded by the group to which he wants most to belong. Rejected children often spend their whole lives trying to prove their worth to their parents. If a child is so motivated, a good grade will not be interpreted as reward unless it gains him love and approval from his parents. Teachers sometimes attempt to reward children by returning good papers to be shown to parents. Rejected children will not interpret this privilege as reward and may destroy or ignore this evidence of achievement. If a child wants love and he gets an electric train, it is not a reward. Exceedingly submissive and conformative children might not enjoy the limelight and might not feel rewarded by being the object of attention, even if favorable.

In many cases, accomplishing a task is its own reward. The boy who repairs his motor scooter may feel satisfaction in fitting the parts together, in completing the task, in improved functioning of the vehicle.

He is rewarded even though nobody is around to hand him a prize or to say, "Well done." Material rewards are not needed when the "yes" reaction comes as a result of finding an answer to something one really wants to know, or of progress in a project which one yearns to complete. Thus, a retarded reader who was fascinated by weather instruments learned new words and improved his reading skills because he found they would help him to read and write about the weather. A girl who found the science textbook too difficult for her learned new words because she needed them to compose a letter of complaint to the state textbook commission.

As previously suggested, the reinforcing reaction is presumed to be much stronger when satisfactions are closely connected with the response. That is, learning is enhanced when the learner perceives the relationship between the situation and the forthcoming satisfaction.

Various historic experiments, reported by Thorndike[58] and Wheeler,[59] illustrate the learning principle that facts which "belong" to each other are more rapidly learned than unrelated facts. Words which make sense in relation to each other are more easily learned than unrelated words or nonsense syllables. The "yes" reaction may be felt as a result of seeing meaningful relationships.

A feeling akin to reward appears to accompany the knowledge that one is doing a task accurately or making gains. The more immediately the individual is aware of his accomplishment, the more profound is its influence. Informing fifth-grade children of their achievement in reading, addition, and multiplication enhanced learning, according to de Weerdt.[60] Similar results were reported by Arps,[61] Johanson,[62] and Book and Norvell.[63] The studies of Lorge and Thorndike[64] support the belief that when individuals are notified immediately after an accurate response, the rate of improvement is more rapid than when this knowledge is delayed or missing.

[58] Thorndike, E. L., *Human Learning*, Appleton-Century-Crofts, Inc, New York, 1931.

[59] Wheeler, R. H., *The Science of Psychology*, Thomas Y. Crowell Company, New York, 1929, p. 246.

[60] de Weerdt, E. H., "A Study of Improvability of Fifth Grade School Children in Certain Mental Functions," *J. Educ. Psychol.*, 1947, vol. 18, pp. 547–557.

[61] Arps, G. F., "A Preliminary Report on Work with Knowledge Versus Work without Knowledge of Results," *Psychol. Rev.*, 1917, vol. 24, pp. 449–455.

[62] Johanson, A. M., "The Influence of Incentives and Punishment upon Reaction-Time," *Arch. of Psychol.*, 1922, vol. 8, whole no. 54.

[63] Book, W. F., and L. Norvell, "The Will to Learn: an Experimental Study of Incentives in Learning," *Pedagogical Seminary*, 1922, vol. 29, pp. 305–362.

[64] Lorge, I., and E. L. Thorndike, "The Influence of Delay in the After-Effect of a Connection," *J. exp. Psychol.*, 1935, vol. 13; 186–194.

An experiment by Greenspoon[65] illustrates the effect of even a perfunctory response on learning. The experimenter asked the subjects to say all the words they could think of, and tape-recorded them. In response to each plural noun spoken, he said, "Mmmm-hmmm." During a second trial, the subjects unconsciously increased the number of plural nouns spoken, while the control group to whom nothing was said showed no such increase.

The value of a positive approach to learning is supported by various experimental data. Positive rather than negative statements or requests were demonstrated to be much more effective in producing acceptable and constructive behavior.[66,67]

Our competitive system of education seems to ensure that the same people are repeatedly rewarded for effort, while the less able pupils receive fewer and fewer of the self-propelling rewards. It is difficult for the teacher to recognize that for Johnny, the retarded reader, the learning of one new word is as great an achievement as reading a whole book is for Sally who has somehow learned to read like a house afire. Sally gets a gold star and a smile from her teacher, but Johnny is lucky if his teacher even notices his achievement. In fact, too often the attitude is "You should have learned this word last year, Johnny." So Johnny feels embarrassed, ashamed, or ignored instead of rewarded. The effect following Johnny's effort is punishment instead of reward. His new word loses part of its meaning, and motivation is lessened instead of increased. His self-esteem gets a blow instead of a boost.

Experiences of failure increase the problems of retarded readers. Investigating the influence of failure upon verbal learning and recognition, Smith[68] found that failure resulted in impairment of learning which persisted throughout the learning task.

The use of the grade card to indicate relative success or failure is virtually a universal expedient. Its advantages and disadvantages are argued pro and con, and the traditional letter grades, E to I, or A to D, are frequently designated the "incentive system" of grading. Would it not be possible to offer a true incentive to a child by giving him the

[65] Greenspoon, Joel, "The Effect of Verbal and Mechanical Stimuli on Verbal Behavior," quoted in Ruch, Floyd, *Psychology and Life,* Scott Foresman, Chicago, 1948.

[66] Johnson, M. W., *Verbal Influences on Children's Behavior,* University of Michigan Monograph in Education, University of Michigan Press, Ann Arbor, 1939.

[67] Meyers, Charles E., "The Effect of Conflicting Authority on the Child," part II, *Authority and Frustration* (by K. Lewin, C. E. Meyers, J. Kalhorn, M. L. Farber, and J. R. P. French), University of Iowa Press, Iowa City, 1944, pp. 31–98.

[68] Smith, Joseph G., "Influence of Failure, Expressed Hostility, and Stimulus Characteristics on Verbal Learning and Recognition," *J. Pers.,* vol. 22, 1954, pp. 475–493.

opportunity to compare samples of his own work, and to decide whether or not this week's work is better than last week's product or whether he has learned new words, new skills, and new facts during the past month? The effect of a letter grade upon the passive recipient is debatable. The effect of self-decision and self-discovery upon the participant is dynamic, whether experienced in the classroom or in the counseling interview.

In applying the principle of reward and punishment to the learning situation, we need to remind ourselves that success and failure are not felt in situations that are too easy or too difficult. If a task is too easy, it is not a problem. If it is too difficult, it is not recognized by the pupil as his problem. Children cannot solve problems they do not have. The implications for teaching would seem to be that attention should be paid not only to the teacher's response to the child's performance and other kinds of rewards, but also to the selection of tasks to fit his abilities and level of achievement. When counseling toward improved behavior, the same principle can be applied. The counselor tries to help the child to take a step forward, but not too big a step.

Reward or satisfaction is presumed to help to fixate a response and thus contribute to learning. Punishment is supposed to have the opposite effect. This is not always the case. An early statement by Thorndike on the law of effect assumed that the strength of a modifiable connection between a situation and a response was decreased when accompanied or followed by an annoying state of affairs. His own research at a later date caused him to abrogate this part of his statement.[69]

When a response is followed by punishment the expected result is extermination of the response, but the response will not be exterminated unless the child has a chance to give the correct response and have it rewarded or confirmed. The possibility that the incorrect response will be eliminated will be less if there are a number of possible responses. In other words, the greater the number of possible responses, the less will be the probability that punishment will be effective. Even in the event that the correct response is reinforced, the incorrect response is punished, and there are no other possible responses, there are other factors which frequently operate to keep punishment from being effective.

Punishment may arouse feelings of guilt, anxiety, or fear, emotions which are not conducive to good or improved behavior. "Strong fear," according to Shaffer,[70] "has little or no utility at any time in life." Fear can produce irrational actions. Acting from fear, the person may jump

---

[69] Stroud, J. B., *Psychology in Education,* Longmans, Green & Co., Inc., New York, 1946, p. 369.

[70] Shaffer, L. F., *The Psychology of Adjustment,* Houghton Mifflin Company, Boston, 1936, p. 368.

into the path of danger instead of away from it. A frustrating emotion, it reduces the ability of the individual to react with his normal efficiency. Threat of punishment puts the person on the defensive, and his energies must be spent on defending and explaining himself.

If the child senses aggression in the punisher and suspects that the punisher is venting his own aggressions on the child, he will respond with aggression. Rebellion and resistance persist in the face of punishment and may spread to other learning situations. Ruch[71] presents evidence that punishment tends to increase aggressiveness, either overt or concealed.

Some objective is sought when an offense is committed. If reaching the objective is more important to the child than escaping punishment, he will have learned to go through the unpleasantness to get the reward. Or he may learn not to get caught. At times, it may serve as a kind of reward, as in the case of the child who receives so little attention that even punishment is preferable to being ignored.

A curious effect of punishment is that it may relieve the offender of feeling responsible for his behavior. Somebody else takes the responsibility when he metes out the penalty. The child feels he has paid for his crime and that is an end of the matter.

Punishment does not produce a favorable change in behavior when it is not connected in the mind of the offender with the offense, follows too late to be associated with the offense, is inconsistent with the gravity of the violation, is the only attention the offender gets, is followed by reward which compensates for the unpleasantness, relieves the offender of responsibility for his actions, interferes with the satisfaction of basic needs, or results in personality damage.

It is not correct to say that the child does not learn as a result of punishment. He learns, but not in the way intended by the punisher. He may learn to think ill of himself, to rebel against society, to conceal natural drives and emotions, to give superficial assent to moral standards, to associate the punishment with the punisher, to evade responsibility, to withdraw from reality and from difficult problems, or not to get caught.

Frequent and inconsistent punishment can render the child incapable of distinguishing right from wrong and reduce his capacity for feeling joy, sorrow, affection, shame, or other emotions.

Among other relevant studies are those of Patrick.[72] He found the

---

[71] Ruch, Floyd L., *Psychology and Life,* Scott, Foresman and Company, Chicago, 1948, p. 462.

[72] Patrick, J. K., "Studies in Rational Behavior and Emotional Excitement: II. The Effect of Emotional Excitement on Rational Behavior of Human Subjects," *J. comp. Psychol.,* 1934, vol. 18, pp. 153-195.

rational responses of human subjects to have been replaced with useless or repetitious responses following electric shock and similar unpleasant experiences.

When disagreeable experiences are associated with language, the effect appears to be inhibiting. In an experiment with 52 college students, the experimenter gave students an electrical shock just after pronouncing a neutral word such as barn. Immediately after the list of words had been presented, the students were asked to recall as many of them as they could. Words which had been followed by shock were recalled by fewer of the subjects than were the other words. Five minutes after the first presentation, the list of words was repeated without using electrical shock. Words which had been followed by electrical shock in the preceding presentation produced emotional responses as measured by a device called a galvanometer. Subjects who had not been able to recall the words associated with shock responded more violently to them than did subjects who had been able to recall them. Emotional responses were also given to words immediately preceding the shock words and to words associated with the shock words.[73] For example, the word "barn" is associated with farming. Thus the association between the shock and the word "barn" might be extended to related words. This study suggests the way in which resistance to language and communication might arise. Similar results are reported by Lysak.[74]

a word regarded as threatening. When given a list of words to decipher,

Perceptual response is apparently delayed when a person encounters

59 students required significantly more trials to identify threatening words than to identify neutral words.[75]

Pleasant associations with schoolroom tasks facilitate learning. Gilbert's[76] review of studies of forgetting suggests that pleasant memories tend to persist while unpleasant ones tend to be forgotten. Of 20 experiments described, 13 support this belief. Three experiments were inconclusive and only four yielded negative evidence. The ineffectiveness of criticism is illustrated by Johnson's[77] references to the childhood ex-

[73] Diven, Kenneth, "Certain Determinants in the Conditioning of Anxiety Reactions," *J. Psychol.*, vol. 3, 1937, pp. 291–308.

[74] Lysak, William, "The Effects of Punishment upon Syllable Recognition Thresholds," *J. exp. Psychol.*, vol. 47, 1954, pp. 343–340.

[75] Cowen, Emory L., and Ernst G. Beier, "Threat-Expectancy, Word Frequencies, and Perceptual Pre-Recognition Hypothesis," *J. abnorm. soc. Psychol.*, vol. 49, 1954, pp. 178–182.

[76] Gilbert, G. M., "The New Status of Experimental Studies on the Relationship of Feeling to Memory," *Psychol. Bull.*, 1938, vol. 35, pp. 124–139.

[77] Johnson, W., *People in Quandries*, Harper & Brothers, New York, 1946, pp. 443–447.

periences of stutterers. In almost all cases, their speech had been criticized.

Retarded readers have commonly experienced punishment in the form of failures, humiliations, disapproval, and rejection. Some have been physically punished. In many cases, punishment was administered by withholding affection and approval. Remediation involves the substitution of satisfactions associated with verbal activities for unpleasant associations.

COMMENTS ON SOME LAWS OF LEARNING

Some applications of the law of effect in learning have been elaborated in preceding paragraphs. Equally familiar to students of education and psychology are the laws or principles of contiguity, readiness, exercise, and recency.

You will remember the statement that if two psychological events occur at the same time or near the same time, the probability is that they will be associated with each other, and that one will suggest the other. Such associations are not necessarily restricted to visible events. In trying to understand the learning processes and reactions of students, we must keep in mind that fear, shame, or joy may have been the vivid experience which occurred contiguously with another event. If two events are associated, the association will be modified according to satisfactions experienced. The reactions of students to learning situations can be better understood if these associations are explored.

Readiness is interpreted to mean that if an individual is in readiness to respond to do so is satisfying and not to do so is annoying. This principle can be used as a criterion for selecting information, experiences, and learning situations suitable for students. The counselor makes use of it when he senses it is not the appropriate moment to press his client for a decision or when he chooses the most favorable time to present new information or alternatives. When an organism is set to respond, almost any stimulus can call forth the response. Understanding this principle helps to make human behavior more comprehensible.

Drills employed in the teaching of arithmetic, spelling, reading, and other basic skills are evidences that the law of exercise or frequency is recognized. Open to question is the belief that if a child is "told" a fact repeatedly, he will learn it. Although practice can facilitate learning, it does not ensure learning. Its effectiveness depends upon whether the learner responds to the situation and the way in which he responds. Some learning takes place without frequency, and, in some cases, repetition has negative instead of positive results. Interesting in this connection is a recent finding that while learning what to do in a given set of circumstances is not transferred to another set of circumstances, learning how to do it may be.[78]

The kind of response called forth by an event depends somewhat on the character of the most recent associations. If a response has been commonly rewarded, but recently punished, some other response may be substituted for the usual one. Hence, although recent experiences are more likely to be remembered than earlier experiences, the law of recency does not operate independently of the law of effect.

The laws of contiguity, readiness, exercise, recency, and effect apply to learning only when the learner is actively involved. Associations are made by the learner not only between visible events and conditions, but with emotions, memories, and unsuspected conditions. When we conclude that the laws of learning fail to apply, our difficulty may be that we fail to see all the aspects of the learning situation including the way in which the child views it.

A pertinent comment on the learning process is made by Gibson,[79] who implies that whenever anything is learned, meaning is involved. Even nonsense syllables or nonsense forms, he says, become meaningful when they become identifiable.

SELF-CONCEPT

The effect of the self-concept on learning and behavior is increasingly emphasized in professional literature. The teacher's role as psychologist, says Sanchez-Hidalgo,[80] has as its greatest challenge that of developing in children and adolescents an objective and full concept of what they are. Cassel[81] names as one of five primary principles of learning, the learner's projection of self. In view of the retarded reader's tendency toward an undifferentiated self-concept, the reading teacher needs to understand its relationship to the learning process.

The individual begins in infancy to build the picture of self and he adds to it as he has new experiences and makes new acquaintances. He sees himself as worthy or unworthy, loved or unlovable, adequate or inadequate, according to the attitudes of his family toward him. If his basic

[78] Bartlett, Frederic, "The Transfer of Training," *Bull. Ass. Int. Psychotechnique*, vol. 3, 1954, pp. 20–41.

[79] Gibson, James, J., *The Perception of the Visual World*, Houghton Mifflin Company, Boston, 1950, p. 202.

[80] Sanchez-Hidalgo, Efrain, "Youth, the School, and the Contemporary World," *Pedagogia*, vol. 1, 1953, pp. 7–15.

[81] Cassel, Russell N., "Primary Principles of Learning," *Peabody J. Educ.*, vol. 31, 1954, pp. 215–222.

needs for love, respect, sociality, physical comfort, and a feeling of growing adequacy are met, he has a good chance to develop a favorable self-
portrait. If he has no role in family life, is ignored, or sharply criticized,
he will learn to think of himself in less palatable terms.

His attitudes toward others will reflect what he sees in himself. If he
feels loved and trusted, he will be able to love and trust others. If he
feels worthy, a person who counts, he can conceive of worth in others.
If he has been rejected or ignored, he will regard his associates with
hostility or fear and will find it difficult to form close affectional ties
with others. If he is doubtful about his own worth, he has no measuring stick with which to judge good in others, in classmates, teachers, or
elders. If he has not been loved and trusted, he will regard the friendly
overtures of the teacher and classmates with suspicion.

The relationship between self-concept and a wholesome adjustment
among high-school students is discussed by Hanlon, Hofstaetter, and
O'Connor.[82] Similarity between the self-concept and the concept of the
ideal person favored a satisfactory total adjustment. A discrepancy between self-concept and ideal appeared related to maladjustment. Fey[83]
found a significant positive relationship between self-acceptance and acceptance of others.

The child finds that some responses work better for him than others. He
relieves tensions aroused by environmental demands and unsatisfied
needs by various modes of behavior. Some are successful and readily
available to him, and he comes to think of himself as a person who likes
to draw, has a temper, sucks his thumb, can dress himself, is always losing something, etc.

He appropriates little pieces of personality from others whom he ad-
mires and from those emotionally close to him. A boy accepted by his
father will probably want to be like him and will be inclined to choose
the masculine goals and activities which society expects of him. A girl
who feels accepted by her mother will probably want to play with miniature stoves, ironing boards, and baby carriages. She will picture herself
as a woman and assume a suitable sex role.

Rejection by either parent makes the process of identification difficult.
Lack of respect for either is also an impediment. If a boy cannot identify
with his father, he may not be able to think of himself in his appropriate
sex role. If, on the other hand, he forms a dislike and distrust for the

[82] Hanlon, Thomas E., Peter R. Hofstaetter, and James P. O'Connor, "Congruence
of Self and Ideal Self in Relation to Personality Adjustment," *J. consult. Psychol.*,
vol. 18, 1954, pp. 215–218.
[83] Fey, William F., "Acceptance of Self and Others, and Its Relation to Therapy-
Readiness," *J. clin. Psychol.*, vol. 10, 1954, pp. 269–271.

opposite sex, he is equally handicapped in formulating a self-portrait which will satisfy the requirements of his role.

When identification with the same-sex parent is impossible, a child sometimes finds a satisfactory substitute parent, as in the case of a boy who spent his summers and week ends on a farm and modeled himself after the farmer who was kind and admirable and interested in him. It does not appear probable that such identification will take place unless the adult shows a warm personal interest in the child. Worship of an ideal character from afar avails few satisfactions to the lonely child who seeks a close, intimate relationship. An unloved boy who was adopted by an elderly couple could not identify with his austere foster father and, denied close contact with any male father-figure, patterned himself after an erring half-brother who was kind to him. This seemed the only available male figure with whom he could identify.

Identification is a complex process. The development of an appropriate sex role may be hampered if there is any distortion in family relationships. For example, one might have expected the daughter of a harsh and rejecting father to become identified with her mother who provided affection, emotional support, and the traditional feminine pattern of behavior. However, the father was the most familiar male figure and thus the prototype for all males. The relationship between father and daughter was so unsatisfactory that she found it difficult to trust or to form a close relationship with any man. Furthermore, she regarded the subservient position of her mother with distaste. If this was the pattern for marriage, why should any woman desire it? Although she felt hostile to her father and perhaps to all males, still he was the "top dog" and held the favored position in the family. She could not picture herself in the relatively submissive role of a homemaker as defined by western society. This kind of experience would not necessarily result in overt homosexuality but could interfere with heterosexual development.

The self-portraits of some people, for lack of a warm, satisfying relationship with any adult, remain undifferentiated, vague, and undefined. Identification is one of the first steps in the process of growing up. When it is interrupted, maturation is delayed, and the learning process is hampered.

And what has this to do with school? If the teacher or counselor understands how the child sees himself, the child's behavior becomes more comprehensible. The child with an unfavorable self-portrait may be helped to express his emotions and to build a respectable self. The child with a respectable self-portrait can be helped to maintain it and add to it. School experiences can be damaging if they reinforce the picture of the child as unlovable, unworthy, or stupid, or shatter the satisfactory self by emphasizing the clumsiness or inadequacy of the new pupil.

Problems of identification can be met with understanding. The child who does not fit well into either sex group may be able to identify with an understanding teacher or an older schoolmate.

The portrait grows as the individual comes in closed contact with the peer group. He is able to satisfy more of his needs through group membership and group experiences. He sees himself in terms of his role in the group, accepted or unacceptable, a valuable member or an outcast. The distress of the reject is reflected in his schoolwork and behavior.

Whether or not group experience is a salutory or damaging one depends considerably on leadership from the school staff. Their attitudes and practices help to set a pattern of democratic participation or of domination by a few. The feeling of belonging to a group remains a very important factor in the lives of most adults. Among young people and children it is essential to wholesome development. Their concerns, problems, and projects are not trivial, and they need help in perfecting the skills of group membership.

The sensitive teacher or counselor may be able to help the reject to become more acceptable or help the group to become more accepting. Through wholesome group experience, every member can develop a meaningful and respected role and learn to work harmoniously with others.

Three factors discussed by Rich[84] as affecting security necessary to the individual's emotional development are the family, the school, and his companions. A feeling of accomplishment is said to be an important factor in security.

As the child experiences success or failure, he adds to his self-portrait. He comes to regard himself, perhaps, as a person who can learn games but not reading, as studious but not athletic, as clumsy or graceful, as poised or shy, as friendly or aloof, etc. These attitudes toward self are reflected in the kinds and amounts of materials he is able to learn.

Learning a new skill is facilitated if the learner can imagine himself performing the act. If he cannot believe that this is possible, he does not know how to begin to try to learn it.

If the child regards himself as a person who cannot learn to read, for example, reading will be difficult for him. Reading does not fit into his concept of self. He will feel that trying to learn to read is useless. If he admits to himself that it is possible to learn to read, he must reorganize his self-concept. The change in one "piece" of personality necessitates a rearrangement of the whole pattern, a difficult process. Although he is not conscious of the problem, he resists disorganization. Until he can make a change in his attitude toward himself, he will make little progress.

[84] Rich, Gilbert J., "Childhood as Preparation for Delinquency," *J. Educ. Sociol.,* vol. 27, 1954, pp. 404–413.

Even though convincing evidence is presented, he will not believe it until his attitude changes. He may recognize the possibility intellectually and talk about it with apparent understanding, but he really doesn't *learn* it until it is a part of his feeling state. This kind of change is not likely to come about unless the teacher and counselor show deep understanding of his emotions and help him to understand himself.

RESISTANCE TO LEARNING

An illustration of resistance to learning is given by Torrance.[85] His successes and most meaningful experiences had been in intellectual areas. He describes difficulties encountered in learning to march.

For example, as an army private in basic training, I was strongly motivated to march in step. I think I really wanted to keep in step as much as I have wanted to learn anything. There was no lack of external nor internal motivation. There was no negativism. I tried every device anyone suggested and practiced during spare moments. Still I was always out of step. It was not until months later in a technical school with men of backgrounds of interests and experiences similar to my own that I 'suddenly' learned to keep in step. Neither lack of motivation nor negativism would seem to describe what had happened to me. Unconscious resistance due to the way I had learned to define myself would seem to be a more adequate way of describing the phenomenon.

A child who was often ridiculed by parents and others because of clumsiness, burst into tears, saying, "I'm just a clumsy lubber." This concept of herself persisted into mature years. Learning to dance was a painful process. Teeth clenched and nerves quivering, she braced herself for each step. Only after leaving home could she relax sufficiently to enjoy dancing. Admonitions ("Try not to get your foot in the mixmaster, honey—try to get hold of the right end of the broom") pursued her into adult life. Years of effort and experience were necessary before she could overcome her resistance to performing household tasks. Because she felt a failure in these areas which seemed so important to family and friends, her motivation was depressed in areas where she was more able.

It is perhaps even more difficult to learn a new fact about one's own emotions and behavior than to incorporate subject matter which seems inconsistent with the self-concept. The aloof, self-sufficient person, determined not to put himself in a position to be hurt, may resist falling in love. The capable executive may disregard his doctor's orders, in the face of convincing evidence. The child who sees himself as inferior cannot recognize his assets.

[85] Torrance, E. Paul, "The Phenomenon of Resistance in Learning," *J. abnorm. soc. Psychol.*, vol. 45, no. 4, October, 1950.

It is difficult for the teacher to understand the many complex factors which operate in this kind of resistance. It is so much easier to assume that the pupil is obstinate, stupid, or lazy. His report card may carry such remarks as: "Johnny wastes times." "Johnny doesn't pay attention." "Johnny is listless." These are symptoms, not causes. Causes must be understood and treated before real progress can be made.

A certain amount of resistance to change and to learning is normal. The astute teacher will expect it and plan ways of meeting it. Any task which requires effort produces resistance. The more difficult it appears to the child, the more resistance might be anticipated.

In each individual there is a desire to be independent and a conflicting desire to remain dependent, to let others decide and take responsibility. People are inclined to resist taking on responsibility, particularly if teachers and parents have performed this function for them. The prospect of unfamiliar responsibilities is especially forbidding and possibly frightening.

When teachers try to use democratic methods of leadership in the classroom or in discussion of playground incidents or program planning, they will find at first that pupils indicate a willingness to have a higher authority make the decisions and take the responsibility. Pupils accustomed to dependency will demonstrate this attitude, "Make us learn. It's your business, not ours." Some classes appear determined to force the democratic teacher into an authoritarian role, in order to be able to fight him.

Although a problem to the teacher, leader, or counselor, resistance is not necessarily abnormal or undesirable. Lecky[86] conceives of resistance as a potentially constructive force, as a desire to maintain a consistent personality. If a student resists learning certain skills or information, it is because, from his point of view, it would be inconsistent for him to learn it. His attitude is a defense against personality disorganization or reorganization. In discussing this question, Ephron[87] remarks, that negativism may be a desperate effort to rescue self or sense of self. Guarding his sense of identity, of integrity, the knowledge of who he is may be more vital than academic achievement to the individual's emotional health and survival.

This obstacle to learning is not easily overcome. Little progress can be expected from exhortations, scolding, artificial incentives, drill, and the like. The answer may be found in the attitudes of the teacher, in the

[86] Lecky, Prescott, *Self Consistency, a Theory of Personality*, Island Press Cooperative, Inc., New York, 1945.
[87] Ephron, Buelah Cantor, *Emotional Difficulties in Reading*, Julian Press, New York, 1953, pp. 13ff.

understanding and sensitivity shown in her relationships with pupils. Understanding resistance, says Redl,[88] should have an important place in education, teaching, leadership training, and attempts to change the performance of management and labor, as well as in attempts to combat prejudice, submission, and group-rut formation. It is obviously an important factor in counseling, in helping any individual to make changes in behavior or attitudes toward self. The moralistic concept of resistance as something which must be broken by stern discipline and punishment has seemed to lead educators into a blind alley, according to Torrance.[89]

If the teacher's determination meets the student's resistance in a head-on collision, little will be accomplished. The student will be obliged to defend himself and explain himself. If the teacher can demonstrate that he understands how the student feels, he may be able to penetrate the defenses and help him make use of his positive emotions.

GUIDED LEARNING

The term "guidance" was perhaps an unfortunate choice of terminology, as it can be interpreted to mean that the well-intentioned teacher or counselor decides for the pupil what is best for him and tells him what to do. This definition of guidance ignores a number of convincing studies and experiments, leading to the conclusion that while some guidance is beneficial, too much is actually detrimental.

Waters'[90] experiment with college students illustrates the point. The control group with no guidance learned a maze in an average of 37.5 trials and in 2,191 seconds. The group given 40 guided trials needed 27.5 additional trials and 43 additional seconds to complete the maze. A group that received 80 guided trials in advance of unguided practice required 23.4 additional trials and a total of 2,833 seconds to accomplish the task. In other words, the unguided students learned in fewer trials and a shorter time than did the guided students. The results of an experiment in teaching handwriting show the same general tendency.[91] The studies of Carr[92] also suggest that too much guidance interferes with learning.

[88] Redl, Fritz, "Resistance in Therapy Groups," *Human Relations*, vol. 1, no. 3, 1948, pp. 307ff.

[89] Torrance, E. Paul, "The Phenomenon of Resistance in Learning," *J. abnorm. soc. Psychol.*, vol. 45, no. 4, October, 1950.

[90] Waters, R. H., "The Influence of Large Amounts of Manual Guidance upon Human Maze Learning," *J. gen. Psychol.*, 1930, vol. 4, pp. 213–227.

[91] Gates, A. I., and G. A. Taylor, "The Acquisition of Motor Control in Writing by Preschool Children," *Teachers Coll. Rec.*, 1923, vol. 24, pp. 459–468.

[92] Carr, H. A., *Psychology*, Longmans Green & Co., Inc., New York, 1926, p. 98.

Some teachers insist that it is their function to ensure that the correct response will be made. On this subject, Carr[93] says, "It is necessary to make and eliminate a certain number of mistakes in order to learn how to execute the act properly." It is his opinion that an act will never be mastered when all possibility of error is prevented. "We learn through correction of our mistakes. The right act is established in part by learning what not to do." There are some evidences that guidance is most effective when introduced after several unguided trials by the subject, or, in other words, when he becomes aware of the need for help.

As the child matures, he learns to try out and discard methods and solutions by thinking about them instead of actually performing the acts. Instead of random trial and error, he refers to past experiences and tries to choose a solution which appears to him to have worked, or one which is similar to a proven method.

The quality of his judgment depends in part upon past experiences of success and failure and greatly upon the number and kinds of occasions in which he has exercised independent judgment. If he has had opportunities to think, choose, act, and experience success, he will be able to make these mental trials. If all of his decisions have been made for him, he will not be able to visualize what might happen as a result of various choices.

Neither the teacher nor the counselor is an oracle who can give the child all the "right answers." With an overabundance of guidance the child feels no need to think and solve problems for himself. Teaching and all guidance activities, including counseling, can be most effective when conceived as joint projects with the pupils actively involved.

SEEING THE STUDENT'S WORLD

In preceding paragraphs, we have tried to show how necessary it is for the teacher and personnel worker to understand how a student feels about himself. It is also important for them to understand how he sees his environment. In order to communicate with him and to know where to begin, to understand what ideas and facts will be meaningful to him, we must try to understand how it looks to him.

We should like to borrow some terms from other authors[94] and describe the environment as the individual sees it, as a field, and the needs, goals, people, and objects known to him as figures in the field. The individual is a figure in his own field, a part of his pictured environment. He sees

[93] *Ibid.*, pp. 236–237.
[94] Snygg, Donald, and Arthur W. Combs, *Individual Behavior*, Harper & Brothers, New York, 1949.

the field from a different angle than does anyone else.[95] He interprets it in terms of his past experiences and his relations with family and friends. The important figures in the teacher's field are not necessarily prominent in the student's field, and vice versa.

The process of selecting what is believed and incorporated and what is rejected by each individual is described by Frank.[96] "Our perception is often warped, skewed, distorted, and amazingly restricted by our emotions and affective responses."

Inability to understand the child's field often brings about misunderstandings between adults and children. For example, a Sunday-school teacher was illustrating the ill effects of disobedience with a sad story about a little boy who disobeyed his mother and took his sled into the busy street. He was struck by a car and killed. The teacher was congratulating herself on making her point until wide-eyed little Danny inquired breathlessly, "Where's the sled?"

Children in the primary grades were beginning preparations for a Halloween play about elves, witches, pumpkins, etc. The teacher said, "Johnny, would you like to try this elf part?" "Who me?" asked Johnny. "Yes. Why not?" asked the surprised teacher. "I want to be a rabbit," announced Johnny firmly. "But there aren't any rabbits in this play," explained the teacher. "Well I don't know about that but what I want to be is a rabbit," and the matter was closed so far as Johnny was concerned. The rabbit in Johnny's field was a very prominent figure, and it was altogether absent from the teacher's field. (Teacher went home and wrote in a rabbit part.)

Self-enhancement remains a persistent drive, and the figures in the child's field are closely related. A bright little girl in the third grade made frequent use of the word "brung." After repeated efforts at correction, the teacher wrote her a note, "Dear Millie, There is no such word as brung." Millie smiled pleasantly and wrote a note right back, "Dear Miss Jones, I didn't get my book report grade this morning." The prominent figures in the two fields were obviously not the same.

As the individual matures, he perceives more figures in the field, more sharply defined figures, and more relationships between figures. If an integrated personality is to develop, these figures should appear to him to be fairly consistent and harmonious with each other. The self, which was originally undifferentiated from the mother or the mother-substitute, comes to be regarded as distinct from others. The field is expanded and

[95] Gibson, James J., *The Perception of the Visual World*, Houghton Mifflin Company, Boston, 1950, p. 226.

[96] Frank, Lawrence K., "Feelings and Emotions," Doubleday Papers in Psychology, Garden City, N. Y., 1954, p. 14ff.

becomes more complex. The self and other figures shift and change positions, as learning goes on. Figures are not necessarily material and concrete. Abstractions, such as truth, beauty, virtue may be incorporated. Needs, goals, threats, fears are prominent.

New learning is possible only if associated with meaningful figures in the learner's field. In counseling and teaching, the adult must strive continuously to understand how the field looks to the pupil and also to convey this understanding.

A cartoon shows a little boy explaining his grade card to a scowling father: "Naturally I seem stupid to my teacher. She's a college graduate." There is a considerable gap between Statistics II and the multiplication tables or between Thomas Mann's *Magic Mountain* and *The Little Red Hen*. The gap can be closed only if the teacher and counselor can learn to feel with the pupil and let him know that they understand how he feels.

SUMMARY

Studies are reported in support of certain psychological principles which might be applied in understanding and helping retarded readers. Major points are these:

1. The degree to which basic psychological needs are satisfied affects the learning process.

2. The learner is receptive to facts and skills which appear to him to be related to satisfactions for basic needs.

3. The need for self-enhancement is recognized as a universal and legitimate need.

4. Most basic psychological needs are social needs.

5. When an individual finds obstacles in the way of satisfying basic needs or reaching goals important to him or finds himself in situations with which he cannot cope, resulting frustration interferes with the learning process.

6. When the threshold of frustration is exceeded, responses become stereotyped, rigid, and primitive, and resistance to learning is raised.

7. Submission to environmental press is a less desirable response than rebellion.

8. Distortion in perception may be related to guilt, fears, unsatisfied needs, insecurity, social influences, and emphasis upon uncritical conformity to behavior standards.

9. Punishment and failure can interfere with learning.

10. The learner's self-concept is related to his attitudes toward others and to the kinds and amounts of materials which he can learn.

11. New facts, ideas and skills will be resisted if they do not fit into the self-concept.

12. Some guidance hastens learning, but too much is detrimental.

13. Communication between teacher and student requires that the teacher be able to see into the perceptual field of the student.

14. Retarded readers have commonly experienced failures and frustrations and demonstrate many of the associated symptoms, including stereotypy, insecurity, and undifferentiated self-concepts.

Overcoming reading disability may involve a rearrangement of the perceptual field and the learner's concept of self. If he is to make improvement, he must have opportunities to feel success and self-esteem. He must make some discoveries and decisions for himself and take an active part in the learning process. Reading, as one of the communicative skills, involves interpersonal relations. A classroom climate of warmth and mutual respect is favorable to learning.

CHAPTER 3

Use of Tests in
Diagnosis and Sectioning

Diagnosis is associated with standardized testing. Other aids to diagnosis should not be overlooked. Test results alone can be misleading. The influence on achievement of factors other than ability is suggested by a study by Hoyt and Norman.[1] They found that the Ohio State University Psychological Test predicts achievement of college freshmen men who make "normal" scores on the Minnesota Multiphasic Personality Inventory more accurately than it does for those who deviate sharply from the norm on the MMPI scales. Thus personal adjustment appears to be an important factor in predicting achievement.

Neidt and Edmison[2] conclude that measurement of attitudes by means of 45 paired statements presented to 342 University of Nebraska students improved the accuracy of prediction of academic success when used with ACE quantitative and linguistic scores.

Data from personal documents with ACE scores added accuracy to prediction of academic survival or non-survival, according to Mrs. Ellen Smith (quoted in the Torrance Report).[3]

Factors affecting interpretation are suggested by this report on a pupil, nine years and nine months of age. The results of three intelligence tests suggested an IQ somewhere between 67 and 80. Memory for information was reported good, but reasoning appeared poor. In the opinion of the clinician, the child was capable of functioning at an IQ level of about 80, but because of reticence and lack of confidence, she often performed

[1] Hoyt, Donald P., and Warren T. Norman, "Adjustment and Academic Predictability," *J. Counseling Psychol.*, vol. 1, no. 2, 1954, pp. 96ff.
[2] Neidt, Charles O., and Lyle D. Edmison, "Qualification Responses Used with Paired Statements to Measure Attitudes toward Education," *J. Educ. Psychol.*, vol. 44, no. 5, May, 1953, pp. 305ff.
[3] Torrance, E. Paul, Summary of Research, Counseling Bureau, Kansas State College, 1945–1950, pp. 11–12.

at a lower level. Experiences of failure and social rejection may have operated to make her distrust her own abilities. Under optimal conditions, this child was believed capable of making a borderline school adjustment. A mental age of six and a half to seven and three-fourths years would place her about second-grade level. If it were possible to get her classmates to accept her, she might have a chance to work up to her level of ability.

On the other hand, school marks do not accurately reflect students' abilities. Teachers' estimates of ability and achievement are not necessarily accurate. " . . . equally able teachers, marking the same essay examinations, may vary from 50 per cent to 95 per cent on the same paper; and the same teacher given a set of examination papers two months after the first marking will vary widely from that first marking."[4] The same essay, marked by 25 teachers, received marks of better than 90 from two teachers, but also marks below 39 from two teachers. Eleven ranked it 70 to 79, but five ranked it between 40 and 49.[5]

Behavior, appearance, and family background can influence the teacher's opinion of a child's ability. The over-conformative little girl who writes when she is supposed to write, turns in all of her papers, and waits for permission to leave her seat may appear considerably brighter to her harassed teacher than the noisy little troublemaker who can't sit still. Neatness in handwriting or grammatical accuracy may be more readily recognized than imagination and creativeness.

A child of average ability may shine in a group of dull normals, or he may appear stupid in a class of pupils of superior abilities. The teacher unconsciously expects a child of well-educated parents to do good work in school, and may underestimate the ability of the unkempt son of a day laborer.

It is difficult for the beginning teacher to know how much to expect of her pupils. If she has her sights too high, she may feel that they are all "dummies." The school marks of other teachers have their influence. A "halo" effect from past years may operate.

The relationship between the child's behavior and teachers' marks can be illustrated by the experiences of two sisters. Gay made average scores on the standardized intelligence and achievement tests, but she was eager to please and behaved well. May ranked in the upper 10 per cent of her age and grade in intelligence and achievement, but she was inclined to ask embarrassing questions of her teachers, to bounce out of

[4] Tiegs, E. W., *Tests and Measurements in the Improvement of Learning,* Houghton Mifflin Company, Boston, 1939, p. 9.

[5] Tiegs, E. W., *Educational Diagnosis,* Educational Bulletin no. 18, California Test Bureau, Los Angeles, 1948, p. 3.

her seat to help a slow classmate, and to exercise her sharp wit at the expense of others. Both girls made a B average in elementary school.

Some factors in over-evaluation of mental ability are suggested by Torrance.[6] Almost two-thirds of a large group of college freshmen who actually ranked in the lower fourth of the group, according to a standardized intelligence test, believed themselves to rank in the upper fourth of the class in ability. Over-evaluators commonly reported faithful participation and leadership in Sunday school, Boy Scouts, 4-H Clubs, and other worthy enterprises. It seems quite probable, as Torrance points out, that teachers, ministers, youth leaders, and parents frequently overestimate the ability of the conformative, conscientious child.

Fallacies in judgments resulting from a limited basis for comparison can be illustrated by the numerous salutatorians and valedictorians from small schools who arrive at college to find themselves near the average in achievement and ability.

Underevaluation of a pupil's ability is also possible. It is speculated that underevaluation over a long period of time may lead the pupil to believe that he is dull and to perform accordingly. For example, a fourth-grader, who slouched down in his seat with his hair in his eyes, was considered dull. He wandered into desks and tables, dropped pencils and books, and seldom finished an assignment. Tests ranked him average in ability, and after a series of success experiences, he began to do better than average classwork. A second-grader who was doing barely average schoolwork ranked superior in tested ability and achievement, and after acceleration competed well in the next grade. A combination of test results and teacher judgment increases the accuracy of diagnosis. The limitations of tests and hints on interpretation will be discussed in the latter part of this chapter.

A rough estimate of how the older student stands can be gleaned by comparing his rate of reading with the average rate for his age and grade. Harris[7] states that the national average is about 225 words per minute, 300 is required for high-school students, and at least 350 for college.

The teacher can observe whether the child reads haltingly or with ease, whether he takes part in the discussion over the reading assignment, whether he blinks, squirms, squints, groans, or otherwise manifests discomfort while reading. Uneven performance from day to day suggests that factors other than ability and competence operate to distract

[6] Torrance, E. Paul, (ed.) "Summary of Research Conducted or Sponsored by the Kansas State College Counseling Bureau, 1945–1950," mimeographed.

[7] Harris, Ruth McCoy, "How Well Do You Read?", in James I. Brown, *Efficient Reading*, D. C. Heath and Company, Boston, 1952, pp. 36–37.

and hamper the student. When the student reads orally, he may reveal reversals, disregard for context cues, phonetic weaknesses, and other errors. One reading clinic has mimeographed some graded stories for use in testing reading performance. As the child reads orally, the teacher circles errors on her copy of the story. If the child makes more than 10 errors for every 100 running words, he is not getting meaning. However, large classes make individual diagnosis difficult. Mass testing can help the teacher of large classes to screen out those who need help and whose problems can be more thoroughly explored by means of individual tests.

The most obvious bit of information to be used in screening students for the reading class is the score on the standardized reading test. This score alone, however, does not show whether or not the student is reading as well as he is able or whether he is capable of improvement. If he reads as well as his classmates in the lower 25 per cent of the class and ranks near that level in intelligence, his problem is not the same as that of the child who ranks in the upper 25 per cent of his class in scholastic ability, but in the lower 25 per cent in reading ability. A fairly accurate judgment can be made from these two test scores, but let us consider further the case of the student who ranks in the lower 25 per cent of the class in both reading and intelligence test scores. Might his intelligence test score fail to represent his true mental ability, since he could not read as well as his classmates? Hence, the kind of intelligence test has something to do with diagnosis. If the test yields two or more scores, for example verbal and non-verbal or linguistic and quantitative, we might examine his rank in the two areas to see if they vary. If his non-verbal or quantitative scores exceed his verbal or linguistic scores by 20 or more percentile points, he may have a chance to improve reading skills. To explore further his potential for improvement, he could be given an individual test of mental ability, such as the Stanford-Binet or Wechsler-Bellevue Intelligence Scale which require little reading. Another possibility is the intercultural test developed by Allison Davis and Kenneth Eells.[8] It is an outgrowth of studies of cultural differences and is intended to test general intelligence regardless of reading skill, school instruction, or speed of response. The Ohio State Psychological Examination is regarded as a power test and places less penalty on the retarded reader than do some of the other intelligence tests.

Sectioning of college students is greatly simplified by the use of a test of mental ability which yields two sectional scores in quantitative and linguistic ability. Using the American Council on Education Psychological Examination, the assigner has merely to look for a quantitative score

[8] Davis, Allison, and Kenneth Eells, *Davis-Eells Games,* World Book Company, Yonkers, N. Y.

20 percentile points higher than the linguistic score to choose a student for the reading class. If there is any doubt in his mind, he checks the student's reading scores. The following examples illustrate how the choices might be made.

Student number I whose scores are reported in table 3-1 reads less well than average, according to the tests, but his Cooperative Reading Test scores are consistent with his ability scores. He might make moderate improvement, but he belongs in a class with students whose problems are similar to his. If sufficient teaching staff is available for remedial work, a separate class might be offered for students with test patterns

TABLE 3-1
STUDENT NUMBER I PRODUCED A FAIRLY CONSISTENT TEST PATTERN

ACE percentile ranks		Coop reading percentile ranks	
"Q"	"L"	Speed	Comprehension
39	40	35	38

TABLE 3-2
THE SCORES OF STUDENT NUMBER II RANGE FROM THE
7TH TO THE 60TH PERCENTILE

ACE percentile ranks			Coop reading percentile ranks	
"Q"	"L"	Total	Speed	Comprehension
60	35	45	7	8

like this one. Methods described in Chapter 5 will work with such students, but only modest gains can be expected.

Student number II, whose scores are reported in table 3-2, is a promising candidate for the developmental reading class. His quantitative score exceeds his linguistic score by 25 percentile points and his Cooperative Reading Test scores fall far below the level of his general ability. In our experience, this kind of student has been the most likely to make improvement.

Students chosen by these criteria have made more progress in reading than students who fell below the 35th percentile in total ACE rank. Groups of reading students with the high "Q" and low "L" pattern of test results also showed more progress by standardized retest than a control group of similar abilities who received no reading instruction.[9]

[9] Woolf, Maurice D., unpublished studies at Kansas State College, 1951–1955.

Two other authors report that students who gained the most in reading classes were those who scored relatively higher in quantitative ability than in linguistic ability.[10,11]

Further support for the practice of sectioning according to "Q" and "L" rank is found in a study of two groups of students. When the "L" score fell appreciably below "Q" score, the reading scores were usually lowered. Two groups of college freshmen, group A with "Q" score 20 or more percentile points higher than "L" and group B with even scores on "L" and "Q" were compared by means of three scores from the Cooperative English Examination and the Cooperative Reading Examination. The mean difference between "Q" and "L" for students in group A was

TABLE 3-3

TESTED LINGUISTIC SKILLS OF GROUP A AND B
COMPARED BY MEANS OF t-SCORES

Group	No.	Skill	Mean RS	$\bar{d}$	$s_{\bar{d}}$	t	P
A	118	English total	143.42				
B	110		178.06	34.64	5.2622	6.58	.001***
A	118	Reading speed	16.81				
B	110		24.79	7.98	1.1716	6.81	.001***
A	118	Comprehension	12.26				
B	110		17.29	5.03	.8693	5.79	.001***

44 percentile points in favor of "Q." In group B of 110 students, the "Q" rank of each was approximately equal to "L" rank. All students in both groups ranked above the 35th percentile in total ACE scores, by local norms. The mean raw score for each group in quantitative ability was 49, which fell in the 81st percentile for the class. Results are shown in table 3-3.[12]

Percentile ranks for the A group in these achievement tests, by local norms, were 49, 50, and 45, respectively, or relatively low as compared with the percentile rank of 81 in "Q." Percentile ranks for students in the B group in linguistic achievement were 74, 74, 73, or fairly consistent with rank in quantitative ability. Differences between the groups in

[10] Torrance, E. Paul, Summary of Counseling Bureau Studies, Kansas State College, 1950–1951, pp. 22–23.

[11] Smith, Henry P., and Theodore R. Tate, "Improvement in Reading Rate and Comprehension of Subjects Training with the Tachistoscope," *J. Educ. Psychol.*, vol. 44, no. 3, March, 1943.

[12] Woolf, Maurice D., and Jeanne A. Woolf, "Is Linguistic Ability Related to Maturity?" *J. appl. Psychol.*, 1955, vol. 39, no. 6, pp. 413–415.

English total and reading speed and comprehension are reliable beyond the 1 per cent level of confidence. Students with high "Q" and low "L" consistently ranked lower in reading speed and comprehension and English than students with even "Q" and "L," and their tested reading and English skills were inferior to their tested general abilities.

The relationship between linguistic ability and reading and language skills is further shown by correlations between the mean scores of 1,051 college freshmen from the American Council on Education Psychological Examination, the Cooperative English Examination, and the Cooperative Reading Examination, as shown in table 3-4.

TABLE 3-4

SIMPLE CORRELATIONS AMONG AVERAGE ENGLISH GRADES AND AVERAGE SCORES OF 1051 COLLEGE FRESHMEN FROM THE ACE AND COOPERATIVE ENGLISH AND READING EXAMINATIONS

	Q	L	T	M	E	R	V	S	Compre.
Grade	.337	.572	.526	.600	.582	.557	.562	.510	.410
Quantitative		.582	.859	.414	.509	.220	.231	.198	.167
Linguistic			.914	.600	.752	.815	.764	.774	.641
Total ACE				.581	.724	.749	.675	.729	.606
Mechanics of English					.616	.584	.551	.577	.457
Effectiveness expr.						.734	.703	.712	.565
Reading total							.857	.948	.864
Vocabulary								.761	.636
Speed									.850

High correlations between the scores on the linguistic subtest of the ACE and all other scores suggest that achievement in English can be predicted from the "L" score. The "L" score correlates with total reading score at .81, suggesting that few students with a high "L" score would need remediation. The correlation between "L" score and grades is higher than any other with the exception of mechanics of English. It appears that students might be sectioned in English classes on the basis of the "L" score alone. People with a low "L" score might be expected to have low reading scores. A high "Q" and low "L" might be interpreted as indicating a potential for improvement as a result of remediation.

Table 3-4 illustrates how tests can be used administratively in setting up the reading program. Attention should be paid to relationships between scores and to the absence of relationships. The table suggests which tests might be eliminated if the mass testing program must be cut down to a minimum. In view of these findings, the reading and English tests might be eliminated from the general testing program and diagnostic reading tests given only to the high "Q" and low "L" people and to others suspected of reading disability.

It is surprising to find that "Q" correlates fairly well with effectiveness of expression. Items included in this section appear associated with mechanics and organization rather than with creativity. One might speculate on whether "Q" is related to powers of organization as reflected in this subtest. This might also be interpreted to mean that some verbal ability is needed to understand parts of the test of quantitative ability.

A comparison of average raw scores from these tests suggests that the "L" score separates the excellent, superior, average, inferior, and failing English students from each other equally as well as any subtest of the English examination or reading examination. Table 3-5 shows grades and raw scores.

TABLE 3-5
AVERAGE SCORES ON TESTS AND GRADES OF STUDENTS
IN WRITTEN COMMUNICATIONS

Grade	No.	Q	L	T	M	E	R	V	S	C	%
A	32	49.6	86.9	136.6	126.2	49.6	116.0	43.3	42.8	30.0	4
B	205	45.0	73.9	118.9	112.9	45.2	90.3	34.2	32.6	24.2	23
C	377	41.8	66.3	108.1	94.5	37.7	69.5	26.9	25.1	17.7	42
D	189	37.1	58.1	95.2	80.0	30.4	52.2	21.6	17.6	12.9	21
E	86	32.6	47.1	79.6	69.9	24.7	36.6	14.4	13.2	9.6	10
Average		40.9	65.2	106.1	94.4	37.0	69.1	26.8	24.7	17.8	100

The distribution of grades in this group of students agrees with the distributions of raw scores from each subtest. These findings suggest that grading practices in these classes are reasonably accurate, in terms of ability levels and performance of students. A teacher can look at a table like this one and see where an individual ranks as compared with his classmates and determine which students are likely to fail. Data showing raw scores are often more meaningful to the classroom teacher than are correlations. "L" scores differentiate between the five groups of students equally as well as any other scores.

If the reading scores are appreciably lower than the linguistic scores, the student also shows promise for improvement. However, this combination of scores is less often found. Usually the linguistic score is fairly consistent with the reading test score.

The interpretation of the high "Q" and low "L" pattern as evidence of a potential for improvement disturbs those who say this assumption is contrary to the theory of individual differences. However, unless we can accept the possibility, we should be obliged to believe that there is little hope for students to improve, since "L" score correlates so well with reading test scores. The tested improvement of the high "Q," low "L" students during four semesters of developmental reading supports our belief that they can make improvement. We might think of each person's intelligence as having a range. The individual may be functioning near the upper range of his potential or at the lower edge. The same may be true of linguistic, quantitative, and other facets of intelligence.

TESTS OF SCHOLASTIC APTITUDE

There are various definitions of intelligence. It is often defined as the ability to learn from experience or the ability to apply what has been learned from experience to a given situation. Some prefer to limit the meaning to ability for academic achievement. Mental ability, as measured by some tests, might be equated to verbal facility which certainly is related to scholastic achievement. However, verbal ability does not necessarily imply creativeness nor abstract reasoning. Older tests give a single score. Intelligence has been lately defined as a constellation of several aptitudes rather than a single aptitude. Pupils with the same total scores may vary in subscores. Twenty-five children with identical IQs were found to vary as much as three to five years in such factors as memory.[13] It might be conceded that intelligence is a combination of numerous factors of which verbal facility is one. Other factors may be problem-solving (not exclusively numerical), memory, judgment, logical reasoning, use of spatial relationships, curiosity, quality and variety of interests, quantitative ability, social sensitivity, and ability to organize facts and ideas, to see relationships, draw conclusions, make plans, use abstract concepts, do independent research.

Although some of these characteristics as yet resist quantification, there are a number of tests on the market which are intended to measure a variety of factors. Even those instruments which rely heavily on verbal ability, when used with other data, contribute to accuracy in predicting academic progress. With continuous improvement, greater accuracy can be anticipated.

Some intelligence tests have been standardized on urban, middle-class school children. Their experiences are presumably different from those of children in rural areas and of other socioeconomic levels. The authors of some of the newer tests have attempted to include experiences which

---

[13] Teigs, Ernest V., *Tests and Measurements in the Improvement of Learning*, Houghton Mifflin Company, Boston, 1939.

are common to children of all these population segments. When employing intelligence test results, the teacher or counselor can interpret them more accurately if these factors are taken into consideration.

Although reading-readiness tests offer valuable information for teachers in the primary grades, intelligence-test results are believed to be a more valid predictor of reading achievement.[14] Mental age is more useful than IQ. For example, the four-year-old with an IQ of 134 would not be as ready to read as a six-and-a-half-year-old with an IQ of 100.[15]

Intelligence-test results can help the teacher understand how much to expect from a pupil, to recognize when a learning situation is too difficult or too easy, to judge how much a child's ability varies from the average for his age and grade, to discover whether or not a pupil's achievement is consistent with his ability, to decide whether or not a pupil is placed in a group where he can benefit most and feel successful, to find support for her own judgments, to choose subject-matter appropriate for her pupils, to discover unsuspected abilities, to eliminate lack of ability as a reason for poor performance. For the reading teacher, the intelligence test which yields non-verbal and multiple factor scores can suggest the extent of a pupil's potential for improvement.

In view of the many textbooks on educational testing, the inclusion here of the descriptions of individual tests may seem a duplication. Case histories and the process of diagnosis can hardly be understood without a knowledge of the tests. We believe that teachers, teachers-in-training, and school administrators who use this book will find it convenient to look up information about tests in the same volume which also treats causes, methods, etc. It is irritating to be told that diagnosis should take into account intelligence, personality, home adjustment, etc., and then to be left with no specific information about how it might be done. We have chosen for discussion some commonly used batteries and tests which may already be available to the reading teacher, some less well-known which we feel are especially suitable for diagnosing reading problems, and some which require expert administration and interpretation but with which the teacher should be acquainted. A choice can be made from among several instruments of each type. Information will be given to help the teacher judge which is within her capabilities and which might be the most useful.

Reviewing a number of late reading studies, one writer remarks that reading is now recognized as an aspect of adjustment toward which all

[14] Kottmeyer, William, "Readiness for Reading," *Elem. English,* vol. 24, Oct. 1947, pp. 355–366.

[15] Adams, Fay, et al., *Teaching Children to Read,* The Ronald Press Company, New York, 1949, p. 138.

available personnel services can contribute.[16] Testing is one of the major techniques of the personnel program and was one of the first to enter the school. While much information on testing is available, its application to the diagnosis of reading problems is often neglected in texts on the teaching of remedial reading.

GROUP TESTS OF SCHOLASTIC APTITUDE

If the school operates a mass testing program, reading and intelligence-test scores are available for screening. We have mentioned the American Council on Education Psychological Examination which has proven very useful in the college reading program. Responsible for the technical work on the tests were L. L. and T. G. Thurstone. A new form is issued each year by the American Council on Education. Although the norms are established on college freshmen, the test is sometimes used for high-school seniors. Each of the six subtests is preceded by practice exercises. It requires about an hour to give. Scoring is simple. It can be scored either by hand or machine. Norms are in the form of percentiles for college freshmen in liberal-arts, teacher-training, and junior colleges.

Although most teachers are doubtless familiar with percentile rank, we are including a brief explanation for the benefit of those who are not acquainted with this term. If a student ranks at the 50th percentile in total score on the ACE, his score is average as compared with the college freshmen on whose responses the norms are based. If he ranks at the 75th percentile, his score is better than those of 75 per cent of the students in the group. Many colleges make a practice of preparing local norms, so that the teacher can see how each student ranks in comparison to others with whom he will be competing.

Studies of rural and urban students suggest that the test is a more accurate measure of the ability of urban students.[17] This factor might be taken into consideration when interpreting test results.

For high-school students, the Educational Testing Service of Princeton, New Jersey, has prepared a high-school form of the American Council on Education Psychological Examination. Editions are available for grades 9 through 12. Linguistic, quantitative, and total scores can be calculated. Each item of the subtest, Directions, must be read aloud by the examiner. The time required is about 65 minutes. More research is needed on norms.

The Thurstone Tests of Primary Mental Abilities, distributed by Sci-

[16] Editorial, *J. of Educ.*, vol. 137, no. 3, December, 1954, p. 27.
[17] Super, Donald, *Appraising Vocational Fitness*, Harper & Brothers, New York, 1949, p. 116.

ence Research Associates, are available for ages 5 to 7, 7 to 11, and 11 to 17. They consist of subtests of verbal meaning, space, reasoning, memory, perception, number, and word fluency. Scores from the subtests are combined to produce verbal and performance scores, so that the teacher can compare the two and use them in screening. No reading is required of pupils aged 5 to 7. The time for administration is about an hour, or two half-hour periods for the youngest pupils. Mental age, IQ, and percentile rank can be determined. Self-scoring carbon answer pads are provided.

The long form, or Chicago Tests of Primary Mental Abilities, (Science Research Associates) for ages 11 to 17 requires from two to four hours. It is scored for six subtests as well as for verbal and number ability. Standardization involved approximately 1,000 children in grades 8 to 10 in Chicago schools. More research has been done on the long form than on the other forms.

The California Short-Form Test of Mental Maturity (Sullivan, Clark, and Tiegs, 1950, California Test Bureau, Los Angeles) is available at five levels, kindergarten and grade one, primary grades, elementary grades 4 through 8, intermediate grades 7 through 10, and advanced grades 9 to adult. All forms yield three mental ages: language, non-language, and total. IQ, percentile, and grade norms are also provided. A diagnostic profile can be constructed for guiding the activities of the pupils. The original standardization of this test was based on 25,000 cases for each level. For many of these cases, Stanford-Binet test results were available for comparison. Since that time, data from over 100,000 additional cases have been used. Factorial analysis and other statistical methods were used in the selection of test items. All forms can be administered to groups, but very young children should be tested individually or in very small groups. The preprimary form requires no reading and takes about 20 minutes. The primary form requires no reading, but demands the application of more discrimination and a higher level speaking vocabulary than the preprimary test. Testing time is about 42 minutes. All forms include subtests on spatial relationships, logical reasoning, numerical reasoning, and verbal concepts. All forms require less than an hour to administer. They can be scored by hand, stencil, or machine. Lacking the time or skills to administer an individual test to each pupil, the teacher will find this test helpful in determining the rank of pupils in some areas of intelligence including the verbal factor. The timing, although not rigidly prescribed, is split up into small units of three to eight minutes, and therefore requires the full attention of the administrator. A stop clock is almost a necessity. However, since this test can be given to groups and since it does give a non-verbal score, it is a useful instrument.

Also available from the California Test Bureau is a pretest for vision, hearing, and motor coordination for grades 1 to 3. It is intended to help the teacher detect difficulties which would put children at a disadvantage in taking a paper and pencil test of any type.

The Pintner Non-Language Primary Mental Test by Rudolph Pintner (Bureau of Publications, Teachers College, Columbia University) for kindergarten and grades 1 and 2 requires no knowledge of numbers, letters, reading, or writing. It can be administered to groups of about 10 pupils. Norms are given in terms of mental ages. It is easy to score. Directions for the test are given in pantomine, and considerable preparation is needed by the test administrator. The scanty research data available on this test makes interpretation difficult. However, it might be of some value in assessing the latent abilities of the deprived child.

The Pintner General Ability Tests: Non-Language Series (World Book Company) for grades 4 through 9 is a later test and is accompanied by a detailed test manual. Standardization involved more than 6,000 children from 9½ to 13½ years of age, selected from schools in different sections of the United States. Some of the activities are reverse drawings, pattern synthesis, and paper folding. Scores can be translated into mental age, deviation IQ, and percentile rank. Scores in the middle ranges are believed more accurate than those at the upper or lower extremes.

In an effort to provide uniform norms for the comparison of an individual's scores in different areas, Bennet, Seashore, and Wesman developed the Differential Aptitude Test battery for the Psychological Corporation. This battery is designed for use in high school and the eighth grade. Test items, time limits, and norms are suitable for these students. The eight tests, which can be given separately, include verbal reasoning, numerical ability, space relations, abstract reasoning, clerical speed and accuracy, mechanical reasoning, and two sections on language usage: spelling and sentences. The total testing time is three hours and six minutes. Percentile norms are available for each of the five grades, for each sex, and for different parts of the country. Large samples of students from representative communities were used in standardization. Unusual care was taken in establishing the internal consistency of subtests. Answer sheets can be scored by hand or machine.

Intercorrelations between subtests support the claim that they do measure different abilities.[18] The items of the numerical ability test are

[18] Froelich, Clifford, and John G. Darley, *Studying Students,* Science Research Associates, Chicago, 1952, p. 236.

in the form of computation exercises in order to avoid language problems. The subtests to measure reasoning, space relations, and mechanical reasoning also attempt to minimize language difficulties.

INDIVIDUAL TESTS OF SCHOLASTIC APTITUDE

If the pencil and paper test scores are in doubt, individual intelligence tests are useful. One of the best known individual tests of intelligence is the Revised Stanford-Binet Scale (Houghton Mifflin Company). Work was begun on the scale around 1904. It has passed through several revisions, eliminating defects and improving norms. Louis M. Terman and Maud A. Merril in their 1937 revision utilized a carefully selected sample of representative school children from 17 communities in 11 states. Subjects in grades 1 to 12 totaled more than 2,000. It is available in two forms and can be used for people from the age of two years through adulthood. Since it is given individually and requires an experienced administrator, it would not usually be given to every pupil, but might be given to every first-grader, non-reader, retarded reader, pupil considered for acceleration, and pupil whose pencil and paper test results are of doubtful accuracy. However, since it is fairly heavily loaded with verbal factors, it might not be as suitable for deaf or foreign-born children or for retarded readers as a performance test.

Tasks such as fitting blocks together, picture completion, puzzles, and mazes are included in performance tests. The Arthur Point Scale of Performance, Revised Form II (Psychological Corporation, 1946) is designed for children from ages 3 to 15. Others which are used both for this purpose and for the study of personality are the Goodenough Draw-A-Man test described in *The Measurement of Intelligence by Drawings* (World Book Company), the Buck House-Tree-Person Test, and the Bender Visual Motor Gestalt which are discussed briefly in this chapter as projective techniques.

The Wechsler-Bellevue Scales of Mental Ability, 1939, and the Wechsler Intelligence Scale for Children, 1949 (Psychological Corporation) yield verbal, performance, and total scores. Results can be analyzed to determine whether the individual is functioning at less than his potential ability, and whether or not impairment is caused by temporary inefficiency. An experienced clinician can interpret results as affected by anxiety, depression, or pathological mental states. One subtest is concerned with visual-motor coordination. Much more work has been done on the adult scales than on the children's intelligence test.

The successful use of performance tests and projective techniques necessitates a high quality of rapport between client and clinician. The administrator must be sensitive to shades of meaning and attitudes of the client as expressed in bodily reactions and facial expression. He must know how to record and judge atypical and unexpected responses. Much study and practice are required in order to administer and interpret the results of these tests. If such services are available, these tests can add evidence which is invaluable, in some cases, in helping to understand a pupil and determine what may be done for him.

READING TESTS

The test included as a part of a battery, given to the entire school population or to freshmen, may or may not be suitable for diagnosis, although it can be used in screening. To determine accurately a student's reading level, one may find it necessary to administer a test several grades below his grade placement. A diagnostic test may provide not only the grade level, but valuable information as to where the student's difficulties lie. One of the major purposes in testing students of any age is to determine their level of comprehension. Among the upper grades, high-school and college classes, speed is also tested. Students of college age usually make their greatest gains in speed. A section on vocabulary recognition is included in most reading tests. Some also include exercises featuring word endings, initial sounds, interpretation of directions, reading for facts, finding the central thought, organization, similarities and opposites, alphabetizing, use of the index, and other aids. Some make a distinction between reading literature, science, social science, and mathematics. National norms are provided for use with standardized tests. The teacher need not feel obligated to force her pupils up to the norm, but she will find areas where the class or individuals need special help.

Among those most useful for high-school and college classes, we believe, are the Diagnostic Reading Tests published by the Committee on Diagnostic Reading Tests, Incorporated, 419 West 119th Street, New York 27. Members of the committee are Triggs, Bear, Bedell, McCallister, McQuitty, Spache, Traxler, and Westover. The survey section is available in eight forms, each of which is intended to measure a range of skills from grade 7 through the college freshman year. Because of the range, one can judge the level of a college freshman's reading skill more accurately than is possible from the results of tests designed for the average freshman class. The usual instrument included in the test battery given to entering college students gives little indication of the actual level or problems of the retarded readers. The score of a poor reader on a test which is too difficult for him is partially a result of chance or guessing. Retest with such an instrument may not show gains. A test with a greater range of levels makes it possible for him to register. The survey section is intended as a screening device to be followed by diagnostic tests (or sections) available separately. Section II includes untimed power tests of silent and auditory comprehension, especially useful in diagnosing the problems of retarded readers, identified by the survey section. Section III is intended to measure rate of reading in general, social science, and scientific materials. Section IV is intended to measure oral and silent word attack. The upper-level test may be less useful for screening seventh- and eighth-grade pupils than for high-school and college students.

The lower-level edition for grades 4 through 6 includes, in two booklets, tests of comprehension, word attack, vocabulary, and rate of reading. Section IV of the lower level, Word Attack, includes test paragraphs for grades 3 through 12. This edition might be useful for diagnosing the reading problems of retarded readers in junior or senior high school. Selections used in the different forms appear to be about the same level of interest and difficulty. Norms are based on the test scores of approximately 30,000 public-school students and 10,000 college freshmen, but norms for some grade levels are based on a very few students. More adequate norms are promised for the future. The skills tested are important ones.

An economical, short, easy to give, and easy to score test of long standing is the Nelson-Denny Reading Test (Houghton Mifflin). Although available for elementary school, it appears most useful in high school and college. Strict timing is required. It is scored for vocabulary and comprehension. Its diagnostic value might be increased if administered without a time limit, providing local norms could be established. Analysis of responses to individual items offers help in diagnosis.

The Traxler High School Reading Test by Arthur E. Traxler (Public School Publishing Company) for grades 10 through 12 yields a rate score and three comprehension scores. It requires 50 minutes of working time. Norms are based on the test results of more than 7,000 pupils. Percentiles are given for each score and for each grade level. The manual contains lucid information regarding interpretation and use. The two forms appear to be equivalent, making them convenient for test and retest. The rate score is easily determined. The items were carefully selected, and studies of the test's reliability are favorable.

A unique function is performed by the Durrell-Sullivan Reading Capacity and Achievement Tests by Donald D. Durrell and Helen Blair Sullivan (World Book Company) which provide a means of comparing the child's hearing comprehension with his reading achievement. The capacity test is less difficult to administer than most individual intelligence tests. Diagnosis is aided by scores in word and paragraph meaning and responses to questions requiring pupils to note details, get the central thought, and locate information. Supplementary tests of spelling and written recall are available. Directions are easily understood. The norms for the intermediate test are based upon 6,000 cases. Two levels are available, covering grades 2 through 6. The format is not particularly attractive, but the test is nevertheless very useful. Since the capacity test leans heavily on language facility, it should be used with caution in cases of underprivileged or foreign children or those with language handicaps.

For individual diagnosis, Gates Reading Diagnostic Tests by Arthur I. Gates (Teachers College, Columbia) are thorough and comprehensive. However, unless the school employs a reading specialist, psychometrist, or counselor, an individual test requiring from 60 to 90 minutes is useful only in a few special cases. Areas tested include vocabulary reversals, word and phrase perception, word analysis, and visual perception. The tester records information about vision, hearing, speech, eye movements, emotional tension, special interests, dislikes, home influences, and school history. Norms are available for grades 1 through 8, and for subtests as well as total score. Diagnosis is thoroughly discussed in the manual.

READINESS TESTS

Readiness-test results, together with data on mental age, social and emotional adjustment, health, experiential background, and maturity, can help the teacher to judge how soon to introduce reading activities. Also of great value are the teacher's observations on the child's use of the language, his willingness to do things for himself, and his attention span. The test results alone cannot predict individual achievement in reading, since some children who are scored as unready will undoubtedly reach the norm in achievement. The purpose of the test is not to tag a child as a slow or fast learner, but rather to try to select those pupils who would be bored by prolonging readiness experiences as well as those who need a period of preparation before beginning reading.

A latecomer on the scene is the Harrison-Stroud Reading Readiness Test (Houghton Mifflin) for kindergarten and first grade, aimed at measuring ability to make visual and auditory discriminations, use context clues, and understand that words stand for ideas. The test situations seem appropriate for measuring abilities which will be used in reading. Test results might be used with other data to determine whether the child should be placed in kindergarten, transition group, non-reading group, or in a slow, normal, or rapidly moving reading group. These tests will become more valuable as further research data are made available on their outcomes.

Also relatively new is the School Readiness Inventory (Educational Test Bureau), a checklist of items based on the works of Gesell, Doll, and Goodenough on personal and social development in children. It is believed helpful, though not infallible, when used with other measures and other data. Although specific behavior items are listed, the score depends somewhat on the teacher's judgment and knowledge.

The Stone-Grover Classification Test for Beginners in Reading (Webster), published in 1933, is intended to measure ability to see likenesses and differences in word forms.

The Van Wagenen Reading Readiness Tests (Educational Test Bureau), focused on language background, cover range of information, understanding of logical relationships, vocabulary, memory span for sentences, discrimination of like and unlike words, and ability to learn word forms. The six subtests are administered individually. Low scores suggest where the child needs help.

Five sections compose the Gates Reading Readiness Tests (Teachers College, Columbia). They are picture directions, word matching, word-card matching, rhyming, letters and numbers. A measure of mental age is needed along with these test results. The Gates Readiness Tests and Manual have recently been reprinted for distribution throughout Australia.

TEST BATTERIES

Reading tests offered in batteries are often useful in screening, and some are diagnostic. When a test battery is used routinely for all students, considerable information about each student is available to the reading teacher early in the school year. Remaining testing can then be devoted to diagnosis of group and individual problems. The battery makes possible a comparison of reading achievement with performance in other subjects.

The Metropolitan Achievement Tests by Allen, Bixler, Connor, Graham, and Hildreth (World Book Company) have the advantage of years of research, careful standardization, and fairly recent revisions in the light of research. The reading test provided with the battery is useful, both for screening and for diagnosis. The tests are available at four levels. Age and grade equivalents, age-grade norms, and percentile ranks are furnished and helpful suggestions on the uses of tests, planning a testing program, and teaching methods are included. Class analysis and error analysis are carefully explained and record forms provided for them. In addition to general norms, special norms are provided for special populations, as Negro, white, and parochial school, cities of 300,000 population, and others. Subtests include reading, vocabulary, and English.

Each test is designed to cover a narrow grade range, a feature which has the advantage of offering more items suitable for a given grade than does a test with a greater range. The difficulty mounts appropriately from test to test, permitting comparability from the cumulative record of several years of test results. Items which were not differential were dropped from revised editions. Revisions have been followed by revised manuals which give excellent data on interpretation. Reading tests can be obtained separately.

The explanations of item selection and standardization, says Findley,[19] leaves no doubt that

. . . a thorough and competent job has been done of establishing a revised series of batteries that (*a*) afford several equivalent forms at each of five educational levels, (*b*) can be used with confidence as equivalent to corresponding batteries of the previous edition, and (*c*) permit continuous interpretation of achievement on the same scales over several grades.

The Metropolitan Primary Reading Test has six subtests, including word recognition, word pictures, word meaning, sentence and paragraph reading, and spelling. The Primary I battery is particularly useful. The readiness test is a group test intended to measure ability to perceive similarities and differences, to identify and relate visual forms, and to understand words and sentences. It requires about an hour and should be given in several short periods. Norms are given for the total test score and for subtests. Revisions have produced improvements in format and procedures. Special instructions are given for administering the copying test to left-handed children. The final items were selected after item analysis from three experimental forms given to 2,600 children in the beginning first grade in different localities. Norms are based on testing more than 15,000 children in 26 states. The readiness scores can be translated into percentile ranks and into letter ratings.

Among the popular batteries are the Stanford Achievement Tests (World Book Company) which include measures of paragraph meaning, word meaning, spelling, and language. Three levels are available. Age and grade norms are provided. The time required is from 65 to 110 minutes. Those for upper levels can be machine scored. Standardization,

[19] Findley, Warren G., Review in O. K. Buros, (ed.), *Fourth Mental Measurements Yearbook*, Gryphon Press, Highland Park, N. J., 1953, p. 17.

which was particularly thorough, followed the usual procedure with the exception that all retarded or accelerated pupils were eliminated. Subject matter tests can be purchased separately. Authors are Kelley, Madden, Gardner, Terman, and Ruch.

The Iowa Every-Pupil Tests of Basic Skills (Houghton Mifflin) contain tests on silent-reading comprehension, vocabulary, work-study skills, use of dictionary, alphabetizing, and basic language skills for grades 3 through 5 and 5 through 9. The section on paragraph comprehension attempts to measure the ability to grasp and understand significant details, the organization of ideas, and the ability to appreciate total meaning. Selections in Part I are from various subject-matter areas. The elementary form includes stories and materials from social studies and science. The advanced form includes no fiction. Words in the vocabulary section are presented in phrases and sentences. Some of the words used in both forms in both paragraph and vocabulary sections are rather unusual and difficult. The manual includes a discussion of individual diagnosis and suggestions for remedial work. Each form appears more suitable for the upper level for which it is intended than for the lower level. For retarded readers in grade 5 through 9, it might be best to use the lower form. The tests are easy to give and to score. Norms are provided in terms of grade, age, or percentile rank. The norms tend to be higher than those provided with some other batteries. The tests were developed by H. F. Spitzer in collaboration with Ernest Horn, Maude McBroom, H. A. Green, and E. F. Lindquist.

The California Achievement Tests (California Test Bureau) offer four equivalent forms at each of three levels, which can be scored by hand, stencil, or machine. The primary form includes reading, spelling, and language. The reading test is divided into four subtests of word form, word recognition, meaning of opposites, and reading comprehension. The 30 items included in the reading-comprehension subtest relate to paragraph reading for facts, interpretation, and following directions. Beginning items in the reading test are simple and inspire confidence. The vocabulary in the paragraph reading is, for the most part, suitable for the primary pupil, but the paragraphs are unrelated to each other. The primary tests have been criticized because they cover such a wide range of abilities (four grades), but when used for diagnosing among third- and fourth-grade retarded readers, the range is an advantage. Simply worded and readily understood instructions are conveniently printed on the tests as well as in the manuals. Aids to interpretation are given.

The elementary battery, grades 4 to 6, and the intermediate battery, grades 7 to 9, cover the same subjects, and the separate tests are available by subjects as well as in the battery. A profile is provided by which one can judge the academic strengths and weaknesses of the pupil (although an error analysis would yield a more refined diagnosis). Group analysis data can also be charted. Preliminary work on the tests included studies of psychological literature and curricula in school districts in various parts of the nation. Norms were developed from testing pupils of differing mental abilities in different localities. A small percentage of the pupils tested during standardization were of minority groups; the majority were Caucasian. Standardization procedures involved more than 25,000 pupils for each grade level. Aside from testing pupils in each grade for which the battery was intended, the authors also gave the tests in next higher and lower grades to establish comparability of scores. Testing time suggested by the authors is 105 minutes for primary, 138 for elementary, and 153 for intermediate, although this is approximate only. The authors suggest stopping within five minutes after 90 per cent of the pupils have completed a section.

The California Test Bureau also publishes reading-readiness tests for kindergarten and first grade. The authors are J. Murray Lee and Willis W. Clark. The first test covers similarities and differences in letter and word formation and presents a series of pictures which are marked by the pupil according to the instructions given by the teacher. The revised edition, published in 1951, was standardized on 5,000 cases selected from approximately 25,000 cases. The test was given within one month after the pupils entered the first grade. Pupils repeating the grade were eliminated. The median chronological age in this group was six years and the median IQ was 100.

The First Reader Test by Lee and Clark (California Test Bureau) includes two sections on word recognition, one on following simple directions, one on sentence completion with three choices, and one section entitled "Inference," requiring the child to read eight sentences and answer a question following each. The vocabulary used in the test was checked against the first 500 words in the Gates list and primary readers. Rank can be determined in terms of age, grade, or percentile points. It was revised in 1951.

The Coordinated Scales of Attainment (Educational Test Bureau) are available in two equivalent forms for kindergarten through ninth grade. These tests are not new, but norms were revised in 1950. More than 50,000 pupils from kindergarten through grade 9 were employed in standardization. Rural, small town, city, and large city schools are said to be represented, as well as various geographic areas and socioeconomic levels. Test items were selected from an analysis of 30 state courses of study and 15 city curricula and evaluated on the basis of the test papers of the middle 20 per cent of the normative population. Each test was administered to the grade for which it was intended and to the grade above and below. Each battery is designed for use in a single grade. The authors recommend that the time be regulated by the point at which each section is finished by 90 per cent of the pupils in the class. The authors of batteries 1, 2, and 3 are Leo J. Brueckner, James A. T. Fitzgerald, and Ullin W. Leavell.

The vocabulary used in the primary battery was checked against Rinsland's basic vocabulary and the Buckingham-Dolch word list. There are four sections of 20 items each in the reading test. The first gives the pupils a choice from four words to match with a picture, and the second offers a choice of four pictures to go with a word. The remaining two sections are devoted to vocabulary recognition and paragraph reading. The paragraphs form a continuous story and each paragraph is followed by multiple-choice questions. The items in each section are of increasing difficulty. However, the first items in each of the primary batteries, particularly the reading test for grade 1, seem a little too difficult to inspire confidence. Some of the pictures in section II are quite small and appear to confuse some children. The first two sections, as well as section III, are concerned with word recognition, which seems to place undue emphasis on this skill as compared with reading comprehension. However, test interpretation could take these factors into consideration. Rank can be determined in terms of age or grade norms and provision is made for error analysis for each class.

The Coordinated Scales of Attainment for the upper grades includes literature and language. The tests can be scored by machine or stencil. Total time for the battery is about 256 minutes. The use of the test results in remedial work is explained in the manuals, and age and grade norms are given. The print in some sections of these tests is very small.

The so-called built-in tests which accompany most reader series need not be neglected in diagnosis and evaluation. They conform to the vocabulary and other features of the readers. Tests are provided two or three times a year by the publishers of *My Weekly Reader*. Among the advisory editors are well-known authorities in the field of reading instruction, Gray, Gates, Horn, Hoakam, Witty, Betts, Leary, Russell, Durrell, Blough, Millett, Strong, and Hefferman.

FACTORS IN INTERPRETATION

Intelligent use of standardized tests requires that one understand their limitations. Some are better than others, but none are perfect. For example, if the "ceiling" of a test or subtest is so low that some pupils make perfect scores, their achievement has not been accurately measured.

This possibility is mentioned in the discussion of the four reading subtests of the Coordinated Scales of Attainment (primary battery).[20]

For most children the average score on the four tests is a fair measure of reading ability. However, for exceptionally able readers, the top of the easiest test is not high enough. For these children it is recommended, therefore, that the average of the three highest scores, rather than the average of all four, be used as the measure of reading ability.

An able third-grader made one error on a test and a perfect score on the retest in vocabulary recognition. Her grade placement on the subtest was 4.5 on the first test and 4.3 on another form of the same test several months later, results which would make it appear that she had lost ground in this area, unless the various factors were understood. At the upper end of the scale for converting raw scores into grades scores, one notes that a difference of one error makes a difference of one grade in rank on the reading comprehension subtest of form B. While perhaps statistically defensible, the interpretation of this part of the scale is confusing to teachers. Another peculiarity of the converted scores for battery 3 is that a raw score of 19 on the vocabulary-recognition subtest, form A, ranks a child at grade 4.5 while 20, a perfect score, on form B ranks him 4.3.

Tests which include unusual words yield debatable scores for children who read well from their readers. These words, taken from a second-grade reading examination would not necessarily be common in their experience: mistress, annoying, pouch, guest, tense, peasants, observe.

Test results of the academically retarded pupils should be given special attention. If the first test is so difficult for a pupil that he fails to register, a retest may fail to show progress. If retardation is suspected, it might be a good thing to use an easier test to begin with. For example, a severely retarded reader scored zero on a second-grade reading test, but according to a first-grade test, given on the following day, he ranked about mid-year for the first grade.

Attention should be paid to the population used in standardization. If the test has been standardized on pupils from urban, middle-class segments of the population, the scores may not be typical of rural children nor of lower socioeconomic levels. In interpreting test results, the teacher of an atypical group can take into consideration whether the scores of these particular pupils might be somewhat depressed as a result of exposure to different kinds of information and experiences from those

[20] Brueckner, Leo J., James A. Fitzgerald, and Ullin W. Leavell, "Coordinated Scales of Attainment," Master Manual, Batteries 1, 2, and 3, Educational Test Bureau, Minneapolis, Nashville, Philadelphia, 1950, p. 11.

common to the group used in standardization. As Allison Davis[21] points out, the parents of children in the middle classes expect them to study at home, to do well in school, and to do their best on tests. This attitude probably operates to their advantage. "To the average lower-class child, . . . a test is just another place to be punished, to have one's weaknesses shown up, to be reminded that one is at the tail end of the procession."[22]

Another feature which might conceivably alter the interpretation of reading comprehension test scores is a difference in the interest value of the stories provided on alternate forms. Form A of one test offers a warm human interest incident involving a man who wanted a doll for his sick child. The story offered by form B for the same grade tells of a father who made a plane trip and brought presents to his children. For some reason, the form B story appears less appealing to children, perhaps because they picture themselves staying at home instead of taking the trip themselves. In this case, it is possible that less motivation operates during testing with form B.

Another feature which might influence results is the accuracy with which pictures in the test proper are reproduced. In some cases, the pictures used in connection with word recognition are very small and appear smudged. They are confusing to the young child who may be a little dismayed by the test situation anyway. Defects in format or type could distort results.

A test feature of importance is the difficulty of the first items. If the first items appear too forbidding to the pupil, he may be so frightened and discouraged that he will not be able to do his best on other parts of the test. Tests of reading comprehension which hang together to make a story appear to be more acceptable to children than those which are composed of separate unrelated paragraphs.

In some batteries, the importance of reading comprehension seems a little underestimated in proportion to the total score. For example, 20 questions out of 80 or 100 items will be devoted to actual reading. These contribute only a fourth or a fifth of the total score. While it is important to include other aspects of reading, such as vocabulary, word form, word meanings, and picture-word association, reading comprehension is probably the most important area measured and thus should probably be weighted more heavily than others in interpreting tested reading achievement.

[21] Davis, Allison, address at the Mid-Century Conference on Children and Youth, 1950, Washington, D. C.

[22] Eells, Kenneth, et al., *Intelligence and Cultural Differences*, University of Chicago Press, Chicago, 1951, p. 21.

Obviously, the conditions under which a test is administered could affect the accuracy of results. Motivation, physical condition of pupils, ventilation, heating, temperature of the room, and emotional tone are possible influences. Strict adherence to the instructions for administration is necessary if the results are to be comparable to national norms. A mistake in timing makes results inaccurate. The person administering the test should be thoroughly familiar with instructions and content. Taking the test oneself in advance is an excellent precaution.

Pupils who are unfamiliar with objective tests can be given special preparation. They might be told something about the form and purpose. A little advance practice in multiple-choice, matching, and completion exercises would be legitimate. Some tests provide practice exercises. If not, some exercises similar to those in the test might be given a day or two before formal testing. Special instructions are necessary if machine scoring is to be used.

The pupils may be told that they are not expected to answer all of the questions and that some will be easy and some more difficult. The test administrator can help the children to feel comfortable and calm in the test situation. The attitude with which the test is approached may have more effect on the reliability of results than do physical factors.

In administering a battery, particularly in the lower grades, the tester should be careful not to try to accomplish the whole task in one day. After completing a section, he might ask, "Do you want to stop or go on?" Signs of fatigue should be noted and some sections postponed if necessary.

For an accurate understanding of results, the testing program should be a continuous one. A single sample of achievement could easily represent a "leveling-off" period in an individual's growth or a temporary spurt of improvement. The growth and development of an individual can be thoroughly understood only by evidence accumulated over a period of years.

Difficulties in interpretation were encountered in one school system when two different batteries were used for the test and retest. One cannot be sure that two batteries have been standardized on the same kind of school populations. One could have been entirely urban and the other selected from a variety of communities, in which case the norms would not be comparable, and evaluation of progress would not be accurate. One test measured word form while the other did not. In one test, 40 items were devoted to word-picture association, a reading skill which was not directly measured by the other test. It would seem that if the test results are to be used for evaluation, two forms of the same test would best serve this purpose. This does not mean that after making a selection, the school system must continue its use indefinitely, but rather that for purposes of evaluation, the norms must be comparable. Improvements are constantly being made in tests. Frequent revisions and the development of new tests make possible a wide selection.

The danger of assigning exaggerated importance to standardized test results is suggested by a study of the relative difficulty of two reading tests. Although both are reputable instruments, a difference of more than one year was found in the grade rank of the same group of pupils on the two tests.[23] The two tests appear to measure similar factors and rank students in about the same order. In the light of this finding, teachers are reminded that it is more important to use the test results to see in which area students need help, which students need help, which might profit by being grouped together, and how much improvement is made, but not to indicate how much a given class or individual is above or below the national average.

Attention should be paid to the test's validity, or appropriateness, that is, to the evidence that it measures what it is supposed to measure. The test manual usually tells what real-life experiences the testmaker used to check validity and how well the test correlates with competence in the area it is supposed to measure.

Reliability or consistency is also an important characteristic. It refers to the degree to which a test will yield approximately the same results upon repeated administration or the degree to which equal parts of the same test agree in results. Reliability coefficients are usually reported in the manuals. A reliability coefficient of .80 or higher is said to be needed for accuracy and stability.

SECTIONING

From one-fifth to one-fourth of the college freshmen at one institution were found to demonstrate the high "Q," low "L" pattern of test results.[24] Since only part of the students could be admitted to the developmental reading classes, those students with the greatest discrepancy between "L" and "Q" were given first place and the assigners gradually worked down to those with "Q" scores 20 percentile points higher than "L." Students who ranked below the 35th percentile in total ACE score were placed in separate classes. Second semester classes were offered for students who ranked above the 35th percentile in total ACE score, demonstrated the "Q" and "L" discrepancy and who were not able to enroll in

[23] Pflieger, Elmer F., "A Study of Reading Grade Levels," *J. Educ. Res.*, vol. 42, no. 7, Sept., 1948–May, 1949, p. 541ff.

[24] Woolf, Maurice D., unpublished study, Kansas State College, 1954.

first semester classes. Similar criteria for sectioning can be applied to elementary and high school.

If individual testing service is available and if remediation is available for all who need it, classes should be offered for those students whose reading skills fall below the level of the general ability as measured by such tests as the Stanford-Binet or the Wechsler-Bellevue.

If students with similar problems and similar range of skills are sectioned together, they will probably be able to communicate with each other and to feel comfortable with each other. Choosing materials and methods is easier. Unfavorable comparison between students is minimized. Progress is more apparent to the retarded reader when he does not compete with pupils of superior skills.

INTEREST TESTS

Judging from data presented in Chapter 1, the interests of reading students are expected to be immature. In the case of the individual, this cannot be assumed. All reading students will not conform to the pattern of the majority. It is important to know whether or not the interests of the individual are similar to those of his reading classmates. Similarity or divergence throws light on his personal characteristics and problems. Using an interest test, along with instruments to measure ability, achievement, and personality, is consistent with our concept of treating and teaching the whole child.

Testing with the Strong Vocational Interest Blank or with some other interest test is desirable for students above the junior-high-school level. If a vocational interest is uncovered, it may prove to be motivating to the retarded reader. A vocational objective requiring reading makes study and drill appear more sensible to the student. Materials can be chosen in the light of the interest test results of individual and groups. Information from the test is valuable in counseling, often affording the best leads for beginning interviews with students.

The Vocational Interest Blank for Men by E. K. Strong (Psychological Corporation) and information on its interpretation are products of about 30 years of almost continuous research. It attempts to measure the degree to which the likes and dislikes of the subject are similar to those of adults who have remained in various occupations for a reasonable length of time and have achieved some degree of status. Criteria for status included membership in accrediting organizations, output, placement in favored positions, and mention in professional yearbooks and directories, necessarily varying from one occupation to another.

Much more work has been done on the men's form than on the

women's form, and it is sometimes used for both sexes. It is very easily administered, but difficult to score. Nearly 300 studies of its use add to the accuracy of interpretation. In addition to comparison with people in 34 occupations, the responses can be scored for groups of occupations and on three non-occupational keys. The occupational level key relates to inclinations toward the professions or toward the trades. The masculinity-femininity key indicates scientific as contrasted with verbal interests. The interest-maturity score was once believed to indicate whether or not the interest pattern might be relatively permanent or subject to change. Recent investigations cast some doubt on this interpretation.[25,26]

Since a comparison of a high "Q" and low "L" group of students (group A) with an even score group (group B) suggests that the former

TABLE 3-6

SVIB INTEREST-MATURITY AND SOCIAL WELFARE SCORES OF GROUPS A AND B
COMPARED BY MEANS OF t-SCORES

Group	No.	SVIB scale	Mean RS	$\bar{d}$	$s_{\bar{d}}$	t	P
A	119	Soc.-welfare	-15.62				
B	110		$-\ \ .77$	14.85	5.1685	2.87	$.01**$
A	116	Int.-maturity	$-\ 8.16$				
B	110		38.55	46.71	14.1390	3.04	$.01**$

tend to yield low interest-maturity scores, the reading teacher should be particularly interested in this SVIB scale.

Each of the A group produced a score in quantitative ability ranking 20 or more percentile points higher than his score in linguistic ability. The mean "Q" score of the A group was equal to the mean "Q" score of the B group. All students in both groups ranked above the 35th percentile in total scores on the ACE. Results of the study are reported in table 3-6.[27]

Group A ranked at the 28th percentile and Group B at the 45th percentile in interest-maturity as compared with 18-year-old men in general.[28] Differences between the two groups were significant at the .01

[25] Stordahl, K. E., "Permanence of Interest and Interest Maturity," *J. appl. Psychol.*, vol. 38, 1954, pp. 339–341, and *J. appl. Psychol.*, vol. 38, 1954, pp. 423–427.

[26] Hoyt, Donald, "Measurement and Prediction of the Permanence of Interests," pending publication in *Counseling Use of the Strong Vocational Interest Blank*, W. L. Layton (ed.), University of Minnesota Press, Minneapolis.

[27] Woolf, Maurice D., and Jeanne A. Woolf, "Is Linguistic Ability Related to Maturity?" *J. appl. Psychol.*, vol. 39, no. 6, 1955, pp. 413–415.

[28] Strong, E. K., *Vocational Interests of Men and Women*, Stanford University Press, Stanford, Calif., 1943, p. 263.

level of confidence. The difference in interest-maturity scores represented by the *t*-score of 3.04 means that there is little probability that the difference is a result of chance. The meaning of a low interest-maturity score is further discussed in Chapter 11.

Neither group indicated a pronounced interest in social-welfare occupations, but the tested interest of group A in this field is significantly lower than that of group B. Only five students in group A produced top ratings on the social-welfare scale (scored for occupational group), but 18 students in group B received top ratings on the social-welfare scale.

Further support for the belief that the high "Q" low "L" group lags in interest-maturity was found by comparing their SVIB scores with those of students who ranked high in linguistic ability and 20 percentile points lower in quantitative ability. The high "L" group was called the C group.

The mean quantitative score of the C group was equal to that of each of the other two groups. Results are reported in table 3-7.

TABLE 3-7
A, B, AND C GROUPS COMPARED WITH REGARD TO INTEREST-MATURITY

A vs. B			B vs. C			A vs. C		
Favors	*t*-Score	Signif.	Favors	*t*-Score	Signif.	Favors	*t*-Score	Signif.
B	3.04	.01	C	.64	no	C	2.73	.01

Interest-maturity scores of the linguistically inferior group are significantly lower than those of the other two groups. Interest-maturity can be conceived as ranging along a continuum with that of the 15-year-olds at one end of the scale and that of the 25-year-olds at the other. The interests of the linguistically inferior students resemble those of the 15-year-olds.

Super and Moser[29] found correlations significant at the .01 level or better between interest-maturity and independence, patterning of measured interests, and cultural stimulation or richness of experience. Ninth-grade groups studied ranged in number from 70 to 135.

VISUAL SCREENING

Some visual problems interfere so acutely with the improvement of reading skills that some sort of visual screening device should be employed. The Snellen eye chart has two disadvantages. The test is given

[29] Super, Donald E., and Helen P. Moser, "Relationships between Interest Maturity in Ninth Grade and Other Indices," Teachers College, Columbia University, New York.

at a distance of 20 feet instead of at the usual reading distance. Some people are able to fuse at the far point but not at the near point where fusion is needed for reading. Binocular vision is not required for reading the symbols on the Snellen chart, but it is required for efficient reading.

The Telebinocular, available from the Keystone Company, of Reading, Pennsylvania, can be used to measure variations of binocular vision. The instrument can be used to measure under-convergence, over-convergence, fusion at near and far points, depth perception, color blindness, phorias, and usable vision in either eye at various distances.

Students with symptoms of these visual problems should be referred to proper medical or optometric authorities.

The Correct Eye-scope, put out by the same company, helps to diagnose the distortion made by a youngster in the process of perceiving and recording a simple picture. The Am-Optical Orthofuser is used diagnostically in industry and has industrial norms for many kinds of jobs.

HEARING EXAMINATIONS

Partial deafness prevents the student from hearing words correctly spoken, interferes with getting meaning, and obstructs correct pronunciation. A study of 1,180 children suggests that loss of hearing can escape accurate diagnosis and that teachers are inclined to misinterpret the behavior of hard of hearing pupils. Eighty-three children were identified by testing with the ADC Pure-Tone Audiometer as handicapped by probable hearing loss. Of this number, teachers named only 13 per cent suspected of having hearing loss, but they regarded 24 per cent of the hard of hearing group as retarded in reading, spelling, and phonics, 28 per cent as retarded in school progress, and 20 per cent as behavior problems. Students diagnosed as poor readers might well be referred for a hearing examination if adequate means of testing hearing is available in the school system.

We recently talked with a woman who discovered at the age of 19 that she was almost totally deaf. Her parents and teachers had always regarded her as a little absent-minded and dull. Physicians diagnosed the ailment as one of long standing, probably dating from infancy. Aside from the possible advantage of early treatment, understanding her handicap would have made a difference in teachers' and parents' attitudes toward her in favorable seating arrangements in the classroom, speaking directly to her, and possibly training in lip reading which might have made learning easier.

It is also possible to mistake an emotional problem for loss of hearing. Pupils who daydream excessively, who are negatively conditioned to the speech of teachers or parents, or who are distractible because of anxiety or depression give the impression that they do not hear well. "A child may seem deaf because he is so emotionally disturbed that he does not want to hear," Drs. A. Bruce Graham and J. Lewis Hill reported at a meeting of the American Academy of General Practice.[30]

PERSONALITY INVENTORIES

As indicated in previous chapters, personal adjustment is linked with learning and with the reading process. Personality tests have been more severely criticized than any other measurement instruments. It would be a mistake to use the results of a personality test to moralize, pin a label on a student, discipline him, or lead him to feel there is something "wrong" with him. One of the dangers is that without experience and careful study of their limitations, teachers or counselors may accept the results as gospel. This is, of course, a fallacy in the use of any test. The counselor or teacher should not assume that the results of any one test or even more than one can give a complete picture of personality. Personality is too complex to be measured with any existing instrument. If one tried to use all available instruments to help him understand a single individual, it might turn out to be a lifetime job. As Williamson[31] points out, there are hundreds of personality tests, and each measures only a few aspects of personality.

It is difficult to prove the reliability and validity of a personality test. Some test authors compare their test results with teachers' judgments to determine whether the tests can distinguish between groups of students believed by their teachers to be well-adjusted or maladjusted. It is a debatable practice, in view of considerable evidence indicating that teachers are not prepared to recognize symptoms of maladjustment. Kaplan[32] found that teachers are more inclined to react to behavior which is annoying to them than to behavior which might be symptomatic of serious adjustment problems. In his study, he used a list of annoyances prepared by 150 elementary-school teachers, which was then presented to 250 experienced teachers for rating. Aggressive behavior was more often noted than withdrawn behavior, although the latter may have more serious implications.

An early study by Wickman compared attitudes of 511 teachers toward

[30] *Science News Letter*, April 16, 1955, p. 249.
[31] Williamson, E. G., *Counseling Adolescents*, McGraw-Hill Book Company, Inc., New York, 1950, p. 155.
[32] Kaplan, Louis, "The Annoyances of Elementary School Teachers," *J. Educ. Res.*, May, 1952, p. 649.

50 behavior traits with attitudes of 30 mental hygienists and found little agreement between them. Although later studies suggest that teacher attitudes have moved in the direction of those held by mental hygienists and clinicians, there are still significant disagreements. (A comparison of ratings of mental hygienists and clinicians in 1928, 1940, and 1951 showed little change.) Two behavior traits rated in 1951 by teachers as most serious were rated by clinicians as least serious. Among the 50 traits rated, there were 16 upon which teachers and clinicians differed markedly. Teachers still tend to be more concerned with transgressions against order and perhaps convention than with some of the more serious symptoms of maladjustment. Among the traits ranked serious by clinicians, but not serious by teachers, were shyness, suspiciousness, dreaminess, fearfulness, sensitiveness, tendency to be over-critical of others, and nervousness. The authors conclude that disagreements between teachers and clinicians are not so great as in 1927, but they are still of the same nature.[33]

In a study of the behavior of junior-college students, more than 200 students were rated by faculty advisers, hall counselors, suitemates, and instructors. Instructors made more use of the column "No opportunity to observe" than the three other groups of raters, and their ratings distinguished least between students diagnosed as maladjusted and students rated as well adjusted.[34] Teachers reported to Cunningham[35] that they felt less well acquainted with children believed to be maladjusted than with those believed to be well adjusted.

These references suggest the value of a truly differential instrument, if one can be found, and they illustrate the difficulties encountered in validation.

Another danger of the personality test is that the counselor may focus his attention on problems suggested by the test and fail to recognize the cues the student is trying to give him about other pressing matters. Some students who need help will not be identified by most screening tests. They may be reluctant to agree to statements which appear to them to be damaging. Some have concealed their problems from themselves. Some will react defensively to test items like these: "Do your classmates think you cannot do well in school? Do you often think that nobody likes

[33] Schrupp, M. H., and C. M. Gjerde, "Teacher Growth in Attitudes toward Behavior Problems of Children," *J. Educ. Psychol.*, no. 7, Nov. 1953, pp. 203ff.

[34] Woolf, Maurice D., "A Study of Some Relationships between Home Adjustment and the Behavior of Junior College Students," *J. Soc. Psychol.*, vol. 17, 1943, pp. 275–286.

[35] Cunningham, Ruth, et al., *Understanding Group Behavior of Boys and Girls,* Bureau of Publications, Teachers College, Columbia University, New York, 1951, p. 259.

you? Test items can be somewhat disguised to minimize defensive reaction, but if they are too subtle, one isn't sure what has been measured.

Another danger, perhaps, associated with personality testing is that the teacher or counselor might assume that every student should fit into a uniform mold. As Snygg and Combs[36] remark, "No individual ever continuously conforms to the norm. His behavior cannot be predicted by norms."

The attitude of the student toward the test could influence the result. If he feels that it might be used against him, or that the counselor or teacher administering the test is hostile, he may not answer frankly.

On the positive side, personality tests can identify a large number of students who need help. A review of a student's responses helps the counselor to prepare for the counseling interview and to understand what the student is trying to say. Both teachers and counselors can get from the student responses, as well as from total scores and subscores, valuable information about how the student regards himself, problems with which he is faced, attitudes toward authority, and his scale of values.

Many items of information gathered by tests can be uncovered in interview and through observation by sensitive teachers with a background of psychology, but ordinarily time does not permit. With personality inventories, this information can be gathered with a minimum of time and effort. If the counselor is acquainted with the student's opinions and problems reflected in test results, he has much better orientation and can save time in interview.

Reading students have difficulty in communicating, especially on subjects of a personal nature. We have found personality tests particularly useful in interviews with them. Apparently, they find it easier to check an item on a questionnaire than to bring up the same subject in an interview. Some who are over-conformative present a portrait of model behavior to the casual observer, but respond to personality inventories in such a way as to yield deviate scores. Judging from our own experience, more reading students are identified and diagnosed by the Minnesota Multiphasic Personality Inventory than by general screening tests, although not all who have serious problems according to clinical judgment are identified by it. Students whose behavior suggests problems but who do not yield deviate scores on the MMPI are consistently those who are constricted, repressed, conservative, and very conventional.

In the case of K. B., however, the test results suggested problems which otherwise might have remained unsuspected. In the classroom, he

[36] Snygg, Donald, and Arthur W. Combs, *Individual Behavior*, Harper & Brothers, New York, 1949, p. 8.

appeared to be an unusually polite, well-behaved, hard-working student. He said he liked to read. His high-school grades were entirely satisfactory. Most teachers, we believe, would interpret his statements as indications of a wholesome adjustment, although they are somewhat stereotyped: "Good people will always continue to be liked. Grown-ups think clearly and quickly. My purpose in life is to obtain an education. It is wrong to over-drink. You should never get angry. Things that make me mad are very few." An MMPI score of 65 on the hysteria scale suggested that he tended to convert worries into physical symptoms. According to screening tests for visual problems, he had no depth perception and had difficulty using his eyes together at the near point. Study and reading brought on headaches. In interview, he mentioned seasickness, carsickness, and ulcers. This combination of data suggests that he was under stress, but that his problems may have been too disturbing to recognize consciously. The MMPI helped the counselor in two ways. With K. B.'s medical history and signs of over-conformity, a good clinician might suspect hysteria, but the MMPI gave support to the diagnosis and made possible a tentative diagnosis at an earlier time than would otherwise have been possible. Further, the test score prepared the counselor to recognize underlying aggressions and to respond when the client faintly expressed the feeling that he might be trying too hard or that he could not do well under pressure. After counseling over a period of four months, the student reported that his headaches had disappeared, and his test results showed a gain of 200 words per minute in reading speed. In such cases, the clinician works closely with medical authorities, as genuine physical ills should not be confused with somatization.

Some personnel workers are so fearful that teachers, or even other counselors, will misuse personality-test results, that they refuse to recommend them and discuss their application reluctantly, if at all. We believe that many teachers will increase their understanding of human beings in general and gain insights into the behavior of their students through using these tests. Although, college classes in testing are heartily recommended as preparation for test interpretation, the use of tests with real students on the firing line makes them more and more meaningful.

Other advantages of the inventory-type test are these: it is easy to administer; can be given to groups; samples several areas of adjustment; may alert the teacher or counselor to trouble areas; is relatively inexpensive. Scores can be compared with those of several hundred or more other people of the same age and grade. Most of these tests are fairly easy to score.

Personality tests are constantly being refined and improved. Current and future research studies will doubtless aid in security and ease of interpretation and in more thorough understanding of the human personality. Users of these instruments should try to keep up with late studies, as findings may alter interpretations and throw new light on the meanings of scores. The clinician may prefer a diagnostic instrument, such as the MMPI or projective techniques, but for screening and for school counseling general tests, such as the California Personality Inventory or the Minnesota Personality Inventory, are widely used.

Introducing their discussion of instruments for screening and understanding emotional and social adjustment, Remmers and Gage[37] explore the relationship between motivation and adjustment and the reasons why teachers should understand the relationship before attempting to interpret the results of personality testing. They list as important motives of all people the drives for social approval, mastery or the urge to excel and succeed, new experience, security, and individuality. Obstacles to fulfillment may be an over-solicitous mother, customs of society, activities of other persons, personal defects such as lameness or ugliness, or conflict between equally strong motives, as the need to be independent as opposed to the need to be indulged and protected. In attempting to understand how well individuals meet these needs and by what modes they attempt to meet them, teachers are cautioned that moralistic, hostile reactions to people who exhibit adjustment problems are incompatible with the belief that maladjustment and undesirable behavior are "caused" by the interaction of the person with his environment.

Five types of pupils should be recognized by teachers as needing special help: unsociable, model, defensive, nervous, and emotional children.[38] Perhaps the least noticeable is the model child who carries neatness, obedience, or other virtues to an extreme. The behavior of the defensive child is often misinterpreted and labeled braggadocio, showing-off, or just plain meanness. Tests can help to call attention to problems which might be otherwise overlooked.

Minnesota Multiphasic Personality Inventory
by Starke R. Hathaway and J. Charnley McKinley
(Psychological Corporation, N. Y.)

The use of the MMPI requires a thorough knowledge of developmental and abnormal psychology, experience in test interpretation, and counseling skill. It is discussed here because it is one of the best yet pro-

[37] Remmers, H. H., and N. L. Gage, *Educational Measurement and Evaluation*, Harper & Brothers, New York, 1943, 1955, pp. 290–293.

[38] Myers, C. R., *Toward Mental Health in School*, University of Toronto Press, Toronto, 1939.

duced and because it is a contribution to understanding the human personality in general as well as individually. This instrument is composed of 550 self-descriptive items which were assigned to various scales on the basis of the extent to which they differentiated 221 classified psychiatric patients from 724 normal persons. Various investigations produced evidence that the scales tended to distinguish between groups of abnormal people with different kinds of mental illnesses. For example, paranoid cases can be distinguished from hypochondriacs, and so on. When subjected to severe tests of validity, the MMPI appeared to have more validity for screening and classifying personality problems than any of the generally available personality inventories.[39] A modification of the instrument for use with younger people is in progress. It may be of value to teachers and counselors who are not acquainted with the inventory to know that, on the MMPI, the higher the standard score, the more serious the problem. A high score on other inventories is more likely to be interpreted as favorable to the client, although not always.

When the MMPI was first used in studying reading students, the assumption was that a particular pattern of test results might be common among them. This was not the case, but a considerable proportion of them do deviate from the norm on one scale or another.

The kinds of adjustment measured by the MMPI are believed to interfere with productivity and self-realization in one way or another. Scores on the scales suggest to what degree the individual tends toward or away from the norm, whether or not he has a serious problem, and whether or not he is likely to be amenable to counseling. A moderate deviation from the norm, for example, on the paranoid key, suggests that the individual is a so-called normal with tendencies toward fixed ideas, inflexibility of purpose and habit, sensitivity, and suspiciousness. A marked deviation from the norm suggests a more serious problem, possibly requiring psychiatric treatment or hospitalization.

Eight of the scales are named for fairly well-known diagnostic categories, which in extreme cases correspond to mental illnesses and are intended to measure the degree to which a subject resembles abnormal people. Since the school counselor would use the instrument to measure trends in normal students, he is wise to avoid naming these trends in terms usually associated with abnormality. Another counselor might understand the incautious statement that the superintendent is a manic or that the track champion is a paranoid, but it is obvious that such indiscretions could cause trouble for the counselor and his clients. It is possible for well-functioning people to have these traits in moderation.

[39] Super, Donald, *Appraising Vocational Fitness,* Harper & Brothers, New York, 1949, p. 505.

These modes of behavior may have developed as a result of unsatisfied needs or as an attempt to satisfy needs or relieve tensions, or as an effort to escape from situations which offer no opportunity for self-realization.

It must be mentioned that there are kinds of maladjustment not measured by the test. For example, some obviously constricted, over-conformative, repressed individuals produce a relatively normal pattern. It is also important to understand that a given pattern might represent a temporary mood of depression, exhilaration, etc. Furthermore, maladjusted people are reluctant to admit damaging facts. Some of the questions arouse the defenses of some clients, and, although their scores can be corrected by various ingenious devices for distortion and defensiveness, the results obtained are not entirely satisfactory. It is, of course, possible for the test pattern to show a combination of deviating scores.

The client is asked to sort all statements into three categories; true, false, and cannot say. A large number of "cannot say" responses invalidate the test results. A moderately large number suggests that the subject's actual score would deviate more markedly from the norm than the results indicate. The lie score is intended to measure the amount of falsification. If the subject is careless or unable to understand the items, these flaws may be revealed in the F score. The K score is intended to reflect the amount of defensiveness. If any of these scores are high, they reveal something about the adjustment of the individual, as well as about the accuracy of the test.

The Hs, or hypochondriasis, scale relates to concern about bodily functions and physical illness. Genuine illness is presumably not reflected in a high score on this scale. The hypochondriac's symptoms are vaguely described. He has escaped from trying situations by imagined illnesses, but he does not know this. He is not faking. A validating study supports the belief that hypochondriacs can be distinguished from normals by their scores on the Hs scale.[40]

A high score on the D, or depression, scale indicates feelings of worthlessness, lack of self-confidence, worry, little hope for the future.

Subjects with a deviating Hy, or hysteria, score have presumably converted their worries into physical symptoms, such as paralysis, ulcers, simulated heart disease, psychosomatic blindness, etc. Headaches, fainting, stomach pains, and nausea are among the symptoms which may appear. Under stress they are likely to become acute. In time, a physical disability may develop as a result of the psychological symptoms. Medical treatment or religious experiences sometimes effect cures, but if the psychological problem remains, the ailment may reappear or the patient

[40] McKinley, J. C., and S. R. Hathaway, "A Multiphasic Personality Schedule: II. A Differential Study of Hypochondriasis," *J. Psychol.*, 1940, 10, p. 255ff.

can develop some other physical symptom. It seems that as the general public becomes more sophisticated about the subject of psychosomatic illness, the more obvious forms of conversional hysteria tend to disappear, and the physical symptoms become more subtle, as if the causes might be more thoroughly repressed.

The effect of counseling, environmental changes, and correct placement upon the pupil's eczema illustrates how these physical symptoms appear related to stress. He was under medical treatment and on a strict diet, but the eczema was apparent on all exposed parts of his body and he was very thin. Judging from observation and his spontaneous comments and writings, he felt himself rather unimportant. His father was quite strict with all of the children, and especially with the boy's older brother who passed the authoritarian behavior on to the younger children. The pupil's daily classroom performance was barely average, but standardized tests ranked him superior in intelligence and in all subjects excepting writing. His teacher hesitated to accelerate him, fearing that he might feel under increased pressure, but after talking with his parents, she advanced him to the next grade. He made a good adjustment to the new situation, academically and socially, and felt very proud of himself. The brother also found satisfying activities and developed leadership abilities. Their father seemed to get a new perspective on his family, and both boys received more praise and attention at home. Counseling for him and his brother helped them to relieve tensions. After two years, he was doing superior work in his new group and his eczema had disappeared.

In the more obvious forms of conversional hysteria, one can see a direct relation between the cause and the illness, as in the case of the soldier who develops paralysis which keeps him out of battle. In cases of subtle somatization, the illness may solve something for the patient, but the connection is disguised.

Subjects with one or more of these three patterns of behavior are said to be common among marginally adjusted people, operating among normals, although they can also be found among institutionalized patients. Some respond readily, others more slowly, and some not at all to improved environment and counseling, depending on the extent and history of the psychological problem, the skill of the counselor and the flexibility of environmental conditions.

The Pd, psychopathic deviate, is characterized by a lack of emotional depth, inability to learn from experience, and disregard of conventions and moral and legal regulations. He appears naïve, repeating offenses and experiencing the same consequences with mild surprise. One often finds a personal history of severe and indiscriminate punishment. People with this behavior pattern are often pleasant, normal-appearing people in the periods between their occasional outbreaks. In contrast with the manic, they do not seem to be power or profit motivated. Studies of delinquents suggest that the Pd scale is quite successful in differentiating them from normals.[41,42] Adults with high Pd scores do not ordinarily respond to counseling. There is more hope for younger clients and those with moderate scores.

The Mf, or masculinity-femininity, scale measures tendencies toward masculine or feminine interests. Although found to be of value in distinguishing homosexuals,[43] the scale should be very cautiously interpreted. Abnormality cannot be assumed on the basis of a deviate score. Little research is available about females who deviate from the norm. The items relating to adjustment to an appropriate sex role are stated in terms of the interests and attitudes of men and women as defined by our own particular society. Research on primitive societies reveals that the roles of men and women vary greatly. In contrast to general practice in western society, art, child care, or domestic duties are definitely assigned to men or shared by men in some societies. In our own culture, we can find contradictions in the common concept of either role. Men are expected to be interested in the sports and sciences, and in mastering the physical side of environment. Women are pictured as quieter and more submissive, more likely to be attracted by the arts or domestic duties. Yet, many men resent the fact that their wives are not interested in their activities and favorite pastimes, or they are attracted to women who are like them in their mastery of sports and liking for the out-of-doors. Men are expected to feel tenderness for their wives and children, and yet avoid any public display of these emotions. Women are presumed to have verbal and intellectual interests, and yet most of them become housewives with little opportunity to indulge this inclination.

Even the experts differ on sex roles. Reik contends that one cannot be a good sweetheart and at the same time a good pal. Maslow[44] interprets his data on self-actualizing people to support the opposite point of view. Moreover he found that either men or women in this study could take the initiative in love-making. Apparently, these wholesome, well-adjusted

[41] Benton, A. L., "The Minnesota Multiphasic Inventory in Clinical Practice," *J. nerv. mental Dis.*, vol. 102, 1945, pp. 416–420.

[42] Capwell, Dora F., "Personality Patterns of Adolescent Girls: I, II." *J. appl. Psychol.*, vol. 29, 1945, pp. 212–228, 289–297.

[43] Benton, *op. cit.*

[44] Maslow, A. H., *Motivation and Personality*, Harper & Brothers, New York, 1954, p. 238.

people were so sure of their maleness or femaleness that they were not threatened by recognizing both facets of personality.[45] His conclusions are not consistent with the common belief that women who are passive and submissive in their relationships with men make better wives.

It may be true, however, that failure to accept for oneself the same-sex role as defined by the society in which one lives can be a liability to satisfactory adjustment. The individual with this handicap may find that he does not fit comfortably into his community, peer group, or occupational group. He may come to believe that there is something "wrong" with him, or he may spend his energies rebelling against the social mores or trying to make them over to suit his needs. A sense of guilt or anxiety may inhibit his productivity. Counseling can help to relieve these pressures to some degree.

The man with a high femininity score might be expected to have a great respect for verbal occupations, the arts, and intellectual pursuits. He probably spends less time thinking and talking about sex than the average male. He may get along very well with women, enjoying their conversation and sharing their interests and work, but his defenses may rise in situations which threaten to become intimate. He may have wished to be a woman, but he may have concealed the wish even from himself. On the other hand, he may have found the proper niche where he can make a contribution to society, realize satisfaction in his work, and feel himself a person of worth.

Women who deviate from the norm on the Mf scale might be expected to like sciences, physical activity, or administrative work. They may be strongly attracted to aggressive women, and they may wish to be men. Some of the women who tend toward masculinity, as measured by this scale, remind us of the rugged pioneer women, glorified in tales of the early history of our country. Rather than wishing to dominate people, they appear to be motivated to master the physical aspects of their environment. Many of them wish to marry and have children.

Another kind of temperament which seems to us associated with a deviate Mf score is that of the woman who has intellectual interests plus a drive toward professional status. She characteristically resents the role of the submissive, domestic female. She enjoys the company of men because she wants to talk politics, philosophy, and business and to demonstrate her knowledge and skill in men's affairs. The physical side of life is a necessary evil which one disposes of efficiently so as not to let it get in the way of more important matters.

A deviation from the norm on this scale could make a difference in choice of occupation and in marriage plans. Two people with a strong

[45] Maslow, *op. cit.*, p. 245.

drive to dominate and manipulate others probably would not be happy together. A man who shows by his scores to have interests similar to those of women might not be happy in marriage.

The Mf scale is of particular interest to people working with linguistically inferior students, since a considerable proportion of those with the high "Q," low "L" test pattern deviate from the norm on this scale. As stated in Chapter 1, the deviation appears to reflect a lack of appropriate identification (undifferentiated self-concept) rather than identification with the opposite sex.[46] The tendency toward masculinity in women reading students appears consistent with their dislike for intellectual and verbal activities. In men, however, the tendency toward femininity is more difficult to understand, since, if it is true that their interests are feminine, it follows that they should like to read. We can speculate that they have a great respect for verbal and intellectual superiority, but have been unable to achieve it. It also seems possible that their response to successive rebuffs and failures has made them behave more submissively than the average male. A deviate score for men suggests tenderheartedness.

It would be unfortunate if a teacher or counselor should regard a deviate score on the Mf scale as an occasion for moralizing. As we have seen, it does not necessarily suggest overt homosexuality. The function of the counselor is not to make the client over into a model of averageness in all areas. He may be able to help the client to understand and accept himself as he is and as he is capable of becoming, understand and accept others, understand and accept reality, see alternative courses of actions, and make decisions which lead to self-realization.

People with a deviate Pa, or paranoid, score usually reveal one or more of the following characteristics: hypersensitivity, suspiciousness, fixed ideas or systems of fixed ideas, unusually logical reasoning, perseverance toward a goal, exaggerated resistance to change and to new ideas. We might observe that the genuine paranoid is so logical as to be unbelievably convincing. Early in life, he has figured things out so as to relieve himself of blame or to explain away unfavorable aspects of environment so that he could live in it without unbearable strain. Once he thoroughly accepts a conviction, he is exceedingly unlikely to give it up. In extreme cases, the paranoid is subject to delusions of persecution or delusions of grandeur.

Some characteristics of the Pa temperament might be considered assets. Persistence toward a goal is a highly admired trait in our society. Logical reasoning can be an advantage in some occupations if all evidence is recognized and accurately assessed. Sensitivity may, in some

[46] Woolf, Maurice D., unpublished study, Kansas State College, 1954, 1955.

cases, help the individual to understand how others feel and to get along with others.

On the negative side, hypersensitivity may operate only in relation to self, producing the conviction that others are exploiting, ridiculing, or harming the person. The rigidity of the paranoid personality is a barrier to learning, to taking on new ideas which appear to threaten the carefully constructed defense. Persistence may become a battle with windmills when efforts would be better spent in an enterprise which promises more satisfaction. The paranoid may be so suspicious of others that he can never form close, intimate relationships, or his suspicions can stand in the way of taking advantage of promising opportunities. Unwarranted suspicions may interfere with his relations with relatives, friends, fellow-workers, or employers. He is quick to retaliate against anyone who appears to threaten or to wish to control him.

The authors of the test state that[47] " . . . they have observed very few paranoid persons who have successfully avoided betraying themselves in the items of this scale." The counselor who understands the Pa personality is aware how very carefully he must handle the case if he is to help the client and at the same time avoid any action or statement which might be interpreted as making him responsible for the client's misfortunes. The person with Pa adjustments yields slowly to counseling, if at all. In our experience, some clients with this problem have made progress toward a more wholesome adjustment, as judged by counselors and others, and as measured by retest with the MMPI. Students of high-school and college age with moderate deviations have a potential for improvement. One adult client with a deviate Pa score fancied that her employer was persecuting her. After having been counseled for about a year and moving to a more favorable environment, she was reported to be functioning efficiently in her job and improving in interpersonal relationships. A score of 80 and above is said to be nearly always significant of disabling abnormality. Scores of from 70 to 80 are sufficiently high to justify referral of the client to a competent authority for clinical diagnosis.[48]

The Pt, or psychasthenia, scale is believed to measure excessive anxiety, worry, generalized fear, distractibility, or compulsive behavior. The person with constant anxiety spins his wheels and accomplishes very little. He is not aware of the source of his fears, but he may allay his anxiety temporarily by checking twice to be sure the brakes are on in the car or running back into the house to assure himself that the stove is

[47] Hathaway, S. R., and J. C. McKinley, Manual, Minnesota Multiphasic Personality Inventory, Psychological Corporation, New York, 1951, p. 20.
[48] Hathaway and McKinley, *op. cit.*, p. 20.

turned off. He is indecisive, vacillating, and aimless. His anxiety may crystallize into excessive fear of a closed room or furry animals or any one of a number of things. He may try to ward off disaster by compulsive handwashing, or by snapping his fingers three times, or by more elaborate ceremonies and rituals. He is almost constantly in a state of unrelieved tension. If the score is above 80, a serious problem is suggested; if between 70 and 80, referral for further diagnosis is wise.[49] People with moderately high scores may respond to counseling, possibly uncovering the source of their fears, relieving tensions, and gaining in productivity.

The schizophrenic, as diagnosed by the Sc scale, has a tendency toward a dream life that helps him to satisfy his needs and ambitions more fully than seems possible in real life. This is not necessarily an abnormal adjustment, but it can be if the dream world becomes more real and satisfying than the real one. A deviate score on this scale tends to be associated with bizarre and unusual thoughts and behavior. It is difficult for the counselor to communicate with a client with this kind of temperament, as his speech and actions do not agree with his thoughts, and he may have very special, private terms and phrases which have meaning for him, but not for other people. High Sc scores are often accompanied by high scores on other scales. A person with this adjustment made the comment quoted previously that reading "seems like something a way off." People with a small share of this component often have vivid imaginations which they may be able to use productively. People with a large share see the outside world and other people as if through a veil. They often feel that the world is spinning too fast for them to catch up. Events happen too fast. They may feel that they are spinning.

A deviate score on the Ma, or hypomania, scale suggests spasmodic enthusiasms, hyperactivity, and self-interest. The manic component, if not great enough to be disabling, may be expressed in the starting of a great many projects, joining every organization on the campus, proposing more ideas can possibly be attempted. The manic has so many irons in the fire that he cannot finish what he starts. In many cases, he is profit-motivated. If not actually interested in financial gain, he may be power-oriented, or eager for prestige, or pushing whatever organization or activity which appears to promise self-aggrandizement. His hyperactivity is the result of both the drive for status and the need to relieve tensions. It may take form of an active interest in social reform or charitable endeavor, but however disguised, his underlying motivation is actually self-enhancement. The manic is very much aware of authority. Very likely he sees himself somewhere on an authoritarian scale, with certain favored people above him and the less important ones below him. He

[49] Hathaway and McKinley, *op. cit.*, p. 20.

seeks to know the honored guests at the dinner party and is especially pleasant to anyone who might be in a position to help him. He doesn't offend people unnecessarily, but he is willing to ride roughshod over anyone who gets in his way. He is often pleasant, a jolly good fellow, the life of the party. At the same time, he is busily anticipating what is coming next. He is intrigued by the new and the exciting.

In some respects he is similar to the psychopathic deviate, but his violations of conventions and the law are calculated risks. He knows the rules and he looks for the loopholes. If he is penalized, he may count the gain as more important than the penalty. If he loses in a gamble, he finds another way around the rule.

In extreme cases, the manic is frantically active and talkative. He wears himself out and tires those around him. His moods of exhilaration may alternate with depression.

In view of the frequency of deviate Ma scores among 300 undergraduate women students studied by Lough,[50,51] the counselor should be cautious in interpreting the results of this scale with adolescents. Possibly, a small share of the manic component is normal among adolescents. They are still in exploratory stages of life, many of them without well-defined goals, intrigued with new experiences, not too well acquainted with their own abilities. The world is expanding for them. Possibilities appear to them to be unlimited. It is normal for them to be vigorous, effervescent, and eager to try new things. It might also be added that in this country a premium is commonly placed on hyperactivity and getting ahead in the world. Perhaps, manic behavior is subtly rewarded and reinforced by the mores.

When a high manic score appears in combination with other high scores, the behavior pattern is modified. For example, an 18-year-old college woman produced a fairly high Pa score, a moderately high Ma score, and a deviation from the norm on the Mf scale. She betrayed very little of the retaliativeness usually noted in the Pa adjustment. This might be explained by the fact that early in life she had adopted the principle that one should never say anything critical of anyone and should never hurt anyone's feelings. Once she had made this standard a part of herself, she adhered to it with the usual rigidity of the Pa adjustment. Rigidity was also manifested in the time limits and other standards which she set for herself and to which she adhered.

[50] Lough, O. M., "Teachers College Students and the Minnesota Multiphasic Personality Inventory," *J. appl. Psychol.*, vol. 30, 1946, pp. 241–247.

[51] Lough, O. M., "Women Students in Liberal Arts, Nursing and Teaching Training Curricula and the Minnesota Multiphastic Personality Inventory," *J. appl. Psychol.*, vol. 31, 1947, pp. 437–445.

Sensitivity was noted to any statement or act which could be construed as criticism or indifference. Subtle hints of suspiciousness could be observed. Although she did many favors for her classmates, she could never experience as much approval as she thought she deserved. While trying to avoid expressing criticism, she cautiously explored the possibility that they might not like her and that they might be trying to get her to do things for them. Her attitudes in counseling interviews were gradually revealed: "I don't quite trust you with my innermost secrets." On some occasions she seemed to be expressing, "What do you really mean when you say that?"

Friendly overtures and favors from others aroused these questions, "Why should they do this for me? What do they want?" If she was obliged to accept a favor or a gift, she could not rest until she had paid it back. Her reasoning seemed to be that one doesn't get something for nothing; for every favor, the donor expects a return; by hastily discharging an obligation, one might avoid having to reciprocate in a less agreeable fashion. She thoroughly resented any person who appeared to be trying to control her. Her father, sister, sweetheart, and some friends and instructors came in this category.

The Ma tendency was reflected in over-talkativeness and constant activity which seemed to give her considerable relief from tension. However, unlike the typical manic, she was able to carry on a number of activities successfully and to finish what she started. Apparently the purposefulness and persistence inherent in the Pa adjustment balanced the flightiness of the manic component. While giving a satisfactory performance in two part-time jobs, she was able to carry a full schedule of classes and to maintain a B-plus average in her college work. She attended church faithfully, took care of her own clothing, participated in sports, and found time for some social life.

The Mf score showed that she preferred the company of men as long as they talked interestingly or played games with her; she was confused and somewhat repelled by amorous advances. Women who had made their mark in the professions or business were greatly admired, but most women appeared to her as frivolous, gossipy, and inconsequential. Since the Mf score for women cannot be assumed to have clinical significance in determining homosexuality, in this case it may reflect an interest in sports and the out-of-doors plus a slight lag in identification with same-sex figures. These characteristics seem relatively normal for adolescents. If more support can be found for the trend toward masculinity, and if it continues, such a girl might be happier in professional life than in marriage.

After several months of counseling, retest with the MMPI suggested that Pa tendencies had declined. If the Ma trend might be discounted as an aspect of adolescence, remaining problems appeared to be inclinations toward hypersensitivity, some rigidity, and the need for self-acceptance. It seems possible that with a favorable environment and wholesome experiences, the Ma and Mf scores might move toward the norm as the client grows older. These brief excerpts from a case history are given to illustrate how important it is to see test scores in relation to each other and how necessary it is to avoid an exaggerated weighting of a deviate score. The deviate Ma and Mf scores, which are not so serious in the case of an 18-year-old, if found in an adult female profile suggest that she may be arrested in emotional development at an adolescent level.

A study of the MMPI as an indicator of success in college suggests that deviate scores above the mean on all scales may be associated with low achievement, regardless of ability. High scores on the manic scale appear to be characteristic of all low-achievement groups.[52]

Among additional areas for which the MMPI can be scored is social introversion (Si), or the tendency to withdraw from social contact with others. High scores on the scale have been found to distinguish between college women involved in few activities and those involved in many.[53]

In general, we might add that the MMPI is a valuable clinical instrument for the experienced counselor, to reflect to some degree how the client has tried to relieve tensions and satisfy his needs and to suggest what kinds of behavior have been rewarded in the past. A total of 283 research studies using this instrument are listed in the third and fourth mental measurements yearbooks. The most ambitious of these is the Hathaway-Meehl[54] *Atlas for the Clinical Use of the MMPI*, which contains 968 case histories with MMPI profiles.

The Bell Adjustment Inventory
by Hugh M. Bell, Stanford University
(Psychological Corporation, N. Y.)

The Bell Adjustment Inventory in two forms, for grades 9 to 16 and adults, is easy to administer and can be scored by stencil or machine. Hand-scoring is quick and easy. The student form is scored for four areas of adjustment, home, health, social, and emotional. The adult form

[52] Jackson, Boyd, and Mary Taylor, "Summary of Research," unpublished study, Counseling Bureau, Kansas State College, 1950, p. 18.

[53] Drake, L. E., and W. B. Thierde, "Further Validation of the Social I. E. Scale for the MMPI," *J. Educ. Res.*, vol. 41, 1948, pp. 551–556.

[54] Hathaway, Starke, R., and Paul E. Meehl, *An Atlas for the Clinical Use of the MMPI*, University of Minnesota Press, Minneapolis, 1951.

yields the same four scores plus a score in occupational adjustment. Opinions vary on the usefulness of this test, but there is some evidence in its favor. When the test results of 119 delinquent children were compared with those of 148 school children, the home and emotional adjustment scores were found to distinguish markedly between the two groups.[55]

Fourteen items from the home scale were found useful in predicting social and emotional maladjustment.[56] When 106 junior-college women who ranked excellent on the home-adjustment section were compared with 105 junior-college women who ranked unsatisfactory on this section, significant differences were found in their behavior. Each student in each group was rated by her adviser, her hall counselor, a suitemate, and one instructor on 37 items relating to behavior. Differential items from the Bell Adjustment Inventory were as follows in the order of their importance: (1) either parent easily irritated; (2) felt that parents did not understand her; (3) either parent became angry easily; (4) felt parents were disappointed in her; (5) felt conflicting moods of love and hate for members of family; (6) felt strong desire to run away from home; (7) either parent insisted on unreasonable obedience; (8) parents had irritating personal habits; (9) either parent frequently found fault with her conduct; (10) either parent very nervous; (11) had to keep quiet or leave the house to have peace; (12) felt friends had a happier home life.

When the four ratings were combined and the two groups compared, the differences between the two groups were represented by critical ratios ranging from 3 to 4.7 on the following items: is supersensitive, expresses hate, mopes by herself, cuts classes, is self-conscious, is listless, expresses feelings of inferiority, cries, has difficulty in making friends, expresses prejudices, misses meals, expresses fear, misses appointments, sulks and pouts, resents criticism, is spiteful.[57]

Leuba[58] and Pederson[59] concluded that the home-adjustment section is the most valid of the four. H. T. Tyler[60] states that the reliability of

[55] Bartlett, Edward R., and Dale B. Harris, "Personality Factors in Delinquency," *School and Society*, vol. 43, May 9, 1936, pp. 653–656.

[56] Marsh, Charles J., "The Diagnostic Value of the Bell Adjustment Inventory for College Women," *J. soc. Psychol.*, vol. 17, February, 1943, pp. 103–109.

[57] Woolf, Maurice D., "A Study of Some Relationships between Home Adjustment and the Behavior of Junior College Students," *J. soc. Psychol.*, vol. 17, 1943, 275–286.

[58] Leuba, C., "An Evaluation of the Bell Adjustment Inventory at Antioch," unpublished report, Antioch College, Yellow Springs, Ohio.

[59] Pederson, R. A., "Validity of the Bell Adjustment Inventory when Applied to College Women," *J. Psychol.*, vol. 9, 1940, pp. 227–236.

[60] Tyler, H. T., "Evaluating the Bell Adjustment Inventory," *Jun. Coll. J.*, vol. 6, 1936, pp. 353–357.

the test is high and approves of the methods used in validation. Students involved in validation were selected as well adjusted or maladjusted, according to the judgment of high-school and college counselors and administrators. Differences between the two groups were represented by critical ratios: home adjustment 7.02; health adjustment 6.58; social 5.52; emotional 5.32. Hanawalt[61] states, "The validity apparently is as good as any of the paper and pencil adjustment inventories. . . ."

Comments on the home-adjustment section are of particular interest to the teacher of retarded readers, since home conditions and parental attitudes toward the child influence his ability to learn. Both the home-adjustment score and responses to various test items help the teacher and counselor to understand the student's behavior and problems with which he may be faced. Other scores are useful to some degree. Our experiences with sophisticated and constricted clients lead us to believe that an excellent score is sometimes open to question. Some students are very skillful in concealing problems. Some deceive themselves. The Adjustment Inventory is much less specific and less diagnostic than the MMPI, but it is simpler to administer and score and easier to interpret.

The Guilford-Zimmerman Temperament Survey
by J. P. Guilford and Wayne S. Zimmerman
(Sheridan Supply Co.)

The Temperament Survey for grades 9 to 16 and adults is a revision of three older instruments. Areas covered are general activity, restraint, ascendancy, sociability, emotional stability, objectivity, friendliness, thoughtfulness, personal relations, and masculinity. It can be scored by stencil or machine, and the stencil scoring is easy. Items are weighted either 0 or 1. Norms for nine of the ten traits were obtained from a college population of 523 men and 389 women. Norms for the thoughtfulness trait were developed from high-school seniors and their parents. The test pattern and the instructions for interpretation emphasize the complexity of personality. The interpretation of this instrument appears to require a considerable degree of professional sophistication on the part of the counselor. The statements in the survey are answered by yes, ?, or no. More than three question marks are said by the authors to mean that the examinee does not understand himself or that he lacks confidence in his judgment about himself. Nevertheless, Van Steenberg[62] reports

---

[61] Hanawalt, Nelson, G., comment in *The Fourth Mental Measurements Yearbook,* edited by O. K. Buros, Gryphon Press, Highland Park, N. J., 1953, p. 29.

[62] Van Steenberg, Neil, review in *The Fourth Mental Measurements Yearbook,* edited by O. K. Buros, Gryphon Press, Highland Park, N. J., 1953, p. 50.

that a number of mature psychologists answered the 300 items and produced, in most cases, more than three question marks.

The Heston Personal Adjustment Inventory
by Joseph C. Heston
(Psychological Corporation, N. Y.)

Another relatively new instrument is the Heston Personal Adjustment Inventory (World Book Company), intended to measure analytical thinking, sociability, emotional stability, confidence, personal relations, and home satisfaction. It can be simply administered and scored, is fairly easy to interpret, and might be used for screening and for cues in counseling. Percentile norms based on results from about 1,900 students are provided for college men, college women, high-school senior men, and high-school senior women. The manual is readable, thorough, and modest in its claims for the instrument. More research is needed to determine exactly what it does measure. Experienced counselors will probably prefer to use a more diagnostic instrument for individual measurement.

Minnesota Personality Scale
by John G. Darley and Walter J. McNamara
(Psychological Corporation, N. Y.)

Darley and McNamara used factor analysis of several earlier instruments in developing this test. It requires only about 45 minutes to give and is easy to administer and score. Test items appear to us less likely than some others to arouse defensive reactions. It is intended for use with students in the last two years of high school and college and with adults. It is scored for morale, social adjustment, family relations, emotionality, and economic conservatism. Answers are given in terms of five degrees of agreement or intensity, as from "strongly agree" to "strongly disagree" or from "almost always" to "almost never." Norms are for 2,000 men and women freshmen at the University of Minnesota. Although economic conservatism appears at first glance to be out of harmony with the rest of the test, a high or low score in this section reflects attitudes and opinions to which the counselor needs to respond in interview and which may be related to emotional needs and problems. A student who consistently answers "Strongly agree" to questions such as "On the whole our economic system is just and wise" might be expected to show resistance to change. His security lies in preserving the status quo. His security needs may make it impossible for him to recognize any flaws in parents, church, or other highly respected institutions.

Lown[63] studied consistency between self-ratings and the results of Minnesota Personality Scale. He found 72.67 per cent agreement between students' statements of social problems and 57.67 per cent agreement between their statements of emotional problems and the results of the Minnesota Personality Scale. Perhaps students find it more difficult to confess to emotional problems. These findings suggest that the MPS may identify more students who need counseling than would be determined by direct questioning.

From a sample of 350 freshmen tested for respect toward human worth and dignity those who showed greatest respect tended to have average or better than average scores on the five sections of the MPS. The mean scores of those who showed least respect were less satisfactory than average by from 8 to 20 percentile points. For example, the mean percentile rank for the "most respect" group on morale was 68 and for the "least respect" group the mean percentile rank was 34. This study is of further interest to reading teachers in view of the fact that the "much respect" group had a high "L" and average "Q" ability pattern, while mean percentile ranks of the "little respect" group were 53 in "Q" and 29 in "L".[64]

When 200 students were retested with the MPS after two years of college, more than twice as many ranking in the upper 30 per cent on the ACE were found to have made improvement on the emotionality scale as occurred among the lower 30 per cent.[65]

Halbower[66] found that sorority women who deviate from the norm on the emotionality scale tend to make poorer grades than those with normal scores. The difference was significant at the .05 level of confidence. Normals among sorority women (per MPS) tended to make higher scores on the Ohio Psychological Examination than deviates, and the difference was significant at the .001 level of confidence. When compared with unaffiliated women by means of the economic-conservatism scale, sorority women appeared to be ultraconservative, while unaffiliated women

[63] Lown, Wilfred, "The Relationship between Claimed Problems of College Freshmen and Problems as Indicated by Objective Test Data," unpublished master's thesis, Kansas State College, 1948.

[64] Torrance, E. Paul, "Summary of Counseling Bureau Studies, Kansas State College, 1950–1951," unpublished, p. 17.

[65] Nelson, Patricia, "Changes in Attitudes, Values, and Personality Adjustment After Two Years of College Experience," unpublished study, Kansas State College, 1951.

[66] Halbower, Charles, "A Study of Developed Differences in Personality, Intelligence, and Scholastic Achievement between Sorority and Unaffiliated Women," unpublished master's thesis, Kansas State College, 1949.

tended to be liberal. Owing to the small number of students tested in this study, the results are not entirely conclusive.

California Test of Personality
by Louis P. Thorpe, Willis W. Clark, and Ernest W. Teigs
(California Test Bureau)

The 1953 revision for grades 4 to 9 provides percentile norms derived from test data for over 4,000 pupils in grades 4 to 8 inclusive in Nebraska, New Jersey, New York, Ohio, Massachusetts, and California. The two major divisions of the test are self-adjustment, or personal security, and social adjustment based on feelings of social adequacy. The test proper includes 144 items. Also provided is an interest-activity checklist of 74 items. The selection of items for the test proper was made from more than 1,000 modes of response to specific situations which confront children. The judgments of teachers and school principals were sought regarding the significance of the items. The reactions of children to the items were studied and compared with those of teachers.

Some of its uses are suggested by various studies. Factors relating to achievement in the first grade were explored by Edmiston and Hollahan[67] who tested 115 first graders. The California Test of Personality appeared to add accuracy to predictions of achievement when used with reading readiness and intelligence tests.

The personal adjustment of pupils with 10 or more unexcused absences was compared with that of pupils who had no absences for a semester. The perfect attendance group of 599 members ranked higher on the CTP than the experimental group of 599 members. Statistically significant differences were found between the total adjustment of these two groups in grades 5 and 10. Economic status and school grades also differentiated between the two groups.[68]

A small number of readily accepted children were compared with those most rejected by their classmates by means of the CTP. The most accepted group were among those who scored highest on the California Personality. Of the 12 isolates, 11 were among the 12 lowest on the personality scale.[69]

---

[67] Edmiston, R. W., and Catherine E. Hollahan, "Measures Predictive of First Grade Achievement," *School and Society*, April 13, 1946, p. 268f.

[68] Edmiston, R. W., M. E. Henlon, and Floyd Raser, "Special Emphasis to Improve Attendance," *J. Educ. Res.*, vol. 41, no. 1, September 1947, pp. 35–40.

[69] McClelland, F. M., and John A. Ratliff, "The Use of Sociometry as an Aid in Promoting Social Adjustment in a Ninth Grade Home-Room," *Sociometry*, vol. 10, no. 2, May, 1947.

This type of test is judged by two authors to be as useful as the interview in gathering information.[70,71]

Fourth-graders who ranked in the lower 25 per cent of their class according to the CTP were retested after a year during which they were given special attention. Retest showed a gain of about 20 percentile points. After another year, they showed an additional gain of 10 percentile points.[72]

The Primary form of the California Test of Personality consists of 96 items and is suggested for kindergarten through grade 3. Three sets of directions are given, one for children too immature to mark their own papers, one for children who need to have the questions read to them but can mark their own choices, and one for pupils who can read and mark their own answers. The norms were derived from test data on 4,500 pupils in kindergarten and the first three grades in schools in South Carolina, Ohio, Colorado, and California. Forms are also available for intermediate, secondary, and adult levels. All forms can be either machine or hand scored.

Wishing Well
(*Bureau of Educational Research, Ohio State University*)

The degree of personal security and need-satisfaction is also suggested by answers to the Wishing Well Test. Some items are: "I wish I felt as though I really belonged to my school group, my class in school really wanted me there, some gang or club would want me to join; other children wanted me to go more places with them."

Checklist of Opportunities in Human Relations
Horace Mann-Lincoln Institute of School Experimentation
(*Teachers College, Columbia*)

A three-point scale provides for marking such items as: "How often do you have this experience: be a member of a team, be a member of a club, be a member of a group which makes its own rules, spend leisure time with friends of own choice." Also provided is a scale for indicating how important the experience is: important, O.K., unimportant.

Another product of the same institute is a Classroom-Distance Scale on which the child can rate others or himself as others seem to treat him

[70] Jackson, Joseph, "The Relative Effectiveness of Paper and Pencil Test, Interview, and Rating as Techniques for Personality Evaluation," *J. Soc. Psych.*, vol. 23, 1946.

[71] Ellis, Albert, "Questionnaire versus Interview Methods in the Study of Human Love Relationships," *Amer. sociol. Rev.*, vol. 12, 1947, pp. 541–553.

[72] Flory, C. D., "Classroom Teachers Improve the Personality Adjustment of Their Pupils," *J. Educ. Res.*, September, 1944, pp. 1–8.

on such items as: "would like to have him as one of my best friends; would like to have him in my group but not as a close friend; would like to be with him once in a while but not often or for a long time; don't mind his being in our room, but don't want to have anything to do with him; wish he weren't in our room."

The Mental Health Analysis (Elementary Series)
by Thorpe, Clark, and Tiegs
(California Test Bureau)

The MHA is composed of 200 items and is scored for mental-health assets and liabilities. Ten subscores are yielded in such categories as behavioral immaturity, feelings of inadequacy, interpersonal skills, social participation, and adequate outlook and goals. Test items were selected on the basis of professional literature and research, reactions of students, teachers, principals, and employees, and the use of statistical computations. Attention was paid to language level. It can be scored either by hand, answer sheet, stencil, or machine. Norms were prepared from test results of approximately 1,000 pupils in grades 4 to 8 in nine school districts in three states. Some disguise in the framing of questions was used: "Do your friends seem to think that you are fair with them? Do you often worry because people do not like you as well as they should? Are you often troubled because your plans do not turn out well?"

The Behavior Preference Record
by Hugh B. Wood
(California Test Bureau)

Six forms are available, two each for elementary, intermediate, and advanced levels. Subscores can be obtained in the areas of cooperation, friendliness, integrity, leadership, responsibility, and critical thinking. Fifteen problem situations relating to home and school are presented. In each case the pupil is asked, "What would you do?" Four choices are given. This question is followed by five to seven possible reasons for the chosen action, and the pupil marks one. The scores of over 8,000 students of average intelligence and achievement were used in developing the norms for this test. Work on the record was begun in 1938. Additional work on norms was done before the printing of the 1953 edition.

Rogers' Test of Personality
by Carl R. Rogers
(Psychological Corporation, N. Y.)

This objective-type pencil and paper test can be given to groups and is untimed. It is one of the few which attempts to measure escape from reality into fantasy and daydreaming. Other aspects scored are feelings of personal inferiority, social adjustment, and family adjustment. Opportunities are given to indicate whether the individual feels the need to be better liked, to get along better with parents, to improve relations with his peers. Information is gathered regarding feelings of rejection or over-dependence. Items are based on the clinical experiences of psychologists and psychiatrists with children. Opportunities for over-statements are deliberately presented.

An interesting part of the test instructs the client to write a sentence describing a fictitious boy or girl with regard to appearance, social acceptability, relationships to parents, and other characteristics. Then the pupil is asked to indicate whether he is just like the character described, or whether he wishes to be like him.

Few references are made in professional literature to the Rogers test. Fleming and Snyder[73] used it with two other measures in evaluating the results of non-directive group play therapy among children between the ages of 8 and 11. The usefulness of the test cannot be determined by the results of this study, because the group was very small. Members of the control group were judged initially less maladjusted than the experimental group, and the improvement shown by members of the experimental group might have been partly a result of their pleasure in a twice-weekly trip to the clinic 10 miles away from the children's home where they lived. However, results of the evaluation agreed with the therapist's judgment. The boys' group of four failed to make significantly more improvement than members of the control group, according to test results and therapist's judgment. The girls' group of three improved significantly more than the control group, as indicated by the three tests and opinion of the therapist.

Responses to the test could be useful in determining how the child feels about himself and others and how he meets frustration. It is one of the few intended for use with younger children.

SUMMARY

The cautious use of standardized measures of intelligence and achievement can contribute to an accurate diagnosis of the retarded reader's potentials and needs. Suggested criteria for screening students for remediation are:

---

[73] Fleming, Louise, and W. U. Snyder, "Social and Personal Changes Following Non-directive Group Play Therapy," *Amer. J. Orthopsychiat.*, vol. 17, 1947, pp. 101–116.

1. Quantitative or non-verbal ability is 20 percentile points higher than linguistic or verbal ability.

2. Total rank on test of mental ability is not less than the 35th percentile for his age and grade.

3. Reading skills rank lower than total score on test of mental ability.

Students screened by these criteria are said to demonstrate a potential for improvement, and studies are quoted in support of this point of view.

Neither test results alone, nor teacher judgment of ability or achievement is as accurate in predicting achievement as a combination of the two. Knowledge of the personal adjustment of the individual adds to accuracy of prediction as well as to understanding his needs and planning remediation.

After screening students by means of mass testing, the counselor or teacher can use diagnostic reading tests, individual tests of ability, and personality tests for a more refined diagnosis. For appraising a student's level of reading skills and particular weaknesses, a reading test should be less difficult than that used for appraising the skills and needs of his class and should measure specific skills as well as general level of achievement. Interpretation of test results should take into consideration weaknesses in test construction and standardization and the conditions under which it was administered.

A thorough diagnosis might include physical examination, tests of vision and hearing, and instruments to measure interests and personal adjustment. All of these tests help the counselor and teacher to communicate with the pupil. They not only indicate where he needs help, but how he sees the world and himself.

CHAPTER 4

Projective Techniques
and Informal Methods

The remarks in the summary of Chapter 3 relate to the uses of pencil
and paper tests and inventories which have been more or less standardized. It is possible to compare the individual's score with those of other
people by means of percentile rank or some other standard. There are
other valuable sources of information about the student's personal adjustment, values, needs, and satisfactions. Among them are some instruments called projective techniques. They are designed so as to permit
free response to pictures, sounds, ink blots, or other stimuli. Considerable
work has been done in classifying and interpreting characteristic responses. They have been widely used and thus comparison of individual
responses with others is possible. The content of these tests is such that
a variety of interpretations can be made by the client, according to his
needs and strivings, to whatever figures in his environmental field are
important to him or whatever problems might be urgent. The services
of experienced clinicians are required for administration and interpretation.

Since the teacher (and, in many cases, the counselor) is not likely to
be trained in the administration or interpretation of such instruments, it
may seem irrelevant to mention them here, but we feel that it is important to recognize that such information can be gathered by specialists.
It is possible in many localities to enlist the aid of child-guidance clinics,
college counseling bureaus, psychologists, psychiatrists, and others who
are trained to use these techniques. When referral is made to specialists,
the teacher or counselor needs some acquaintance with the instruments
in order to cooperate fully.

While they are believed to measure some of the same tendencies
tapped by pencil and paper inventories, the two types of information do
not duplicate each other, but supplement each other.

There are a number of reasons why projective techniques are valuable sources of information. In the first place teachers' observations and even many inventory-type or pencil and paper tests of personality are not certain to identify children with concealed hostility, repressions, tendencies toward withdrawal, anxiety, insecurity, and less obvious, but nevertheless serious, symptoms. Teachers recognize outward aggression and hostility, but commonly overlook these less apparent problems. Well-adjusted children more readily admit damaging things about themselves than do maladjusted children. Unless the pencil and paper test is skillfully prepared, the results may be misleading. Children with serious problems not only avoid those questions which appear to them to invite self-criticism, but also those which come too close to painful subjects. They shrink from admitting even to themselves, for example, that home is other than normal or that affection is withheld. In many cases, the child assumes that his home is typically normal.

Projective techniques permit the expressions of concealed feelings with a minimum of threat. Responses to some can be given in the third person and thus are less painful and threatening to the client. The subject is not limited to the items included by the test-maker, but is free to respond in terms of his most vivid impressions of reality or his most troublesome problems. Intensity of emotion can be expressed, and answers are not limited to "yes" or "no," or to a limited number of choices.

The world of the teacher is not the same as the world of the pupil. The reading, spelling, and language lessons which loom so large in the teacher's mind are rearranged in the child's world to make room for other important figures which are just as real or more real to him.

The individual who has too often found himself in dilemmas for which there is no acceptable solution may have shut out or distorted a part of his perceptual field. Instead of restricting the child's answers to the adult's view of the field, projective techniques leave him free to respond in terms of the figures he sees as important, desirable, or threatening.

Distortion of perception interferes with appropriate reactions to environment, people, subject matter, inanimate objects. Projective techniques give us some idea of the character and amount of distortion and help to make the disturbed child's behavior comprehensible to us. They may reveal the kinds of stimuli to which he can respond, kinds of information which might be meaningful to him, kinds of responses which would convey understanding.

Often, the client's responses to the pictures, ink blots, or other projective stimuli give the counselor leads to use in interview. The client may progress from his third person response to a non-threatening item to more personal matters. While projective techniques are perhaps most useful in studying the child's emotional climate, some can be used to suggest the level of intelligence. In the case of a child with latent verbal skills, this information is invaluable. Most intelligence tests require verbal ability, but other important areas of ability can be tapped by means of instruments which do not emphasize verbal skills.

The Rorschach
(*Grune and Stratton, Inc.*)

The Rorschach ink-blot test, for example, can be interpreted in terms of intellectual activity. Before discussing it briefly, we want to point out that Rorschach spent 10 years working on this test before his death in 1922. Bell[1] cites 798 references on its use. Other studies are now in progress.

The test is made up of a series of 10 or more ink blots to which the subject can respond by telling what he sees. Although open to free interpretation, they call forth certain responses more often than others. Some blots are commonly interpreted by clients to be animals, others to be human beings, etc. Digressions from the usual are noted by the clinician. The cards present symmetrical figures, some in varying shades of gray and some in red and other colors.

In scoring for intellectual activity, the scorer gives a better rating to responses which show that the subject perceives forms clearly than if he makes vague responses. If the blot is seen as a whole, this indicates abstract or theoretical ability, according to some authorities, with the exception that a preponderance of simple popular wholes may indicate superficiality.

Attention to major detail may suggest a practical, concrete approach. Ability to see relationships between portions of figures is noted by some scorers, and seems to suggest the degree to which the client is able to use his abilities (whether handicapped by anxiety, etc.). The order in which the client reports what he sees is weighted in scoring and believed by some to be related to intellectual control. A preponderance of animal responses may indicate immaturity, stereotypy, or possibly intellectual limitations. Original responses are said to be evidence of superior and differentiated intelligence, but at times, if extreme, may indicate distortions in perception or emotional disturbances. A preponderance of popular responses (or exaggerated attention to form) is believed to indicate stereotypy, or over-conformity and perhaps inflexibility or prejudice.[2] A

[1] Bell, John E., *Projective Techniques,* Longmans, Green & Co., Inc., New York, 1948.

[2] Anderson, Harold H., and Gladys L. Anderson (eds.), *Introduction to Projective Techniques,* Prentice-Hall, Inc., Englewood Cliffs, N. J., 1951, pp. 105ff.

low number of popular responses is interpreted to mean resistance to conformity. The total number of responses is also believed to be significant. More than 50 is considered an indication of superior ability (possibly creative ability), although some disturbed clients also produce quantities, usually of inferior quality. More than 75 are rare.[3] If the client sees human movement in the figures, his score is raised, and this response may be related to creative energy and imaginative ability. If movement is reported with good form, organization, originality, and attention to detail, superior ability is suggested.[4] If human movement is seen in some area where it is not commonly reported, the client is believed by some to show originality and creativeness.

Inferences are also drawn from the way in which the client holds the card, the location of the part of the figure which stands out to him, whether he reports on the light or dark portions of the card, rejection of cards, responses to color, or in terms of color, and from the behavior of the client during testing. Uneasiness, exclamations denoting emotion, comments showing stress or defensiveness, hesitation, fidgeting, decline in quality or quantity of response, deviation from pattern of response, reports relating to shading or texture or perspective or distance are all regarded as meaningful by some authorities. Importance is attached to the proportion of responses relating to form, wholes, movement, color, detail, fine detail, unusual detail, shading, dimensions and perspective, light and dark.[5] For example, if the number of responses relating to wholes is twice the number relating to movement, a sense of personal inadequacy is suspected.[6] Shading and dark responses seem related to tensions, morbidity, depression, fears, anxiety, and painful emotions.[7,8] If the client responds to color without reference to form or if color responses dominate form responses, emotionality, excitability, and sometimes suggestibility are suspected.[9] If animal movements are reported in quantities, the subject may wish to disguise feelings or habits.[10] Animal movement may be related to primary needs or emotions. "Eyes looking at me" is said to be a typical paranoidal reaction.[11]

The order in which the client reports what he sees is recorded. For example, a common sequence is for the subject to report first the form

[3] Bell, *op. cit.*, p. 119.
[4] *Ibid.*, p. 124.
[5] *Ibid.*, p. 122ff.
[6] *Ibid.*, p. 125.
[7] Anderson and Anderson (eds.), *op. cit.*, pp. 111ff.
[8] Bell, *op. cit.*, pp. 127ff.
[9] *Ibid.*, p. 123.
[10] Anderson and Anderson (eds.), *op. cit.*, p. 116.
[11] Bell, *op. cit.*, p. 129ff.

or whole, then major detail, then minor detail, with occasional variations in sequence. Frequent digressions from this order or rigid adherence to sequence are noted. Confusion or lack of order can be meaningful to the operator. This brief discussion of interpretation suggests the complexities involved in the use of the Rorschach and the obvious necessity for experience and training if satisfactory results are to be achieved.

Support for the use of the Rorschach is found in a number of studies. When teachers' ratings of 30 preschool children were matched by the analyses of an experienced Rorschach worker, agreement was significant at the 1 per cent level of confidence.[12] When psychiatric diagnosis of 26 children was compared with Rorschach examination, 88.5 per cent agreement was found.[13] Bell[14] describes three studies showing that "blind" interpretations of Rorschach responses (without seeing the patients) agreed with psychiatric diagnoses. In a study of 46 cases, complete agreement was reached in 39 and comparable diagnoses made in 7 cases. In one study of 16 cases, there was 100 per cent agreement. Another review of 50 patients showed 66 per cent complete agreement, 20 per cent essential agreement, and 12 per cent partial agreement. The use of the Rorschach in diagnosing neurotics and schizophrenics is described by Bell.[15] A combination of five out of nine common characteristics of neurotics appeared significant: fewer than 25 responses, human movement restricted to one response, number of responses in which form (not high quality) was emphasized over movement (FM) greater than number emphasizing human movement, color shock (present in 98 per cent of neurotics), shading shock, refusals to one or more cards, form responses higher than 50 per cent, animal responses higher than 50 per cent, not more than one form plus color response. Another study suggests that a high percentage of responses related to anatomy is significant in the diagnosis of neurosis.

Responses apparently significant in the diagnosis of schizophrenia were: sensitivity to rare detail; detail dominating the report of wholes; infrequent reports of normal wholes, normal detail or commonly reported small detail; inconsistencies in sequence (confusion in order); high percentage of color or color dominating form; low percentage of form dominating over color; low quality of form responses; low number of popular responses; reversal of figure and ground; change of tempo in response; contaminations; complete rejections; self-reference; unintelligi-

<hr>

[12] *Ibid.*, p. 136.
[13] Siegel, M. G., "The Diagnostic and Prognostic Validity of the Rorschach Test in a Child Guidance Clinic," *Amer. J. Orthopsychiat.*, vol. 18, 1948, pp. 119–133.
[14] Bell, *op. cit.*, p. 135.
[15] Bell, *op. cit.*, pp. 138–141.

ble language; unrelated words. Depressives commonly responded with many forms of good quality and many animals; decreasing numbers of wholes, human movements, and color responses; and reduction in total number of responses. Manics showed a low percentage of clear form responses and a high percentage of human movement, color, whole and original responses, though of low quality.

Thematic Apperception Test
by Henry A. Murray
(Harvard University Press, Cambridge, Mass.)

The original TAT was composed of a set of 20 pictures around which stories could be written or told. A set of 30 now includes 10 for males, 10 for females, and 10 for either. The pictures are sufficiently ambiguous to permit the person to respond with what might be uppermost in his mind and feelings. Telling these stories in the third person permits the person to describe feelings and incidents which otherwise might be concealed. Attributing his own feelings and characteristics to a character in the story, the person reveals how he sees himself and he also gives clues to how he perceives his environment. Distortions may be detected. The storyteller can emphasize or ignore some feature of the picture. Omissions, repetitions, exaggerations, elaborations, inconsistencies often indicate trouble areas.

The clinician observes the behavior of the client during testing: excitement, tears, distaste, side remarks, aggressiveness, silence, hesitancy, rejecting pictures, facial expression, self-reference, self-derogatory remarks. Each story is supposed to have a past, present, and future. Ignoring or over-emphasizing one of these has significance.

Although most of the pictures show adults, the TAT has been used effectively with children. A Children's Apperception Test (CAT) is available for children between the ages of 3 to 11 years. Animals are pictured in some of the common problem situations of children. Some workers believe that children respond more readily to pictures of animals and find it easy to identify with them.

A few hints on interpretation will illustrate some of the uses of the TAT. Depressives are commonly observed to be slow in reacting, and to give brief or monosyllabic responses.[16] The tone of their stories may be gloomy, moralistic, or punitive, and may include mention of physical or mental illness.[17] At times, however, they go to extremes in sentimentality.

[16] Schafer, Roy, *Clinical Application of Psychological Tests*, International Universities Press, Inc., New York, 1948, p. 60.

[17] Rapaport, David, *Diagnostic Psychological Testing*, Year Book Publishers, Inc., Chicago, 1948, p. 441.

Moralizing is also frequent among subjects with paranoid tendencies.[18] Caution, rigidity, logic, reasoning, intellectualizing, and rationalizing are usually noted. Suspiciousness may be obviously or subtly expressed. "Eyes looking at me" or people watching may be described. A free flow of imagination and fantasy is impossible. In addition to the more obvious indications, the paranoid-inclined may misrecognize the sex of figures in the pictures and ignore pictures in which aggression is obviously expressed.[19,20] The student described as yielding a deviate score on the paranoid scale of the MMPI gave these responses to projective techniques: ignored situations where a struggle was obviously going on, ascribed only the purest motives to villianous-looking characters, showed some indications of confusion about sex role, made frequent references to moral and religious issues, offered proof for conclusions, and questioned the motives and the remarks of the examiner. Although this subject carefully avoided expressions of aggression and criticism, she displayed her aggressions by frequent questions, "Why do you ask this? Why is this true? Can you prove it is true? What makes you think so?" Nothing could be accepted as true unless she could find proof of its validity for herself.

Among the pictures are several showing a young person with an older man or woman. These often inspire stories which reveal resistance toward authority or submission to domination. One card for boys and men shows an older woman turned partly away from a younger man. Resistance to domination is suggested by this response, "The young man respects his mother, but he expects to carry out his plan in spite of her opposition." Almost all stories by this subject reflected his awareness of authority and aggressions toward people, self, and environment or impersonal forces. Authoritarian figures were introduced into others. For example, the response to picture 1 (a small boy looking at a violin) was, "He is wondering whether his mother will be displeased. . . . "

As in the interpretation of other projective tests, one looks for repeated expressions of the same attitude or emotion, loneliness, hostility, submissiveness, etc. If, however, most of the stories from a subject are on the same theme, a deviating story may call attention to an important event, goal, or facet of personality. A series of gloomy stories was interrupted in one case by this response to the silhouette of a person in a window: "The man has been in darkness, but he is coming into the light."

From the volumes of materials on the interpretation of the TAT, one can readily see how one could spend a semester in class on this test

---

[18] *Ibid.*, 446.
[19] *Ibid.*, pp. 447–448.
[20] Schafer, *op. cit.*

alone and require repeated experiences with it in order to catch subtle meanings and recognize deviations from the usual. Records of clinicians have helped to indicate popular and unusual responses and those which are common among patients diagnosed as mentally ill.

Even though the counselor makes no attempt to interpret the TAT, he can often find in the stories a starting point for counseling. He can ask about a pertinent story or part of a story, "Would you care to tell me more about this?" He can check his interpretation with the client, "Would you say that the mother has tried to dominate her son?" He can respond to feeling, "The boy resents the attempts of others to dominate him." In summarizing a series of stories, he might go so far as to say, "It seems that many characters in these stories feel that life is a struggle against hostile forces." If he has good rapport with his client, he might ask, "Does this mean that the man has been depressed, but now sees a ray of hope?"

Conflict may be openly expressed or may appear through inconsistencies within or between stories. Conflict appears fairly clearly in this statement, "He doesn't know whether to come out into the light and take a chance on being hurt, or stay in darkness." The first story in one client's series reflected submissiveness, dependency, and desire for parental approval. The hero in a later story expressed aggressiveness and desire to dominate. Less structured cards toward the end of the series are believed to permit more freedom of expression.

Clichés, stereotypes, stories drawn from folklore may reflect evasiveness and defensiveness. In response to the picture of the dragon with rock walls in the background, a client produced this story: "The setting is about the time of King Arthur. A knight is returning with loot and the dragon frightens his beast of burden, so the knight is trying to subdue the animals and rescue his loot." The client later revealed distrust of the clinician, and related to another examiner the first story which had occurred to him: "The man is having a fight and is in a hell of a spot. In front of him are his adversaries between him and the castle (rock walls). Behind him is the dragon, so he cannot retreat." This story suggests the battle for existence with hostile forces, and the castle is seen as a refuge. A more sophisticated interpretation would require a knowledge of symbolism and the application of Rorschach techniques, as well as ample experience with projective tests.

Variations of the TAT Technique

The Michigan Picture Test for children (Michigan Department of Public Health) is composed of 20 pictures selected from about 1,000 used in preliminary research. The final set has been administered to more than 300 school children and appears to distinguish between well-adjusted and disturbed children.

Reactions to frustration may be studied by means of the Rosenzweig Picture-Frustration Test (Saul Rosenzweig, 1948). A form for children depicts 24 conflict situations. The remarks of one person in each picture are given, and the subject being tested supplies the remarks of the child in the picture whose desires appear to be frustrated. Scoring takes into account whether or not the child aggresses toward self or environment. It differs from the TAT in that it is limited to the study of reactions to frustration.

Other adaptations of the TAT explore the individual's reactions to group membership, to minority groups, and to people of other races and cultures.

Bender Visual Motor Gestalt Test

Nine geometric designs are given in this test, and the subject is asked to reproduce them. Interpretations are made from the position on the page, the accuracy of reproduction, the quality of line, size of figures, proportions, distortions, embellishments, flattening of curves, sharpening of angles, extended lines, elongation of figures, closure, erasures, retracing, overlapping of figures, omissions, substitutions, reversals, sketching strokes, and the behavior of the subject during testing. Erasures, crowding, very light lines, interrupted lines, retracing, very small figures, small openings left where lines should meet, drawings which cling to the edge of the page, and lines drawn around each figure appear to be related to anxiety, insecurity, and constriction, perhaps to perceiving the world as hostile and threatening. Enlarged figures are interpreted by some to suggest over-compensation. Sharpened angles are presumed to suggest irritability. Very heavy lines that cut the paper are said to show aggression. Flattened curves and angles are suggestive of shallow emotions or excessive control of emotions. A change in the position of the axis of the figure is said to be frequently associated with psychosis, but opinions of researchers are by no means unanimous on this point. Also judged indicative of serious maladjustment are dissociation, elaboration, confused order, inversion, unusual use of space, reversals, marked condensation, substitution of loops for dots, or circles for diamonds, etc., consistent extension of lines, fragmentation of figures, inconsistencies in size, gross distortions. Some types of errors are believed associated with organic involvement. Among them are: vagueness and sketchiness, marked perseveration (tendency to repeat patterns or to give each new figure some characteristics of the preceding ones), loss of detail, fragmentation, difficulty with acute angles, overlapping and other difficulties in spatial orientation, splitting of figures which are joined, difficulty in reproducing the diamond, and the bell-shape, sweeping lines which are carried on beyond the point where they should end. Depression is sometimes read in the dropping of lines beyond the point suggested by the test figure. Inconsistencies in size or in strength of stroke may suggest ambivalence, conflict, vacillation, and instability.

Observations on the client's behavior include attention to degree of interest and cooperation, flushing or other indications of tension, self-criticism, dependency, reluctance, refusal, fatigue, delays, unusual amount of time, etc.

There is considerable disagreement over interpretation of this test. Writers caution that one deviation is not to be considered significant. The age of the child must be taken into consideration. Bender[21] offers a chart showing the ages at which children can normally reproduce these figures with relative accuracy. Most of them can apparently be reproduced with a fair degree of accuracy by the ninth or tenth year. It is obvious that its use requires much study and experience, as in the case of other projective tests described. A pattern running all the way through the test responses, together with other data, gives the experienced counselor information about how the person sees himself and his environment. For example, if heavy lines, jabbing, sharpened angles are interpreted as hostility, the observer will seek confirmation in other data, stories in which aggression is expressed, playground incidents, etc.

Markedly compressed records on the Bender appear to be an indication of a tendency to perceive the world as a hostile place.[22] If organic involvement, visual-motor incoordination, or serious maladjustment is suggested, referral to a specialist seems appropriate.

The use of the Bender is particularly interesting to remedial-reading teachers in view of their students' customary constricted use of space and responses suggesting insecurity, as described in Chapter 1. Improvement in reading skills appears to be accompanied by improvements in their responses to the Bender. If the Bender truly reveals distortions in perception, it would be even more valuable in understanding the reading student. Distortions in reproduction would suggest that the reading student does not see the world as it is perceived by other people.

[21] Bender, Lauretta, *A Visual Motor Gestalt Test and Its Clinical Use*, Research Monograph no. 3, American Orthopsychiatric Association, New York, 1938.

[22] Torrance, E. Paul, "Analyses of the Bender Gestalt Drawings Compared with Scores on the Minnesota Multiphasic Personality Inventory," unpublished study, Kansas State College, 1950.

Test and retest with the Bender seemed to reflect accurately a change in reading student, D. S., from painful shyness and feelings of inferiority toward self-confidence and self-determination. He was ignored by his family, and the scapegoat of his peers. In early counseling interviews, he expressed confusion, loneliness, feelings of inadequacy, and a sense of worthlessness. In later interviews, he began to make plans to conquer his shyness, take part in social affairs, and choose a suitable curriculum. Like many of his classmates, on the second Bender test, he doubled the size of his pictures, improved in accuracy of figures, and distributed them over the page instead of crowding them into a small space. At the same time he demonstrated improvements in skills and use of abilities, as shown in Table 4-1.

TABLE 4-1

PERCENTILE RANKS OF READING STUDENT D. S. FROM TEST AND RETEST
WITH THE ACE AND COOPERATIVE READING EXAMINATION

	February percentile	April percentile
Quantitative	78	93
Linguistic	7	17
Total ACE	28	47
Speed	14	62
Comprehension	15	59

The progress shown by retest of ability, achievement, and personality reflects total growth. This observation is in harmony with our belief that learning involves the whole person.

HOUSE-TREE-PERSON

The House-Tree-Person technique was proposed by J. N. Buck. The subject is given a minimum of instructions during his drawing of the three objects and is then asked to tell about them. Some interpret each drawing to be a self-portrait. If the objects are small, the person is suspected to feel inferior and inadequate. Omissions, exaggerations, special attention to detail, erasures, faint or heavy lines, and crowding are scored. Cooperativeness, mannerisms, attention span, and remarks are also recorded.

Agreement is not general over whether each drawing does constitute a self-portrait. Lack of ornamentation or shrubs around the house or bare branches on the tree are said to mean a barren life, lack of interesting experiences, perhaps lack of affection. Small shrubs are interpreted by some to mean siblings. Scars and defects on the tree trunk are presumed to mean damaging childhood experiences. If the tree appears to be floating, unrooted, without a ground line, the effect suggests insecurity.

If the approaches to the house are omitted, or if the door is small or the windows barred, the child may be expressing restriction or difficulty in making contact with the outside world or with other people. Complexities in the house, many wings, gables, corridors, etc., may reveal the way in which the child sees his complex environment, or baffling problems which confront him. Sometimes the house is drawn as the child would like it to be. Chimneys are believed by some to be phallic symbols. Thus, omitting the chimney or over-emphasizing the chimney may indicate a conflict in this area. However, if the child is accustomed to gas heat, he may have seen many houses which have gas vents instead of chimneys and might be expected to draw what he sees.

It the child draws a human figure very different from himself, he may wish to be different, or it may be the way in which he sees the inner self. Preoccupation with self is suggested by small figures in the upper left of the page, or stick figures. Insecurity and inadequacy are suggested by emphasis on the mid-line of the body, as in the case of rows of buttons or an emphatic mark down the front of the blouse or coat of the figure. Rigid posturing may imply difficulty with social contacts, restrictions, conformity. Over-emphasis on clothing may be a clue to the need for concealment, overconformity, conventionality. Belt buckles denote dependency. Buttons and pockets are said to be common in the drawings of the mother-dependent and deprived children.[23] The treatment of hands and feet, as contact points with the environment and with people, may reflect guilt, fear, and insecurity. If omitted or mutilated in the picture, these problem areas might be further explored.

Exaggerated noses, hats, hair, mountains, cigarettes, pipes, guns, large neckties are believed by some to be symbols of sex.[24] A strong nose is masculine and assertive. If mutilated, a problem in this area is suggested.[25] The belt marks off the sexual area. If very tight it suggests an effort to subjugate the body. If the area below the belt is not drawn, this may be a conflict area.

A side view is considered a symptom of evasiveness or desire for self-protection. If the opposite sex is drawn in response to the request to

[23] Machover, Karen, "Drawing of the Human Figure: A Method of Personality Investigation," in Anderson and Anderson (eds.) *An Introduction to Projective Techniques,* Prentice-Hall, Inc., Englewood Cliffs, N. J., 1951, p. 359.

[24] Dr. Leon H. Levy of Ohio State University reports a study which indicates that these symbols are not universally associated with sex. *J. consult. Psych.,* February, 1954.

[25] Machover, *loc. cit.,* p. 355.

draw a person, the client may have trouble identifying with the appropriate sex. Large breasts are believed to suggest a dominant mother.

Mind-body conflict is suggested by a very small neck. The impulses of the body are thus cut off from the head. Restraint and inhibition are implied. Sometimes the eyes are closed, crossed out, or missing, as if to shut out the world.

Goodenough used the "Draw-a-man" Test as an IQ Index. The House-Tree-Person Test is also used to appraise intelligence, with special reference to details, proportion, perspective, organization, quality, and the subject's comments. Although the establishment of norms on this kind of test is difficult, is would be a valuable instrument in cases of non-readers and children with other verbal handicaps. Some believe it gives some indication of social intelligence. The H-T-P is reported in one study to correlate .472 with the Wechsler-Bellevue Performance Scale.[26]

The changes made in drawings by reading students are briefly mentioned in Chapter 1. The drawings of student D. F. seemed to agree with his behavior in class and interview. His first drawing of the human figure was the head of a woman in profile. He had drawn the eye, but had erased it. From observations of his behavior, conversation, and family relationships, one could make a tentative assumption that he was inclined to be identified with his mother who was the dominant parent. Alternating light and heavy strokes suggest that he vacillated between aggressiveness and submission, an assumption that was borne out by occasional aggressive outbursts in class as contrasted with frequent references to conventional and moral behavior. Narrowness of views reflected unwillingness to see some aspects of environment (also suggested by difficulty in drawing eyes). Great respect for the intellectual side of personality and disregard of the physical was consistent with his strict Puritan upbringing and behavior standards. Mounting aggressiveness and masculinity were demonstrated in his classroom contributions as well as in the heavily drawn masculine head offered at the close of the semester. The eye was included in the final portrait, suggesting that he could perceive more of his environment. He was openly critical of the reading class in discussion, interview, and writings. Although his final reading test showed no progress, he gained 22 percentile points on the linguistic section of the ACE, showed gains on daily progress charts, and showed marked improvement in other classes. It seems possible that, knowing the purpose of the reading test, he unconsciously or deliberately set out to prove by making a low score that he was correct in his assertion that the class was no good. On the ACE, which he knew was not a reading test,

[26] Sloan, W., and W. H. Guertin, "A Comparison of H-T-P and Wechsler-Bellevue IQ's in Mental Defectives," *J. Clinical Psychol.*, vol. 4, 1948, pp. 424–426.

he may have demonstrated his true ability. A year later, he returned voluntarily to tell the instructor that the class had been very helpful. At that time, he was making superior grades in college. He drew his second tree and house with added foliage, shrubs, and ornamentation, and tripled the amount of space used for the Bender. The Bender figures were greatly improved in accuracy, and the pencil strokes in all drawings were uniformly firm.

Various evidences of mounting aggressiveness were seen in other cases as students began to make improvement in reading skills, to take part in classroom discussion, offer opinions of their own, and assert themselves.

SENTENCE COMPLETION TESTS

This type of measure, also called incomplete sentence, may be an outgrowth of the Word Association Method of studying the individual, used by Galton as early as 1879, and later by Wundt, Jung, and others. It has the advantage of offering considerable freedom of response, and, at the same time, providing the same stimuli to all people in a group. It is easy to give and very inexpensive. Interpretation is not so complicated as that involved in the Rorschach. Use of Sentence Completion Tests is apparently increasing in the armed forces, industry, and schools, judging from more frequent references to it in professional literature. Although it is possible for the teacher or counselor to construct such a test, the Psychologial Corporation offers a manual for the Rotter Incomplete Sentences Blank, by J. B. Rotter and J. E. Rafferty, and a revision of the Payne Sentence Completions Blank and manual, by Amanda R. Rohde and Gertrude Hildreth. Among others available is the Sacks Sentence Completion Test, described by Joseph M. Sacks and Sidney Levy in *Projective Psychology: Clinical Approaches to the Total Personality* (Alfred A. Knopf, Inc., New York, 1950). Various systems of scoring on the basis of needs, environmental press, inner states, and other interpretations are derived largely from the work of H. A. Murray.

When using a test which has been subjected to research, the interpreter can make use of the findings, experiences, and observations of clinicians and psychologists. If it is necessary to use a homemade test, the examiner can still find valuable information about how the student sees himself, men, women, children, laws, his environments, threats, satisfactions, and favorable or hostile forces. Clichés and stereotypes, imagination, avoidance responses, or straightforward expression are as meaningful as such responses to other projective instruments. Phrases introducing such subjects as criminals, delinquents, or mentally ill may elicit punitive, moralistic, sentimental, realistic, or charitable responses. Attitudes toward parents, school, or authority in general can be tapped.

Items beginning "I wish . . . ", "I would like . . . ", "I need . . . ", or "Most people hope for . . . " are often quite revealing. Wishes about home, school, classmates, friends might be included. Items beginning, "People should . . . " or "Everybody should . . . " may bring forth expressions of moralism or over-conformity, or, at times, expressions of aggression. Understanding of the individual is sometimes enhanced by responses to these: "My most important experience . . . " or "My most painful experience. . . . "

When constructing a homemade test, the examiners decide what they wish to measure and state items accordingly, trying to make the statements as clear as possible and at the same time to avoid statements which might arouse defensiveness.

INTERPRETATIONS OF CREATIVE EXPRESSIONS

Some of the principles employed in the interpretation of projective techniques can be used in understanding the stories, remarks, paintings, and other expressions of the pupils. Tone, volume, organization, spontaneity, and other aspects reflect the individual's values, attitudes, needs, and strivings. Repeated expressions of self-respect, satisfaction, hostilities, aggressions, or other emotions are meaningful.

Some of our best clues to personal adjustment are found in original stories, writings, and speeches. An impression of over-conformity and self-righteousness was given by these selections from the writings of an eighth-grader:

Boys and girls should keep the playground clean, play fair and not cheat, not fight on the playground and take good care of equipment. I always help my mother around the house and my dad in the shop. I try to help my teacher. For my community, I try to take part in community doings such as church and clubs. I help my country by being a good citizen. The personal appearance of people affects me this way. If they are clean and neat and pleasant, that is the kind of people I like. I would like to change some of the ways the children act at school. From high school I expect to get a good education.

This boy's parents expected him to be perfect. He was unable to meet their standards and felt dissatisfied with himself. His security lay in conforming to a rigid set of behavior standards, and in dominating younger siblings and classmates. He constantly set himself up as the enforcer of rules and morals, and tried to impose his values on his schoolmates.

A story of the wolf stalking the deer produced in response to Beethoven's *Moonlight Sonata* revealed some of the problems and fears of a fourth-grade boy. The life of this farm boy and his parents was an endless struggle to make a living. His writings appeared to reflect his fears that they could not survive. Resignation was suggested in his comment, "The wolf was hungry and he got fed." When his class decided to dramatize the story of Prokofiev's *Peter and the Wolf*, the boy volunteered to play the part of the duck which was eaten by the wolf. Perhaps he thought of himself as a perpetual victim. His drawing, illustrating the story, showed a scene which occurred after the duck was eaten. His comment was, "The duck is in the wolf's stomach." The character which he chose to play was left out of his picture as he may have felt he was left out of the scheme of things. The wolf was portrayed with a long red tongue and wicked fangs, looking hungrily at the cat and the bird. The boy wrote, "The wolf is looking at the cat and the bird." In other words, the wolf looks for other victims. Fences in this picture suggested social isolation and barriers to communication with others. The world seems a hostile place where the strong devour the weak.

The loneliness of an adolescent in a world of adults seems the theme of a story written by a seventh-grade boy about the *Moonlight Sonata*. He apparently represented himself as an insignificant little water-drop in a river of adults. Although he could not cry, the water-drop cried. With cues like this, the counselor is ready to respond when the occasion arises with, "You feel lonely. You wish for more friends of your own age." When the pupil was involved in dramatizing the story of *Peter and the Wolf*, he asked to play the part of Peter. To illustrate the story he drew a picture of Peter as a little pig. There is nothing in the recording to suggest this. The boy was very fat, and it seems likely that he thought of himself as a little pig. (After moving to a school where he was happy, he lost weight.)

The *Moonlight Sonata* reminded another child of a "cowboy riding all alone in the dark." He was rejected by his schoolmates and made a scapegoat. His story suggests how much he felt his rejection. When he drew an illustration for the story, *Peter and the Wolf*, he failed to include the grandfather which part he played in the dramatization. His comment was, "I just left myself out." Then he asked to be permitted to add the grandfather to the drawing. Doubtless, he felt himself an unimportant member of the group, but he was trying to find a role for himself.

Understanding of values, problems, and past experiences can be enhanced by noting the parts of a story which attract the attention of pupils. A group of older boys and girls in developmental reading class were discussing the novel, *The Gentle House* by Anna Perrot Rose (Houghton-Mifflin Company, Boston, 1954). Some of the comments were:

1. I was interested in the way the boy was treated by his foster parents who were wealthy but not very affectionate. (*The speaker comes from a stern, undemonstrative family.*)
2. I liked the part where the boy made friends with the fat middle-aged teacher. I've known teachers like that. This part sounds real.
3. It was surprising that the boy could forget the bombings and starving he knew in his own land and remember only the pleasant parts, but then other people push unpleasant thoughts down and try to forget them.

Response number 3 agrees with many remarks made by reading students in class and interview to the effect that unpleasant memories have been either deliberately or involuntarily forgotten. Many say that they remember little or nothing about childhood, school, parental relations, etc.

The counselor can gain an understanding of his clients by observing the number of positive and negative responses in their speech and writing. A favorable emotional climate is reflected in these answers given over a period of several months by an eight-year-old girl: "My home is pretty; I am glad when school starts; people are good; a baby is good; it is fun to play; school is good; my father works; I like food; I like people; I like children; I like Alice because she is funny; I like people who help me; I like people who talk to me nice; I like school; I like to go to school; my pony is nice; I like to swing." She expressed few wishes, laughed and smiled frequently, and appeared to feel successful in schoolwork and social contacts. So much emphasis is placed on detecting and responding to negative expressions that the counselor or teacher is in danger of forgetting to watch for positive ones. The foregoing remarks give hints as to how the pupil feels about herself, about others, and about school and suggests how the counselor or teacher might respond to her. Contrast them with these expressions from a second-grade boy: "My friends are crazy; people are crazy; a baby is bad; school is bad; my father is bad."

A comparison of earlier with later attempts at writing can show the way in which a child's skills, imagination, and social sensitivity have been developing. A September paper from a third-grader states: "At school I work and play. I do reading, writing, spelling, arithmetic, science. I play games." In May she wrote: "I have learned a lot about people this year. The people in school are nice to me. I have learned about music. I have learned many pretty songs such as 'The Rose of Tralee,' 'Steal Away,' 'Beautiful Dreamer.' I have learned to play baseball, basketball, football, soccer, clap in and clap out, and many other games and square dancing. I have learned how to write writing, spell, read better. We have learned interesting things in arithmetic."

In September, a second-grader wrote, "I want school to help me read."

In May he wrote, "I have learned to do arithmetic better, I have learned to do reading better. I have learned to spell. I can draw better pictures. I have learned many new games and many new songs. I like the cowboy songs best. I have learned more this year than last year. People are nice to me and I try to be nice to them."

A non-reader who contributed nothing original in early months of the school year and merely copied obediently from his books or the blackboard produced this in March, "I liked the story about the horses. I liked when the horses were turned into mice."

Even a child of marginal ability, after a year of experience in writing his own wishes and thoughts, was able to dictate this letter: "We are having a picnic on Monday. I wish you could come." Earlier efforts were confined to, "I am fine and hope you are the same." He waxed enthusiastic when he wrote: "I like to be on a farm. I like to unload the truck. I like to get cobs and wood for my mother. I like to help my brother do the chores." His remarks indicate the way in which some of his security needs were met and some degree of family solidarity.

Improved discrimination, sensitivity, and flow of ideas are sometimes noted. From early attempts of this nature, "I like Dotty because she is a good girl," a fourth-grader progressed to this stage, "Dotty likes other people and she likes me I think because she told me she did. She is kind to other people. She helps me when I need help. She is thoughtful and honest and has respect for others. I have never heard her say very many bad words. When she gets mad she really fights."

Although original stories cannot be scored objectively and compared with norms, they do give clues to children's inner feelings. Psychiatrists and psychologists have for many years invited creative storytelling from child patients to obtain data regarding conflicts, anxieties, wishes, fears, needs, etc. "Briefly stated, it is felt that given a relatively unstructured topic, the story told will reveal this kind of information where direct questioning would not."[27]

Three major themes are found by one author in children's stories:[28] what the child is *afraid of* (anxiety); what the child *wishes* (wish-fulfillment); and what he *fears he might do* (sadism). A common theme determined by the child's conflicts could be detected running through all stories told by the same child.

Topics for five stories are suggested by Bell:[29] (1) a child five years of

[27] Morris, W. W., "Other Projective Methods," in Anderson and Anderson (eds.), *op. cit.*, p. 518.

[28] Bell, John E., *Projective Techniques*, Longmans, Green & Co., Inc., New York, 1948, pp. 59–60.

[29] *Ibid.*, p. 62.

age or under; (2) an ideal family; (3) best friends; (4) a romantic story; (5) story about a hero. Classification was made according to (1) whether the stories were pertinent to the suggested title and situations were created and solved adequately; (2) partial fulfillment of these criteria; and (3) dysfunction or refusals, changes in title, unresolved plots, rambling, presentation of animals in the main role, etc.

Story completion is also suggested as a projective technique. A dramatic situation is used as a starter and the resulting development evaluated for reflections of environmental press or unsatisfied needs.

As previously suggested, a means of evaluation of either original stories or story completion would be a search for recurring patterns or response: happiness, satisfactions, and success or anxiety, guilt, hostility, submission, ambivalence, compromise, rationalization, etc., also intensity of expression. The kinds of motivations to which the child responds can also be noted: material rewards, affection, praise, feelings of success, satisfactions in interesting activities, possessions.

Some suggested situations are:

1. A boy is on his way to school. He is thinking that this is the day for the spelling test. A car stops beside him. What happens next?
2. A group of children are playing. One girl is sitting by herself. What happens?
3. Two boys are scuffling on the ground. A grown-up comes. What happens?
4. This child is going on a trip. What happens?
5. This child is having a dream. Tell about it.

Other persistent characteristics which might have meaning for the counselor are these. A loose organization, lack of synthesis, unprecise or approximate terms, excessive use of personal idioms (phrases which have special meanings for this individual alone), might, with other evidence, suggest a tendency to take refuge in a world of fantasy. References to color might suggest emotional undertones. The clinician might look for evidences of integration or harmony with fellows and with environment and for evidences of spontaneity. If spontaneity is high, the individual may be demonstrating ability to cope with the press of environment. Stereotypy suggests efforts to conform to a restrictive environment, or, in some cases, may be associated with mediocre ability. Also meaningful may be: identification with a character in the story, atypical association, irrelevancies, evasions, references to punishment or violence, attention to detail, unusually logical development. Unusual attention to detail might indicate anxiety or over-concern for the practical. Unusually logical development or over-abundance of proof may be associated with a tendency toward fixed ideas, suspiciousness, feelings of persecution, or attempts to rationalize and explain the press of environment.

When teachers or counselors first attempt to elicit a free expression of opinion from children, they may find that the first responses are stereotyped (in terms of what they think teacher expects). One third-grade group responded to the first invitation with remarks like this, "I like science. I like reading. I like to write." One boy who wrote, "I like science," later confided that he really "hated" science. In response to an invitation to write "Why I Like This Person," many children wrote such sentences as this, "I like Danny because he is a good boy." One child wrote, "I like tomatoes." These efforts were accepted without criticism, but the teacher continued to encourage free response, and later in the year the pupils began to feel freer to express their real feelings, to use spontaneous and creative ideas, and to use more definitive terms.

In contrast to these conventional responses was this effort by an eight-year-old in the same group: "I am writing this story at school. I am going to tell you about it now. The first day we went to school was Tuesday and our mothers had to come. And that day we had to find our own desks." This child was able to break away from the conventional response and he also indicated recognition of responsibility. He implied, "After today mother will not come and I will be on my own. I have begun to take responsibility by finding my own desk." He may have expected the teacher to assign him a desk.

This poem by an eight-year-old shows creativeness, but also suggests a problem: "I can see everything, almost everything. I can see footrace and sometimes a hiding-place. I can see everything, almost everything. I can see everything . . . but my own FACE."

An opportunity to express mild aggressions toward boys (probably her brothers) was seized by a 10-year-old girl. Other classmates obediently made unrelated sentences and underlined verbs, but she composed this gem (with verbs dutifully underlined) which shows imagination and humor, but also suggests a slight problem.

Mothers *work* and fathers *work*. Girls *help* their mothers. They *wash* dishes and *scrub* floors and *iron* clothes. Fathers *plow* and *drive* the tractor. Mothers *cook* dinner and *clean* the house. Girls *sew* and *mend*. Boys *play* ball and *ride* bikes. They *fish* and *swim*. They *eat* all of the time and *track* in mud. Boys *are* not good for much of anything.

Obviously, the counselor or teacher can make use of such statements to encourage exploration of family relationships and attitudes toward self and others.

Special interests are suggested by some writings and remarks. A third-grade boy wrote: "What I like best in school is science. I like best why we have day and night." Other indications of a scientific bent were suggested by his writings and paintings. Subjects for painting were waterfalls, volcanoes, machines, Indian villages, the world going round. Stories made frequent mention of telescopes, microscopes, trucks, and caterpillar tractors. Although somewhat retarded in writing, reading, and spelling, he began work on a "book" about war. A passage from this story shows imagination and a verbal potential: "Well folks, it all started one morning when Captain Tongues was speaking to his squad at the squad tent. They were telling about the fight that happened last night. There were shells that lit up the sky so that the enemy could see our troops." After seeing some colored slides of Japan, he wrote: "Some people in Japan are very poor. The thing that I like best is where a church would be in an alley. The church is about the size of a window. The people would pull a ribbon to call the attention of the God." The vocabulary used in this story seems rather remarkable in view of the fact that early in the year he was unable to write more than one or two sentences using the simplest words.

One day, he asked if he might give a report on the beginning and the end of the world. Permission was granted and he talked for about 15 minutes, showing his own drawings and pictures cut from magazines. His classmates were much interested and he was invited to give the same talk in some of the upper grades.

His imagination was evident in other responses. When most of his classmates were writing that the music of *Liebestraum* made them think of church music, he wrote: "It makes me think of when a story ended. It makes me think of dancing music." Of *Carousel Waltz*, he said: "Elephants are moving. It sounds like bagpipes."

These opportunities to express his feelings in speech and writing helped the teacher to understand his interests, creative ability, and feelings, and we believe they also contributed to progress in reading and spelling. November reading tests ranked him below the third-grade level. In five and a half months he raised his vocabulary-recognition score from a grade rank of 1.7 to 4.3, spelling rank from 2.5 to 3.9, and reading comprehension from below third grade to grade 4.

These two selections from an eight-year-old girl obviously indicate unusual imagination, originality, and verbal potential (she taught herself to typewrite and used capitals for emphasis):

THE EARTH

It takes people three years to walk around the Earth, and we *think* it takes two million years to walk around the sun. Now do you see how much bigger the sun is than the Earth? Some people think that the world was once part of the sun. That, of course, was a long time ago. Then there were no people, trees, houses, plants, grass or dirt, and many things we now have. All that was on the Earth then was: violent explosions and boiling lava streeming from bursting ret-hot mountains. After that cooled (which took quite a lot of years) there came the first rain. It poured and poured for over a week, until soon there was just a few sprouts. They grew and grew and kept shedding their seeds and soon there was a whole bunch of them. Soon out of the water grew very small fishes. There were many of them, and all growing until they became about like frogs and crawling upon land. They kept on growing and growing until they became like monkeys. Then like apes, with fingers like we have now. Then came early man. The Early Man had skin like we have now, but with more hair on it. The Early Man dressed in bear skins and lived in caves. Very, very, VERY slowly, things started to improve, as more things were invented. After millions and millions and millions of years there was me.

THIS STORY IS ABOUT HENRY THE CAVE MAN

Once about a time, when there still were cave men in the world, there happened to be a town of cave men known as Clubbemdeadville. Now there was a particular cave which was the biggest in Clubbendeadville and that belonged to Henry A. Bone. Now Henry A. Bone was president of the town's leading social organization—the Hairy Brute Society. This honor came to him because he had clubbed more wild animals to death than anyone else with his club. Henry Bone was very proud when he killed a small deer. Now one night when everyone in Clubbendeadville was asleep, except Henry A. Bone, there came into the town a huge dinasaur (meaning in Greek, terrible lizard) which came to wreck the town of Clubbemdead, UNLESS......Henry A. Bone did something about it! The first thing Henry did was wake everybody up very quickly. Then all the strongest men got all there strongest tools and climbed a strong tree, ready to fight the dinosaur and save their town. Henry's plans were to hide up in the strongest branches of the strong tree and jump down on the beast when he came to the gates of Clubbemdeadville. There plan worked out ok, but one man got a broken leg and one man got a broken arm, but it was ok. For being so cleaver, Henry A. Bone got a new piece of lion skin, a new piece of smooth rock, and a bear skin rug. Henry A. Bone and his family were very happy.

Most of these illustrations have been taken from written stories. Storytelling works very well in the counseling interview and has the advantage of allowing the child greater latitude in use of vocabulary and length of story. The young child might not be able to write all he would like to say or might grow tired of writing before he has fully expressed his ideas and feelings. Storytelling can also be used in the classroom, but some children are inhibited from "letting themselves go" by the presence of classmates. Some children enjoy keeping their ideas and feelings "private" in diaries or handing them in to the teacher, but not reading them aloud. In the primary grades and remedial classes, children can dictate their stories or get help with troublesome words. A joint story can be composed by the class with each individual adding his own special ideas. This entails considerable individual help, but it is highly productive. Some pupils are willing to look words up in their readers, spellers, or dictionary and work fairly independently.

UNDERSTANDING ART WORK

Although, it is generally unsafe to lay down rules for interpreting children's art work, some characteristics appear to suggest certain tendencies. Omissions and distortions suggest incomplete or distorted perception and areas of conflict, which might be checked against other evidence. Excessive attention to detail may indicate the same tendency in daily habits, meticulous attention to clothes, orderliness, etc. Excessive neatness and geometric designs may be associated with over-conformity.

Violent clashes in colors, sharpened angles, heavy lines, pencil jabs may reflect aggression and hostility. The use of space, location of figures on the page, omissions, size and proportions of figures may be meaningful. Very light lines, crowding, erasures, and retracing suggest anxiety or constriction. Heavy frames around pictures suggest desire for concealment or protection from a hostile world or the desire to nail everything down, to keep things from getting out of hand. Excessive use of shading in sketching is believed to represent anxiety or depression. Exaggeration of some part of the human figure may call attention to preoccupation with that part. Omission of a part suggests this is forbidden territory. Some of the principles and practices described in connection with the House-Tree-Person and Bender Visual Motor Gestalt tests apply to the interpretation of art work.

The drawings and paintings of a patient in therapy are described by Levy.[30] The 12-year-old boy had been referred for treatment because of disobedience, negativism, difficulty in making friends, and undue sensitivity to criticism. Among his nine landscapes, some were obviously associated with violence, fire, people, falling down a cliffy ledge, storm, and ships in storm. This author believed storms were associated with death. Drawings of animals were concerned with capture and prey, in which the child appeared to be identified with the victim. Among his titles were: angry horse left behind; panther and prey; frightened rabbit; eagle, its eggs are stolen; hunter killing an animal; and knight and dragon.

[30] Anderson, Harold H., and Gladys L. Anderson (eds.), *An Introduction to Projective Techniques*, Prentice-Hall, Inc., Englewood Cliffs, N. J., 1951, pp. 678ff.

Cat and dog pictures appeared to be associated with himself and his sister of whom he was jealous. A picture of a duck and a cage is said by the author to be associated with imprisonment. Crime was the subject of many drawings of people. One series of 12 drawings depicted the exploits of a gangster, killings, capture, and death. There were three drawings of suicide, one of a funeral, and one of pirates. Levy[31] explains, "In general, the drawings portray a competitive dog-eat-dog existence in a world full of danger and violence, in which the patient is struggling along in the form of a helpless, abandoned victim, trying to escape from the enemy. . . . " Anxiety is suggested, according to Levy, by chasms, steep rocks and cliffs.

Montague[32] observes that schizophrenic children often depict rhythmic action and circular movements. (These remarks apparently do not apply to finger paintings, because most finger painters use circular motions. The illustrations given were of pencil drawings.) Diagonal stripes may be used. Figures may be depicted dancing or swinging their arms. Human figures are sometimes shown flying. An inner impulse to whirl is said to be the source of these drawings. Detached body parts may be drawn. He suggests that the patients might fear the loss of an arm or leg or the possibility of being hurled into space by centrifugal force. This fear may also show up in efforts to define boundaries, in emphasizing the outlines of a figure or picturing it in a cape or other protection. The patient expresses his fear of disintegration, that parts of him are in danger of getting away. Rigid posturing may suggest this fear. Pictures showing human figures merging into circular lines or into the background appear to show inability to define self, or possibly personality disintegration. The faces in these drawings may appear vague or ghostlike.

Elongation and distortion of hair, fingernails, ears, eyelashes, extremities, and other bodily parts are said to be common in the drawings of schizophrenic children. The anxiety felt by the child is sometimes reflected in his drawings of faces.

Machover[33] suggests questions which might be asked in connection with the child's drawing of the human figure. A child's drawing and his answers are given together with the author's interpretations.

In his discussion of finger painting, Napoli[34] describes scrubbing, scribbling, scratching, and slapping at the paper as symptoms of disturbances. The painting of dead animals is said to reflect a lack of atten-

---

[31] *Ibid.*, p. 688.
[32] Anderson and Anderson (eds.), *op. cit.*, p. 378ff.
[33] Anderson and Anderson (eds.), *op. cit.*, pp. 346ff.
[34] *Ibid.*, pp. 406ff., 401.

tion and affection. A finger-painting record form, equipment, and methods of administration are described by Napoli. The significance of colors is discussed. He believes an adequate sampling would require a series of at least six finger paintings at the rate of about two a week.

SOME USES OF TESTS IN COUNSELING

One of the more important uses of test results is to help the counselor prepare for counseling. He may have learned from his client's teacher or from his own observations how the pupil behaves in class. He may suspect the nature of the problem, but he needs to know the depth of problem and how the pupil sees the situation. Personality tests of various kinds can help the counselor understand how the pupil feels and whether or not counseling is indicated.

Suppose his interview is to be with Audrey, a quiet third-grade girl of average mental ability who is retarded in reading, spelling, and arithmetic. Her teacher says that she recites in whispers. She is not invited to play with the other boys and girls. Her parents do not permit her to learn folk dancing, wear jeans, or play rough games. She has four brothers and sisters. Two of them are outstanding pupils and one has a beautiful voice. The two younger sisters require considerable care from their mother. Audrey is clean and well fed, but opportunities to feel successful and important are lacking. How does she feel about herself?

Some clues are found in some of her responses to a personality inventory:

Is it easy for you to talk to your class?   **No.**
Do you feel bad when you are blamed for things?   **Yes.**
Do the children think you can do things well?   **Not very often.**
Do most of the boys and girls like you?   **I don't know.**
Can you do things as well as other children?   **Some things.**
Are the children glad to have you in school?   **They don't know when I'm there.**
Do you need to have more friends?   **Yes.**
Should you mind your folks even when they are wrong?   **You should always mind your folks.**
Do you say nice things to children who do better work than you?   **Yes.**
Do you help new children get used to the school?   **No.**

The counselor suspects that this pupil is lonely and timid. She probably feels very insignificant, but perhaps she is not ready to say so. She would probably like very much to be permitted to do the things that her classmates enjoy, but she also wants to please and obey her parents.

Although the personality inventory is helpful, some of the questions arouse her resistance. She feels she cannot answer either yes or no. It would be painful for her to acknowledge that she feels the boys and girls do not like her or that she cannot do things as well as other children.

In Audrey's folder are some of her sketches and paintings. One of them shows a boy standing before a big house. (Her brother is an important member of the family.) It is rather significant that there are no girls in her pictures. She may feel that girls are less important than boys. Outside the picture in the margin is a small bug. Perhaps Audrey feels that she is, like the bug, very small and insignificant. Perhaps she feels she actually is a bug. This may be the place to begin, "Would you like to tell me more about this painting?" Then if the pupil fails to respond, the counselor can say, "The bug feels very small. Is the bug lonely?" The child may find that she can express her feelings in the third person. Finding the counselor friendly and accepting, she may become able to talk openly about herself.

Reviewing a case history before a counseling interview, a counselor noted that his client showed a high score on the defensiveness scale of a personality inventory. Although her grades were satisfactory, she ranked below average in reading speed and had been referred to a remedial-reading class. Her personality test results suggested that the client would resent placement in the class and would resist counseling. The client mentioned the reading class and continued: "They put me in there on account of those tests, but I wasn't feeling well the day I took the tests."

> COUNSELOR: You feel that the test does not show how well you can read.
> STUDENT: I get along all right. I don't need any help. I make my grades.
> COUNSELOR: You feel as if this class is not necessary for you.
> STUDENT: I just don't like any of it. I don't like for people to act as if something is wrong with me.
> COUNSELOR: It's as if somebody is accusing you of something.

The student is expressing resentment, but, since she is on the defensive, she may not be prepared to acknowledge it. The words, resentment and defensive, would probably be interpreted as criticism, so the counselor tries to choose words that will express how she feels without exciting resistance. He is prepared for her attitude by the test results.

This client later discussed her achievement-test results with her counselor. She found that they suggested superior ability in science and numerical reasoning, but less than average achievement in linguistic skills. Her resentment decreased and she was able to direct her efforts toward improving reading skills.

Cues for counseling are also found in informal expressions. Second- and third-grade children responded to Liszt's *Liebestraum* with a variety of remarks: "It makes me think of way out in the desert." "It makes me think of when a story ended." "It reminds me of a wedding . . . church music . . . dance music . . . of home . . . music in town last year . . . leaf music . . . play music at Caroline's house." The counselor finds leads for opening remarks, "Can you tell me more about this?" He can respond, "This makes you think of a happy time (or a lonely time)" or "The music makes you think of a day when something important happened to you." When he is getting acquainted with the pupil or when the interview bogs down, he can ask, "Can you tell me more about this?"

Some test scores help the counselor predict how the student will behave in the counseling interview. A person with a high score in defensiveness, or one who manifests defensiveness to projective techniques may have a hard time getting started. Depressed people usually talk very little. Aggressive people may express resentment against the class, teachers, parents, roommates, etc. People with a high Sc score might be expected to be dreamy and uncommunicative. A high Pa or Ma score may be reflected in talkativeness at a superficial level. A person with either deviation may wish to avoid discussion of feelings. The manic usually loses interest unless counseling moves along rapidly. He will be likely to give the impression of impatience to get the conversation over and get on to the next event of the day.

None of these remarks should be interpreted to mean that the counselor can ever predict definitely how the client will behave. He should be prepared to accept and respond to the client's expressions, whether or not they conform to his expectations. Factors outside the counselor's knowledge influence behavior. Recent events may operate to make a change in the usual behavior of the student. Depressives may have periods of elation, and manics may be temporarily depressed. Combinations of deviations, such as anxiety plus Pa, may reflect modifications of the usual behavior of either. A high Sc score is the result of so many variables that behavior may not conform to the usual pattern. The counselor may expect from a deviation on the Pa scale that the client will be retaliative, but if his logic and fixed ideas have taken the turn that "good people do not express aggressions," the client will not appear retaliative, or retaliation may take the form of excessive sweetness and martyrlike tolerance. Asking questions is sometimes a form of aggression.

Progress in counseling or classwork depends on the degree to which the client can make use of the situation. People with extreme rigidity are slow to respond. The client may appear to make progress in one interview, and in the next to have reverted to his former stage of adjustment. Uncommunicative and constricted people may take several interviews or an entire year to get going.

Outside factors operate. If the student achieves enough success in other classes or in social contacts to satisfy him, he may refuse to believe that he has a problem. The behavior of parents, classmates, dates, roommates, and other instructors have their impact on the student. The depressive may begin to feel accepted by members of the reading class and instructor, but failures in other experiences and in interpersonal relations may convince him that he is worthless after all. A student who was making progress in counseling and classwork was forbidden by her fiancé to continue the counseling interviews. After terminating counseling, her classwork deteriorated and symptoms of anxiety increased. The benefits of counseling and remediation sometimes become apparent a year or two after the services are terminated. The uses of test results in counseling will be further discussed in the chapter on counseling the retarded reader.

Hamrin[35] describes an unusual application of the Bell Adjustment Inventory. The mother of a client was asked to answer the questions exactly as she thought her son would respond to them. When she found that his answers differed greatly from those she imagined he would give, she was helped to a new understanding of his attitudes and problems.

ANECDOTAL RECORDS

Although the keeping of records can become a burden, certain kinds of observations can be of great value. Grade-school teachers have more opportunity to observe behavior than anyone else, and their comments can be helpful to the counselor. Teachers will often be surprised, in reviewing their notes, to find illuminating incidents which they have forgotten and to see evidences of progress in behavior and classwork. Teachers need some briefing on what to record. Otherwise, the task is too laborious, and the meaningful information is lost in a mass of detail. With experience, they become more discriminating in choosing information to record.

The following notes on a retarded reader in the second grade appear to reflect progress:

OCTOBER 1—Dannie often appears to feel tired and sick. He responds a little better than at first.

[35] Hamrin, Shirley, *Chats with Teachers about Counseling*, McKnight & McKnight Publishing Company, Bloomington, Ill., 1950, p. 190.

OCTOBER 15—He finished arithmetic and spelling assignments today . . . is learning new words in reading.

NOVEMBER 1—He took part in the play and seemed to enjoy it. He made no objection to wearing the costume, smiled frequently through the evening. He looks as if he feels better. Acts rebellious at times but almost always works away at written work. Seems to get meaning from reading.

NOVEMBER 10—Dannie was the only one in the class to recognize the word "hurry" today. He read some extra pages in a primer and did fairly well. He knew enough words to feel pretty successful.

In this informal record, kept on the inside of a manila folder, the teacher can find items to include in remarks to parents and to mention to the pupil.

Dependency and home problems are reflected in these notes:

SEPTEMBER 5—Kay's mother reports that she cried for five hours last night about school. Mrs. T. says she had a nervous breakdown after her third child was born and says Kay is nervous, too. Kay waits to be given detailed instructions before beginning work on anything, brings everything to me for approval.

SEPTEMBER 9—Kay had another crying spell at home. Her mother kept her at home a half day, but has decided to send her regardless from now on.

SEPTEMBER 29—She helped to fill the water jars for everybody during art period and spent the whole period keeping them full.

Maturity seems reflected in this anecdote about a second-grade boy:

OCTOBER 2—Got hurt on the playground, but did not blame anyone else and did not cry.

Notes on a college freshman suggest the kind of information which might be kept:

DECEMBER 18—Superior in quantitative ability, inferior in linguistic ability, reading scores range from 3d to 40th percentile. Says he always had trouble with reading and words. Is worried about statistics and English examination. Says if he fails, the army will get him. Has trouble reading physics exercises. Tested interests in medicine and engineering.

APRIL 2—Quite depressed over physics, says he makes stupid mistakes. Made a B on English theme once when he wrote down outline first.

APRIL 7—Feeling better. Will study hard for physics exam, rest on Sunday, and see what happens. Says he knows the stuff, and if he doesn't feel pressure of exam too much he can recall.

MAY 8—Passed his English test and two other tests with safe grades. Very happy. Doesn't feel really safe yet, but says he's "getting the hang of things."

Can write with better organization. Looks as if he can stay in ROTC and in school. Will write a theme on air power.

Notes should be dated and initialed. A description of an incident is better than an opinion. For example, "Cried yesterday and today" is more accurate and meaningful than "Is moody." Aggressions are likely to be noted, but withdrawn behavior is equally important and should be recorded. For example, "Janie declined to take part in the play. She is often so deep in a daydream that I have to touch her arm to get her attention." If Jane should suddenly volunteer to take part, it would be an important incident to record. Items of value would include notes on: how well the child gets along in a group, whether he is an outsider, on the fringes, a leader or an accepted member; whether or not and how he attempts to become a member of the group; occasions when he feels successful or unsuccessful; whether he blames self or others for his misfortunes; favorite games and the child's role in play; incidents showing attitudes toward authority, etc.

CASE FOLDERS

The individual case folder should contain all test data, samples of the student's work, his daily progress reports, personal data, health information, grades, information about home, and notes from teachers and counselors. If a full-scale testing program is operating, tests might include one or more measures of mental ability, a general screening test of reading, diagnostic reading test, achievement tests, a personality inventory, an interest test, and one or more projective tests. One intelligence test would be the instrument administered to the entire school. A second might be an individual test or a pencil and paper measure of power, non-verbal ability, or performance. Signs of progress, plans for the future, letters and remarks from parents, and copies of letters sent to parents could be of value. An autobiography often adds valuable information.

POOR MAN'S PROGRAM

If handicapped by limited funds for testing, the school can make a start toward studying the retarded reader. Students suspected of reading problems might be selected by teachers for special testing. The test battery might include a measure of verbal and non-verbal ability, a diagnostic reading test, and either the House-Tree-Person or a sentence-completion test or both. Each student's folder would include relevant information from school records, teachers, parents, family physician, and interviews with the student. The daily progress chart, autobiography, autobiographical questionnaire, problem checklist, and samples of the student's work can be assembled with little expense. The inside of the folder can be used to record interview notes, observations of behavior, and incidental information.

Some students who need help will doubtless be overlooked, but if the interest and support of the teachers can be secured a record of this kind can be quite successful in identifying the majority of those who can make improvement and in providing a running record of progress. With in-service-training, teachers will become more skillful in identifying retarded readers and in furnishing information.

In special cases, where individual testing is needed, sometimes the cooperation of the state psychologist or college faculty members can be secured. Retest with the reading test would be desirable, but, if this is not possible, some idea of progress can be obtained from the daily progress chart, the student's opinions, opinions of other teachers, carry-over to other classes, grades, etc. Retest with the H-T-P or sentence completion test contributes to an appraisal of the student's personal development.

PREPARING TEACHERS FOR THE TESTING PROGRAM

It is obvious that the support of the teachers is needed for a successful testing program. They cannot be expected to cooperate fully unless their consent is obtained before involving them in giving tests, perhaps scoring and interpreting them, furnishing information, and using the information gathered. Faculty meeting time can be used to good advantage to present information, weigh advantages, invite opinions, and reach decisions. Testing should be done during the school day, and it is perfectly legitimate to use school time for this important service. It should not be added to the school day for either teacher or student.

We are reminded of an experience which illustrates "how not to introduce a testing program." All decisions were made and tests ordered before the teachers were informed of their added responsibilities. No attempt was made to eliminate duplication in records. The meeting at which the tests were distributed was largely devoted to entertainment. A clever comedian told funny stories, led group singing, and drank a glass of water while standing on his head. At the close of the meeting the teachers departed with nothing to guide them in their new duties except the tests, the test manual, and little understanding of their purpose. Their resentment was reflected in chance remarks showing that they intended to put in the minimum amount of time and effort. Most of them were unacquainted with the administration, timing, or interpretation of standardized tests. The scoring, recording, error analysis, and extra study were unwelcome and laborious tasks. Much of it was done in a perfunctory fashion, and little use was made of test results.

The school counselor will be expected to advise the administration and faculty regarding the selection of tests, the scheduling of mass testing, and the choice of record forms. In planning stages, he may be asked to explain the merits of various tests, to tell what they can do for the faculty, and to help decide how much testing is practical in view of available clerical help and the amount of time which the faculty can give to the guidance program.

It would be a mistake for the counselor to be placed in a position of telling the faculty "what is wrong with the school" or even "what is right with the school." Such conclusions may be drawn, but they should be faculty decisions. The counselor is a helper and consultant, but not judge and evaluator. Evaluation is the right of the whole group, and action in terms of evaluation will follow only if the faculty participates in making the decisions.

Following the recording of test data, teachers may welcome an opportunity to talk over with the counselor, administrators, and with each other, the results of testing. Questions can be raised and discussed, and sample cases might be reviewed.

PATTERNS OF DATA

Diagnosis is not accomplished in one sitting. It is a continuing process. A tentative diagnosis is made from whatever data are first available. As more evidence is gathered, appraisal is refined or altered. Points of agreement and disagreement are explored, and missing information sought. Test data are compared with other information. As a pattern emerges, the counselor or teacher has a frame of reference from which to view and try to understand the student and prepare to respond in interview and in classroom discussion. Some of the data might be gathered in interview, but this is time-consuming and requires just as much preparation, as a well-organized testing program, if not more.

The following case records illustrate the process of diagnosis:

CASE OF M. L.

JANUARY 31, INFORMATION AVAILABLE BEFORE INTERVIEW: M. L., college freshman, age 18. Quantitative ability—82 percentile (upper 20 per cent of her class); linguistic ability—43 percentile (lower half of class); total ACE—61st percentile; reading speed—37 percentile; comprehension—45 percentile. Entrance theme—C.

TENTATIVE DIAGNOSIS: Reading problem, especially in speed; comprehension is lower than total ACE score. ACE shows uneven mental development often associated with emotional problems.

PROGNOSIS: Good chance for improvement with remediation, but vision or emotional problems interfere. Might be expected to like math and science.

INFORMATION NEEDED: Personal adjustment and visual performance.

FEBRUARY 6, INTERVIEW: Liked typing in high school, likes math, but not other classes; liked high school, but college is disappointing.

VISUAL SCREENING: Left eye, farsighted; right eye, nearsighted; right eye sees picture larger than left eye; car-sickness, nervousness, and some eye strain; symptoms suggest that eyes do not work together; wears glasses, but has not seen physician for 1½ years; suggested investigate convergence, fusion, aniseikonia, lenses, visual training.

PERSONAL ADJUSTMENT: MMPI, depression, standard score of 72; social introversion, 71; psychasthenia (anxiety), 68; schizophrenia, 69; suggests marked emotional disturbance, depression, and anxiety, interfering with attention and concentration; probably short memory span, low morale, poor opinion of self and others, insecurity, tendency to withdraw, shyness, difficulties in communication, possibly daydreaming.

SENTENCE COMPLETION: Attitudes toward others—people make me nervous, used to think all people were good, don't trust every person, hurts when others criticize; doubt if braggers are as good as they think. Attitudes toward authority—some grownups think all children are bad. Attitudes toward school —if I were a teacher, I'd help students to find pleasure in school life, most important thing is studying hard, hardly ever miss a class, not sure I like college, hate English class, time when school is to close is drawing near, wish for summer to come, difficult to make high grades, afraid of taking tests. Concealment or stereotypy—when I was little I played with paper dolls, purpose in life to achieve my goals, people who go to church hear the word of God, eyes are brown, good people love their neighbors, people should count ten before losing temper.

REVISED DIAGNOSIS: Progress may be hampered by emotional problems and visual problems; emotional and social adjustment probably interfere with full use of native abilities; counseling recommended.

MARCH 15, INTERVIEW: Says she likes to go home; likes nieces and nephews, but does not like the way her family treats her, nieces, nephews, brother; exams look like mountains, dreads them, worries, works part-time, says she likes it, likes the money, has gained 40 words per minute according to progress chart. Feels she can concentrate better.

ANALYSIS OF DATA: Fears, anxieties, feelings of inferiority, expressed in interview and sentence completion test support the MMPI scores on the depression and anxiety scales. The rather pessimistic responses to the sentence completion, classified as attitudes toward others, are similar to those expressed by people scoring high on the depression scale. Tendency to withdraw is seen in some responses, agrees with the deviate scores on the Si and Sc scales, but there is little evidence of fantasy, and she seems relatively in touch with reality. The interview and sentence completion test would not have indicated the depth of the emotional problems as well as did the MMPI, but they add support and give additional information. Attitudes toward authority appear to be a combination of resistance, resentment, avoidance, and submission. She does not like school, but seldom misses class and thinks it important to study hard. She states, "Some grown-ups (may mean parents, teachers, others in authority) think all children are bad." Responses suggest vacillation between resistance and submission, a state which produces anxiety. The hints of home problems, given in responses to sentence-completion items, are amplified a little in interview. Improvement noted on progress chart and her remark that she can concentrate better suggest that she is making increased use of abilities and has a chance for continued improvement.

OBSERVATIONS OF COUNSELOR: Her remarks show almost a complete lack of spontaneity and strong feelings of insecurity. She makes veiled references to sibling conflict.

MARCH 22, INTERVIEW: M. was punished by second-grade teacher, still remembers how scared, didn't learn to read; brother treats her like a child, does not like this; is aware that she does not communicate well; hints at the feeling that she is rejected, but cannot express it openly.

APRIL 14, INTERVIEW: Depressed over English grade, hurt, very upset, doesn't like art and English instructor, feels she is doing better than grades show.

MAY 17, INTERVIEW: Has broken off with boy friend, feels badly, doesn't know what is wrong, still likes him; wanted door shut so it would be private, then talked much better.

MAY 26, INTERVIEW: Feels she will make passing grades, could use more counseling. Still finds it hard to like teachers.

FINAL CRITIQUE OF THE CLASS: "I feel that I have benefited a great deal from this class. When I enrolled in it I was rather skeptical. It is one where everyone can come with gripes and learn what others have banked up inside of them. I learned to know most of the students in the class and found them to be quite friendly. I learned to know the professor and found that all professors are not bad and hard to get along with. Thank you for all you have helped me with and all you have taught me."

FINAL SENTENCE COMPLETION: I like to talk; most people are thoughtful and kind; used to think I did not like my father; people should enjoy their occupations; the best time is now; things that make me mad are few.

REVIEW OF DATA: Progress chart shows a gain of 110 words per minute. Although improvement has been made, in reading skills and personal adjustment, further counseling is indicated. Signs of a more hopeful outlook are found in the final critique and sentence completion items.

CASE OF R. S.

In the following case summary can be seen agreement between test data and the counselor's observations.

NOTES ON R. S.: "Q" score above average; "L" score and reading scores far below average. Enrolled in ag. engineering. Likes athletics. Failed English, is trying again, working hard. Says he is afraid of English exams, butterflies in his stomach, can't get rid of the feeling; things go on that he ought to know about, but he can't catch on . . . misses the boat. Events are vague to him.

BENDER VISUAL MOTOR GESTALT: His figures are less than an inch high and crowded into the upper left of the page, in about one-eighteenth of the space usually required, evidences of erasures, and retracing, each figure surrounded by a heavy frame (extreme insecurity, feelings of insignificance, anxiety). Dark shading (depression). Some figures are incomplete, some inaccurately drawn, some tilted on the axis, all surrounded by loops and swirls (suggests distortion in perception, incomplete perception, great effort expended in control, attempt to keep things stabilized and to keep self stabilized, feels things and perhaps self are in danger of flying apart, events are going round too fast and he is going round too fast).

COMMENTS OF INSTRUCTOR: Needs counseling. Symptoms of instability should be checked by further testing and perhaps referral for clinical diagnosis and treatment.

CASE OF B. N.

Various signs of insecurity, anxiety and vacillation are seen in the case data on this 18-year-old college freshman, female.

NOTES FROM THE CASE FOLDER OF B. N.: September, "Q," 50 percentile; "L," 31 percentile; total ACE, 38 percentile; reading speed, 28 percentile; comprehension, 11 percentile. Bender is reproduced in about half the usual space, with erasures and retracing (insecurity); alternate light and heavy strokes (ambivalence, probably anxiety). House-Tree-Person, human figure is very small, cannot tell whether a man or woman, but probably male, (feels insignificant, problem in identification); lines are mostly faint with a few sharp, heavy strokes (ambivalence, probably anxiety); shading (anxiety, depression) tree is bare and house has little ornamentation (drab life); backview of human, stick figure and shutters suggest defensiveness and self-protection; house is shuttered and path does not lead to the door (social communication is difficult). Uneven performance shown on daily progress chart suggests disturbance, perhaps distractibility. Speed varies, 260, 230, 210, 330, 270 words per minute in first five sessions. Comprehension also fluctuates between 70 and 100 per cent.

INTERVIEW NOTES: Says she has trouble with concentration, has headaches, liked high school but does not know about college, still trying to make up her mind, is taking nursing and home ec.

VISUAL EXAMINATION (OPTOMETRIST): Some astigmatism, accommodation fatigue, over-converges.

COUNSELOR'S COMMENTS: Anxiety, vacillation, and ambivalence are suggested by projective test results, uneven classroom performance, and conversation. All point to feeling that she and all people are insignificant. She is probably not using her full ability. She has trouble getting started in counseling interview. Counseling may help her to relieve her feelings of anxiety and unresolved aggressions.

B. N. CASE SUMMARY: January, Bender figures are more accurate, stroke is firmer, fewer erasures and retracings (more maturity, confidence). House has shrubs; tree has leaves (life a little more interesting); pencil strokes more uniform and firmer (less anxiety, more confidence); less shading (anxiety may be somewhat relieved); human figure is side view (slightly less self-protective and defensive); figure has an eye (sees more of environment), is walking (might mean a more active attack on problems), figure is still a stick figure and looks like a male (defensiveness and problem of identification remain). Gains shown by retest:

	Percentile rank	
	February	April
Quantitative	50	93
Linguistic	31	43
Total ACE	38	69
Reading speed	28	62
Comprehension	11	59

Progress chart shows continued fluctuation, but the average speed for the last five sessions is 298 words per minute and average comprehension score for the last five sessions is 91 per cent. Eyeglasses prescribed by physician. Says she likes them. Was more communicative in April and May interviews. Says she reads much more easily now. Probably should continue counseling.

CASE OF K. A.

Some uses of the Diagnostic Reading Test and other instruments are shown by the case history of K. A., college freshman, age 18, male, enrolled in Arts and Sciences.

SEPTEMBER TEST RESULTS:

	By local norms	
	Raw score	Percentile rank
ACE quantitative	59	95
ACE linguistic	50	25
ACE total	109	59
Coop. reading	19	7
Vocabulary	9	9
Speed	6	10
Comprehension	4	8

K. was placed in developmental reading on the basis of the above percentile rankings. Additional information was gathered by the reading specialist as follows:

DIAGNOSTIC READING TEST (Survey section)	BY UNIVERSITY OF DENVER NORMS Percentile rank
Rate of reading (277 w.p.m.)	40
Story comprehension	7
Vocabulary	56
Comprehension (studies)	8
Total comprehension	26

MMPI STANDARD SCORES: psychopathic deviate 65 (disregard for conventions and laws or rules, shallow feelings flattening); manic 78 (excitability, bursts of enthusiasm, many projects, lack of persistence, over-talkative, great respect for power or money, likely to be authoritarian, shallow feelings).

BENDER VISUAL MOTOR GESTALT: figures very small, crowding, heavy frames, erasures, retracing (insecurity, doubt of one's own worth, constriction); shading (anxiety or depression), inconsistent pencil stroke, light and heavy (ambivalence, aggression vs. submission).

COMMENTS: Reading disability is clearly shown by all scores. A potential for improvement is indicated by the high "Q" score and total ACE rank. Personal problems, indicated by personality test results, may stand in the way of improvement. People with pronounced deviations from the mean on the Pd scale do not respond readily to counseling. People with high Pd and Ma scores tend to communicate at the surface level. They do not feel deeply, so deep communication is not possible. Improvement will depend on the degree to which this student can make use of the service, experiences, and opportunities to which he is exposed.

CLASSROOM BEHAVIOR: Reluctant to show approval at first, but gradually became cooperative; appeared shy, did not talk much at first, but later participated in discussion and initiated conversation with the instructor; class schedule did not permit counseling at the hours when the counselor was available, no counseling except informal talks before class, and responses to feeling when expressed in discussion.

FINAL TESTS IN JANUARY: Indicate gains.

DIAGNOSTIC READING TEST (Survey section)	BY UNIVERSITY OF DENVER NORMS Percentile rank
Rate (338 w.p.m.)	79
Story comprehension	40
Vocabulary	56
Comprehension (studies)	59
Total comprehension	61

PROGRESS CHART: First four scores between 210 and 300 words per minute; last four scores 370 to 390. MMPI, psychopathic deviate 50, manic 50 (average scores, improved adjustment).

Bender Visual Motor Gestalt, larger figures, less crowding, increased space, frames are retained but lighter (improved security, self-confidence, expansiveness, self-esteem); no shading (less anxiety or depression); pencil stroke more consistent, firm but not heavy (less ambivalence).

Case of D. J.

The case data on this third-grader reveal adequate ability, academic handicaps, and emotional problems.

Notes on D. J.: Age, 8 years; girl; 2 younger and 2 older siblings. Good health. Recites in a whisper, mother says she was ridiculed by former teacher, writes well, but never finishes assignments, reads very poorly, very slow, timid, does not play with other children. Mental age, Stanford, 8.1 years. Reading test, grade 1.9.

Interview notes: Talks more in interview. Sang a song and her voice was sweet and true. Wants to be like her brother who is a good student and an artist. Says she loves her baby sister and likes to take care of her.

November notes: D. talks aloud a little more. Her compositions show imagination. Artwork is good. All pictures of people are boys. Finishes more assignments. Took part in public performance and did well. Plays house and card games with classmates. Told me a joke, "There was a terrible fight. A cat licked his paw." Can answer some questions over reading.

Comments of counselor: With remediation and continued success and approval, this child may be able to overcome her academic handicaps. Should be supplied with first-grade materials.

Case of M. S.

M. S. is a low ability pupil, but his test results suggest that he is **not** reading as well as he is able.

Notes from case history of M. S.: Age, 15 years; male. Mother says he was very small until the age of 9 years when he began to grow. He did not eat well until about that time. Although he is undersized, he seems to be healthy. California Short-Form Test of Mental Maturity and Non-language Section: mental age, non-verbal scale, 13 years; mental age, verbal scale, 6.9. California Achievement Tests, Primary Form AA for grades 1 through lower fourth:

	Grade rank
Reading vocabulary	2.5
Reading comprehension	4.2
Arithmetic reasoning	4.4
Arithmetic fundamentals	5.3
Total arithmetic	4.7

Performance on the reading test was uneven. When asked to read orally from a different test, he was able to recognize words that he had apparently missed on the written test. He called accurately such words as distant, far-away, blossom, flower, and trouble. When he worked alone at the written test, apparently he was unsure of his responses. Performance on the California Vision, Hearing and Motor Coordination Test for Elementary Grades suggests good motor control except when speed is a factor or when under strain. California Test of Personality, Primary Form AA, satisfactory scores in self-adjustment: self-reliance, sense of personal worth, sense of personal freedom, feeling of belonging, withdrawing tendencies, nervous symptoms; and social adjustment: social standards, social skills, antisocial tendencies, family relations, school relations, and community relations. The examiner checked frequently to see whether or not he understood the questions and he apparently did, as he was able to give illustrations of why he believed his answer to be the correct one and to give definitions of various terms. In spite of satisfactory scores, some responses reflect loneliness and lack of social satisfactions. Significant responses were:

Are you lonesome even when you are with people? **Yes.**
Do you feel you need to have more friends? **Yes.**
Do the boys and girls often try to cheat you? **Yes.**
Do you often feel so bad that you do not know what to do? **Yes.**
Should you mind your folks even when they are wrong? **You should always mind your folks.**
Does it often make you angry when people stop you from doing things? **Yes.**
Are there many bad children in your school? **Some.**
Do the people near your home seem to like you? **No.** (*His mother says they have neighbors who quarrel with everybody.*)
Do you have more fun near your home than other children do near theirs? **Yes.**
  Do you feel bad when you are blamed for things? **Undecided.**
  Do you have to tell some people to let you alone? **Undecided.**
  Are you punished for many things you do? **Undecided.**

House-Tree-Person: In all three pictures, house, tree, and person, M. expressed ambivalence. The house was split into two equal wings, the tree into two large branches, and the person looked as if he were going in two directions. (His remark, "The boy is going somewhere, but he doesn't know where he is going.") These expressions may reflect his present uncertainty as to whether he wants to go away to school or stay with his parents. Person is a male figure (masculine identification); house has no path, door is recessed, hands of figure are in pockets, face is in profile, eye has no pupil (awareness of difficulties in communicating with others); tree has bare branches, no foliage around house (barren life); figure has small neck, arms are close to sides (effort expended in self-control; impulses from the body must not get into the head; constriction of arms suggests control).

This pupil was also given the Szondi Triebdiagnostik, a series of 48 photographs of patients in an institution for the mentally ill. Each of eight kinds of maladjustment is represented in each set of pictures. The client is asked to choose from each selection of eight pictures—two which he likes best and two which he likes least. Interpretations are drawn from the choices and from the remarks or stories of the client about the pictures. While the Szondi is vigorously criticized, the responses of this client to the pictures appear to lend support to other data about him. The following information is derived from the results of the Szondi. His responses follow a pattern common among the general population but also said to be given by feeble-minded children. The need to be dependent, to receive maternal affection and care, but also a growing need to feel independence and to assert his masculinity are indicated. Frustration of oral needs (feeding problems, block in communication, etc.), lack of social satisfactions, sadness, loneliness, and withdrawal are suggested. The response pattern from which this interpretation is drawn, however, is also said to be characteristic of children who are trying to relinquish strong ties with their mothers. If Szondi results are manifestations of the child's search for independence, he might be expected to seek security in the construction of objects, exploration of their practical usefulness, etc.[36] If interpreted as lack of social satisfactions, he might be expected to seek security in surrounding himself with material possessions. Other characteristics suggested by results of the Szondi were: ambivalence toward parents, opposing drives toward control and discharge of emotions (sometimes associated with fear of violating the conventions or with guilt and fear related to sexual needs). The Szondi is supposed to measure the degree to which basic needs are satisfied, and, therefore, six administrations are recommended to get a complete picture of adjustment. The above report is based on only one administration.

From parents and teachers, the following information was secured about M. He can take his motor scooter apart, repair it, and put it back together, and he can find his way to any part of town and back again. He has regular household duties and performs them adequately and willingly. He appears to get along well with other children in school and gives his teachers no trouble. His reading tutor believes him capable of improvement.

CASE SUMMARY: Public-school classes have been so crowded that his teachers could not give him the individual attention he needed. He has had few opportunities to converse with anyone. His parents understand his handicap, but hope that he can learn a trade and improve reading skills. Several sources of information suggested ambivalence, inadequate social satisfactions, effort expended in self-control, growing need for independence, masculine identification. Test results and other data pointed to non-verbal ability adequate for some trades.

The following recommendations were made for helping M. S. to develop latent verbal ability:

[36] Deri, Susan, *Introduction to the Szondi Test,* Grune & Stratton Inc., New York, 1949, pp. 141–142.

1. Frequent conversations about motors, machines, sports, adventure, likes, and dislikes.

2. Opportunities to write brief papers about likes and dislikes, motor repair, etc.

3. Daily reading at third- or fourth-grade level followed by conversation: (Is there someone in the story that you like or would like to be like? What part did you like best? What would be a good name for this part of the story if it were a story by itself?).

4. Occasional reading instructions for building model airplanes, motor repair, etc., followed by discussion.

5. A minimum of drill until interest mounts (he has had too much drill with consequent dissatisfaction in reading).

6. Visits to factories, garages, machine shops, zoo, etc., with subsequent opportunity to describe and discuss these experiences.

7. Occasional tape or wire recording of his own stories if possible.

He was sent to a special school where he was given machine shop training and remedial reading. Reports a year later indicated that he had made considerable progress.

SUMMARY

Projective test results, when added to other data, can help the counselor and teacher to understand how the student sees himself, others, and his environment. Distortions in perception, repressed feelings, needs and the way in which the student tries to satisfy them are sometimes suggested. Clinical interpretation of projective techniques require considerable training and experience, but with study and experience teachers can use some of them to understand students and to initiate conversation in interview.

The Rorschach, TAT, and variations of the TAT technique are explained to give the teacher some ideas as to the kinds of information which might be supplied by specialists if their services are available. Suggestions are given for the uses of the Bender Visual Motor Gestalt, House-Tree-Person, Sentence Completion, and interpretations of art work, original stories, and other expressions of students.

Test results and responses to certain items can help the counselor to predict the client's attitudes toward counseling, how he will respond, whether or not he is amenable to counseling, and the rate of progress. Anecdotal records add valuable information to the case history.

Teachers will make use of test results if they are informed and consulted before the testing program begins. They should study the tests and their uses and help to make the necessary decisions.

If funds are not available for a full-scale testing program, a beginning can be made by testing only students referred by teachers. The "poor man's program" includes measures of verbal and non-verbal ability and reading skills, a simple projective test, work samples, autobiography, progress charts, and anecdotal records.

Diagnosis is not accomplished in one sitting. As more data become available, the diagnosis may be refined or altered. The process of diagnosis and the uses of different kinds of data to support each other are illustrated by analysis of data from the six case histories of reading students.

CHAPTER 5

Methods, Materials,
and Organization

Multicausal factors in reading problems have been discussed, and evidence has been presented to illustrate how the individual learns with the whole self. In this chapter, we shall present a multiple approach to the reading problem, describing methods and techniques which have been tailor-made to suit the particular needs of the student with uneven intellectual development. Included will be drills and exercises aimed at improving skills, but emphasis will be placed on those experiences which involve thinking, reacting, and expressing emotions.

This approach is based on wholistic psychology. We work with the total personality when we work with a retarded reader. We must take into account not only the student's intellect, but his emotions which operate to facilitate or hamper progress. A change in reading habits means a personality change. Such a change does not come about overnight. For years, the individual has been building a picture of himself, attitudes toward reading, habits of resistance to communication. He cannot and should not make an abrupt change in the only stable self he has been able to achieve. Learning about *self* goes along with learning new skills. Psychological principles apply to both kinds of learning.

Reading is a part of the constellation of verbal skills and is related to speaking, writing, and spelling. A deficiency in one area is usually related to deficiencies in all. Students with high quantitative ability and low linguistic ability not only rank far below students with even linguistic and quantitative abilities in reading skills, but in total scores on the Cooperative English examination. The differences in these scores between two groups of students matched for quantitative ability but differing in linguistic ability were statistically significant far beyond the .001 level of confidence.[1] There is virtually no probability that the differences are a result of chance.

[1] Woolf, Maurice, D., unpublished study, Kansas State College, 1954.

These students commonly raise barriers to communication between themselves and others. As explained in Chapters 1 and 2, defenses developed to protect the individual from exposing real or fancied shortcomings can be extended to interfere with communication of all kinds. Remediation will not achieve the desired results if the teacher regards reading as a separate skill or tries to treat the problem apart from other aspects of personality. Since the retarded reader has not responded to customary teaching methods, it appears that other methods must be sought.

The two facets of the multiple-approach are group experience and individual treatment. In our opinion both are needed in most cases. In the group, the student learns to respond to and communicate with his fellows. The exchange of ideas and shared experiences in group thinking stimulates motivation, builds self-assurance, and helps the individual to understand that he is not alone in his problems. Individual diagnosis and counseling is focused on the unique problems of each student. With his counselor, he can bring up questions too private or intimate to be discussed in class, check to see if his interpretations of various class discussions are valid, learn about his own potentials, and make plans for the future. Some questions are the concern of the whole group. Others of a more personal nature would not be of interest to the group or are best discussed in private to avoid embarrassing the individual. In the class, the student takes his part in a miniature society. In the counseling interview, he enjoys the entire attention of the counselor and receives the unspoken reassurance that he is a person of sufficient worth to deserve help in making decisions, overcoming obstacles, and understanding his own personal world.

The first part of this chapter will be devoted to a description of a program which can be applied to all levels of students except those who read less well than the average third-graders. Even beginning readers respond favorably to almost all techniques described, with the exception of speeded reading and analysis of propaganda. Modifications are, of course, necessary in some cases. For younger pupils, materials, spelling lists, tachistoscopic slides, vocabulary exercises, comprehension tests, and subjects for discussion would be chosen to suit their levels of competency.

The latter part of this chapter will give some additional techniques, particularly suitable for elementary-school pupils. We have no wish to duplicate unnecessarily the information given in texts on the teaching of beginning reading and in the teaching manuals which are provided by publishers of readers. However, brief mention will be made of the ways in which some aspects of the word-recognition method, work-experience technique, and other techniques can be applied to remediation in the grades.

ORGANIZATION

While considerable merit can be claimed for voluntary participation in reading classes, we find more practical advantages in regularly scheduled classes, offered as a requirement for those students who need extra help. An understanding instructor can avoid the ill effects of regimentation by providing opportunities for other kinds of decisions regarding the conduct of the class, setting the goals, evidences of progress, the value of various experiences, etc. When the class is offered as a part of the academic program, students expect to be given assignments, to meet certain requirements, and to attend class regularly. Although some valid arguments can be given against the use of grades, credits, and penalties for absences, the instructor often finds that without such props he is in competition with traditional classes for the time of the student. Furthermore in the regularly scheduled class, the processes of enrolling students, evaluating gains, and recording progress are greatly simplified. Therefore, we are presenting a plan of organization which integrates remediation into the academic curriculum. After students are selected for remediation, as explained in Chapter 3, they substitute the developmental reading class for the regular reading class in the elementary school or study reading in connection with English class in high school or college.

The procedure followed in a scientific-technical college is to assign college students to a special English reading class if they demonstrate the high "Q," low "L," low reading-ability pattern by standardized testing. People with low reading plus low general ability test scores are sectioned separately. Each special English reading class meets five days weekly. It is taught on alternate days by a reading specialist and on remaining days by the regular English teacher. The instructors are in constant communication with each other, sharing decisions regarding the conduct of classes, evaluation processes, grading, and the like, and exchanging information about students. The cooperating English instructors are chosen for their understanding of human nature, interest in students, resourcefulness, and willingness to give individual attention when needed. The usual attendance regulations apply to these classes. Three hours of credit are given for one semester's work.

Most of the work on reading is actually done during the class period, although a few outside assignments are made. Since outside study is less demanding than in other classes, students come to accept the time spent in counseling and individual diagnosis as legitimate aspects of the class and, in time, regard them as privileges. The reading instructor periodically passes around a sheet of paper giving his office hours, suggesting in a matter-of-fact manner that students indicate the 20- or 30-minute period when they want to see him. Any student who fails to make an appointment receives a note indicating that an appointment with the instructor is a course requirement. In spite of a slight authoritarian flavor in this routine, it has worked quite well. Students accept the requirement readily, and many show progress toward stability and mental health.

The amount of time required for improving and fixating reading skills deserves mention. Although improvement is sometimes reported as a result of intensive training, it often develops that individuals making such rapid gains were already average, or better than average, readers. We have tried various arrangements. Less than nine weeks appears to yield few permanent gains. Classes meeting five times a week do only slightly better than those which meet three times a week. Some students continue to improve during a second semester of remediation. In such cases, the degree of motivation appears to have a great deal to do with the amount of gain, but, of course, motivation is always an important factor. Among those who wish to continue are some students who have already made satisfying progress, but also some who have used the whole semester trying to make up their minds that it can help them.

There are a number of reasons why a "quick conducted tour" leaves little enduring impact. In the first place, these students have spent from three to eighteen years developing reading habits and attitudes toward reading which are not quickly overcome. Second, a good, solid, mutually satisfying group relationship is not built in a few short weeks. Third, a multiple approach, covering many activities, requires time. Thorough testing for diagnosis and evaluation can easily consume eight or ten days. Training in group procedures, orientation processes, and personal development discussions take time. Some class periods are spent in interpreting test results and discussing a graph showing the average scores of the class.

Some students in the elementary school have shown marked improvement during 50 lessons, or about 16 weeks of study, meeting three times a week. Some continued to make improvement during 50 more lessons. Others made fewer gains during the second half of the year and some appeared to stand still. It seems reasonable to assume that the value of prolonging remediation depends upon the needs and attitudes of the individual as well as upon the sustained interest and skill of the instructor.

The progress of students meeting twice a week was less satisfactory than that of classes meeting three times a week. Possibly, interest and skills are lost in the longer interval between class meetings.

The addition of counseling to group treatment boosts gains in many cases. The most effective arrangement, in our experience, has been a class meeting three times a week for one semester, plus counseling. The resulting combination has the advantages of a sustained, secure relationship, group experience, and individual attention.

ORIENTATION TO THE NEW CLASS

The characteristics of a harmonious and integrated group do not develop by accident. One of the aims of the instructor is to make a group out of the class. His first efforts are directed toward making the members feel comfortable and at ease with each other. He begins by introducing himself and telling a little about himself. Then he asks the members to introduce themselves and tell whatever they choose about themselves, where they live, what activities they enjoy most, etc.

Since the methods and techniques will probably be new to the students, it is well to give them a little preparation for the new experience: "You may find that this class is different from any you have ever taken. Sometimes you will think it is easier than other classes. Sometimes you will think it is more difficult, because I shall expect you to take considerable responsibility for making decisions and working for improvement. Sometimes you may feel that we are wasting time because you cannot see the relationship between some of our activities and improving reading skills. The methods we shall use have been tested in other reading classes and found effective."

Some mention might be made of the reason for including discussion: "Reading is a kind of thinking. If you are not thinking, you are not reading. Talking with others about what you have read helps you to think while you read the next time. When you form your own opinions and hear yourself express them, you are increasing your general verbal skill and your ability to think while you read."

Students will appreciate an explanation of why they are chosen for this class: "You have been assigned to this class because your test results show that you are not using your full abilities in your reading. By your performance on standardized tests, you show that you can make improvement in reading skills. Some of you already knew that you were slow readers; others are surprised to find themselves in the class. Some of you are average readers, but you are not reading as well as you are able. This class is for people who show what we call a 'potential for improvement.'" As in other classes, an explanation of the grading system and requirements is appreciated.

These bits of orientation are best given in small doses. Given all at once, they are too much for students to absorb, and too much lecturing discourages participation by the class. The sensitive teacher discerns when a note of explanation will help the class on its way.

Most students, by the close of the primary grades, if not before, have a comparatively fixed idea of what a teacher is like and what a class is like. If the conduct of the class deviates markedly from their preconceived ideas, they may get the impression that it is going to be a "breeze," or that the teacher is an "oddball" (or whatever the current equivalent expression may be). Some will be impatient to get on with the class, feeling that these preliminaries are a waste of time. For these reasons, the teacher works into early sessions some exercises which will conform to their expectations. A gradual transition from traditional to new methods meets with less resistance from the class than does a revolutionary change. The process can be helped along if the teacher occasionally reflects what the class is thinking and feeling. "This surprises you. You feel that this is a waste of time. You are not sure that these conversations will be helpful. You feel this is not an appropriate subject for the classroom. You are not used to doing things this way. You feel doubtful, etc., etc."

The instructor should also be alert to opportunities to respond to positive expressions: "You find this new method interesting and challenging. You like this way of doing things. You enjoy having a share in making decisions."

Sometimes he will be aware of differences in opinion among the class: "Some of you like this. Others do not approve. Shall we talk about it?" He may recognize a student's feeling of ambivalence: "You feel two ways about the class. You like some things, but you question other things." In defining each situation, the teacher orients the students. Reflecting feeling and redefining the situation from time to time is, in part, orientation. The instructor explains: "This is the way it is now. This is what is going on." Or he checks with the class to see if they understand each other: "Is this the way you see it?"

With respect to the role of the instructor and the roles of the members, this might be said: "You will have many opportunities for participation, for judging the effectiveness of procedures, offering opinions, making suggestions, and helping to make decisions. I am not abdicating my responsibility and my role as leader and teacher, but I intend to give each of you an opportunity to play a leader's role and to make more and more decisions as you demonstrate your ability to do so. Each of you has something to give to the class, and I also have something to contribute." The instructor's role varies in different kinds of sessions. As each new activity is introduced, the instructor defines his role and those of the members.

Retarded readers are usually quite dependent. Their attitude toward responsibility is something like this: "I'm here. Teach me. Make me learn to read. You do it." Learning to take responsibility, to work on their own problems, is essential to improvement.

On the subject of responsibility, one instructor makes this statement to his class: "The rate of your improvement will depend heavily on whether you are willing to take responsibility for making decisions and working to overcome obstacles. I am willing to take 50 per cent of the responsibility if you will take the other 50 per cent." He adds: "If you crowd me, I might even take 51 per cent."

GOAL ORIENTATION

Early in the term, on the first or second day, the instructor invites the members of the class to help set the goals of the class. "What do we hope to accomplish in here this year?" He encourages all members to offer suggestions, and he adds his own. Together they state and write down the goals. After two or three weeks, the goals should be reviewed. As the class becomes familiar with methods and techniques and their own needs, they may want to add, delete, or refine their earlier statements. The stated objectives serve as a standard toward which to work and by which progress can be measured. The assumption is that if students share in formulating goals, they will take responsibility for reaching them. By taking part in setting goals, the students become teammates with the instructor and with each other. A step is taken toward harmonious and coordinated group effort, toward consolidating group spirit, and in the direction of placing responsibility for progress on the students themselves.

Goal orientation can be used with young children. At first, they will state their goals in general terms, " . . . to get through the reading book . . . to learn to read better." When goals are reviewed, they begin to state more specific objectives. They love to help make out a schedule and to follow up by checking off with satisfaction those items which they have accomplished.

A NOTE OF EXPLANATION

In the remainder of this chapter, you will find numerous references to reading materials suitable for developmental reading classes. Although there are many excellent scattered selections, it is difficult to find in one book exactly the right combination of easy, interesting articles and stories of a suitable length. We are still searching for such an anthology.

Some which include delightful and interesting materials are limited in value by difficult vocabulary. Some offer materials suitable for personal development discussions, but fail to include materials on propaganda or controversial issues, and vice versa.

THE DAILY GRIND

An outline of the everyday class period will be followed by explanations of the more involved procedures and by a description of other procedures which can be introduced to vary the daily routine. Interest is maintained through a variety of activities. This routine is designed for a 50-minute period. Parts of it must be eliminated when incidental activities are introduced, or when the school period is less than 50 minutes.

1. Tachistoscope drill, 7 to 10 minutes. Slides for the Tachistoscope are available, using words of various lengths, phrases, sentences, and numbers of varying lengths. The simplest words and numbers are used in beginning. Difficulty is increased and time of exposure reduced as speed of recognition improves. The Keystone company provides a manual explaining the use of the machine. This is one of the most popular features of classwork. Aside from the effect of practice, the exercise excites and motivates the students. They believe that it is helping them. Alone, it is actually quite limited in effecting improvement, but with other activities, it is a very useful device.

2. Skimming exercises, 5 minutes. Appropriate materials for skimming can be found in the book section of the *Reader's Digest, Omnibook, Coronet, Pageant,* and similar magazines.

Some of the selections reproduced by Glock[2] are suitable for skimming: "My Experience in a Gambling Saloon" by Bret Harte, "Why I Failed Botany" by James Thurber, "The Insanity Plea" by Fredric Wertham, "Dear Sir, You Cur," by John Crosby, "An Actress Reminisces" by Cornelia Otis Skinner, "How to Write a Letter" by Cameron Shipp, "The Fireman Who Conquered Niagara" by Ralph H. Major.

Selections for this purpose should be relatively light, interesting, easy, and occasionally humorous. A flowing, rapidly moving style of writing is best for skimming.

The students are told, "Read the first paragraph and then the topic sentences. When you find out what a paragraph is about, go on to the next paragraph." A student with a reading problem is accustomed to reading slowly. Skimming helps him learn to adapt his pace to suit the materials.

[2] Glock, Marvin D., *The Improvement of College Reading,* Houghton Mifflin Company, Boston, 1954.

When timing skimming exercises, the instructor explains that skimming speed usually exceeds study speed. The reading is stopped after five minutes. The students are requested to record the number of words per minute on the back of their progress charts.

If time permits, a brief discussion follows. The instructor asks, "Did you find anything interesting or funny in this story? What did you like best? Is there anything worth remembering? What do you think the author is trying to say?"

3. Speeded reading, 5 to 10 minutes. This time, the purpose is comprehension, though it is timed too. Rather than limiting the time, the instructor records the stop-watch time on the blackboard as each student raises his hand to indicate that he has finished a selection. After the first few students raise their hands, the instructor can record the number of seconds every six seconds for easy calculation by the students. For example, when the first student raises his hand, suppose the stop watch says, "1 minute, 42 seconds." Write it down. We use the nearest tenth of a minute, six, twelve, eighteen seconds, etc., for the convenience of the students and to save calculation time. Otherwise, dividing 60 seconds into, say, 39 seconds becomes too involved and laborious; class time is lost and the better students are bored. To maintain interest, activities must move along rapidly. It may be a minute or more before the next student finishes. When he does, write down the time to the nearest tenth of a minute and then begin writing every six seconds, as "2 min., 6 sec., 12, 18, 24," etc. This method of timing permits each student to finish the selection and produces less tension than limiting the time, to 10 minutes or 5. At the close of the speeded reading, each student calculates and records the number of words per minute he has read that day. The instructor has already determined the number of words in the article and recorded it on the blackboard or on the comprehension test page. Accurate speed testing requires materials fairly constant in level of difficulty.

4. Comprehension testing. A brief objective test of comprehension is then given, in order that comprehension will not be sacrificed for speed. Completion, multiple-choice, and true-false items can be used. Some students prefer multiple-choice items, but probably variety in form stimulates thinking.

5. Daily progress records. The student records his words per minute and percentage of comprehension score on a Progress Chart such as the one in Fig. 6, p. 348. Thus, he can compare his daily scores with past scores and see whether he is making progress. He need not be embarrassed by comparison with more favored students. Putting down his own scores gives him considerable satisfaction. Instead of waiting until the

end of the six-week period or the semester to find out how he is doing, he checks daily or several times a week to discover exactly how he stands. The effect is increased motivation.

Teachers are sometimes surprised to learn that students grade their own papers, record their own progress, and are trusted not to read the timed articles before class. We have had no trouble with student "cheating" in reading classes conducted in this fashion. Obviously, there would be little point in it. Student's understand that the daily record is principally for their own convenience, and most of them are very much interested in improving skills and in discerning their actual rate of progress. An explanation of grading, given early in the course, makes clear that grades will be determined by many factors: regular attendance, completing assignments (including personality tests, counseling appointments, etc.), effort expended, cooperation with other students and with instructor, and the degree to which the student fulfills his potentials, taking into consideration such handicaps as physical disability and emotional blocks. If periodicals are used, students know they can find them on the newsstands and in the library, but they are told which articles will be used for testing and they are careful to avoid them.

6. Group discussion. On some days, speeded reading is followed by discussion. For example, the class might break into small groups to discuss one or more questions, as: "What point is the author trying to make? Do you agree with the author? What would you do about the problem presented in this article? Have you ever had an experience like this? Do you think this is a true and complete picture of the situation?"

The instructor should make the first questions for discussion quite specific. Otherwise, inexperienced students will flounder and fail to make efficient use of time. Each group is told that their conclusions will be reported to the whole class and is asked to choose a recorder and a leader. These roles are explained. The recorder of each group keeps a record of opinions expressed, points emphasized, agreement or disagreement of members, conclusions reached, etc. The leader keeps the group talking, trying to ensure that every member has a chance to voice an opinion or make a contribution. The instructor warns the group when the end of the time is near. The recorder checks his summary with his own group and makes corrections if necessary. The class reconvenes and hears the report given by each recorder. At this point, the instructor makes a general summary of all reports showing points of agreement and disagreement.

As might be expected, students need preparation for the roles of leader, recorder, and group members and for evaluating group efforts. Training for effective group membership and leadership is described in a later chapter.

This activity is an exceedingly important one, as we have mentioned before. Through voicing opinions, judging the author's intention, evaluating the content of an article, differing or agreeing with classmates, the student is stimulated to *think* about what he has read. In conducting discussion, the instructor constantly returns this question to the students, "What do you think about this?" Practice in judging and weighing evidence is preparation for getting the meaning next time. The reading class can become a class in general education. Through properly conducted discussion, process, skills, and mechanics of reading are seen in their proper perspective as aids to getting meaning.

Experience in communicating with others is related to improvement in reading. As one of Marion Monroe's pupils said, "Reading is only talk wrote down." Retarded readers do not know this. They learn it by talking as well as by reading. When they do learn it by virtue of their own experience, reading becomes less formidable.

People live and work and play in groups, and they learn through reacting to and with other people. The student's peer group probably has a more profound influence on his thinking and behavior than any other group. Group learning among one's peers is a permanent kind of learning. If the potential and motivations within the group are ignored, the teacher is losing a valuable ally. A one-way flow between teacher and pupil is not effective; a two-way flow between the teacher and pupil is little better. An all-round kind of participation, sharing, and multiple reactions between class members is a dynamic experience. Counseling and tutoring can help the retarded reader, but nothing can take the place of group experience.

Since reading students are often shy and uncommunicative, they talk more freely in small groups than before the entire class. "Buzz sessions" have been over-worked and often used inexpertly. People are so tired of them that some say with tongue in cheek they would not be surprised to find commencement exercises conducted by buzzing the audience. A librarian, rebelling against a plethora of book reviews, claims she intends to fill her next engagement by buzzing the audience on the question, "What books have you read?" Nevertheless, dividing the reading class into small groups increases opportunities for participation and gives the shy member a chance to make his contribution.

Group discussion should also be encouraged among younger pupils. When they have an opportunity to say whether they like the story and the people in the story, what they think is coming next, what is the most interesting part, etc., they see a purpose in reading. They like to tell which character they would like to be, how this story could be made into a play, what is new in this story.

WARM-UP

Occasionally, a brief warm-up period of reading is substituted for the skimming exercise, or encouraged in the few minutes before the class begins. Students themselves often suggest that they would like to use the interval between classes to read the jokes and shorter articles which are not suitable for speeded reading or discussion. The more able readers also like to read while they wait for the slower ones to finish the speeded reading.

The magazines are distributed before the students come into the classroom. Certain articles are earmarked for class use. Students are free to read any others they may choose.

The trust demonstrated by the instructor may be a factor in improvement. A substitute teacher, failing to understand the routine, used the usual classroom approach to testing, distributing the materials immediately before speeded reading, instructing students not to turn the magazine over until she so indicated, etc. A murmur of surprise rippled over the class, and one student voiced the sentiment of the class: "She doesn't trust us!" The teacher inquired how the exercise was usually conducted. A chorus replied, "Our teacher trusts us."

VOCABULARY STUDY

Many words have come into cognition of the reading student with a negative connotation. He resists learning them. Looking up words in a dictionary has been a meaningless and often futile experience. There has been little or no cumulative effect. The teacher, therefore, is obliged to do more than present a list of words for study. The words for study should be chosen from among those which can have some relevance for the students. When possible, vocabulary study should cover words which can be found in the reading for the same day. Word lists for this purpose offered in standard English textbooks are often too difficult for retarded readers and without meaning for them. Some are so rare and so infrequently used even by college professors that they do not make sense to the struggling reading student. Few students are likely to have any occasion to use "veridical," "decennary," "ellipsis," or "hemachrome" in daily conversation. Give them words they can use often and make the drill as much fun as possible.

After studying a word list, the students should be permitted to select the words they anticipate they will be able to use. The teacher adds suggestions, and together they agree on a final list. After further study, the relevance and use of the words might be the subject of discussion, followed by a test requiring sentences using the words. Students will enjoy discussing the test after it is scored.

Word games, finding synonyms, and other vocabulary drills can be used about twice a week. The instructor says, "I am thinking of a word which means . . . What is it?" Later, he invites the students to offer definitions for response by the rest of the class. This activity is popular among students, and it is amazing how quickly they begin to improve. It requires very little class time.

In time, the vocabulary exercise becomes spontaneous. It is amazing to watch the transformation. Students learn to think quickly, to offer a definition, to respond to the definition offered by others. At this point, the instructor can sit back and watch the show.

Younger students rise to the challenge to "find the word on page 30 which means beautiful (or small or big, etc.)." Completion exercises are useful. In the lower grades, vocabulary study may precede reading, to prepare the pupils to meet new words.

The teaching aids which come with most graded textbooks usually contain word lists and suggested exercises. New words are indicated, and at times suggestions are given as to which of the new words are likely to occur most frequently in reading, so that the teacher can choose those on which it will be most profitable to spend time.

Some teachers encourage their students to keep lists of words which are new to them. Some help the student choose a list which he thinks he can use to say the things he wants most to say. Students may be intrigued by the idea of keeping a list of especially meaningful and expressive words, as "Ten Dollar Words" and "Five Dollar Words."

SPELLING

Most poor readers are also poor spellers. When possible, spelling drill should be closely related to reading and to creative writing. As will later be explained, students are most motivated to learn to spell those words which help them write something they really want to write. If possible, part of the list for study should be made from errors made on papers, or at least from the daily reading selections. Numerous spelling lists are available for use at upper educational levels. A book for this purpose is *The University Spelling Book* by T. C. Pollock and W. D. Baker (Prentice-Hall, Inc., Englewood Cliffs, N. J., 1955). In addition to a list of most frequently misspelled words, this text includes sections on the use of the dictionary, spelling rules, prefixes and suffixes, words that sound alike, and memory devices. Included are some ingenious exercises in proof-reading and supplying missing letters in commonly misspelled words.

PERSONNEL SERVICES

Counseling, group therapy, and play therapy are personnel services which can facilitate remediation. They are best offered by professionally trained workers. Role-playing and new methods of group leadership also demand special training. Descriptions of these services cannot be detailed enough to prepare a teacher to give them, but the teacher will get a glimpse of how they might be of use.

If teachers understand how the specialist can help them, they will be willing to seek out and make use of their services, be more alert to symptoms which suggest the need for remediation and be prepared to co-operate with personnel workers to bring about improved personal adjustment whenever possible. Understanding personnel methods helps teachers to communicate with the specialists. The informed teacher is prepared to welcome the services of new staff members.

Even though no such services are available, knowledge of their processes helps teachers understand and respond to their pupils. Personnel principles can be applied to teaching. Adequately trained specialists working with both teachers and students would be the ideal arrangement. In-service training with professionally trained workers as consultants is valuable. If professional services cannot be procured, for financial or other reasons, summer-school classes and workshops for the classroom teacher are partial solutions. Teachers already give some of these services. In many schools, there is no other resource. Whatever help they can get to make this work more effective is all to the good. Evidences of the value of personnel services to the retarded reader are given in Chapter 1 and throughout this book.

GROUP PROBLEM-SOLVING

Since reading students are commonly troubled by personal, social, and emotional problems, some time should be given to discussing related subjects chosen by them or indicated by their responses to questionnaires and tests. After some group solidarity has been achieved, the instructor explains that most of the students have indicated concern about a number of non-academic questions and that solving such problems can lead to improvement in reading skills. The students are told that talking these questions over together can lead to a solution, and they are invited to list those they would like to discuss. The instructor writes them on the blackboard, calling attention to those which are stated more than once and to some which might be classified together. Then he asks if he may add some of the problems indicated by their responses to tests and questionnaires. Through teacher-student planning, the agenda for future meetings is prepared. A certain period or part of a period is set aside each week for the purpose of discussing and trying to solve personal problems common to the group.

Some of the same subjects are suggested by class after class. The instructor can almost predict that social inadequacy will be listed. Popular items are study habits, what to talk about on a date or at a party, lack of ability to concentrate, desire to make friends or to hold friends. The instructor knows from test data that feelings of insecurity, inadequacy, and inferiority are certain to be present. If they are not openly expressed, he is prepared to recognize hesitant statements in this direction.

Group problem-solving may take at least three forms: (1) discussions provoked by reading selections on non-personal issues, such as the growing of rice in India, or the religious beliefs of the Druse; (2) exploration of problems agreed upon by the class; (3) discussion growing out of the reading of articles which touch on their personal interests and problems.

In all of these sessions, the students are encouraged to express their own thoughts, opinions, and feelings. An effort is made to help them weigh evidence and arrive at conclusions, but in each type of class the instructor plays a slightly different role. In academic discussions, the objectives are getting meaning, increasing speed, learning new facts, and exercising critical thinking. In this context the instructor is leader and resource consultant. The personal development sessions are focused on learning about self and others and human nature. During these periods, an important function of the instructor is to help the students to relieve themselves of worries and fears and to work through questions which do not ordinarily arise in the classroom. Communication beyond the surface level becomes increasingly possible. Exchange of opinions among class members leads to their discovery that they are not alone in their problems. They learn that they can be themselves and still be liked and accepted. In time, the students begin to respond to feelings expressed by classmates and to exhibit increased understanding of self and others. Questions arising in class are brought up in the counseling interview. Some begin to feel the need for counseling and welcome the opportunity to pursue a subject in privacy or to introduce more intimate problems.

Reflection of feeling is the instructor's major technique in the personal development discussions. It can also be used incidentally during class periods devoted to skills. Occasionally, response to feeling leads quite naturally to digression from the daily routine. If the question is important to the entire class and if they agree to take time right then to discuss it, that is the time when it is most interesting and most urgent to them, the discussion is most likely to be of benefit. The students might be asked if they want to pursue the subject immediately, save it for the weekly personal development discussion, or whether in their opinion it is of interest to only a few members. If it is not of concern to the majority of the students, the instructor can suggest that it be brought up in interview. While such a digression can lead to unusual spontaneity and insights, the instructor must be alert to the real sentiments of the class. Some students prefer not to deviate from the regular routine and grow impatient to get on with the work. Others may purposely interrupt the class to enhance their own sense of power over the group or to escape the routine. If the class agrees on the daily routine and on setting aside time for discussing personal problems, the instructor is taking a privilege from them if he lets one or a few members disturb the usual schedule. He violates his own principles and takes responsibility which he has voluntarily given to the students unless he ascertains the wishes of the group.

The third type of discussion, growing out of selections on personal problems has the advantage of a third-person approach to matters which may trouble most of the students. They may feel more comfortable discussing a problem impersonally. Students need not accept the author's solutions. They can raise questions, "Is this a problem to many people? Do we agree with the author's analysis, statement of causes, solutions? Can we use this? Can we apply what he says to our own experiences? Can we offer other explanations and arrive at our own conclusions?"

Group problem-solving will be more thoroughly explored in Chapter 5. Various approaches will be described and actual examples of class discussion will be reproduced. Suitable materials for priming personal development discussions will be named and suggestions given on how to use them. Meeting resistance and other emergency situations will be explored.

ROLE-PLAYING

Spontaneity and interest in personal development discussions can be aroused by role-playing. Insights develop into the feelings and behavior of oneself and others. Shy students can explore threatening experiences and prepare for social events. Sometimes the student plays himself, and sometimes he plays the role of another person.

Suitable situations for role-playing are suggested by student statements of problems. Situations which usually provoke a wholehearted response are: starting a conversation with a new acquaintance; making conversation with a professor at a dinner party; asking a girl for a date; talking on the way to the movie; interviewing a prospective employer. Relationships with parents, brothers and sisters, and roommates lend themselves to role-playing. The instructor gives a brief description of the situation, asks for volunteers or chooses the cast, and leaves the lines and actions to the actors. The little scene is followed by discussion from the audience, and the actors who tell how they felt while acting out the incident. The instructor reflects the feelings expressed by students.

One class agreed that starting a conversation was to them a formidable situation. The instructor explained, "You two boys are standing on the steps taking a break before your next class. You don't know each other, but I know both of you, so I introduce you." He made the introduction and left the situation with them. After several sessions of role-playing, the class made the surprising discovery that to make conversation one isn't required to offer world-shaking pronouncements and that success in small talk depends on friendliness, seeing the other's point of view, on listening as well as talking. Many students remark that the reading they do in reading class gives them something to talk about.

Talking on the way to the movie and talking on a Coke date are two favorite role-playing situations. Male students state repeatedly that these situations present real problems to them, sometimes restraining them from asking for a date for fear they will "run out of talk." Role-playing presents enough of a challenge to be interesting and is real enough to facilitate learning. Yet the threat of failure is not so great as in the real situation.

Characters in the scene "asking a girl for a date" became somewhat heated when the girl refused. During the conversation which followed, the girl explained that while she couldn't go, she was glad to be asked. The boys who sympathized to a man with the rejected suitor were greatly surprised. They had not thought very much about how the girl feels. In the ensuing discussion, the boys discovered that refusal did not necessarily imply that they were unacceptable. Previous relations between boys and girls in the class had been somewhat strained. An improvement in group cohesiveness was observed to follow this experience.

Role-playing is especially suitable for young children. They enjoy acting the roles of the teacher, parent, visitor, big brother, or themselves in different situations. The teacher can get insights into how she appears to the students. Pupils learn how others feel. Children can be helped to meet new situations: welcoming a new pupil, visiting an industry, giving a party. Home problems come to light in the small dramas. Discussion following role-playing help the children to understand the behavior of others and themselves.

Puppetry is also a useful device. Anonymity is preserved in the puppet theater, and the children are free to express their real feelings. The teacher can help by responding accurately to these expressions.

PLAY THERAPY

The conduct of play-therapy sessions is believed to require intensive preparation, although one university instructor says that he has been able in one semester to train elementary-school teachers, school nurses, and school principals to use it effectively. The play therapist provides toys, modeling clay, paints, crayons, and other materials through which the child can express his feelings, wishes, and thoughts. As the child uses them, he may talk freely. The therapist responds both to the talk and to other expressions. If he hits or breaks the doll he has made of clay, the therapist says, "You are angry with the doll." If the child gives it a name, the therapist uses the name. If the doll represents the child's mother, brother, or playmate, the therapist reflects the aggressions or love or pity expressed toward the person by the child.

Some expressions will be inconsequential. The therapist tries to recognize and respond to those which are significant. He follows the child's expressions closely and does not get ahead of the child. If the doll is not named, he does not give it a name, although he may suspect what person it represents.

Through observing behavior in a relatively free situation, adults come to see the world as the child sees it. As in the counseling process and group therapy, if therapy is successful, they observe a rise and decline of negative and destructive emotions and the beginnings of positive emotions. When allowed to express what he really feels, the child may be able to rid himself of disabling fears and resentments and work through his problems to more productive use of his energies. In a climate of acceptance, he has a chance to begin to feel that he is a person of worth. The toys and creative materials present a third person situation in which the client can project his fears and other feelings without embarrassment or fear of punishment or reprisal. Play therapy is often accompanied by contacts with parents, who may be the source of the trouble.

Therapy sessions can be conducted for more than one child at a time. The advantage is that the therapist can respond to the interaction between the children: "Tom wants the truck and Barry wants it, too." Some say they can handle as many as 10 or 12 in play therapy, but ordinarily two or three small children are enough to handle. With more, the situation is likely to get out of hand, and the therapist finds it difficult to follow and respond to all that is going on. The feelings of aggressive children are more readily recognized than those of withdrawn children.

The limits of the situation are clearly explained. Harmful acts to the therapist, to other children, or to self are not permitted. While cheap toys can be destroyed, such equipment as a tape recorder or permanent fixtures are "out of bounds."

In meeting violence, the therapist responds, "I know you want very much to do this, but no . . . ." If necessary the child is restrained by force, but the therapy should be terminated for the day at this point. The therapist should remember that there will be times when he can say, "I know you want very much to do this, so go ahead."

References on these subjects will be found in the bibliography. Classes in play therapy are given in some universities under a variety of course titles: elementary-school guidance, individual clinical treatment, practicum with children, projective techniques, and others.

ANALYSIS OF PROPAGANDA

The stereotypy of reading students is appalling. Ability to get meaning is severely limited by the narrowness of thinking. To expand horizons a little and to encourage critical thinking, it is well to offer the class some information on propaganda techniques.

One approach is a lecture on the devices of card stacking, glittering generalities, name calling, plain folks approach, double question, testimonials, and various transfer techniques. Explanations of propaganda devices appear in the following texts: *The Challenge of Democracy* by Theodore P. Blaich and Joseph C. Baumgartner, Harper, 1947, pp. 532–534; *The Analysis of Propaganda* by William Hummel and Keith Huntress, William Sloane, 1949, pp. 51–69; *How to Understand Propaganda* by Alfred McClung Lee, Rinehart and Company, 1953, pp. 58–75; "How to Detect Propaganda" by Clyde R. Miller.[3] Similar information can be found in numerous texts on logic, philosophy, and psychology.

Illustrations of the various propaganda devices, taken from current newspapers and magazines, will help the students to understand how they influence thinking. For example, a newspaper story used a direct quotation from the governor of the state. Although the quotation was accurate, it was taken from a speech favoring one bill before the legislature and placed in juxtaposition to a discussion of another bill to which the governor was opposed. Reading students, presented with this illustra-

---

[3] Miller, Clyde R., "How to Detect Propaganda," reproduced in James I. Brown, *Efficient Reading*, D. C. Heath and Company, Boston, 1952, pp. 33ff.

tion, were aghast. Apparently, they had assumed that anything in print must be gospel truth.

Also impressive to reading classes is a study of the effect of propaganda on the thinking of college students. In this experiment, a large group of college students was asked to read editorials favorable to Hughes, the Prime Minister of Australia during World War I. Another group was exposed to editorials unfavorable to Hughes. After reading 15 of these articles, the students were tested with an attitude scale. Of those who had read the favorable editorials 98 per cent were biased in favor of Mr. Hughes. Of the group who had read the unfavorable articles, 86 per cent were biased against him. When the attitude scale was given again after an interval of four months, the bias of each group was almost as strong as it was at the close of the experiment.[4]

After hearing a brief lecture describing various propaganda devices and reviewing illustrations of their use, a group of reading students were given an article and asked to identify the devices used by the author. The class was divided into small groups for discussion, and their recorders reported the conclusions of each group to the class. As an outside assignment, the members were asked to write a critique of the article, explaining the use of propaganda. Variations of this comment were common, "If a person didn't know anything about propaganda, this article would be very misleading."

Analyzing the article, "The Controversial Mr. Strauss," condensed from *Fortune* magazine in *Reader's Digest,* students offered the following comments:

"The title of the article is propaganda. It suggests a controversy and there is none mentioned in the article as it is entirely favorable to Mr. Strauss."

"I noticed these glittering generalities: deeply religious, naturally sociable, one of our generation's outstanding Americans, extraordinary successful private business career, saved the United States from disaster, recognizable prototype of Western man, optimistic, shrewd in business dealings, humanistic, unshakable moral equanimity."

"The author uses the plain folks approach when he tells that Mr. Strauss worked as a simple shoe salesman, worked for Hoover for nothing, lived on his small savings, later raised cattle and grain, lived with his family in a modest brick row house."

"This article contains testimonials from Eisenhower, Hoover, and a

---

[4] Annis, A., and N. C. Meier, "The Induction of Opinion through Suggestion of Means of 'Planted Content,' " *J. soc. Psychol.,* vol. 5, 1934, pp. 65–81. Reproduced in Floyd L. Ruch, *Psychology of Life,* Scott, Foresman & Company, Chicago, 1951, pp. 655ff.

Navy officer. Hoover called him a jewel of a secretary. The author builds Strauss up more by telling that he was a close friend of Robert Taft and a full partner in a firm rated as worth a million dollars."

"This author makes Mr. Strauss look very good. He started as a shoe salesman and got to be a member of a million dollar firm. He is religious and intelligent and modest and generous and a hard worker and a good scientist. He worked for Hoover without pay. He is supposed to be patriotic and very wise. I wonder if anybody is really this good."

To carry analysis further, the instructor can introduce articles which present opposing points of view. Although, the search for suitable materials and their adaptation for the use of retarded readers is time-consuming, student response is very rewarding. A good discussion and much interest was provoked in several classes by a series of articles on academic freedom. The arguments for controls were presented in two articles. The case for freedom was presented by selections from the Bulletin of the American Association of University Professors and a digest of an article by Robert Hutchins.[5] The latter were cut and partially rewritten in simpler vocabulary. Among the various possibilities are these subjects: Federal aid to education, public vs. private power, public vs. private schools, the role of the United States in the world community.

COUNSELING

There will be an entire chapter on the subject of counseling, but it should also be mentioned here as one of the major methods of helping the retarded reader. As we have described in previous chapters, reading disability is often complicated by social, emotional, and personal problems, as well as questions of educational and vocational choice. Individual interviews give the student an opportunity to review his progress with the teacher, ask questions, discuss problems, work out plans, blow off steam, etc. He may want to discuss his test results, elaborate on a problem discussed in the class, or explore his relationships with his wife, roommate, or parents. Married students come to talk about reading and return to relate the problems involved in adjusting to their new responsibilities. Freshmen, away from home for the first time, confide homesickness and difficulties involved in learning new rules. Others are dismayed to find that they read only half as fast as their roommates. Some seek the reassurance that somebody is personally interested in them. The importance of the counseling relationship is demonstrated when former and current students drop in to share the news that they

[5] Hutchins, Robert, "Are Our Teachers Afraid to Teach?" *Look Magazine*, March 9, 1954.

passed a difficult examination, received an invitation to an important social event, found a way to go home for the weekend, cleared up a misunderstanding with another teacher, etc.

Younger students have their problems, too. Stevie has a new baby sister; he has three other sisters and hoped this one would be a boy. David's father told him he mustn't bring home any more books to read; he must help with the farm work after school. Linda's little brother tore her spelling workbook and she is worried about it. Jim's mother was up all night watching for baby pigs and she couldn't give out his spelling words to him. Debby's mother wants her to be perfect. Consequently she can never be satisfied with her achievements. Little Paul has bad dreams. He was once tied to a chair, and in his dreams he can't run; he can't get away. All of these matters are real and serious to these pupils. They are just as important as family illness or the loss of a job would be to an adult.

These excerpts from case notes suggest that progress may be accelerated by counseling:

CASE B. G.: No increment in speed and comprehension apparent until after mid-semester when student began counseling interviews. Following a series of counseling interviews, she made a gain of 40 words per minute during the remaining weeks of the semester without loss of comprehension and stated that she was able to apply improved skills to other classes.

CASE S. S.: Salutatorian of his high-school graduating class. Scores below the 21st percentile on the first standardized reading test. In interview, discussed limitations, demands of college classes, plans for future. Ranked in the 50th percentile on the second reading test.

CASE T. M.: After three interviews, showed her first gains in speed and comprehension on daily progress chart. Standardized test and retest showed a gain from the 35th to the 50th percentile in speed and from the 40th to the 88th percentile in reading comprehension by end of semester.

VISUAL TRAINING

It is very difficult for a student with certain visual problems to make progress in reading even though he may be endowed with adequate mental ability. If visual training is given by an optometrist, orthoptist, ophthalmologist, or oculist, there should be some means of communication between the teacher and the physician or therapist. Changes in visual performance require changes in the nervous system and affect the whole personality. Each person working with the student has information which will help the other to understand his needs and behavior.

Some physicians and optometrists are interested in working with teachers and counselors on problems of retarded readers. Five- and six-year courses in optometry are now offered by a number of leading universities. As much or more psychology is required for a degree in optometry as for a teaching certificate.

LECTURES

No lecture to retarded readers should consume an entire period. Talks should be informal, concise, and brief. Occasionally, as we have mentioned, it is desirable to make explanations, to give information, or, as the students say, "to give the pitch" for discussion. Used in this manner, lecture serves a useful purpose. It also satisfies the students who expect the teacher to play a decisive role. Brief talks on problems of reading students, the class procedures, roles of leaders and group members, understanding human nature, emotions and the learning process, propaganda devices, have been highly rated by reading students when evaluating the effectiveness of teaching methods.

It is perfectly legitimate to take time to tell a joke or an amusing anecdote occasionally. A college professor adds this comment on effective teaching, "In order to hold the interest of students it is sometimes necessary to indulge in amateur theatrics (hamming, that is)." He is one of many teachers who can use such tricks successfully. Others, less skillful, merely embarrass their classes. These devices should be used sparingly. There is danger that the teacher will become the "star" of the class, leaving little time or opportunity for those who need it badly to become involved and to shine.

CREATIVE WRITING

Creative writing is described here as an adjunct to reading. Its aim is neither polished performance nor preparation for professional writing, but rather the encouragement of spontaneity and interest. Words and grammar make sense to students only when they use them to say things they really want to say. A word which says exactly what a person thinks or feels gathers meaning to be applied in reading. Grammar is seen as a real need if it ensures the writer that he will be understood. The desired result is not forthcoming if the student has little to say on a subject or cares nothing about saying it. Some of the stereotyped subjects which dog the footsteps of the unfortunate English student dull the appetite for writing and inhibit the imagination. People learn to write and spell by writing, and they learn other skills that carry over to reading. The reverse is also true. English instructors report that reading students improve in writing performance, both skill and length of composition, equally as much as students who take the traditional English class instead of reading. That is, students who spend three days weekly in reading class plus two days in English class are reported to make as much progress in theme writing as students of similar abilities who spend five days a week in English class. Probably, the experience of creative thinking contributes to improvement in both writing and reading.

Some hints have been given regarding coordinating writing with reading. Students usually enjoy writing critiques pointing out the use of propaganda, because they are proud to be demonstrating new skill and they find it rather exciting to be "in the know." They often welcome the opportunity to write a critique of the class, telling what parts have been most helpful to them and how they think it might be improved. One of the most popular subjects for reading students is "Things That Make Me Angry." Good responses are made to these titles: "Things I Like, People I Like and Why, Wishes, Why I Agree (or Disagree) with This Author."

Younger pupils show much more interest in writing when they are permitted to write about ideas they want very much to convey. A second-grader who had shown little interest in any schoolwork was galvanized into new effort when he fell in love with a little girl in the next grade. In contrast with the teachers of yesterday, the teacher helped him write his love letter. He had always spelled the word "love" as l-i-v-e. In this important epistle, it had to be correct. After that there was no more trouble with the spelling of love. Obviously it became more meaningful in terms of his feelings. The experience of actually conveying something he wanted to say was very rewarding. This child had received little affection. He had never before in the presence of his teacher expressed affection for anyone. This was a very important learning situation.

Another letter of supreme importance to him was written to his grandfather. He was a rejected child, living with unsympathetic, punitive relatives. His dearest wish was to visit his grandfather. He wanted to write the letter asking to visit him plainly and accurately and neatly in order to be sure that his grandfather would be able to read it and would be favorably impressed. After being encouraged to communicate ideas which were important to him, he greatly increased his volume of writing. His first stories consisted of one laborious sentence each. By the close of the school year, he would voluntarily write a page or more. Although these experiences in communication were not the only aids given him, they contributed greatly to his progress in reading. During the year, he made gains in reading skills at one and a half times the rate of the average second-grader.

A very illuminating incident occurred in a third-grade class. A retarded reader suddenly became interested in forecasting the weather. He set up a radio station in the first-aid room with an old telephone, a map, and other appropriate props and recruited three other third-grade boys. They spent all of their recesses for days forecasting the weather, consulting maps and the encyclopedia, and assembling thermometers, make-believe barometers, strings, and wires. The teacher obligingly postponed the study of night and day during the science period to explore the mysteries of high and low pressure areas, clouds and rain, etc. A real barometer was procured; daily records were made. A visiting science teacher spoke on the subject and brought along an anemometer and a rain gauge. The interest of the class was captured. During the study, they wrote and wrote about the weather. The leader of the movement had hardly been able to recognize the difference between "sat" and "saw." All at once, he began to read. At the close of the term when standardized tests were given, he could recognize words such as barometer, thermometer, weather, instrument, etc., and even spell some of them. The project was a learning situation only because it was pursued while the students were interested. At a later date, their interest would not have been so intense, and less learning would have taken place. This transfer of skill from writing to reading appears to us to occur only when the student feels that what he is writing is worth saying.

Pupils of all ages appear to enjoy writing about how music makes them feel. Upon hearing the Beethoven *Moonlight Sonata*, elementary-school pupils produced these varied responses:

SEVENTH-GRADER: Once upon a time there was a very sad little water drop. He hadn't anyone to play with and he was very lonesome because he lived in the big river. All the other water drops were older and didn't like him.

FIFTH-GRADER: It makes me think of a lullaby. The second part makes me think of a little girl skipping.

FOURTH-GRADER: The slow part makes me think of a wolf creeping through the woods trailing a deer. The fast part makes me think of the wolf killing the deer. Then the slow part again makes me think of the deer dead and the wolf eating it.

THIRD-GRADER: It makes me think of water. The last part makes me think of Jesus when he found out he would have to be killed.

SECOND-GRADER: The first part sounds like a cowboy riding along on a horse. When it gets to the loud part some robbers are after the cowboy.

FIRST-GRADER: I like it. This is fun. Thank you Mr. Beethoven.

Facets of personal adjustment are revealed in these writings. Loneliness, happiness, threatening forces, and spontaneous pleasure are expressed. Equally important is the fact that the pupils felt they were saying something important. They were communicating their thoughts and feelings to a receptive reader. What does it matter that they weren't inspired to write about moonlight and romance?

Group compositions of the work-experience type help to build vocabulary and facilitate communicative skills. Although this technique is most commonly used in the primary grades, it can be effective with upper grades and even with retarded readers of high-school age. Following an interesting group experience or discussion, the group dictates a story or report or critique which is written on the blackboard by the instructor or a class member. Each member is given an opportunity to add to the story. Then the students copy whatever parts they choose and add any other ideas that occur to them. New words are introduced. The students are actively involved. They think about what to say and how to say it, hear themselves say these things, see their thoughts correctly written, and write some of them. Correct spelling, form, and grammar are presented. The finished product represents the coordinated efforts of the group. Excursions, audio-visual aids, talks by visitors, pictures, and story-telling can be used as springboards to work-experience lessons. The same sort of use can be made of play-days, programs for the public, playground incidents, new school equipment, parties, and exhibits of the children's work. Diaries, autobiographies, records of the school year, and letters to children of other nations can be valuable. Activities encouraged in the Junior Red Cross program arouse interest.

Children in one school derived a great deal of benefit from a study of local history and the writing of stories about events in the lives of their ancestors. The final product, illustrated and bound by the children themselves, represented satisfying group activities in many areas of learning.

Another group saw new value and meaning in words as throughout the school year they revised and rewrote a set of playground rules. Opportunities for learning new words occur frequently in teacher-pupil planning for special events, daily lessons, or daily routine.

In these examples from classroom experience, the primary teacher will recognize a variation of the work-experience technique which can be applied to groups of all ages. One of the advantages of the technique is that it is a real experience as contrasted with the artificiality of the usual language lesson. Another is that the teacher gets a glimpse into the world as seen by the students. No less important is the satisfaction felt by the teacher when the pupils gain in enthusiasm, spontaneity, and skill.

RECORDING

A recorder was made available for use in a remedial-reading clinic. The clinician asked the parents of her pupils to take them to various spots of interest; museums, lakes, art galleries, industries, etc. Each child dictated a story of his experience into the recorder and heard his own voice telling the story. It was then typewritten. The pupil studied the story, helped by a tutor until he knew the new words. When he could read it, he was permitted to take it home to read to his parents. All pupils who participated were greatly interested in this project, and there is no doubt that they learned to recognize new words. The printed word took on more meaning, and motivation was improved.

INSTRUMENTS AND MACHINES

Among the variety of machines on the market to improve reading skills is the Viewlex. It is arranged to project a page of print on a screen. Phrases become distinct to the reader as with a smooth, even pace a shaft of light moves across the projected page, focusing on a part of a line of print at a time. Some similar instruments perform the same function, but some move jerkily. This machine is very smooth. Selections of varying difficulty are available. The pace can be adjusted to suit the comfort of the reader and increased as desired to improve speed.

Similar in effect are the Stroud films, distributed through the State University of Iowa Bureau of Audio-Visual Instruction. A set of 14 films is presented at increasing rates of speed. The first film is run at the rate of 270 words per minute. The rate is increased with each lesson to 447 words per minute for film 14. After the 14th lesson, instructors often show the first film again to demonstrate to the students how their reading speed has increased. The films are supplemented by three manuals which include film-comprehension tests, supplementary reading materials and tests, keys, and instructions. Materials include stories from *Nature Magazine, Pageant, The Saturday Evening Post, Coronet, The New York Times, American Magazine,* and other publications. They are well-chosen, interesting selections, related to the interests of students in the upper grades and high school. Films and teaching aids were prepared under the direction of Dr. J. B. Stroud, professor of education and psychology at the State University of Iowa.

Other devices for increasing reading speed are the Harvard films, the reading rate controller, and the Metron-O-Scope. One clinician says that the reading rate controller is his favorite gadget. It has the advantage of being the same distance from the eye as the printed page. It is designed for individual use, and the student can regulate his speed by moving a bar down the page. The Metron-O-Scope, distributed by the American Optical Company, controls left-to-right movements by a triple shutter arrangement which exposes a third of a line of print at a time. The rate of speed can be regulated.

All of these instruments and materials have their virtues when used wisely. They are secondary in importance to activities which emphasize getting meaning, but they excite interest and provide practice in rapid recognition. Students usually like them. The instructor needs to know the needs and abilities of his students before choosing one to use. Some of the reading materials used on the films are too difficult for severely retarded readers. Other techniques, such as group discussion, counseling, comprehension testing, and analysis of propaganda should not be neglected. Book and story films can be followed by discussion.

DRILLS AND EXERCISES

Too much drill is deadly. However, used with caution, exercises can be valuable. For example, a class consistently made errors in pronouncing and spelling word endings. This appears to be a common problem among retarded readers of college age as well as younger pupils. Using drills and exercises designed to emphasize differences in endings, their teacher helped them to overcome this handicap. Some illustrations are presented here: What is a word almost like chicken which means more than one? Find a word on page 30 which is almost like hunt, but which tells what the boys in the story did yesterday. The words, started and starting, are alike in some ways and different in some ways; how are they alike and how are they different? If you change the ending of this word to "ing" how does it change the meaning?

Also helpful are completion exercises requiring the pupils to write the same word with different endings. We favor completion exercises over matching, multiple-choice, and true-false items, because writing the word helps to fixate the correct impression. The other three can be used occasionally for variety's sake. Many students say they prefer multiple-choice items.

Some pupils in the lower grades experience difficulty with certain sounds or combinations of sounds. Such a class might be asked to make a list of all the words on a page beginning with the letters *st* or *th,* or whatever sounds seem most troublesome. Discussion might follow on how these words are alike and how they are different.

Similar exercises are available in workbooks, but in order to meet the particular needs of a class of retarded readers, the instructor often finds that he must prepare additional assignments, tailor-made especially for them.

Some attention should be paid to context cues: "What word would make sense here?" For emphasizing meaning, these assignments are suitable: "Write the words in your reading assignment which mean pretty _____, sad _____, big _____, high _____, etc. Make up a good name for page three of the story." The first efforts at choosing a suitable title for a paragraph or page may be disappointing, as, "A Good Story." First attempts may be a reproduction of the first sentence in the story or a phrase from the story or a few words which reflect only a small part of the meaning. With practice and discussion the pupils will become more discriminating.

Teachers trained in the teaching of reading will remember to give the pupils something to read for, "What happened to the lost boy? Why were people surprised when the circus performers knocked at their doors? Why did the lion take a trip?"

Glock[6] uses the same idea in his volume of readings and exercises for college students. A statement of purpose precedes each selection. For example, he asks the students to read to determine the author's feeling toward the lawyer; to learn some important facts about comets; to find out what causes forgetting. Some selections are devoted entirely to the process of reading. Glock asks the students to read them to find out how words communicate meaning, to find suggestions for improving ability to concentrate, to find out how to develop effective study skills.

Finding the little words which make up a big word is an aid to understanding word structure. Techniques relating to structural analysis and word form are explained by Gray.[7] Flash cards and other word games can be used among severely retarded readers whose tested ability falls below the third-grade level. Among the numerous other possibilities are these: illustrating a story and labeling the pictures, matching words with pictures, following instructions for drawing or for action, finding in the reading lessons the same words which appear on the blackboard, finding how many times a word appears on the same page.

OTHER PROCEDURES

Classroom routine can be varied by an occasional panel discussion, symposium, round-table discussion, or brief reports given by class members, followed by group discussion. As their stage fright diminishes, three or four students may be willing to prepare on a subject and discuss it informally before the class. A variation is to ask each participant to prepare, for his colleagues on the program, a list of items on which he feels well enough informed to answer questions, or to prepare a list of questions for other panel members to ask him. This sort of program is best conducted with informality, permitting occasional interruptions and "off

[6] Glock, Marvin D., *The Improvement of College Reading*, Houghton Mifflin Company, Boston, 1954.

[7] Gray, W. S., *On Their Own in Reading*, Scott, Foresman and Company, Chicago, 1948, pp. 67ff.

the cuff" remarks and questions. With practice, grade-school pupils can learn these procedures.

A very popular and motivating activity among elementary-school pupils is "making a play out of the story." They form committees, hold meetings, assign parts, decide what the lion or the clown or the princess should say, what to leave out, and what should come next. They become aware of the values of reading skills as they consult the book to find out just exactly what happened.

Choral reading, learning new songs, preparing for public performances, and choosing a play afford opportunities to learn new words and to attach meaning to reading. Visits to the library promote interest in reading.

The uses of the dictionary, encyclopedia, index, table of contents, and subtitles can be meaningful if there is something the students really want to find out. Otherwise these exercises are drudgery. For example, the children who became interested in the weather were eager to make use of these aids to locate the information they needed. Picture dictionaries are useful for non-readers and pupils retarded below the third-grade level. Phonics workbooks for occasional drill are found to be effective in some cases, even among fourth- and fifth-graders if introduced with care. For example, one fifth-grade girl became interested when she was asked to help some first-grade pupils with their phonics exercises.

Teachers are doubtless familiar with multiple-choice items such as this: "Which of the following sentences best states the main idea of paragraph one? Choose one of four responses." Or this: "Check the four main points of the article in the following list of eight statements."

Both skills and interest are aided by questions like this: "Choose the word or phrase which best describes the boy in the story: friendly, selfish, brave, sad." Interest is usually stimulated by the assignment, "Write what you think might have happened next."

Questions which can be used either in written exercises or discussion are: "How did the girl in the story feel: excited, happy, frightened, worried?" "How did the story make you feel?"

Some teachers like this exercise: Give the number of the page and the number of the paragraph where these questions are answered. Some workbooks offer selections in which the paragraphs are numbered for the convenience of the students. Open-book tests over reading materials can also be used.

FREE READING

Recreational reading helps to increase interest and speed. Science and math students must read slowly and need to balance this kind of reading with a lighter fare. Although college students have only limited time for casual reading, some will welcome lists of light, easy books with a few comments on the nature of each. A bookshelf in the classroom often inspires students to increase their volume of reading. When encouraging outside reading, the instructor can help the slow reader to work up enthusiasm and courage to begin by telling or reading the first few pages.

Cues to the kinds of materials most interesting to retarded readers can be found in their interest-maturity scores. Judging from the results of the study quoted in Chapter 1, we can expect most of them to like stories of adventure, exploration, and feats of physical skill and daring. Attention to individual tastes can stimulate interest. One nine-year-old boy, for example, improved noticeably after being provided with books about boats. A fifth-grade girl was stimulated to read when she discovered a number of interesting stories about horses. Funny stories are always popular. A slow seventh-grader got his start with a Richard Halliburton book. During the remainder of the year, he read 23 books.

Hints as to the characteristics which appeal to retarded readers are given in their remarks about stories. A third-grader says of his reading book, "Well you don't have to wonder very much what's coming next." Another, taking care not to hurt his teacher's feelings, said cautiously, "Well it doesn't seem very logical. I don't believe it could happen." If he liked the story, he said, "That was a good one. I liked that." True adventure was the major interest of a sixth-grader. He always asked, "Is there such a thing? Did it really happen?" If the story was not true, he lost interest.

The level of difficulty should be appraised when selecting materials for an individual or a group. Obviously, a book ceases to be interesting if it requires painful effort.

The comments of Harris[8] on the selection of reading materials apply also to recreational books. For beginning remedial treatment, he recommends using materials one or two grades below the pupils' apparent reading level. As he points out, one cannot always rely on the grade-label of the reading book, as there is a tremendous range of difficulty among readers intended for the same grade. He offers criteria for judging the difficulty and suggestions for preparing pupils to read materials on unfamiliar subjects.

One of the measures of difficulty is the degree to which the reader manifests strain, blinking, yawning, squirming, nervousness, etc. However, such symptoms can also mean that the subject is not interesting to

[8] Harris, Albert J., *How to Increase Reading Ability*, Longmans, Green & Co., Inc., New York, 1940, pp. 203–207.

the pupil. Retarded readers have been known to demonstrate unsuspected skill when confronted with a story they really want to read.

There are numerous interesting stories in easy vocabulary, and the supply is rapidly increasing. Some books in the American Adventure Series (Wheeler Publishing Company) offered at levels from second to tenth grades, are interesting enough to hold the attention of adults. Picture books designed for young children are often witty and clever and appealing to adults. Among the many which might be mentioned are *Andy and the Lion* by Daugherty, *Young Mr. Meeker* by Miriam Mason, *Marshmallow* and other cat stories by Clara Turley Newberry, *Misty of Chinchoteague* and other horse stories by Marguerite Johnson, *Little House on the Prairie* and all of Laura Ingals Wilder's books. Some books are chosen solely because they are fun to read, some because they appeal to special interests of individual pupils, and some because they help the retarded reader to express emotions which he needs to express. For example, *Lutie* by Margot Austin is about a little mountain boy who did not want to go to school. He threatens to make an "awful scene," and he does, several times. Thus the reader is able to enjoy the vicarious expression of aggression without threat, although in real life he might restrain himself for fear of losing status and security with parents or teacher. *The Pirate's Apprentice* by Peter Wells serves a similar purpose. *Timid Timothy* by Williams tells about a kitten who learned to be brave. *The Big Lonely Dog* by Harris is the story of a dog whom nobody wanted. Both express feelings which may be problems to retarded readers, and both contain just the right amount of repetition, enough to help the pupil learn words, but not enough to be monotonous. Conrad Richter's *The Trees, The Fields,* and *The Town* are popular, and selections from them have been used with success among elementary-school, high-school, and college students. Especially appealing to boys are the adventures of the pioneer family as they crossed the Appalachian Mountains on foot, two boys who went to the mill with corn loaded on the back of a reluctant calf, the boy who cut off his own finger after being bitten by a snake. These and other incidents lend themselves to dramatization which is a valuable and enjoyable learning experience. The importance of the balance of nature is painlessly taught in the Richter books by dramatic illustrations which can be related to science units. *The Way West* by A. B. Guthrie and *Tales of the South Pacific* by James Michener excite interest. Students characteristically remark that they never knew before that reading could be so much fun. Some teachers and librarians are inclined to frown on picture books which contain little reading, but they are exactly right for pupils who dread the thought of plodding through a whole page of print. They approach a short paragraph with more courage and feel a sense of accomplishment when they finish the book.

MATERIALS FOR CLASSWORK

The *Reader's Digest* offers a variety of topics for high-school and college classes. Also available is a teacher's manual with exercises, tests, vocabulary drill, reading time chart, and other aids. A junior edition is published by the *Reader's Digest* for younger readers. In order to counterbalance a possible bias on political and other serious issues, it is well to provide some other periodical or paper, such as the *Christian Century, St. Louis Post Dispatch, Washington Post, Reporter, Christian Register,* or *Christian Science Monitor.* If the students are consistently exposed to only one periodical, there is a decided possibility that they will become indoctrinated with one point of view. The reading teacher has a responsibility to avoid indoctrination and to encourage self-decision.

Popular story books can be used in tutoring or in the reading class if the number of pupils is small. A lesson plan can be made over this kind of story just as easily as over the selections in the reading book. The principal difficulty is securing enough copies for a class. Libraries can sometimes supply more than one copy of the same book to be used with those belonging to the school. Some of Margaret Friskey's stories have appeared in reader series. The originals contain 18 labeled pictures inside the cover. A copy of the original can be used with good effect along with the reading book. Portions of *My Weekly Reader* and the *Junior Red Cross Magazine* are suitable for reading classes.

We usually find that poor readers react adversely to the traditional type reader. It is associated in their minds with failure and embarrassment. If so, recreational books are more welcome. At least, if a reading book is used, it should be different from those used previously for a particular group or individual.

Older students like to read about the educational problems with which they are faced. Short and fairly simple materials on this subject can be found in some textbooks, for example, "Proof That You Can Read Faster," "Reading for Main Ideas," "Getting the Author's Point," "Why Building a Reading Vocabulary Is Easy."[9] Also suitable are "Basic Reading Attacks," "How to Read an Essay,"[10] "Vocabulary Development," "Vision and Reading," "Concentration," and "The Problem of Meaning."[11]

[9] Lewis, Norman, *How to Read Better and Faster,* Thomas Y. Crowell Company, New York, 1951.

[10] Shaw, Phillip B., *Effective Reading and Learning,* Thomas Y. Crowell Company, New York, 1955, Chap. 4.

[11] Glock, Marvin D., *The Improvement of College Reading,* Houghton Mifflin Company, Boston, 1954.

Articles on controversial issues arouse interest in further reading. If the instructor has time, he can find appropriately belligerent statements in newspaper and magazine articles. Some other articles that raise questions are these: "Race Purity" by Adolf Hitler, "But for Grown-ups Laughing Isn't Any Fun" by Dr. Seuss, "Evolution" by W. F. Pauli, "The Amenities of Wealth" by Oliver Wendell Holmes, "The Ignoring of Contexts" by S. I. Hayakawa, "The Monster" by Deems Taylor, "Red Spy Masters in America" by J. Edgar Hoover, "The Strategic Freedoms" by Sidney Hook, "Education in the Army" by Robert M. Hutchins, "The Freedom to Search for Knowledge" by Robert M. MacIver;[12] "Faith for Freedom" by Barbara Ward, "The Decline of Conscience" by Willard Sperry;[13] "What Price Freedom" by Robert Maynard Hutchins, "Peace through Law" by William O. Douglas.[14]

Discussion is usually stimulated by a series of articles such as these: "Negro Rights," "His Vote and Your Daughter," "The Federal Role (in the Negro problem)."[15] Several points of view on an issue can often be found in letters to the editor. Especially good sources are *Harper's Magazine* and the *St. Louis Post Dispatch*. A variety of opinions are expressed in such columns in journals for men such as *True* magazine, *Outdoor Life*, and *Field and Stream*. Interest in reading and discussing can often be stirred by focusing on a question of immediate concern to the community or state: public vs. private power, preservation of national forests and public lands, the right of labor to organize. Closer to home may be these questions: working mothers, young couples who live with their parents, college housing for young married students.

A book sometimes used in college classes is *Readings for Opinion* by Earle Davis and William C. Hummell, Prentice-Hall, 1952. The editors offer selections which treat a number of subjects from more than one point of view. This is an excellent idea. The students find, often to their surprise, that some matters have not been settled, that two or more perfectly honest and intelligent opinions can prevail on the same subject. They can decide to take sides with one author or another, or state their own opinions which may differ from either.

The basis for friendly argument can be found in these selections: "The Football Scholarship" by Lyle Owen, "Honor System" by John R. Rober-

[12] *Ibid.*

[13] Wise, J. Hooper, J. E. Congleton, and Alton C. Morris, *The Meaning in Reading*, Harcourt, Brace and Company, Inc., New York, 1953, pp. 209ff.

[14] Brown, James I., *Efficient Reading*, D. C. Heath and Company, Boston, 1952, pp. 140–143.

[15] Lewis, Norman, *How to Read Better and Faster*, Thomas Y. Crowell Company, New York, 1951.

son, "Why I Quit Working" by Jennifer Colton, "College Women Ten Years After" by Mary Morris, "Needed: A College Revolution" by Harold Taylor, "All Things Considered" by Howard Vincent O'Brien.[16]

Challenging questions are raised in the book, *Strange Lands and Friendly People* by William O. Douglas. Farm boys and girls will be interested in the soil-conservation problems of Persian and Arabian farmers. Efforts of some Arab leaders toward land reform are thought-provoking. Douglas describes how some of the border peoples feel toward Russia. His suggestions regarding our relations with the Arab nations might be used as a starting point for a friendly debate. The adventures of his young son on this journey make interesting reading.

The values in incidental reading are known to many teachers who make use of instructions for building model airplanes, planning parties, playing games, or learning a new square dance. Other resources are catalogues, advertisements, travel folders, and book reviews. Reading can be encouraged by liberal use of bulletin boards for notices, announcements, school news, items about students, newspaper items, cartoons, programs, scheduled school events, reminders, jackets from new books, jokes, pictures, riddles. Additional materials are listed in the Appendix.

ATTITUDES OF THE INSTRUCTOR

Reference has been made to the importance of the instructor's attitude toward his students. As described in connection with the discussions of group leadership and counseling, the ideal relationship with the class is one which reflects permissiveness, acceptance, and respect for each member. Belief in their ability to improve is an important factor. Progress may be slow, so the instructor needs patience and sensitivity to small evidences of progress. Ability to sense how each students feels and to convey this understanding is practically indispensable to the teacher of developmental reading.

As one of our psychologist friends remarked, "The word 'elephant' taught by a sour-puss, comes into cognition with a negative flavor." The importance of the teacher's attitude can be seen in simple, everyday learning experiences. Two men were talking about their earliest training in farm work. One had been taught by his competent but hard-driving father who showed impatience with his son's awkwardness. This boy was made to feel that he should be ashamed of himself because he knew so little and could do so little. He felt he was just a nuisance to his father.

[16] Jones, Everett L., *An Approach to College Reading*, Henry Holt and Company, Inc., New York, 1953.

At the same time, he felt resentful because he knew it was unreasonable to expect him to be expert in tasks which were new to him. The other was inducted into farm work by an understanding grandfather who made him feel, "This is a secret and I'm letting you in. I am going to help you learn to do this, because it will be fun for you to know." The grandfather had the sensitivity and interest to explain small steps which he had mastered, but which would be difficult for the beginner. His grandson felt that he was accorded a rare privilege. He further sensed that his grandfather regarded him as a person of worth who deserved to be taught these valuable skills. The first boy felt that his father's motive was to make the farm pay, to turn his son's labor into profit. The other boy felt that he was being taught skills which would help do things he wanted to do.

Ability to enter into the small triumphs of the students is a valuable asset to the teacher. Think what it means to a non-reader when he actually recognizes a new word. Success is more profoundly experienced if somebody else shares the excitement of the moment. Coexperiencing, as we have indicated, is a very dynamic force in learning. A young mother tells us that she will never forget her little daughter's excitement and wonder when she learned that tables and chairs are made from trees. Sharing this delightful discovery made it much more important and meaningful to the child. First-grade teachers know what it means to their pupils for the teacher to join in the self-congratulation and enjoyment when they learn that this word actually means *boy*, or when they read for the first time. Older reading students have been somewhat dulled by failure, but occasionally these vibrant incidents occur to enliven the class. A sensitive teacher will recognize their possibilities. Improvement which comes about during counseling, tutoring, or remedial classes may be a result, in part, of the fact that the student feels, perhaps for the first time, that someone is interested in him as a person.

Although conceding that reward produces more learning than punishment, some teachers are very sparing in their recognition of progress, especially with retarded pupils. As one junior-high-school principal remarked at a teachers meeting, "People are inclined to find fewer things to praise than to criticize." Retarded readers have commonly experienced fewer rewards for schoolwork than the average student. Recognition of their small successes can be very motivating to them.

Praise is most helpful when it is given for a specific achievement. "You are doing fine," means little. More meaningful is this, "I noticed that you are now reading 50 words a minute faster than when you entered the class," or for the non-reader, "Today you could recognize the word, 'that.' It is a new word for you, isn't it?"

Although you have "heard this tune before," let us reiterate that the instructor must start where the pupils are. If a high-school student ranks at the fourth-grade level in reading, it is of no earthly use to give him a volume of Shakespeare, or even James Fenimore Cooper. Offer him *Mr. Tootwhistle's Invention* by Peter Wells or *Pilot Jack Knight* (third-grade level). If he reads them, progress has been made. Non-readers use the words "dog," "cat," "church" in daily conversation. A word in print means nothing to them unless they can use it freely in speaking. Reading begins with the words they know. Other aids include attaching meaning to unfamiliar words.

RELATIONSHIPS WITH PARENTS

The roots of some reading problems are in the home. Contacts between the instructor and the parents of college students are not usually practicable. They are more easily arranged with the parents of public-school pupils.

A change in attitude on the part of the parents can be very helpful. Often the visiting teacher, school social worker, counselor, or remedial instructor can help the parent to understand the way children see things, the kinds of problems they face at school, and what the school is trying to do for them. A social worker was sent to visit the mother of a fifth-grade girl who was somewhat overburdened with the care of her younger brothers and sisters. The social worker mentioned that the girl was very good at sewing and coloring. The mother, formerly apathetic, showed a spark of interest and eventually came to feel pride in her daughter. Such a change in family relations can help the child to feel pride in himself and to face the world with more courage.

The parents of a fourth-grade boy cooperated with his teacher by arranging his room so that he could read in bed. With a good bed light, a nightstand, and a supply of inviting picture books, he developed the habit of reading a little while before going to sleep. After talking with the teacher, the parents made a change in attitude toward the boy from, "We know you can do it. Why don't you?" to "We believe in you." These developments, along with special instruction, contributed to his improvement in reading skills.

A rather indifferent mother was aroused to interest in her son when he demonstrated that he was beginning to read. Although a third-grader, he was a non-reader. When after a few weeks of remediation, he was able to read to her from a primer, she was so surprised and pleased that she ran out and bought ice cream for the whole family. Sharing his success with his family seemed very important to the boy's continued improvement. If the mother had not had several sessions with the school psychologist, she would not have been able to recognize the small signs of progress.

If an interview with the parent cannot be arranged, the next best device is an occasional note, commenting on progress. A decided change in attitude came about in the mother of a second-grade boy after receiving several notes from the teacher. Early in the school year, it was evident that he was a rejected child. His mother had a rigid, punitive attitude. She expected the worst from him and was seldom disappointed. The boy refused to carry the first note home, apparently having had unpleasant experiences with notes from the teacher. At first, the teacher watched closely to find small marks of progress. In time, his behavior and schoolwork improved noticeably, and it was not so difficult to find good things to say. Near the end of the school term, the mother visited the school. In contrast to her early fears and criticisms, she voluntarily praised his progress.

Very little, if anything, is accomplished by notes in a negative vein. The following letters, taken from case files, illustrate the kind of statements which have produced good will toward the school and parental understanding of children. You will notice that they are not necessarily about reading.

SEPTEMBER 30—Dear Mrs. A: John prints very neatly and he nearly always finishes his assignments. This morning, I noticed that he had learned many new words. One of his new words is 'through' which is a hard one for many second-graders.

OCTOBER 25—Dear Mrs. A: John is learning to square dance. He learns very quickly, and the children are glad to have him in the group. He seems to enjoy it.

DECEMBER 1—Dear Mrs. A: I thought you would like to know that John stood behind Miss B's chair today and seated her at the lunch table with a flourish. His classmates admired his good manners.

APRIL 4—Dear Mrs. A: Today I repeated an informal reading test which I gave in October. On the first test, John made 23 errors for every 100 running words, using the first semester second-grade reader. Today, he read in the first semester third-grade reader with only 14 errors for every 100 running words.

In the case of Tommy, the problem was not rejection, but parental indifference. He was middle child in a family of eight. His mother did not willfully neglect him, but the older children needed clothing and the little ones demanded constant attention. Tom slouched in his seat and daydreamed; his shock of long, untidy hair was always in his eyes. After receiving some favorable notes from the teacher, his mother began to take more interest in him, and he improved in many ways. Here are some of the notes sent to her.

NOVEMBER 10—Tommy made a perfect score in spelling today. All the children clapped. He looked very happy. This is his first perfect paper.

DECEMBER 16—You will be glad to know that Tommy is working much faster than ever before. He nearly always finishes his assignments. He is planning to take home a book from the library for outside reading.

FEBRUARY 12—You have probably noticed that Tommy stands and sits straighter since he has begun to feel proud of himself. He washes his hands before lunch without being reminded. In September he read less well than average for his age and grade. The last tests suggest that now he is reading at least as well as the average third-grader.

Counselors and teachers will receive more satisfactory cooperation if they spend some time with parents, preparing them to understand and accept remediation. Sometimes this process requires more than a single interview or more than one group discussion. A brisk review of facts may leave the parent with the determination to prove that the evidence is just not valid. As in the case of parents of mentally deficient children, they may spend energy and time going from one authority to another in the hope of getting someone to agree with their point of view. Some parents are affronted by the idea that their child has a reading disability. Some feel a sense of guilt for having permitted the problem to develop. Parents need to work through their own emotional problems and defenses before they can help their children. One mother, for example, insisted on enrolling her six-year-old in a private school. Two years later, he was still having difficulty with the first-grade reading book. Parental rejection is a basic problem in this case, but the mother cannot permit this explanation to occur to her. The school may not be at fault, but, if she recognizes the reading problem, she feels that she must admit to an error in judgment in sending her son there, so she refuses to believe that he is a retarded reader. The simplest solution for her is to ignore the problem.

It takes time for parents to accept unsavory facts, to be relieved of guilt feelings, to understand the remedial program, to make plans, and to change habits of long standing. Discussion meetings and counseling for parents are important factors in remediation.

Parents can also be enlisted in prevention. Orientation activities for the school beginner can include parents' discussions of the many new situations which the child will face and the resulting emotional strain experienced by many first-graders. Many parents do not understand the range of reading readiness or the methods of teaching reading. They may be apprehensive about the first year and wish to be reassured that their children will be taught by tested methods. Understanding the range of reading readiness will help parents to avoid putting undue pressure on first-graders. Discussion of handicaps to learning might be cautiously introduced to help the parent understand the complicated process of learning to read. Such activities, if properly handled, can make a team of parents and teachers, and may help to avoid the unfortunate situation where the parents glower accusingly on one side and the teachers take a defensive or patronizing attitude on the other. The teacher's role is not that of the expert. The best results will accrue if the teachers can convey the idea that " . . . we are working on these matters together."

A start has been made in some schools toward orientation of beginners and their parents. The usual schedule of events includes a meeting for the parents, the distribution of a booklet about the school, a physical examination for each child, and perhaps one or more psychological tests. Sometimes, the children are given an invitation to visit the first-grade in the spring of the year before. All these are helpful, but they are not enough. Perhaps, some incidents from actual experience will make clear the differences in the teachers' and the parents' point of view. A radio program on the orientation of school beginners was being arranged. A first-grade teacher who was interviewed was firmly convinced that all possible questions of parents had been answered in the booklet and in the meeting. The mother of a first-grader had left the meeting without an opportunity to raise most of her questions and she had failed to find the answers in the booklet. In answer to a question by one mother, the teacher remarked, "Let the school worry about social adjustment. Just you get his galoshes a size larger than his shoes so I can get them on and get him home." One can certainly understand that this comment suggests a formidable daily task for the first-grade teacher. On the other hand, social adjustment is a joint responsibility, which cannot be fully realized without the wholehearted and intelligent cooperation of the parents.

Even if it were true that all questions of parents were answered in one meeting and an orientation handbook, as teachers, we surely know that having the answers does not mean that parents accept them. Any learning by anyone involves a process of emotional acceptance of information. Just having information does not ensure acceptance. A series of meetings and individual conferences with parents, while time-consuming and complicated to arrange, represent a good investment in terms of prevention of reading disability, emotional problems, and parental hostility. Along with remediation, the school has a responsibility to make every possible effort toward prevention. The wrecking-crew operation is the only course for those pupils who have lagged along the way, but a preventive program is less costly for school, pupil, and parent.

Individual interviews with parents offer opportunities to take up questions which are not of general interest to the group or which the parent might feel embarrassed to ask in front of a group. These vary from questions about level of the child's ability to what toilet terms are acceptable to the teacher. Test results can be explained in interviews, and problems which are suggested by the test results can be explored.

If counselors or visiting teachers are employed, they can serve as a link between the home and the school, although some contact between teacher and parent is also desirable. If the teachers must make all of the contacts, they should not be required to do it on their own time. School time should be set aside for the activity, and it is important enough to all concerned to use school time in this fashion. If teachers make the contacts, they should have some preparation. A young teacher began her first interview with the mother of one of her pupils, "Well Jimmy is not as much of a problem as I thought he would be." Such an approach is not calculated to cement pleasant relations between school and parent. A series of teachers' meetings on the purposes of teacher-parent contacts is in order. How to conduct an interview might be a suitable subject for discussion and demonstration. Beginning teachers will profit, but experienced teachers might also welcome an opportunity to talk over their experiences and to learn from a counselor or visiting teacher.

DEFINING STAFF ROLES

A successful developmental reading program requires cooperation among staff members. Administrative support is, of course, a very important factor in its effectiveness. The administrative role is that of leadership in determining the need for remediation, inviting opinions of faculty and parents, acquainting the board of education and the public of the needs of the school, recommending adequate budgetary provisions, and making other necessary administrative arrangements. The astute administrator will recognize that the program will fall short of expectations if it is added to the duties of an overloaded faculty. His attitudes toward the program and toward the faculty will be reflected in their receptiveness toward the new services.

Advance study of the needs of the school, the measures taken by other schools and the possibilities and limitations of the local situation will contribute to a maturely conceived and carefully planned program. Involving the faculty all along the way in study and planning invites their support and understanding of objectives and operation. One of the first steps might be to ask the help of the faculty in appraising the needs of the students. After evidence is gathered, the faculty can share in making decisions. If specialists can be employed, the faculty will be prepared in advance to accept them readily and to cooperate. The administrator is the proper person to promote the idea of in-service training for teachers, to secure outside speakers and consultants, or to organize group discussions with the help of the staff.

Our contacts with public schools lead us to believe that the classroom teacher is very much aware of the problem of reading disability. If the program is built as a result of teacher interest, it has a better chance to be effective than when it is imposed upon the faculty from above. The alert administrator recognizes in their manifest interest the most fruitful opportunity for introducing the developmental program.

The project will not function smoothly unless the administrator assists in arranging for mass testing, adequate supplies and equipment, usable record system, scheduling, and evaluation. Many helpful suggestions will arise from the faculty if they are consulted on these matters. Joint planning will help the faculty to see the problems involved from the viewpoint of the administrator, and they will be helped to understand why some of their ideas cannot be put into practice.

The attitudes of the administrator and faculty toward retarded readers influence the success of the classes. If the students are led to feel that the class is for "dummies" or "oddballs," they will resent being placed in it. If they receive the impression that counseling is only for "queers," they will avoid the service. Parents may also resist the new program, if they feel that placing their children in these classes is a reflection on their abilities or on their own status. The administrator can smooth the way through effective public relations with students and parents. Parent-teacher meetings, mothers' clubs, visiting teacher contacts, school visits, parent-teacher conferences, assemblies, homeroom discussions, faculty advising can all be utilized to good advantage in preparing students and parents to make the fullest use of the services.

In many schools, some form of remediation has been given for years. In expanding to a full-scale program, care must be taken to integrate the new activities into the old program without appearing to threaten present staff or cast reflections on previous efforts.

The most common approach to reading problems appears to be to make the classroom teacher responsible for remediation. In this case, the teacher plays the major role, with help from specialists if they are available. Observations on classroom behavior would be passed on to the counselor and case conferences held with specialists about students who present unusual problems. The counselor would supply information gathered about each student from test data and interview. An important function of the teacher would be the referral of students to the counselor and, in some cases, to other specialists. The teachers would contribute information about students' progress for evaluation purposes and for inclusion in an annual report to the administration and faculty. If visiting teachers are employed, they will depend on the classroom teacher to furnish information which they carry to parents.

Aside from counseling students, the counselor trains teachers to interpret test results and to see the relationships between data. He prepares the teachers to recognize the symptoms of maladjustment, to make referrals and to prepare the student for counseling. The leadership of inservice training may be given to the counselor. If the faculty members choose a leader from among their ranks, the counselor acts as consultant, helping to plan the meetings, to choose suitable topics for study and to assemble relevant professional literature. He may be called upon to demonstrate counseling, to arrange for pseudocounseling demonstrations, to suggest evaluation techniques, and to train faculty members in new group techniques. In this role, the counselor is expected to be an expert in three areas: counseling, group processes, and diagnosis. Most counselors are prepared to test, diagnose, and counsel. Few are prepared to demonstrate leadership techniques and other group processes, but this kind of preparation is increasingly recognized as essential to school personnel workers. An early concept of the counselor, isolated in his cubicle with individual students, is gradually giving way to the belief that the counselor is most effective when he works part of his time with teachers. Among his duties may be the conduct of group therapy, personal development classes, role-playing, and play therapy, or he may be recruited to train faculty members in these techniques. If the counselor is an expert in remediation, he may actually conduct the reading classes, or he may be the head of the program, training the teachers in these special techniques as well as in personnel methods. In all of these functions, he finds that a knowledge of group processes is invaluable.

REFERRAL

When the teacher or administrator decides that a student should see a counselor, he should explain to the student why he is making the suggestion. If possible, during this interview, he should telephone or take the student to the counselor and fix the date of the first appointment. If this cannot be arranged, he should send a note to the counselor, explaining that the student has been asked to make an appointment. The teacher or staff member making the referral then provides such information as he deems valuable to the counselor: grades, evidences of progress, behavior in class, reasons for referral.

Referring a student does not relieve the teacher of his responsibility for the student. He merely shares it for a time with the counselor. He expects to find in the counselor's reply clues to understanding and helping the student.

Occasions will arise when it seems advisable to refer students to other agencies, such as speech clinic, child-guidance clinic, optometrist, physician, social agencies, etc. There are service clubs that furnish eyeglasses for deprived children, finance trips to state and regional remedial centers, and carry on other charitable projects. Staff members should be aware of the resources of state and community and know the proper channels for securing their help when it is needed.

SUMMARY

A multiple approach to reading problems is needed in view of the many interrelated causal factors. Drills, exercises, and mechanics of reading are described as necessary, but secondary to activities which involve thinking, reacting, and expressing emotions. Two facets of the multiple approach are group experience and individual treatment. A typical daily routine might include tachistoscopic drill, skimming, speeded reading, comprehension testing, and discussion. Each student keeps his own record of daily performance. Variations of the routine include personal development discussions, analysis of propaganda, spelling, vocabulary study, word analysis, dramatizations, creative writing, panel discussions, round-table discussions, reports. The authors recommend a regularly scheduled class, meeting three times weekly. Counseling is said to be an important factor in improving reading skills. Goal orientation and orientation to new classroom methods are strongly suggested. Training in group leadership and group membership is given in preparation for the group discussions. Illustrations are given of how reflection of feeling can be used in the reading class. Some materials are named, and suggestions are made as to how they might be used. Criteria for selecting stories and articles are given.

The attitudes of the instructor toward his students are said to be equally important or more important than methods and materials. Suggestions are given on improving relationships with parents, and the effect of parental attitudes on reading progress is discussed. A brief comment is made on the prevention of reading problems. The support of the administrator and his attitudes toward his staff and toward the program are linked with its success. The roles of administrator, teacher, and counselor are defined. Suggestions are made on how to refer a student to a specialist or an outside agency.

CHAPTER 6

Group Procedures

In Chapter 5, we introduced briefly some group procedures which can be used to facilitate the improvement of reading skills among retarded readers. In this chapter, we shall enlarge upon these suggestions and give examples from classroom experience.

One of the first steps is to help the students understand their own problems and the multiple goals of the class. After defining and exploring the problems, they begin to understand that the act of reading involves thinking, feeling, and talking as well as seeing and to accept the notion that talking about personal problems can help to overcome reading problems. In an early class session, the problems and goals of the members are discussed. Some classes delay the mention of personal problems. Others take advantage of the opportunity to discuss them.

Problems listed on checklists or autobiographical questionnaires are usually repeated and usually agree with results of personality testing, but stating them in class helps to commit the students to work on them. The list varies little from semester to semester. As problems are stated, the instructor writes them on the blackboard. With the help of the class, he combines those which are essentially the same. If some are overlooked he asks, "Would you mind if I make some suggestions? You may decide whether these items shall be discussed." All decisions are approved by the class. Some expressions of aggression can be expected. The instructor defines them, but does not permit the aggressors to disrupt the discussion.

DEFINING PROBLEMS AND GOALS

Excerpts from an early classroom session are given here. All initial testing has been completed. The discussion begins with a brief statement from the teacher.

TEACHER: We can work more effectively together if we know what we hope to accomplish and what obstacles stand in the way of reaching our objectives.

You understand that you were assigned to this class because your reading skills are not equal to your other abilities, so you would probably agree on problems related to speed and comprehension in reading. Sometimes personal problems interfere with reading. If you are worried, it is hard to concentrate and to remember what is read. If there is something that you want very much, you may think about it instead of thinking about what you read. Perhaps, in listing problems, you will want to mention some of these personal matters in addition to those directly concerned with reading and study. After making a list of the problems you would like to discuss, we can decide together which to discuss first. If you like, we can set aside class time for the discussion of personal problems.

STUDENT No. 1: Can they be just any kind?

TEACHER: Anything that we might talk about in class.

STUDENT No. 2: You mean if we can't get a date here at this college, we can talk about that?

T: Yes, if there are enough in the class who think the same way.

S. No. 2: It's a problem, I think, to most men.

T: We will list this as a problem. After we name several, we can go over the list and decide on those we want to work on in class. (*Writes problem on the blackboard.*)

S. No. 3: Is this going to be a Lonely Hearts Club?

T: It's satisfying to you to make light of this sort of problem.

S. No. 3: I was only asking a question.

T: You feel a bit cynical about it.

S. No. 3: (*Looks around for support; mumbles.*)

T: What other problems shall we put on the agenda? (*Long silence.*)

S. No. 4: I don't know whether others have this problem or not. I'm not so far along as trying to get a date. I just have trouble talking to anybody . . . you know . . . just carrying on an ordinary conversation.

T: We will add this to our list of problems. (*Writes.*) Are there others?

S. No. 5: I can tell him what to do on conversation. Just ask the other person what he is interested in.

T: We will be glad to have discussion about these later. Today, we are just naming them.

S. No. 6: I don't seem to be able to talk in company, especially if there are lots of people around. I don't seem to know what to say.

T: Shall I list it, "Fear in relation to conversation"?

S. No. 6: Yes . . . it's kind of a shyness, too.

T: I suspect we all feel a certain shyness or reluctance to talk in the presence of many people.

S. No. 7: If a student can't talk and carry on a conversation, he doesn't belong in college.

T: You feel unsympathetic toward this matter of social relationships between students. Perhaps you feel it is a waste of time to talk about it in class.

S. No. 7: This is the sort of thing that fraternities and sororities do. Why waste class time?

S. No. 1: Some of us don't belong to fraternities and sororities and may never belong. We need to get it somewhere.

S. No. 7: What has this got to do with reading? I came in here to learn to read better.

T: This subject seems pretty remote to you and you feel sort of hostile to it.

S. No. 7: Oh well. . . .

S. No. 8: I don't know anybody yet. I don't get acquainted very easily. I need to know more people.

T: I see. Too few social contacts. Shall we list it?

S. No. 9: I don't seem to have the confidence I ought to have when I read. Well, this seems to apply to some other things, too. I'm not very sure of my·self in other ways. Maybe it's not important enough to list.

S. No. 10: That's the way with me, too. I think it should go on the list. (*Others nod and murmur agreement; teacher lists lack of self-confidence.*)

S. No. 1: I have trouble expressing myself, too, but I have trouble with study. I don't use my time very well. The time passes and is gone and my lessons aren't done. (*Others nod; teacher lists study schedule.*)

S. No. 11: My problem is spelling. I just got a theme back with a low grade because I misspelled six words.

T: This sort of frightens you.

S. No. 11: Yes, because I don't know that I'm misspelling them.

S. No. 2: I have the same trouble. Sometimes I spell a word right and other times spell the same word wrong. I can't tell the difference. When a word has an *i* and an *e* in it, I usually make them both *e* and put the dot halfway be·tween. That way, the teacher can count it right if she wants to.

S. No. 11: People tell me to use the dictionary, but you have to know how to spell before you can find the words.

T: It's discouraging, isn't it? Do others have this problem? (*Several nod, and he adds it to the list.*)

S. No. 12: It's the words I don't know that bother me. Some of the words in my lessons, I have never heard of before. By the time I look one up, I've forgotten what the sentence was all about and have to read it over, and some-times the definition has another word in it that I don't know.

T: Shall we put down vocabulary as a problem?

S. No. 13: My problem seems to be different. When I read, my attention wanders. I go down the page and turn the page, and all at once I realize I don't know what I've read and I was thinking about something else. Then I have to go back and read it again.

T: It's hard to concentrate. (*Writes.*)

S. No. 14: It's hard for me to get started, to make sense out of things. Some-times, I spend a good deal of time settling down. I think of getting a drink of water and maybe washing my hair or dashing down to the drugstore for a tube of toothpaste, or something.

S. No. 15: It's hard for me to get started, too.

S. No. 9: Me, too. And even when I do understand something, I'm not sure I'm right. Then I go over it again and never get to the last part.

T: Some of you feel as if you have to make yourselves settle down to work. Other things take your attention. Maybe this is related to concentration, and comprehension, too.

S. No. 15: I don't like to read. I just never read anything that isn't assigned. I mean, I never check out a book. I read very slowly, and I just skip reading if I can get out of it.

T: There are two problems . . . slow rate of reading and lack of interest.

Students in this class listed 25 problems, then combined and eliminated items, and agreed on a final list of 12. There was about 80 per cent agreement on the final list of items.

The goals of the class were then stated by the students in terms of the problems: to improve speed, comprehension, concentration, interest, vocabulary, study habits, spelling, self-confidence, social skills, and ability to analyze and appraise articles; to identify and correct ocular defects; and to explore how feelings relate to efficiency in reading. Part of one class period each week for 12 weeks was set aside for the discussion of these problems, as agreed by the class. On problem-solving days, a drill of some kind, usually speeded reading and comprehension testing, required about 15 minutes of class time, and the remainder was spent in discussion. The instructor closed the goal-setting discussion by explaining, "We can try out some procedures designed to help us reach these goals. After the try-out period, the class will have an opportunity to discuss whether we are making progress and which of them seem most suitable for this class." Although group decision is employed constantly in the reading class, we feel that the introduction of new methods, techniques, and materials is not inconsistent with democratic processes, as students are not prepared to make a decision on such matters until they have had some experience with them.

LEADERSHIP

In any classroom, the teacher is a leader and has more effect upon the classroom climate than any other one person in the group. The kind of leadership exerted in the reading class is important from two points of view: (1) it can either hasten or retard learning; and (2) it is a factor in training for citizenship which is a function of the reading class or any class.

In preceding chapters, we have stated that retarded readers need practice in participation and in verbal communication as well as in reading. The ability to think while reading is said to be enhanced by experience in exchanging thoughts and opinions about the materials read.

The degree and quality of participation by students depends largely upon the skills and attitudes of the teacher.

The effectiveness of leadership is measured not by the degree to which the leader is able to influence the members to agree with him but by the degree to which the group takes part in making use of all available information on a subject, makes use of the abilities of all members, and arrives at a decision which represents the consensus of the group. In the group-centered class, each member has an opportunity to experience leadership as well as membership, and the teacher gradually relinquishes leadership responsibilities to the students.

This kind of leadership requires not only belief in the democratic processes, but skills as well. Although, as a nation, we are committed to democratic principles, we are not agreed on a definition of democracy. In practice, in home, church, school, and community life, leaders are as often authoritarian as democratic. Reading students, after 12 years of schooling, know little about democratic procedure and are seldom able to distinguish between democratic and authoritarian leadership. Like many adults, they are confused by inconsistencies between belief and practice.

We shall present some techniques and examples of classroom experiences through which they can learn to distinguish differences and learn to make use of the democratic group climate to learn and grow. The techniques can be applied in other classes, extra-class activities, church groups, and group projects of various kinds. They have been used effectively with high-school, college, and adult groups in this country and with college and adult groups in Japan.

Among the various kinds of leaders, you will find the person who: (1) is forthright in his defense of authoritarianism and who openly dominates the group (hard-boiled dictator); (2) gently and skillfully maneuvers the group to adopt his decisions (benevolent autocrat); (3) interprets democratic leadership as relieving him of all responsibility (*laissez-faire* leader); and (4) helps the group to make its own decisions, but makes his own contribution (democratic leader).

Evidence is accumulating in support of cooperative classroom and group efforts. When the behavior of children led by democratic, autocratic, and *laissez-faire* leaders was studied, those in the democratic groups were found to work harder, produce more, use more originality, go ahead with purposeful activity in the absence of the leader, express less hostility and aggression, and talk less about themselves.[1] A similar

[1] Lewin, Kurt, Ronald Lippitt, and R. K. White, "Patterns of Aggressive Behavior in Experimentally Created Social Climates," *J. soc. Psychol.*, vol. 10, 1939, pp. 298ff.

study comparing the results of autocratic and democratic leadership in a children's camp shows that membership in the democratic groups doubled and these groups were rated superior in enthusiasm, persistence, efficiency, self-discipline, and quality and quantity of output. Leaders trained in democratic procedures also showed improved morale, initiative, and satisfaction. Belief in democratic procedures is said to have been strengthened. Leaders in training came to feel more calm and poised as they discovered that group discipline was not dependent on constant vigilance.[2] The effects of dominative versus integrative behavior on 55 kindergarten children is reported by Anderson.[3] Such behavior as commands, direct refusals, postponing, disapproval, blame, warning, threat, etc. was termed dominative. A dominative response is described as rigid, inflexible, tension producing, resistant to change and growth. Integrative behavior is spontaneous, dynamic, flexible, voluntary, respectful of differences between self and others, capable of reconciling differences and expending energies with others. He concludes that dominative behavior by a person does not produce integrative behavior in others, but dominative behavior is dynamically related to integrative behavior.

Perkins compared group-centered with leader-centered learning. Group-centered groups were markedly superior to leader-centered groups in their greater use of supportive evidence to substantiate their views. Student statements in the leader-centered groups were more subjective and self-involved.[4] People involved in group decision apparently make greater changes in behavior than those given the same information in lecture or individual instruction.[5,6]

Horrocks[7] found that by using socialized recitation and group-centered procedures over a two-quarter period, students improved in personal adjustment and tended toward better grades when compared with other

[2] Bevelas, Alex, and Kurt Lewin, "Training in Democratic Leadership," *J. abnorm. and soc. Physchol.*, vol. 37, no. 1, January, 1942, pp. 115–119.

[3] Anderson, Harold, "Domination and Social Integration in the Behavior of Kindergarten Children and Teachers," *Genet. Psychol. Monogr.*, vol. 21, 1939, pp. 287–385.

[4] Perkins, Hugh V., "Climate Influences Group Learning," *J. Educ. Res.*, vol. 45, no. 2, October, 1951, pp. 117–118.

[5] Deutsch, Morton, "An Experimental Study of the Effects of Cooperation and Competition upon Group Process," *Human Relations*, vol. 2, no. 3, July, 1949, pp. 199ff.

[6] Lewin, Kurt, "Group Decision and Social Change," in Newcomb and Hartley (eds.), *Readings in Social Psychology*, Henry Holt and Company, Inc., New York, 1947, pp. 330ff.

[7] Horrocks, Winifred Bellinger, "A Sociometric and Psychometric Analysis of Results of Optimalizing Classroom Interpersonal Relationships," dissertation, Ohio State University, 1949, p. 203.

classes using more conventional procedures. Experiments by Deutsch and Jenkins indicate the advantages of cooperation over competition.[5,8]

Cooperation, companionship with fellow-workers, participation in the discussion of common problems are believed to have brought about increased productivity among industrial workers in the Hawthorne plant of the Western Electric Company.[9] Fox and Scott[10] studied problems of management in three companies and concluded that the comparatively low rate of absenteeism in one of the three was a result of the fact that the company encouraged teamwork more than did the other two. Whittemore[11] compared the results of competitive with cooperative work situations. The number of mistakes increased in competition. The performance of graduate students in competition and in cooperation was tested by Watson.[12] The average score of the group was greater than the best score of any individual working alone.

Recent studies suggest that group discussion alone is much less effective than group decision in making changes in behavior.[13,14] In the group studies described, facts were given by experts, but decisions were left to the groups. Haire[15] concludes that passive or apathetic groups do not make good use of group decision, but such opportunities stimulate interest in participation and eventually reduce apathy.

The experiments of Maier[16] have shown that the skill of the leader is a factor in the quality of group problem-solving. He believes, however, that an unskilled leader can promote a high quality of problem-solving by using democratic leadership.

The work of Paul Torrance[17] with 57 combat air crews in training suggests that a structured non-authoritarian method of conducting group

[8] Jenkins, D. H., "Research in Group Dynamics," *Soc. Educ.*, vol. 12, no. 8, December, 1948, p. 347.

[9] Roethlisberger, F. J., and W. J. Dickson, *Management and the Worker*, Harvard University Press, Cambridge, Mass., 1939.

[10] Fox, John B., and Jerome F. Scott, "Absenteeism: Management's Problem," *Business Research Studies*, Harvard University, Cambridge, Mass., no. 29, 1943.

[11] Whittemore, I. C., "The Influence of Competition on Performance," *J. abnorm. and soc. Psychol.*, vol. 19, 1924, pp. 236–253.

[12] Watson, J. B., "Do Groups Think More Efficiently than Individuals?" *J. abnorm. and soc. Psychol.*, vol. 23, 1928, pp. 328–336.

[13] Haire, M., "Some Problems of Industrial Training," *J. soc. Issues*, vol. 4, 1948, pp. 41–47.

[14] Hendry, C. E., *A Decade of Group Work*, Association Press, New York, 1948.

[15] Haire, *op. cit.*

[16] Maier, R. F., "The Quality of Group Decisions as Influenced by the Discussion Leader," *Human Relations*, vol. 3, 1950, pp. 155–174.

[17] Torrance, E. Paul, "Methods of Conducting Critiques of Group Problem-solving Performance," *J. appl. Psychol.*, vol. 37, no. 5, 1953, pp. 394–398.

discussion produces problem-solving superior to the unstructured non-authoritarian method. However, his report suggests that some of the leaders of so-called unstructured non-authoritarian groups were actually authoritarian. Methods of conducting class described in Chapters 5 and 6 might be most accurately described as structured non-authoritarian, as the instructor takes considerable responsibility for choosing materials, suggesting procedures, and defining limits, but provides ample opportunities for participation, free expression of opinion, approval by the class, group decision, and for experiencing acceptance by the instructor and the group.

The attitude of the individual toward group membership is related to performance, according to Torrance[18] who studied 80 bomber crews, a total of about 900 men. Pretests showing how individuals perceived the group indicate that crews which gave superior performances in simulated survival situations differed from those which gave poor performances in that they more frequently perceived harmonious relationships, less frequently perceived status differences within the group, and accepted more fully the decisions of their crew.

Communication among aircraft crew members is discussed by Torrance[19] as an important factor in survival. Analysis of approximately 200 interviews with Air Force personnel who had been downed over enemy territory during World War II or during the Korean conflict showed that in almost every story of 100 per cent survival, good communication among crew members had been maintained throughout the experience. A high percentage of non-survivors appeared linked with a breakdown in communication. Torrance's comments suggest that communication is impeded by consciousness of status, competition, hostility, and weak affectional linkages. The importance of achieving a stable group structure during training is noted.

These studies lend support to our hypothesis that learning, performance, communication, and group harmony are interrelated.

The ill effects of authoritarian discipline are suggested by numerous studies of parent-child relationships. Two authors report that students with adjustment problems come from dominating homes.[20,21] Junior-

[18] Torrance, E. Paul, "Perception of Group Functioning as a Predictor of Group Performance," Research Studies of the State College of Washington, vol. 21, no. 3, September 1953, pp. 262–265.
[19] Torrance, E. Paul, "The Behavior of Small Groups Under the Stress of Conditions of 'Survival,'" Amer. Sociological Rev., vol. 19, no. 6, December, 1954, pp. 752–755.
[20] Watson, Goodwin B., "Comparison of the Effects of Lax versus Strict Home Training," J. soc. Psychol., vol. 5, 1934, pp. 102–105.
[21] McKinney, Fred, "Personality Adjustment of College Students as Related to Factors in Personal History," J. appl. Psychol., vol. 23, 1939, pp. 660–668.

high-school pupils whose parents were described as nagging, over-critical, and punitive were not well liked by their classmates, according to Anderson.[22] Ayer and Bernreuther[23] conclude that children subjected to severe punishment were less attractive, less able to face reality, and more dependent upon adult affection. Prejudiced people are said to have been reared in authoritarian homes.[24] Homes where democratic freedom prevailed are reported favorable to intellectual, personal, and social development among children studied over a period of years.[25] The persistence of children in the face of difficulty is associated with moderate discipline, according to Thelma Wolf.[26]

The results of these and other studies suggest that a democratic classroom climate is conducive to learning. Characteristics of retarded readers are similar to those found among people reared in autocratic homes: adjustment problems, dependency, and some confusion in recognizing reality.

DEMONSTRATIONS OF LEADERSHIP

Because of the confusion arising from inconsistencies in our beliefs and practices, the reading students need help in identifying the different kinds of leadership. If the students understand the differences and make a choice, they are then committed to make the chosen method work. Discussion of the concepts of democracy may be helpful, but the impact of actual experience is more convincing. One way of beginning training is to arrange for demonstrations of different types of leadership. Four students are chosen, and each is given a description of the role he is to play. The following descriptions of leadership might be used.

The Hard-boiled Dictator has already made the decisions and the meeting is merely for the purpose of letting him make announcements

[22] Anderson, John P., "Study of Relationship between Certain Aspects of Parental Behavior and Attitudes and Behavior of Junior High School Pupils," thesis, Teachers College, Columbia University, New York, 1940.

[23] Ayer, Mary E., and R. G. Bernreuther, "Study of Relationship between Discipline and Personality Traits in Little Children," *J. genet. Psychol.*, vol. 50, 1937, pp. 165–170.

[24] Adorno, T. W., E. Frenkel-Brunswik, D. J. Levinson, and R. N. Sanford, *The Authoritarian Personality*, Harper & Brothers, New York, 1950.

[25] Champney, Horace, "Parent Behavior as Related to Child Development," paper read to American Association for Advancement of Science, December 1939.

[26] Wolf, Thelma, "The Effect of Praise and Competition on the Persisting Behavior of Kindergarten Children," University of Minnesota Institute Child Welfare Monograph, no. 15, 1938.

and assign tasks. He asks all committee heads to "check with him" on details. He may make a few rules, "Anybody who is late will be left behind. All cars will leave promptly at 3:30 P.M. The contest will be so and so." If he asks for a vote, it is merely to confirm what he has proposed. He believes that he must think for the group, make them function efficiently, and exert a firm hand. He works hard and makes a point of saving time. He points out past mistakes and errors in thinking, and he maintains his power by outworking, outthinking, and outtalking others.

The Benevolent Autocrat is kindly, good-tempered, and courteous. He lets the group members think they are helping to make decisions. He may believe that he is genuinely democratic because he lets everybody express opinions and make suggestions and inserts his own decisions when they will do the most good. He manipulates, maneuvers, and appeals to authority. Characteristic remarks are, "Now you're young and you haven't had the experience that I have. I'm sure if you knew all the facts you would agree with me that. . . . That's a good suggestion, but on the other hand. . . . This is the way we do things. . . . We want everybody to be happy about this. . . . I'm sure you wouldn't want anything bad to happen. . . . Probably you haven't thought of this. . . . " The members are regarded as children, nice, but irresponsible. A good many arrangements have already been made, "I called Mr. so-and-so. . . . If you'll see me, I'll tell you how to. . . . Just drop into the office and pick up the necessary information. . . . " This leader believes that he is doing what is best for the organization or the group. Running it is a game, and he loves to match wits with anyone who differs with him. He makes the members personally loyal to him instead of to the organization, "I'm sure you won't let me down. . . . You are one of my best helpers. . . . This is the way I like it. . . . "

The Laissez-faire Leader sits helplessly in the chairman's seat while the meeting falls apart. He does not state the purpose of the meeting nor ask for suggestions. If all talk at once, or if a few dominate, or if the time is spent on irrelevancies, he makes no attempt to see that talking time is fairly distributed or to help the group come to a decision. He offers no information and makes no suggestions. If asked his opinion, he answers in generalities, "Anything's O.K. with me. I'm sure everything will work out."

The Democratic Leader acts as a good host, asking if the members know each other and introducing those who are new. He states the purpose of the meeting or asks a member to do so. He asks for ideas and information and receives them with respect. He summarizes the contributions of the group, stating points of agreement or disagreement or asks a member to do so. He sees that every member has an opportunity to talk. If information is lacking, he asks where it might be found. The group makes all decisions, time, place, food, transportation, division of duties. He assigns tasks only if permission is granted by the group. He checks with the group to see if he is interpreting their wishes correctly. If the discussion breaks down into argument or irrelevancies, he summarizes what has been said and asks for further comments. If questions arise, he refers them to the group.

After the students have studied their roles, the instructor may confer with each on how to play his role. The democratic leader, in particular, may need to talk with the instructor. The types of leadership are not named or defined for the remaining students.

Four or five class members are asked to volunteer to act as committee or group members for the demonstration. The subject for discussion may be planning a party, picnic, or other project. Each leader takes the same committee through a brief discussion of five to ten minutes. The class is then invited to comment on the four types of meetings, evaluating effectiveness, tone of the meeting, interpersonal relations among the members, differences in leadership. The class might be divided into small groups for about a 10-minute discussion. Each small group is asked to choose a recorder to report the discussion to the class. After reports from the small groups, the instructor summarizes, clarifies, and asks for general discussion. Members of the demonstration committee are asked to report how they felt under each type of leader.

Students usually respond to the demonstrations of four kinds of leadership with considerable enthusiasm. The audience gets involved, excited, and often amused. All can participate. There are four demonstration leaders, four committee members, four small group leaders, and four recorders. Others have opportunities to express themselves in the small group meetings and general discussion. An illustration of this classroom experience is given here.

TEACHER: We have already talked about the importance of discussing what we read. Each of you will have an opportunity to lead discussions in this class. It seems a good idea to try to come to some decision about what kind of leadership is agreeable to the class. Today, we are going to have four demonstrations of how leaders can work with groups. We need four students to sit around the table up here and play the parts of committee members. (*Recruits the required number.*) This is a committee of high-school students from . . . shall we say, the 4-H Club. O.K.? They have been chosen at the last meeting of the 4-H Club to plan recreation for the next month. Each leader will meet with this committee. The committee will stay until the four leaders have performed . . . until the four demonstrations are completed. The class will have an opportunity to discuss the demonstrations. See if you can describe each of the kinds of leadership you have observed. The different leaders in the demonstration will use different techniques. You may want to talk about the differences.

The four students who play the roles of the leaders have made some preparation. The committee members have had no rehearsal, so whatever they say is off the cuff. Derral Jacobs is leader number 1.

DERRAL: I've called this group together to decide on a social event for the 4-H Club. I've looked up the records for the last two years and they show we have had a picnic and that both were successful. It looks this way. If we want a successful party, we'd better have a picnic. Any objections? (*Doesn't wait for an answer.*) Well that's settled. To get on with this . . . . The best place and the closest is Kluwane Lake. I've asked the caretaker and he says it's O.K. Bill, you see to the transportation. Mabel can collect the money and buy the food. Just charge everybody 50 cents. Shall we say the date will be two weeks from Friday at 4:00 in the afternoon? Any comments?

MEMBER: (*A bit shocked at the tempo.*) Aren't we going pretty fast?

DERRAL: I like to get things done fast. No use wasting time when we can get it settled. Time is worth a lot. Oh, Mabel, just buy wieners, buns, bananas, onions, apples, and pop. That will be fine. Temple Grocery is the best place.

MEMBER: What if it rains?

DERRAL: If it rains we will have it in the gym. Well, that's it. We got a lot done in a short time, didn't we? Oh yes. Check with me about everything once or twice before the day of the picnic. Thanks. That's all. Is there a motion for adjournment?

TEACHER: Leader number 2 is Marie.

MARIE: This nice committee of boys and girls have been asked to decide on some kind of recreation like a picnic for our 4-H Club. You know how much fun we had last year out at the park. Don't you remember the games we played? Everybody had such a good time. The park is such a grand place. I'm sure we can decide these matters without very much work for anybody. Ruth, what do you think? Should we go to the park?

RUTH: I don't know. Think I'd just as soon go somewhere else. Maybe we should have a . . . .

MARIE: Let's be democratic about this. What do some of the rest of you think?

BILL: Let's make it a swimming party and go out to Lake Kluwane.

MARIE: Oh, do you think it would be safe? You know our mothers . . . . What do some of the rest of you think?

SALLIE: Well maybe the park . . . .

MARIE: I'm so glad you agree with me. Of course, the rest of you are new on the committee. I've had a little more experience. We had such a wonderful time last year, and we have that to go by.

JOE: I just don't want it too tame. I want plenty of eats including ice cream.

MARIE: We'll make a note of that, Joe. Let's try to think what's best for everybody. The park has wonderful facilities, swimming pool, fireplaces. It's safe . . . life guards, no poison ivy . . . not far from the school building. Isn't this a wonderful committee! Such good ideas. I'm so glad you agree so well. Just to make it democratic, Sallie, will you make a motion that we go to the park next Saturday afternoon, since that's the only free time . . . say about 2:30 in the afternoon.

(*Moved, seconded and passed.*)

MARIE: Oh, yes. The food. Does anyone object to the food we had last year? Ruth did such a wonderful job with it last year. Shall we just appoint Ruth to do it again. Everyone was so pleased with her work. Ruth, you would help us again, wouldn't you? (*Ruth nods.*) That's fine. I'd hoped you would. Now Joe, could you see about the cars? You are so good about organizing things.

JOE: (*Reluctantly*) I guess so. We won't need many since the park is walking distance.

MARIE: Yes. That's one thing that's so nice about it. You have all been so nice. I just know we'll have a good time . . . with such a cooperative committee in charge. If anything comes up, just let me know and we'll do something about it. Thanks just loads. I'll see you at the park.

TEACHER: Leader number 3 is Sue.

SUE: I guess you know why we're here, since you were all at the last club meeting.

(*All talk at once; then silence.*)

RUTH: Maybe we ought to get started.

SUE: O.K.

JOE: Maybe we ought to all go out for coffee instead.

⟨*Silence.*⟩

RUTH: The good old 4-H Club is depending on us, gang. What shall we plan for them?

BILL: You got any ideas, Sue?

SUE: Whatever the rest want is all right with me.

JOE: Yeah, but how do we know what we want when we haven't even talked about it.

BILL: Maybe we ought to flip a coin.

RUTH: Over what?

SALLIE: I think we ought to get down to business.

RUTH: Who's going to do the work, Sue?

SUE: Why, all the kids are nice people. I'm sure everything will be all right.

SALLIE: Shall we square dance?

SUE: That would be fine if that's what everybody wants.

BILL: Maybe we ought to decide if it's going to be a picnic or a party or a dance or something. What do you think, Sue?

SUE: Well, what do you think?

(*And so on and so on until the teacher remarks that the time is up.*)

TEACHER: Pat is leader number 4.

PAT: Hello, people. Since our club is such a big one, we may not know each other very well. Suppose we introduce ourselves and tell a little about ourselves. I'm Pat Smith from Winfield and I'm sort of a newcomer to 4-H. I joined last year and had a project on home improvement. Sallie and I met first at an exhibit, and she showed some beautiful canned vegetables. Tell us a little bit about yourself, Sallie.

SALLIE: I'm Sallie Scott from Newton. I've been in 4-H Club work for more than five years, mostly cooking, canning, and homemaking, but one year I had a calf to raise.

RUTH: I'm Ruth Barr from Washington County. I liked the projects in homemaking, but I liked the square dancing and leadership training, too.

BILL: Bill Moore from near Strong City. I raised sheep last year for my project.

JOE: Joe Tully from Brookville over by Salina. Had a wheat crop of my own last year. I'm interested in farm machinery, too. I called the square dances for two years in our club.

PAT: Now that we can call each other by our first names, we are ready for business. Our job is to plan the recreation for next month. Are there any suggestions?

BILL: I suppose first we ought to decide what kind of an event to have.

PAT: Does the committee agree that this is the first question?

(*All nod.*)

JOE: Let's go to the lake. We can swim.

PAT: A swimming party has been suggested.

SALLIE: A picnic is what we had last year.

RUTH: Let's have a square dance.

PAT: These three ideas have been suggested, a swimming party, a picnic, and a square dance. Bill, have you anything to say?

BILL: I talked to other members to see what they would like best. I believe most of them expect a picnic.

PAT: Bill is reminding us that we represent the whole club. Let's see if we can remember what people said at the last meeting.

RUTH: They talked about a picnic, but they left it up to us to decide.

JOE: We might combine the swimming party with a picnic. It's too hot to square dance.

PAT: What do the rest of the members think?

SALLIE: I can string along with Joe's idea. We could play games. There would be something for everybody to do.

PAT: Are there any more ideas? (*Silence.*) Are we ready to decide? (*Nods from all.*) Will someone put the suggestion into the form of a motion?

(*Moved, seconded, and voted.*)

PAT: How shall we divide the work?

BILL: Sallie and Ruth can be in charge of food, and Joe and I can get the cars arranged and plan games.

PAT: Is this agreeable to all of you? (*All agree.*) Maybe the next question is the time of the picnic. Any suggestions?

(*Meeting continues in this manner.*)

TEACHER: The class will now divide into small groups for the discussion of these types of leadership. Begin numbering on the first row, 1, 2, 3, 4. Group number 1 will meet in this corner, group number 2 in that corner. . . . Each small group will choose its own leader and recorder. The job of the leader is to see that everybody gets to talk and that every member understands the purpose of the discussion. The recorder will take notes on what the members say and report their comments to the class. You will have 10 minutes to talk. Each recorder will have about one minute to make his report. The questions for discussion are: "Can you see any differences between these types of leadership? Have you any opinions on their effectiveness?"

(*After 10 minutes, the instructor calls the class together and asks for the reports of the recorder.*)

RECORDER OF GROUP NUMBER 1: Our group though that the first leader was pretty bossy. He didn't give anybody else a chance to say anything. He had his mind made up and told people what to do. The second leader was full of flattery and tried to make people do what she wanted by flattering them. She let people talk, but she got them to do what she wanted. The third leader just let things fall apart. She really wasn't a leader at all. The fourth got the meeting going and let everybody have a part. She tried to help them do what they wanted to do and what they were supposed to do. Some of our members thought that the first leader was the most efficient, but most of them thought the fourth leader was the one they would like best.

RECORDER OF GROUP NUMBER 2: The first leader didn't need any group. He did everything himself. The rest could just as well have stayed at home. The second used all the arguments she could to get her own way. She was polite, but she made them think her way was the best, or at least they gave up trying and let her decide. The third leader was not doing anything. There was no way that anybody could count in that group. She probably thought she was being democratic, but nothing was accomplished. The fourth leader wanted everyone to know each other and seemed to be able to get the kids going on the work even when they were pretty well pitched off at the leader just before. Some of our group think that leaders are supposed to get the group to follow them by tricks like leader number 2, but most of our group thought that the last committee would follow up on the plans.

RECORDER OF GROUP NUMBER 3: Our group thought the first leader took too much responsibility and too much authority, most all of it. He just told them what was going to happen. The second leader was just like the first, only smoother. She wanted her own way, but she wasn't so rude about it. We felt about the same as the other groups about leader number 3. The fourth, we liked because she really wanted to find out what the members wanted to do.

RECORDER OF GROUP NUMBER 4: We agree with the rest that the first was a dictator and second was like him only with better manners and more logic. We thought we had seen lots of leaders like the second and third. The second leader was polite, but the fourth one had more real respect for other people. The committee members felt more important. She didn't try to be the big shot, but she didn't let the meeting go to pieces, and they got something done.

TEACHER: There is considerable agreement among the four group reports. All mention that the first leader made the decisions and told people what to do. The second leader actually made the decisions but tried to make the committee think that they had a part. The third, as you say, did not lead at all. The fourth tried to create a friendly feeling, stated the purpose of the meeting, acted as if the suggestions of the members were important, gave all a chance to talk. All reports favor the fourth leader. Class, do you agree with this summary? Am I stating your opinions correctly? (*Some classes agree at once; others want to talk more about it.*) I would like to ask the people who acted as members of the committee how they felt while working with each leader.

RUTH: I felt like it was real, and I didn't like the first leader. I felt so useless.

BILL: Took me a while to find out what was going on. He should have sent us a memo.

JOE: His plans were not so bad, but I just didn't feel cooperative.

RUTH: I had some ideas, but I never did get to say them.

TEACHER: Sallie, do you have a comment?

SALLIE: I was just overwhelmed. The meeting was over before I could get going.

JOE: I just felt like, oh well, if I don't do this, he'll see to it.

BILL: I felt like he'd be around to check up.

TEACHER: You all felt a little resentful toward the first leader. Is this true?

BILL: Yes, but I was even more browned off at the second leader.

SALLIE: I wasn't as much, but I did think I'd just let her do it if she wanted to.

JOE: For a while I thought she was O.K., such a nice bright cheerful manner, and everything seemed reasonable. I didn't mind, but I would have if we had kept on going.

RUTH: I was confused. I didn't know whether she wanted my ideas or just to give us hers. I wasn't certain she knew best for everybody, especially me.

BILL: I didn't like the political slant.

SALLIE: She was real nice, but I got so I felt there wasn't any use to offer any suggestions. It was going to turn out her way anyway.

TEACHER: Bill felt resentful toward the second leader, and the rest of you were either confused or willing to let her have her own way. (*They nod.*) How did you feel about leader number 3?

BILL: Disgusted.

JOE: I felt like making wisecracks.

BILL: I felt like walking out.

SALLIE: I thought she was kind of nice, but we weren't getting anywhere.

RUTH: I got so impatient just waiting for something to happen.

TEACHER: Sort of unsatisfied and impatient? What about the last?

RUTH: I was so disturbed by the others it took me a while to find out she really wanted to know my ideas.

BILL: I felt like goofing off at first, but more like working later.

JOE: I liked the way she helped us get acquainted. It helped to get things started.

SALLIE: It was a good thing to review what people had suggested. Then we knew how far we'd gotten and we could make a choice.

BILL: I felt like there was a reason for my being on the committee, that I could help.

RUTH: She remembered that we were acting for the whole club. That's important, too.

TEACHER: You felt as if the fourth leader respected your ideas and you could count in this committee meeting? (*Affirmative responses from students.*) Are there any comments from the rest of the class? (*Comments usually show that members of the audience were identified with committee members. They are always able to distinguish between the roles played by the four leaders and the majority favor the democratic leader.*) This class favors democratic leadership. It is the hardest role to play. Would you be interested in learning more about it?

LEADERSHIP TRAINING

Following agreement by the class on their choice of leadership techniques, suggestions for leaders and recorders are distributed to the students. The materials are discussed in class. After they are put into practice, the students observe and comment on the skill of the various students in the leader role.

The leader and recorder, in each session, then understand what is expected of each and the members also understand their roles and responsibilities. When training students in leadership techniques, obviously the instructor should observe the principles and employ the techniques he is trying to teach.

Suggestions for the leader include the following: The leader acts as a good host, making sure that members know each other and that each has an opportunity to talk. He is doing all he can to promote a friendly feeling in the group. He states the question before the group or the purpose of the discussion. He asks for comments from each member, and reminds the group that everybody should have a chance to respond. It is his responsibility to keep the group talking. If a silence occurs, he restates the question and summarizes what has been said, or asks a member to summarize. He tries to see that relevant information is introduced, states points of agreement and disagreement, and asks for clarification on points which seem vague. If any member attempts to bring an issue to a vote, he asks the group if they are ready, if all comments and information have been offered. If he contributes information, he does not try to force his opinions on the group. Each member is important, has something to contribute, and should be treated with respect. The leader also has something to contribute, but he should not use his position to take more than his share of talking time or force a decision. If a member wanders from the subject, the leader reminds the group of its purpose and asks if they want to take time for a digression. If a member tries to monopolize the conversation, he reminds him that everybody should have a chance to talk. He does not dominate, but neither does he allow one or a few to dominate and he permits no railroading. If a conflict occurs, he states both sides of the question and asks the group if more discussion is needed, if the conflict can be resolved, or if the group wishes to go on to another topic. He may ask the recorder to review the discussion. He may remind them how much time is available at about the midpoint of the meeting or near its close, and he gives the recorder an opportunity to check his report with the group for accuracy.

The recorder makes notes on the remarks of the members, summarizes comments, reviews his report with the group to see if he is representing them correctly, and reports the comments and decisions of the small group to the class. He notes all opinions and reports those which differ from his own as well as those with which he agrees. The recorder must condense the remarks of his group and report them briefly.

When dividing the class for small group discussion, the instructor arranges for each member to work with each other class member sometime during the year. If the boys outnumber the girls, as is the usual case in reading classes, he asked the girls to distribute themselves among the groups. These procedures can be used in the discussion of subject-matter articles, personal problems, the goals of the class, or progress toward goals. Following the reports of the recorder, the instructor summarizes and asks for general discussion from the class. After discussing the conclusions, the students might then appraise the efficiency of procedures, the interpersonal relations which operated, and the performance of the various members.

After the class has practiced the procedures for a time, the instructor may want to distribute more detailed suggestions for leadership. The following outline might be used.[27]

---

[27] Modeled after materials from Division of Adult Education, Schenectady, New York.

The Role of the Discussion Leader

When the leader hears or observes	He seeks to	In these terms
New members or a new group	Make them acquainted with each other and himself	Introducing self and members, or asking the members to introduce themselves or each other
Ideas	Welcome them, show respect for the idea and the contributor, relate them to the agenda if necessary, record them or have them recorded	A friendly, cordial, encouraging manner, as few words as possible, without making a judgment on the idea
Confused or inexpertly worded ideas	Clarify by restating them, asking a member to restate, or asking for definition or elaboration	"Do the other members understand this point? Let's see if we understand each other. . . . Could you tell us a little more about this. . . . Is this what you mean?"
Two or more ideas included in one contribution	Distinguish between the two ideas, checking with the contributor, ask the group if they want to consider them separately	"Are there perhaps two ideas in what you have said, this . . . and this . . . ? Do you agree? Does the group want to take them up one at a time?"
Ideas unrelated to the subject	Recognize the nature of the idea without discouraging the contributor, determine the wishes of the group	"As Mr. J. says, religion can be related to world peace, but it is not mentioned in our article. Shall we take time to discuss his idea, or shall we go on with our comments on the article?"

Some important ideas are not being contributed	Encourage further exploration of the subject	"Have we covered the subject thoroughly? Are there other points which might be discussed? Is the group satisfied that all important ideas have been presented?"
Signs of inattentiveness or boredom	Stimulate interest or relieve fatigue	"Can we bring this down to our own experience? Could somebody give an example?" or "Maybe we are tired of this topic. Should we move on to another?" or "Is it time to take a break? What does the group want to do?"
Information is lacking	Have information introduced	"Is there someone in the group who can add to our information? Are there outside resources where more facts could be found? Would one of you volunteer to look this up?"
Wasteful repetition	Call attention to what has been accomplished and what is yet to be done	"Can a member (or the recorder) summarize what has been said? Have we covered the main points? Is it time to move on to the next point?"
Significant agreement	Call attention to it	"The group agreed that . . . ? Am I interpreting you correctly?"

Significant dis-agreement	Get the group opinion on the next move	"We seem to have a difference of opinion on this subject. One point of view is . . . . Shall we discuss this further, or record the disagreement and move on to another question?"
Signs of strong emotion	Recognize it and prevent a breakdown in morale	"One or more members feel very strongly that . . . . Others believe just as strongly that . . . . " (Define feeling states, disgust, excitement, hostility, etc.)
Signs of domination	Build up the confidence and ability of the group to resist domination	"Certainly every member's viewpoint counts in this discussion. Let's see what the rest think about it." Or "Miss B. has some information on this. Let's see what she thinks."
Two or more people talking at once	Make sure that everyone gets to talk and to hear	"We don't want to miss any of this. Could we have your comments one at a time?"
Opinions presented as facts	Distinguish between the two	"How do the rest of you feel about this? Do we have evidence to support this opinion?"
Members treat the leader as an expert and appeal to his authority	Involve the group	"Does anyone in the group have an answer for this question?"

Shy member nodding his head, sitting on the edge of his chair, etc.	Give him a chance	"Mr. G. looks as if he has something to say. Can you help us, Mr. G.?"
Non-contributing member	Bring him into the group	"You are taking American history, aren't you, Mr. J.? Could you tell us where to find the answer to this question?"
Periods of silence	Decide whether it is productive or non-productive	(Give them a few minutes to think things over) or "Have we run out of ammunition on this? What shall we do next?"
Time is running short	Remind the group	"We have five minutes left. What conclusions shall we report? Would you like to hear the notes of the recorder?"
Horseplay	Throw the responsibility on the group	"It seems that the group has a problem. What shall we do about it?"
Uncertainty or ambivalence	Define feeling	"You are not certain. You are trying to make up your mind." Or "You feel two ways about this. Part of the time you think it is right and part of the time you think it is wrong."
Hostility toward the leader	Define feeling	"You feel hostile toward me."

SUBJECT-MATTER DISCUSSIONS

The described procedures were employed among college freshmen in conducting discussions of selections, such as Douglas MacArthur's article, "Can We Outlaw War?" from the May, 1955, issue of the *Reader's Digest*. The students, after completing the reading and recording their speed, were given a comprehension test of 10 questions.

CAN WE OUTLAW WAR?

Reader's Digest, May, 1955   p. 39   No. of Words 1560   TIME____WPM

True + False −0

___ 1. The article implies that war is no longer a medium of practical settlement.
___ 2. If war could be outlawed, it would mark the greatest advance in civilization since the Sermon on the Mount.
___ 3. If there were no war hundreds of billions of dollars could be spent to abolish poverty from the face of the globe.
___ 4. The real problem is how to whip Russia.
___ 5. The little people in most countries are opposed to war.
___ 6. There is a definite objective cited by those who recommend 50 years of military preparedness.
___ 7. MacArthur likes the doctrine of limited war.
___ 8. MacArthur believes peace to be a universal wish and necessity.
___ 9. He feels that war augments progress toward civilization.
___10. MacArthur made this speech to the American Legion in Los Angeles.

After answering the questions, scoring the test, and recording the percentage of accurate responses, the students were divided into small groups to discuss the following questions: "Are MacArthur's arguments valid? What other alternatives can you propose?" After discussing for 10 minutes, the recorders made their reports.

RECORDER FOR GROUP NUMBER 1: Our group thought that most of his arguments were valid. New weapons make mass destruction possible. Since it is possible, if both sides have them, it will be difficult for anyone to win anything or settle anything. We all agreed on this. His argument that if the billions spent on war were spent in solving the problems of poverty was a good one, but we wonder if this isn't pretty idealistic, and probably it wouldn't be spent this way. We didn't understand his remark about limited war. It sounds as if he thinks all-out war is better than limited war. Some of us think that there might be times when limited war is necessary. We couldn't think up any good alternatives except perhaps working through United Nations.

RECORDER FOR GROUP NUMBER 2: We think Russia is a determined nation and will not let up until she accomplishes her goal of world revolution and communism for all. The Russians haven't changed much in 30 years . . . maybe in the way they go about it, but not in aims. We have to keep up with Russia in bombs, tanks, guns, and airplanes. General MacArthur is idealistic and sounds logical, but we think just saying we are for peace won't solve anything. We agree that it is wrong to saddle coming generations with a big war debt, but we think he makes it too simple. Maybe this article will do some good, because it will make people think about the problem and they will be surprised to read such statements from a famous general.

RECORDER FOR GROUP NUMBER 3: Our group believes in these statements of MacArthur: (1) that mass destruction can lead to no victory for anyone, now that we can wipe out civilian populations as well as armies; (2) that the money now spent for preparedness could wipe out poverty and reduce international tensions; (3) that the ordinary people of all countries do not want war; (4) that agreements between nations must be profitable to all or they will not last. We do not agree that war is a scientific problem, but think it is a moral one, and moral forces in the world should be more active. General MacArthur was not clear on what measures to take. He did not say anything about trade policies, tariffs, supporting democratic forces in the world, working through United Nations. He stated the problem, but he did not say how to solve it.

RECORDER FOR GROUP NUMBER 4: It is always hard for the last speaker to say anything that has not been said before. Some of our ideas are like the others that have been reported. We agree fairly well with MacArthur. We do not think it is necessary to have full scale conscription in peacetime. My boy friend is in the army and we can't get married until he is out. I'm sure most of the girls don't like this kind of a situation unless it is absolutely necessary. One of the men who fought in Korea was in our group, and he said that machines and equipment that are a few years old are obsolete and that right now he couldn't get any of the new planes off the ground. He would have to be retrained. MacArthur didn't offer any proposals of how to solve the problem except to say we are for peace. We think religious groups could help solve the problems of war. We agree with other groups that United Nations could help. We think FAO, World Health Organization, and UNESCO help and should keep going. We think the International Farm Youth Exchange program is a good thing and other programs like it.

TEACHER: All groups appear to agree that world peace is desirable and that finding the way to peace is a big problem. None is entirely satisfied with MacArthur's solution. Most of us feel that while MacArthur stated the problem, he failed to offer many practical suggestions about solving it. Two groups discussed moral and religious forces as aids to peace. Three groups mentioned working through United Nations, or its agencies. One group mentioned tariffs, world trade, and supporting democratic forces in other countries as factors in peace and war. One group states that we must keep up our armaments as long as Russia does the same. Their views are not exactly in accord with those of the other groups. Two groups agree that newer weapons which create mass destruction make victory impossible for either side, and that the billions spent for preparedness could wipe out poverty in the world, and a third group also mentions the war-debt as a burden on future generations. Personal problems produced by our preparedness program were mentioned by group four, and they questioned the value of military training in a time when science and technology are moving so rapidly as to make recently developed machines and weapons obsolete. The class appears to be interested in this question. The recorders report not only MacArthur's remarks but the thinking of the students. Is this an accurate summary of what has been said? (*Class agrees.*) Since group 2 does not entirely agree with other groups, would someone from the group like to say more about your point of view?

STUDENT FROM GROUP 2: We think military might is the only thing that Russia understands and that going soft would just encourage her to run over the weaker nations.

STUDENT FROM GROUP 3: MacArthur said this was an idea of both Russia and the United States, but that as far as the ordinary people are concerned, they both want peace. We don't believe war brought peace this time, so we should start talking about something that will.

STUDENT FROM GROUP 2: I doubt if you can trust the Russians. We have always had war and we might just as well get used to the idea that all that's kept Russia from striking is our store of H-bombs.

TEACHER: We have two points of view. One group feels strongly that we must protect ourselves against Russia. Another believes that the ordinary people on both sides want peace and that it is safe to start talking about outlawing war. Do we have other points of view?

STUDENT FROM GROUP 4: It might be that what's been going on is a stage in development. Maybe we had to have destructive wars to find out something. Maybe the war had to come and be fought to show us they didn't solve much . . . maybe to open the way for other methods to be tried. I don't think anybody would object to other methods if they work.

TEACHER: I believe you are reluctant to stop talking about this, but our time is nearly up.

Although it may seem that this procedure is time-consuming, with practice the students become progressively able to make efficient use of the time. The discussion following the reconvening of class is often the most productive part of the hour. In a typical session, students contributing during the last 10 minutes of class totaled 16, and the teacher responded to each. The importance of participation has been emphasized. In the session described in preceding paragraphs, there were four leaders and four recorders. Four students contributed remarks in the closing moments of class. All had opportunities to participate in the small group discussions. Among the 25 students, nearly all had something to say. In succeeding sessions, the leader and recorder roles were taken by others. The effect of participation on learning can be illustrated by the remark of a college professor that he took three classes with the same professor and recited once. All that he remembered from the three classes 20 years later was his own contribution.

Habits of inattention or fluctuating attention can be caused by emotional strain, but they are encouraged by the kinds of classes which prevail in high school and college. Students sit through class after class without a chance to contribute anything or even ask a question. Reading becomes purposeless. In the reading class, the student has opportunities daily to talk about what he has read. Reading has a purpose, because in the next few minutes, he will answer written questions and then offer opinions.

One of the most important contributions of the instructor in sessions such as the one just described is the summary statement. When disagreement is recognized, the students realize that the instructor acknowledges their right to hold differing opinions. When agreement is recognized and restated, the class gains in feelings of solidarity.

Although we have emphasized the importance of group decision, we should not like to leave the impression that unanimity of opinion is urged or desired. Democratic leadership recognizes the right and the need for minority opinions. Sometimes, several sessions are needed for a group to arrive at a decision. Some questions are not decided in one semester. Obviously, the instructor does not expect final decisions on the weighty matters which continue to baffle world leaders.

DISCUSSING SELECTIONS ON PERSONAL PROBLEMS

After the group has achieved some solidarity and skill in group processes, the instructor might deliberately introduce an article intended to provoke conversation on a subject known to be of concern to the students. In presenting an author, the instructor avoids giving the impression that this is the last word on the subject. Rather he asks, "How does this strike you? Is this the way you find it?" Testing his understanding of students' reactions, he may find himself responding to them, "You can't buy this," or "This makes sense to you." Selections presenting personal problems often stimulate expressions of emotion to which the instructor responds by reflecting feeling. Because of their defenses against revealing self, some reading students seem to prefer to approach the discussion of personal problems as if they were talking about other people and gradually lead into the first person singular. The instructor should explain that students are free to disagree with the author. Indeed, the discussion will be better if some do.

Genuinely helpful discussion sessions have followed the reading of the article, "How to Overcome an Inferiority Complex," by Norman Vincent

Peale, first published in *Town Journal* and condensed for *Reader's Digest,* February, 1955. Although solving the problem is not so simple as the good pastor suggests, students were able to make use of his comments on its sources. Some found in the article incidents and conditions which applied to their own lives: the young man with the brilliant older brother, the woman who remembered her impoverished childhood, the braggart who covered up his feelings of inadequacy, etc. Generalizations gradually gave way to discussion of their own experiences and feelings.

The usual routine of reading, testing, and recording scores was followed by discussion in small groups. The following are recorders' reports of the small group discussions in one class. The questions for discussion were, "What do you think are the causes of feelings of inferiority? How well do you agree with the author's suggestions for overcoming them?"

RECORDER OF GROUP 1: Our group has the following points to make: Sometimes feelings of inferiority are caused by experiences at home; too much criticism makes people feel, "I can't do it . . . I'm afraid of failure." If a person is ignored too much, it is almost as bad as criticism. We agree that Mr. Peale's suggestions might help. If a person is not religious he might not be able to use the suggestions, and maybe he should see a counselor.

RECORDER OF GROUP 2: We discussed and had some disagreement over feeling inferior and what it does to you. Some in our group have this feeling and others do not, or at least not much. We are not trying to evade the question. We are just trying to understand better what inferiority feeling is and how it might work. We agree with the author that these feelings do have a damaging effect on personality, that they keep you from doing things you would like, keep you from being yourself, that is, growing and becoming mature. We discussed home training and came to about the same conclusions as group 1, that the way you are treated at home while you are small has a lot to do with an inferiority complex. We would agree with the author that the belief that God can help would be good to help overcome an inferiority complex. Counseling might help, too. Mr. Peale counsels people.

RECORDER OF GROUP 3: Many of us know what inferiority feelings are like. They make you mad at yourself. You want to do something and you are afraid to do it. Later you know you could have and you feel disgusted with yourself. The cause, we think, starts, as Peale says, way back in childhood. When parents have the attitude that a child should be seen and not heard, we think it helps to produce feelings of inferiority. It makes us . . . . it makes children feel that they haven't anything to say worth listening to, so they don't talk and they never learn to carry on a conversation. It makes them feel as if they don't amount to much. We think feelings of inferiority are hard to cure. Norman Peale's remedies might help some people. But most of us thought a person would have to be successful doing something for a long time before those feelings would go away. Some people would not feel they could do something just by being told they could. Some people have been told and it didn't help.

Some have probably tried these other things that he suggests and they didn't help. People don't get confidence as fast as this article sounds like they would.

RECORDER OF GROUP 4: We think inferiority complexes are caused in childhood. Sometimes a child feels that he does not belong at school. He feels left out of things. Maybe he isn't treated very well because he comes from the wrong side of the tracks or doesn't play games very well. Maybe he comes from a broken home or is an orphan or doesn't know how to do the things that other children do, or maybe he doesn't have anybody to love him. He's probably afraid people won't like him or will make fun of him. We think Norman Peale should have talked more about prevention.

TEACHER: You are essentially in agreement that most feelings of inferiority begin in childhood, probably as a result of experiences in the home and perhaps in the school, of being ignored or criticized or ridiculed or shut out of the group or made to feel unimportant or of not being loved. They go along with not being able to feel proud of yourself, fear that others won't like you, fear of failure. One group links these feelings with difficulty in communicating. There is also general agreement that Dr. Peale's suggestions might help, although some feel that overcoming this handicap would require success over a long period of time and others say that more should be said about prevention. Some of you have experienced these feelings . . . afraid to try for fear of failure or ridicule . . . afraid people won't like you . . . .

STUDENT: That sounds like me, and then I feel ashamed of myself for not trying, but sometimes I do try and fail, so I think "What's the use?"

T: You feel as if you can't win either way.

S. No. 1: I sure do.

S. No. 2: I always think of the cleverest things I might have said when it's too late to say them. It's disgusting.

T: You feel disgusted or mad at yourself.

S. No. 3: I can often say things well and do things well when I'm by myself, but with other people around they never come off.

T: Somehow, it scares you or holds you back to have people around. (*Several nod.*)

S. No. 4: I think what somebody said about children not feeling important has something to do with it. You feel all the time like you're in the way; you're a nuisance, somebody that has to be looked after but never does anything right; you don't deserve to have anything; you haven't got anything to say that anybody wants to hear, so you just get to feeling that you're not worth much.

S. No. 1: And they think you're going to make good grades and make people like you and join things, and when you don't, you feel like they're disappointed in you, even if you couldn't help it.

T: You think people need to feel that they are worth something, that they belong somewhere. And when you can't measure up to what people expect of you, that interferes with self-confidence, even though you feel their expectations were unreasonable.

S. No. 5: And then you get to thinking that if you just keep your mouth shut, nobody will know, nobody will find out what it is that makes you inferior. Maybe you don't really know yourself what it is, but you're afraid that you'll give yourself away without knowing it.

T: It's safer just to keep still. Our time is nearly gone. Would you like to continue this discussion next Friday?
(*Class agrees.*)

It is obvious that these students were deeply involved in their discussion, discovering, learning, and understanding. The students acted as if what they were saying was very close to them and that their findings were significant. There was a good deal of nodding and, now and then, a murmur of agreement. Some students seemed to be surprised and relieved to find others like themselves. Perhaps this kind of a session could not be said to be therapeutic, but it sets the stage for a therapeutic session and gives the class a feeling that something worthwhile is going on. The students feel closer together, and morale is improved.

To a certain extent, the teacher appears authoritarian and manipulative in the selection of the article and statement of questions for discussion. However, the plan of operation has been approved by the group.

Also helpful in starting discussions on personal problems have been articles on what a man expects of a wife, dating, student government, vocational choice, problems of boys facing army service, and the like. Films on mental health might also be used to stimulate discussion.

Suitable for priming discussion on personal problems are the following: "What If I Don't Get Married?" by Virginia Hurray, "Retaliation Reaction" by James Sonnett Greene, "The Return of the Hairbrush" by Betty M. Scott, "Self-Respect and Self-Confidence" by Douglas Remsen, "Cheer Up" from *This Week* magazine, "The Best Learning" by Cyril O. House.[28] References to childhood experiences and their effect upon personal development may be found in such news stories as "Language Ills Related," "Difficulty in Reading May be Due to Individualism,"[29] "Major Cause of Delinquency Pin-Pointed by Child Authority."[30] *The Rights of Infants*[31] offers interesting possibilities. Adaptations could be made of some of the reports of the White House conferences on children and youth. Interest is stimulated by such articles as "The Cult of Super-Sex" by Ted Berkman.[32] Also appropriate are "The Mask We Wear" by Oliver

---

[28] Lewis, Norman, *How to Read Better and Faster*, Thomas Y. Crowell Company, New York, 1951.

[29] *Science News Letter*, April 2, 1955, p. 213; May 8, 1954, p. 292.

[30] *Kansas City Times*, June 3, 1955.

[31] Ribble, Margaret, *The Rights of Infants*, Columbia University Press, New York, 1934.

[32] *Coronet*, June, 1955, p. 149ff.

Wendell Holmes, "Primitive Parents and Their Children" by Robert H. Lourie, and "Reading and Mental Health" by Marvin D. Glock.[33]

Depending on the class, good use might be made of all or parts of Gilbert A. Highet's article, "Teaching, Not Facts, But How to Think."[34] Aside from meaningful comments on the nature of attention, he discusses some of the vitally interesting and absorbing matters which invade the thoughts of the student even while he is in class, the most demanding, of course, being love. In his remarks are found any number of sentences which could spark the conversation. About his students, he says, "I sometimes look at them with real astonishment, and wonder what keeps them in their seats when every one of them is a mass of explosive forces." He describes the apparently studious fellow who divides his attention between the lecture and the thought that perhaps he is too unattractive to catch a real beauty and the brisk note-taking of the young married woman who is wondering whether she is pregnant. Prevailing attitudes toward love are stated: puzzled by its power, saddened by its cruelties, terrified by its dangers, exultant at its delights, lonely, searching for someone lovable or loving. The great experiences of life are presented as the baby's discovery of the world, youths' discovery of love, and the adult's discovery of art and religion. Sentences such as this could start a challenging discussion: "Very few students ever go through a course without wondering at least half a dozen times whether they ought to drop it."

Excerpts from the writings of Ruth Benedict and Margaret Mead can lead to exciting discussions. Especially stimulating are portions describing disciplinary practices of mild-tempered primitive tribes and their attitudes toward cooperation in the community. Courtship and marriage in other cultures is a subject sure to arouse interested comments. The account of life among the Zuñi Indians offers items of information practically guaranteed to provoke interest; Zuñi children are not punished; economic affairs are secondary to other considerations; the men like to take care of babies, hold them, and fondle them; farmland is jointly farmed for the common storeroom; cooperation and moderation are very important values.[35] Similar customs are described by Margaret Mead.[36]

[33] Glock, Marvin D., *The Improvement of College Reading*, Houghton Mifflin Company, Boston, 1954.

[34] Reproduced from *The New York Times Magazine*, February 25, 1951, in J. Hooper Wise, J. E. Gongleton, and Alton C. Morris (eds.), *The Meaning in Reading*, Harcourt, Brace and Company, Inc., New York, 1953, pp. 20ff.

[35] Benedict, Ruth, *Patterns of Culture*, Houghton Mifflin Company, Boston, 1934, pp. 69–105.

[36] Mead, Margaret, *Sex and Temperament in Three Primitive Societies*, William Morrow & Company, Inc., New York, 1935.

Among the selections which present questions of interest to young people are these: "Men Never Make Passes . . . " by Rhie Thomas, "Dating Behavior of College Freshmen and Sophomores" by Ruth Conner and Edith Flinn Hall, "Education for Marriage—In the Classroom" by Samuel Harmon Lowrie.[37]

Sometimes questions will arise quite naturally in the course of discussing subject-matter selections or defining goals or appraising the progress of the class. While discussing selections from *The Gentle House*, a student volunteered, "Some people might not think this school teacher was real, but I knew a teacher like that once."

T: You sort of enjoy thinking about her.
S: Yes, I do. She was sort of fat, like this one, but she was a real good teacher . . . not too easy; she expected you to work, but you felt like she was "for you."
T: That did you a lot of good.

This was followed by similar comments from other students. Another comment on this book also offered an opportunity for reflection of feeling, "You know, when this boy was living with the rich family, he had enough to eat and good clothes and toys, but they didn't really like him. That's the way it is sometimes."

T: It sounds real to you.
S: I can think of people like that. It causes a lot of trouble.
T: You feel it isn't a wholesome situation.
S: No it couldn't be. I can see why he didn't act very good.
T: You feel a kinship for the boy.
S: I know just how he felt.

GROUP PROBLEM-SOLVING

During the discussion of social, emotional, and personal problems, divergent opinions will be expressed. As in previously described class sessions, the instructor summarizes, "Differing opinions have been offered. Some feel . . . and some feel . . . . Shall we talk about this further?" The instructor in this situation deals almost wholly with attitudes and feelings, reflecting both, redefining the situation when a shift occurs.

A discussion of this kind usually calls forth expressions of hostility, aggression, or embarrassment. They arise from: (1) the resistance of students to accepting new responsibilities; (2) the adjustment to unac-

[37] Jones, Everett L., *An Approach to College Reading*, Henry Holt and Company, Inc., New York. 1953.

customed freedom in the classroom; (3) threat experienced when discussion approaches an intimate problem; (4) reluctance to discuss or disclose a problem regarded as intimate or painful. The member most threatened by the approaching discussion may be the one who tries to appear the most sophisticated. If hostility is not recognized, it will be repeated. The instructor can respond, "You feel threatened." If the student denies the validity of the interpretation, the instructor can ask, "Can you tell me how it is?" This kind of student reaction often indicates the need for counseling. Some of the pseudosophisticated, aggressive students adjust to the class in time. If the morale of the class is seriously threatened by an aggressive student, he might be excused from the class and counseling substituted. Among nearly 500 students enrolled in reading classes over a period of three years, we have found only two who disturbed their groups to this degree. In one case, the progress of the entire class seemed retarded by the aggressive behavior of one member, although he made considerable progress himself. One girl toward whom many of his outbursts were directed seemed to suffer damage to her self-esteem. Two other girls became disgusted with the waste of class time and lost interest in the work. We feel, for the sake of the class, that a student who persists in ignoring the wishes and welfare of the group might be assigned to a more traditional type of class and given an opportunity through counseling to rid himself of disabling aggressions.

On the other hand, the expression of aggression, when it does not damage another member or the class or when it reflects the sentiments of the class may be an aid to progress. Many reading students have underlying feelings of resentment toward authority which they need to express, analyze, and discuss. The conflict produced by concealed aggression cannot be resolved until it is brought into the open.

Expression of aggression can be a wholesome and favorable development, reflecting growing self-confidence. Many students manifest new forcefulness and aggressiveness as they improve reading skills. Thus the reading class demands a sensitive instructor who can discern the fine line between helpful and harmful expressions of aggression.

Some classes are particularly plagued with horseplay. It may be a subtle display of aggression or just natural exuberance. Sometimes, the roisterers quiet down after this reflection, "You just don't feel like getting down to work. You would like to put it off."

These responses do not mean that misbehavior is condoned or that classwork can be avoided. They merely mean that the instructor is trying to understand and communicate.

Reflection of positive expressions should not be neglected: "You like this story. You feel we are getting somewhere. You feel proud of yourself today." Students like to share their feelings of success, pleasure, and growing self-esteem, as well as to confide their troubles.

Group problem-solving works very well with younger children. They can express their feelings much more readily than can the older student who has consolidated his barriers against what he conceives to be a hostile world. Therapy sessions with young children should be brief. When interest lags, the instructor says, "Maybe you'd rather talk about this some other time," or "Shall we go on with the reading class?" A discussion of social relations or playground problems or personal problems can be made a regular part of the weekly schedule or it can grow out of any expression of feeling during the regular class period. Some come about quite naturally as a result of a chance remark or an interpersonal conflict between students. The teacher reflects how they feel: "Billy feels angry and Tommy feels angry, too," or "That made Milly feel bad," or "Monte feels tired, today." Again, the teacher must take care not to give the impression of censure. He merely states what is going on.

Sometimes, the threatened member turns his aggressions on another class member and makes a scapegoat of him. This development should be recognized and defined, "You feel as if you would like to hurt someone else." Another disruptive member is the clown who must assure himself that he can command the attention of the group. The instructor may say, "You like to be the center of attention. You enjoy making people laugh." Or he might say, "Somehow you get considerable satisfaction from disturbing the class or holding up the show."

It would be a temptation to the instructor to inject sarcasm or disapproval into these remarks, but their effectiveness depends on stating them objectively and of trying to see how the situation looks to the various students.

The instructor is wise to have ready a reading exercise which he can substitute if the conversation falls flat. He can check with the class. "Maybe you are tired of talking about this," or "Would you rather not talk about this now. What shall we do next?" If the first session is unsuccessful, the instructor need not be discouraged. He can give the idea a rest and try again at a later date.

The first session may be a little stiff and awkward. By high-school age, the social façade is usually erected. Young people are afraid of ridicule, of losing face before their peers. It may take some time for these doubts and anxieties to come to the surface. Some classes, however, welcome the opportunity to talk about their problems, and all groups indicate they feel greatly relieved after successful sessions.

Expert use of reflection of feeling encourages genuine communication beyond the surface level. Students begin to understand that they are free to express feelings and opinions, even aggressions, without fear of reprisals or humiliation. In time, the students begin to use the technique themselves, reflecting the feelings of their classmates and indicating increasing understanding of other people.

Such sessions make heavy demands on the instructor. He must be alert to the expressions of every member of the group and to cross-currents and interchanges between members. Basic to success is the instructor's attitude of respect for every member and his desire to discover as nearly as possible how things seem to the students. Rather than parroting their expressions, he is taking a look at the world through their eyes and trying to convey to them that he understands how it looks to them.

Some of the class sessions on personal problems are similar to group therapy, but there are some differences. Students in the reading classes are seldom psychotic, prepsychotic, or neurotic, but they do have resistances and problems which restrain them from using their abilities and from working with others. Some aspects of the problem-solving sessions are borrowed from group dynamics, but they go further in the reflection of feeling and exploration of personal problems.

Probably the most difficult situation (because it is the most threatening to the teacher) is reflection of hostility toward the teacher or the classroom procedure. In some classes, it can be handled by incidental reflection of feeling. In others, it reaches proportions where a class session is devoted to discussing it.

The students have been accustomed to teachers who were figures of authority, who took the greater share of responsibility and gave directions. When these conditions are not present, the student feels insecure and somewhat hostile. Even though the students have accepted intellectually the idea of discussing their problems and working out the answers, they have not accepted the idea emotionally. The old attitudes persist: "You do it. You are the leader . . . lead! Tell us what to do."

Even the students who resist authority feel secure in it. When the pressure is withdrawn, they resent the fact that their attitudes and actions are now inappropriate. As long as the pressure is on, it excuses them from doing anything constructive. When it is removed, they flounder. Students will go a long way toward making the teacher get back in his traditional role, even though they have agreed to take responsibility and to use the teacher to help them think through their problems and explore their attitudes.

The handling of this transition period by the teacher is the most difficult stage in forming a democratic group. The democratic teacher is in danger of becoming a scapegoat, a recipient of the aggressions which cannot be safely directed toward more authoritarian teachers.

The teacher is likely to experience deep feelings of insecurity. The new approach, however delightful and idealistic, may appear impractical at this point.

Negativism, in some form, is predictable and is likely to occur in the first four or five sessions. When it is survived, positive feelings, security, pride in the group, adequacy, and a feeling of accomplishment begin to be manifested. Then they can work, play, and talk together without being threatened. In other words, the group is formed in a real sense.

THE GRIPE SESSION

The teacher can sense the building up of tension in the group, and when it is obvious he can precipitate the release of hostility and tension at an appropriate time. Excerpts from a group discussion among college freshmen illustrate the situation with which the teacher is faced and the role he can play.

TEACHER: Early in the course, we set up our goals and agreed upon an agenda for discussion sessions. Among other subjects, we agreed to take a look now and then at progress toward goals and to discuss the effectiveness of procedures. Do you have anything you want to say on this subject?

STUDENT No. 1: Well, maybe it's all right, but seems to me we waste an awful lot of time.

T: This bothers you.

S. No. 2: I've been looking at my progress chart, and I'm not getting anywhere very fast.

T: You're disappointed.

S. No. 2: Yes. Another thing, I don't seem to get on to the ways of doing business in this class. I don't see how they help.

T: Tell me more.

S. No. 2: Well, for example, I can't see this discussion business. It just takes up time that we could be reading. That's what we came in here for.

THREE STUDENTS: That's what I was going to say. I think so, too.

T: Some of you feel doubtful about the discussions or you feel they do not help.

S. No. 3: Well it seems to me, too, that we would learn to read by reading instead of talking.

T: Doesn't seem practical to you.

S. No. 4: They don't to me either. My progress chart looks better, but maybe we'd go faster if we spent more time in reading and using the tachistoscope.

T: Some parts of the class seem useful, but others do not.

S. No. 5: (*Very aggressively*) You can talk and talk and talk and that doesn't make you read any better.

T: You feel very strongly that the discussion is a waste of time. You're fed up.

S. No. 6, FEMALE: Well look, when we broke up in small groups, it worked O.K. a time or two, and then the boys began to horse around . . . interfering with discussion and not taking responsibility . . . The boys make the girls do all the work and make it as hard as they can.

S. No. 7: Discussions might work in some classes, but in this one there are some people that take advantage.

T: You think they might work, but in here some people keep them from being successful. You feel that failure to take responsibility and scapegoating the girls prevent them from being successful.

S. No. 1: Maybe it could work, but it isn't now.

S. No. 6: When we get together to discuss, the boys outnumber us and they vote us in to lead and record and then they don't take their turn leading. They just don't take responsibilities.

T: You don't like the boys' attitude. You feel they get out of their duties and make it hard for you.

S. No. 7: I just get so tired of waiting for something to happen and the class goes on and on and nothing happens.

T: You feel impatient.

S. No. 8: Sounds to me like the girls want to blame this on the boys. That's the way with girls.

T: You're suspicious of them.

S. No. 8: Well, I've gained about 50 words a minute, but I think it's the tachistoscope work that does it. I don't know about the discussions. They take up a lot of time.

T: You feel doubtful about the discussions, but you think the T-scope does some good.

S: Yes.

S. No. 7: One day, you couldn't help seeing how lightly our group was treating the subject, but you didn't do anything about it.

T: It's your feeling that I should have disciplined the group . . . straightened it out.

S. No. 7: Something ought to be done.

S. No. 6: Why don't you just assign so much work to be done by the next class and make us do it?

T: You would like for me to take more responsibility.

S. No. 1: Well, a teacher is supposed to teach, instead of trying to get us to do all the talking.

T: A teacher should get in there and earn his money. He gets paid for teaching. You are not liking it because I don't teach like the traditional teacher.

S. No. 9: We are not used to these methods, and we don't understand them . . . what good will they do? Seems to me we haven't got very far.

T: It's hard to have faith in these methods. You feel insecure with these class procedures.

(*Period of silence.*)

S. No. 10: I've been listening and its seems to me that the relations between the students themselves are not too good . . . not exactly respectful. We agreed to have these sessions and I think since it's new to us and we are not very good yet at leading, some of us feel uncomfortable and we just horse around.

T: Let's see where we are. We have a situation which is relatively new to most of the group. Some feel very insecure and some deliberately waste time. Some feel we should return to a traditional classroom procedure. It has been mentioned that perhaps the boys express resentment toward the girls by trying to assign them most of the work.

S. No. 11: Maybe it's because boys can't really do it well and it's a way of getting out of a spot.

T: I see what you mean. To continue, some feel that when things are not going well the teacher should step in and straighten things out. One student explained that we are new to each other yet and there is little warmth between the members of the class. Some of you haven't spoken yet. Maybe you have something to say.

S. No. 12: I don't think we have given our procedures a good try yet. None of us are very good discussion leaders yet. When you feel you aren't doing very well, you just try to get out of it. We had one very good meeting and one pretty good one. I really like talking in the small group. I think the discussions are good for us . . . saying how things really are.

T: You feel that we haven't had enough experience to decide. You sort of favor the discussions.

S. No. 13: I don't think it's exactly accurate to say that we don't know each other well enough or that we aren't warm to each other. This is the friendliest class I have. I know more people in here than anywhere.

T: You feel most of the students in this class are friendly.

S. No. 14: I know some of us felt that these procedures were beneath our dignity. We thought we knew about democratic leadership and are surprised to find out different.

T: There is a little shock connected with it.

S. No. 14: Yes. I think there is something to it though. If we could get over the hump, it would work.

T: You would give it another try before deciding to give it up.

S: (*Nods.*)

S. No. 12: It seems to me that sometimes the sessions work, and other times the students are not serious, and they don't work.

T: Success depends on the attitudes of the students.

S. No. 6: Sometimes I think it's working and other times not.

T: You feel two ways, sometimes favorable and sometimes disappointed.

S. No. 15: I do think we are slow to talk. That's why we are in here . . . because we are low in reading and verbal ability . . . seems to me this is one way to develop it. I don't understand why we're griping.

T: We have three points of view so far . . . negative, positive, and divided toward the class. Perhaps a few feel indifferent. Quite a few, although you don't feel positive attitudes toward the procedures, are reluctant to give them up. What are some of the things we could do?

S. No. 1: We could have more reading and more tachistoscope and less discussion.

S. No. 6: I think we have enough of that, but I think we need more vocabulary work.

S. No. 2: What if we'd vote just to have a straight class like most teachers teach?

T: If that is the opinion of most of the class we could do that.

S. No. 16: Well I like the reading. It gives me something to talk about and it's not so hard to take part in a conversation.

S. No. 15: Yes, but saying it in the small group is kind of a rehearsal. I don't think I'd use the ideas in conversation without a kind of rehearsal.

T: You think talking things over in here prepares you to talk other places.

S. No. 7: We might keep the discussions about the reading, but cut out the discussions about problems. We don't get very far on those days.

S. No. 17: But that's the part I like the most. We don't get to do it anywhere else.

T: There is still a difference of opinion on what we should do. Some like some parts of the classwork and some like others.

S. No. 17: Well, maybe that's a sign that there is something for everybody in this class.

T: Is the class ready to make a decision?

S. No. 15: I say we should try it like it is for a while and see how it works.

S. No. 14: That's my opinion, too.

S. No. 12: I know my progress chart shows progress. I wonder how many others do. Would it be all right to have everybody who can see progress on the chart to hold up their hands?

(*All except two hold up their hands.*)

In the next "gripe session" this group did decide to continue all activities. Resistance gradually declined and they made progress toward forming a group in the real sense. In the class period following this one, students were noticeably more serious and worked harder on the reading and in the discussion period. Although not bursting with enthusiasm in class periods immediately succeeding the first "gripe session," the students' interest and enthusiasm mounted, and they began to understand the role of the teacher. Some classes form a group without this kind of release. Others seem to need it to get over the hump. Three classes in the spring semester of 1955 moved smoothly into participation in group discussion with little indication of hostility. Two groups of graduate students also made the transition with little evidence of tension. None of our classes have voted to use traditional methods. If a group should agree on this move, it seems appropriate to conform to their wishes, since the teacher has made it clear that the group has the power of decision. If the class should vote to use traditional classroom methods, students who feel the need of the problem-solving sessions might be encouraged to take counseling. However, if the leader is skilled in the techniques and prepared for some hostility, this eventuality is not likely to arise.

DISCUSSING PERSONAL PROBLEMS

Considerable time in the problem-solving sessions is spent on social relationships, boy-girl relationships, lack of self-confidence, shyness, and home adjustment. Since these are illustrated elsewhere, we have chosen a discussion of study habits as an example of a personal-problem session. It is a popular item and the students attack it with interest. It is usually regarded as one of the "safer" topics and is often chosen as the first item on the agenda. The discussion of study skills is often rated highly in critiques and on other evaluative instruments at the close of the class.

TEACHER: The class has agreed to talk about study habits today. Who wants to start the discussion?

S. No. 1: My trouble is that I can't get it all done. They say you should spend two hours outside of class in study for each class you take. Who can find that much time?

S. No. 2: Me too. I'm on the hill about 30 hours a week, counting labs. If you studied 30 to 35 hours, you wouldn't do much else.

T: You feel it's almost impossible.

S. No. 3: Teachers act as if their class is the only one you're taking.

T: Seems unreasonable to you.

S. No. 1: I'm being rushed by a fraternity and they take your time. I belong to the YMCA and that takes time, too.

T: You feel pressed for time and a little bit worried about how you will work it out.

S. No. 4: I have trouble getting started. I mean, after I've decided to get to work. I'm not sure what the instructor wants. I know I'm not making myself clear. . . . It's like this. There ought to be things that stand out . . . that you would recognize as important to the lesson.

T: Kind of confusing. It's hard to see how what you read relates to the class . . . to pick out what is important.

S. No. 5: Look how long it takes to write a theme. I can waste an hour getting started and then I have to do it over a time or two and by that time I haven't time to get my other lessons.

T: It's discouraging.

S. No. 6: Some of us attended a lecture on how to study. It sounds O.K. He said to make a study schedule and stick with it . . . review on weekends. But I don't know.

T: You are doubtful.

S. No. 5: The trouble is, you can't just decide, "I'll do this in 30 minutes." Maybe it takes longer and then you're schedule is all off.

S. No. 7: So many unexpected things come up. There's a house meeting or the boys come by and say, "Let's go to the show. Let's get culture tonight." (*Class laughs.*) So I go out with the troops. Social life is important, too, they say.

T: You want to study, but you feel you have to belong to your group of men at the house. You don't want to be left out.

S. No. 8: I'm working 20 hours a week at a filling station. I have to. My father doesn't send me a nice, fat check every month. I know it's nobody's fault, but I have a tough time trying to get everything done. If I don't work, I can't stay in school. If I do, I'm not learning much.

T: Seems to you you can't win either way.

S. No. 8: I know I'm not the only one working, but the ones who don't have more time to study, have time to do others things, too. I feel like I'm missing something.

T: In a way, you resent the position you're in . . . seems pretty tough to you.

S. No. 8: I don't mean to whine or feel sorry for myself, but teachers and other students don't seems to realize how it is.

T: You would like for somebody to understand.

S. No. 8: Yes. (*Others nod.*)

S. No. 9: I think that's a real problem, but actually most of us don't really do as well as we might. I think it's our own fault. If a person can't make himself study, he ought not be in college.

T: You feel some students don't do as well as they ought.

S. No. 10: I spend the time, but I don't know what I've read. It doesn't stick. I think I'm doing the best I can.

T: Discouraging.

S. No. 11: I sit there, too, but I'm really listening to the conversation in the hall or thinking of other things.

T: Hard to pay attention.

S. No. 11: For instance, girls. (*Class laughs.*) I know there isn't much danger of a man getting many dates, here, but I like the idea (*Class laughs.*) compared to study.

T: Study versus social life. Two conflicting interests.

S. No. 12: I don't really like to study, but I don't want to fail either. I do study, but I can't say I enjoy it.

T: Neither prospect is very pleasant. Your strongest motivation is not to fail.

S. No. 1: Sometimes I think the simplest thing would be to fail and have it settled.

T: Then you would have this decision made for you.

S. No. 12: I think maybe it would be easier to study if I knew how it would be used in the future. I'm not sure any of this is going to be very useful. I don't know yet what I'm going to do.

T: You're not sure how meaningful the classes are. There are several problems . . . conflicting activities like social life or work, distractibility, worry, lack of motivation, lack of study skills, uncertainty. Are there other comments?

S. No. 13: I think many of us were surprised how different college is from high school. We thought we could get by the same way that we did there. I've just been putting off the painful day when I really have to go to work in earnest. I hope it's not too late.

T: You're about to decide there's no other way. It sort of helps to state the situation like it really is.

S. No. 13: Yes, but it kind of obligates me, too.

T: You feel you have to do it, but you resist it, too.

S. No. 13: Yeah.

S. No. 14: Seems like I stumble along . . . take too much time and I don't get enough out of it.

T: Sort of spin your wheels . . . not enough profit from the work.

S. No. 15: I had the same trouble and it helped me to underline important sentences in the book and go over them a time or two before class and at the end of the week.

T: A suggestion about study has been made. Maybe there are others.

S. No. 16: I always study my lesson as soon after class as possible and as nearly on schedule as possible, although I do break over occasionally. It's a funny thing. When that times comes, I find myself thinking about biology or English, or whatever I usually study then.

T: Helps you get started.

S. No. 17: I go to the library to study, so there are no interruptions and others are studying and there's nothing else to do.

S. No. 18: I found that reading or skimming a chapter to find out what it's all about helps . . . like we do in here . . . gives you a general idea. Then you can go back and read it carefully. Makes more sense.

S. No. 13: One thing that helps me is when the instructor makes a big point of something, I write it down and look it up in the book. If he thinks it's important, it'll show up on a test.

S. No. 19: Maybe I should have brought this up before, but exams scare me. Even if I study like they say, I just forget it when I walk in the room to take it.

T: The pressure of the test interferes with your giving your best performance. Are there other comments?

S. No. 20: We're in a bigger league now. It's the freshman year that separates the students from the others. We have to learn to be more efficient and it's hard to do, so we squawk.

T: Part of the pain of growing up.

S. No. 20: Yes.

S. No. 8: I guess anybody could think of this, but I always look over the assignment carefully before I start. I know some just start reading without any particular purpose or point in mind.

S. No. 3: Won't we automatically study better as soon as we learn to read faster? (*Several nod.*)

S. No. 4: Doc, couldn't you give us some pointers? (*Others nod.*)

T: First I want to go over what has already been suggested and see whether you think you can use these practices. They are: underlining the main points, studying as soon after class as possible, studying the same thing at the same time, study in the library, skimming topic sentences, and rereading after you find what the lesson is about, making notes of the instructor's main points, studying up on them, and using the assignment as a guide. I would like to make a suggestion. Systematic weekly review of all underlinings, notes, old exams, etc., of all material covered might help. Can you use these ideas?

(*The students debate. Some express approval. Most of them take notes.*)

S. No. 5: When you get behind, is it better to spend your time on the lesson for the next day or read the back chapters to try to catch up.

S. No. 20: I get the one for the next day.

S. No. 6: Yes, but if it's economics or geometry, you gotta know what has been left out or you can't get your lesson.

T: Depends on the kind of lesson.

S. No. 8: I try to catch up on Sundays, but, of course, it means no fun.

T: You do it, but you don't like it.

S. No. 9: I get the lesson for the next day and then try to spend a little time on the back lesson.

S. No. 13: I've decided to get up early and study when I'm fresh. I've tried it twice and it works pretty well.

S. No. 11: I've decided that I'll promise myself if I have a certain amount done by nine o'clock, I'll take a break. If not, I won't.

T: Sort of reward yourself if you do well.

S. No. 4: I think maybe a break is O.K., too, especially if you are yawning and rubbing your eyes.

S. No. 9: I just say to myself, "Unconsciously, you're finding excuses for not studying. You're tricking yourself." And then I start again.

T: Understanding yourself helps you get started again.

S. No. 12: It would be so much easier if I really was interested.

T: Our time is nearly up. Are we ready to make some decisions? Would you like to try those which seem most useful and then have another session to report whether or not they work? (*Class agrees.*) Which of them do you think you can use?

S. No. 13: I think underlining might help. (*Assent from several.*)

S. No. 7: I might try studying at the library, but I sure hate to think of it.

S. No. 11: Guess maybe the library might help me, too.

S. No. 1: Could I come in and talk to you about a study schedule, Dr. ____? I don't know as I can make one by myself.

T: Certainly. Just write your name on the appointment calendar.

S. No. 5: Most of us could use skimming, now that we've done it in here.

(*The class finally agrees to try skimming, underlining, and using the instructor's summary as a guide. Some individuals state they will try study schedules and review.*)

T: Some students have mentioned problems of motivation and interest and difficulty in relating subject matter to their needs. Would you like to have another session to discuss these angles? (*Class is undecided.*) Students with these problems can bring them up in counseling if they wish. Would you like to think about this and talk it over later? (*Class agrees.*)

This class responded with a number of useful suggestions. One of the students had discussed study habits in the counseling interview, and he repeated what he had been able to apply. A few had attended lectures on the subject. Some referred to techniques practiced in the reading class. In some other reading classes, the students waited for the instructor to offer suggestions, some of which were acceptable to the class.

ROLE-PLAYING

Role-playing in the reading class serves two purposes. It gives the members experience in roles they will be playing without the threat of failure or punishment which they feel in a real situation, and it prepares the group for discussion. Incidentally, the instructor learns about the attitudes and feelings of his students. The following is an account of a role-playing session followed by discussion. The discussion is an important part of the session.

TEACHER: Last time we role-played a situation where the boy called up a girl and asked her for a date. This time, let us reverse the roles and see what happens. The girls have planned a formal dance and have agreed to invite boys to the party. Bill, will you play the part of the boy who is called? Mary, will you make the call and see if he is free to accompany you? Each of you take your place in a corner in front of the room with your backs to each other. Chairs are the only props we have. Are we ready to go? (*Teacher rings a bell.*)

BILL: Hello.

MARY: This is Mary O.

BILL: Oh! How are you, Mary?

MARY: All right . . . Bill, we are having a party a week from Saturday night and I wondered if you would be free to go with me. It's a formal dance.

BILL: I'm afraid I can't make it.

MARY: Oh, I'm sorry . . . I guess I waited too late to call.

BILL: Oh, no. (*Silence.*)

MARY: Is there some difficulty, like a tux or something?

BILL: No, I just don't want to go.

MARY: (*Flushes.*) Oh. Well oh, that's too bad . . . Well I'm sorry. Good-bye.

T: (*To Bill and Mary.*) Just keep your places but face the class.

STUDENT NO. 1, MALE: That's not the way it usually comes out. The girls can get anybody they want.

S. NO. 2, MALE: I think Bill was playing hard to get because he resents the general situation here, the boy-girl ratio of three men to one girl.

S. NO. 3, MALE: Yes, I think it's his way of letting her know how it feels to be turned down.

S. NO. 4, FEMALE: Bill took advantage of the situation. When boys call, most of the girls really do have dates and Bill didn't.

S. NO. 5, FEMALE: Bill made it too hard on her. She was nice and polite, and Bill knows how to be nice, but he wasn't.

T: You girls feel sympathetic with Mary and a little resentful toward Bill.

S. No. 6, Male: Maybe Bill was a bit rough on her, but you know a lot of us men are more or less waiting for a chance to get even.

S. No. 4: Even with Mary?

S. No. 6: No, not her, exactly . . . .

S. No. 4: Who, then . . . .

S. No. 6: Maybe not any one person. What makes me mad, I'll call up and a certain girl keeps me dangling for about a week. Then when it's too late, she calls, "Sorry I can't make it," and shows up with another guy. How do you like that?

T: That makes you pretty mad.

S. No. 4: Has this got anything to do with Mary? She isn't the one.

S. No. 7: No, it's just that a lot of girls play that game. They wait to see just how good a deal they're going to be offered. When they finally refuse, you know you've been dropped for somebody they think is better, or a party that looks better to them.

S. No. 8: I've known cases where the girl after making a date calls up and breaks it just before a dance and shows up with someone else. Bill at least was honest. He gave her a point blank, "No!" She had time to find somebody else.

T: It's obvious that the boys resent the dating situation here, and they feel some girls take advantage of the situation. Some wish there was a way to get even. They want the girls to know how it feels to get turned down. Mary, do you mind telling us how you felt?

MARY: I felt awfully funny. It was unexpected. I guess in real life, I wouldn't have pressed him to explain why . . . just ended the conversation when he refused, but I know Bill very well. I couldn't think what to do.

T: It was a shock.

MARY: I had no doubt but what he would accept if he were free.

T: You were surprised and embarrassed.

MARY: Almost like it was real. At least, if it was real, nobody would know about it. I felt kind of let down.

T: Like the props had been yanked from under you? (*Mary nods and tries to smile.*) Bill, would you care to tell how you felt?

BILL: I have to work awfully hard to get a date and sometimes there are so many ifs and ands that I wonder if it's worth it. I don't have anything against Mary. I just wanted to get my idea across.

MARY: You acted like I had wronged you some time.

BILL: I know. It probably seemed like I was taking it out on you.

MARY: I didn't know what I had done to be treated that way.

S. No. 9, MALE: Some of us boys have given up dating. We're not very good at social things and conversations, so we just go to athletic events, shows, and the beer parlors. Sometimes we play cards.

T: Decided to give the girls a good leaving alone.

S. No. 9: Well, there's no fun in it the way it is.

S. No. 10, MALE: You ought to belong to a fraternity. Then you wouldn't have any trouble.

S. No. 9: Who me? A frat rat! I hope not. If I get a date, it's going to be because I'm me and not because I belong to a frat.

S. No. 11: The frats just about have the girl population reserved, don't they . . . sort of an unwritten agreement.

S. No. 10: All I'm saying is that it's easier to get a date if you belong to a frat.

T: We have a complicated social situation . . . too many men and too few girls. The boys resent the attitudes of the girls and some resent the advantage that the fraternities have. Fraternity members defend their organizations. Mary feels as if she was made a scapegoat, and I think Bill has slight feelings of guilt about today's incident. Some men feel like giving up dating. I suspect the girls in the class are surprised somewhat at the revelations made today.

S. No. 11: All you need to get a date here is a Cadillac convertible, 10 suits of clothes, a shiny frat pin, and plenty of money . . . and of course several hours of extra time to spend on the telephone.

S. No. 4: That's not so. If I like a boy I go with him whether he has money or not. One trouble is, that, they wait until the night before to ask you and then get mad if you're dated up.

S. No. 7: You can't always win, even if you ask in plenty of time. I think the girls should have some kind of honor code . . . something the men can depend on.

S. No. 4: Well some of us do . . . take the first that asks us, not break a date except for some good reason like sickness, be polite to everybody and not hurt anybody's feelings, and so on, but, after all, should a girl accept a date with a boy she really doesn't care for? The boys at least have some freedom about who they ask, but the only way a girl has of choosing is to turn down or accept dates. She doesn't issue many invitations.

S. No. 5: Some of the boys are so suspicious that if you do have a good reason, like maybe your mother has come unexpectedly, that they don't believe you even when you can't help it.

S. No. 11, MALE: I don't have any trouble, because I don't depend on girls here. I have a girl at home. But I wonder if the men aren't too quick to feel offended when the girls don't go with them. I wonder if there aren't a lot of girls over at East Hall that don't have dates tonight.

T: You feel part of the difficulty is in the attitudes of the boys toward themselves. They don't feel sure of themselves and are quick to feel rejected.

S. No. 4: Even if you haven't got a date when a boy asks you, you can't go out every night, even if you'd like to. You have to study and wash your clothes and your hair and clean up your room.

S. No. 11: I think many of us are shy and self-conscious. We call up somebody a time or two and nothing happens. We feel like we're not good enough, and we resent the whole deal.

T: I see. It hurts your pride and self-esteem.

S. No. 12, MALE: Maybe, we get in the habit of calling the same girls and don't think of other girls that might be free.

S. No. 13, FEMALE: I know nice girls who don't have dates.

S. No. 14, MALE: Yes, but how do you get to meet girls? There isn't much way, here.

T: You're beginning to feel as if there might be more girls available for dates if there is some way to meet them.

S. No. 12: I think I understand more about this situation now. A man hadn't ought to be too innocent, because he might get the run-around, but, on the other hand, he hadn't ought to feel insulted if he gets turned down. Maybe the deal here is kind of hard on girls, too. They can't help it if there aren't enough girls to go around.

S. No. 11: Yes, and maybe there really are girls who would be nice and like to have dates, if we just knew where they were, and in classes like this we get acquainted better.

T: The men are changing their minds a little bit about the behavior of the girls.

MARY: I feel a little different, too. I didn't realize that maybe a boy has to get his courage up to ask for a date and feels almost as bad as I did when he gets refused.

S. No. 5: I know a little bit more about how the man feels, too, but I don't know what to do about it.

T: The girls understand a little more about how the boys feel, but the problem is hard to solve. The men have shown some hostility toward the women. This session threatened the women pretty badly, and produced anxiety. They feel as if they had to take it because they are here, and the girls who caused these feelings aren't here. Some of the boys feel that part of the trouble is in the social adjustment of the boys, that their attitudes toward themselves are part of the cause of the strained relations with the girls. Do you agree that while this session raised the tension of our group, we understand the situation and each other a little better?

The class agreed, and in succeeding sessions they showed more understanding and camaraderie.

INCIDENTAL PROBLEM-SOLVING

One morning, a class dragged in and slumped down in their seats with somewhat less than their usual enthusiasm.

T: You look whipped this morning.

S. No. 1: We are. (*Nods and agreements from others.*)

S. No. 2: Shall we tell him.

S. No. 3: I think we can tell him. I can talk to him.

SEVERAL: O.K. You tell him.

S. No. 3: We're in trouble with another teacher. Almost all of us are in this other class, too. We're discouraged. He just doesn't seem to understand us.

T: Does the class want to take time to talk about this now? (*All agree.*)

S. No. 2: Well, he doesn't seem to like us. He doesn't care about us.

T: You feel he's indifferent.

S. No. 4: I feel all the time like he's making fun of us.

S. No. 5: He never hands our papers back on time.

S. No. 6: But worse than that, he acts like he thinks we don't know anything. If I did know anything, I wouldn't say it in there, because you never can tell when you've made yourself ridiculous.

S. No. 2: Or he makes you feel ridiculous.

S. No. 7: And the grades. I think it's the toughest in school. You just can't make a dime.

T: You're upset and worried and disgusted. Things are all fouled up.

S. No. 5: You can say that again.

S. No. 8: You not only feel that he thinks you don't know much, but that you aren't going to learn much. He thinks we're hopeless.

T: You resent his attitude and you're discouraged, too.

S. No. 3: What do you think, Doc? Can you help us?

T: You'd like me to do something about this.

SEVERAL: Yes, we would. Could you talk to him?

T: You think it might help if I'd talk to him. You'd like for me to take the responsibility.

S. No. 6: Well, somebody ought to. Would you?

T: That would be one way to handle it. Are there any other ways?

S. No. 6: Nobody else to do it . . . except one of us.

T: You think that might help.

S. No. 1: Actually I don't, but maybe we ought to try it.

S. No. 6: I guess it is more our responsibility.

S. No. 9: We might elect someone.

S. No. 10: We might elect a committee.

S. No. 11: Why not ask for volunteers?

S. No. 12: Why not all of us?

S. No. 6: When he comes to class, let's just ask him if we can talk about our relationships with him.

They agreed to do this. At the next meeting of the reading class, one of the students reported, "Mission accomplished. No casualities. We came out O.K. Things are all cleared up."

At times, the students themselves took care of questions. A group of students were discussing problems of communication. Student X insisted that it is a simple matter: You just speak and the other person hears.

STUDENT Y: But you haven't communicated unless what you say is received. Hearing what you say doesn't mean it is received.

X: Nuts . . . . You just . . . .

STUDENT Y: For example, what you are saying now isn't being received. Can't you tell?

Five other boys looked at X and nodded.

This group developed a sensitivity to the feelings of others and skill in communication beyond the selection of the "right" words.

Sometimes, the group was rough with a member, but, on the other hand, a naïve question was handled rather gently, as in the case of a girl who was just beginning to date boys.

STUDENT A: What does a boy mean when he says, "I'll see you."

B: What did you think he meant?

A: Well I thought I really would see him. I thought he'd be back to see me.

B: Well when you leave a girl after a date, you have to say something. You try to think of something that will be polite.

C: It's something to say instead of goodnight . . . . He wouldn't say, "I won't see you."

B: No and he wouldn't say, "Maybe I'll see you around sometime." He doesn't want to hurt your feelings.

C: He wants to say something friendly, but not too definite.

This girl wrote, "I think the discussion on dating was very interesting. I believe they helped many of us solve problems that were bothering us."

The opinions of peers is often seen to be more influential than anything said by the instructor. A semester of counseling had made little impression on an immature girl. A schoolmate said to her gently, "Come now. Don't act like you're 10 years old." There was a visible impact at the time, and a change in behavior was noticed following the incident.

If the group decides to take care of a disciplinary problem, its actions are often more salutary than those of the instructor. For example, a troublemaker in a college class was finally quelled by a classmate who asked, "What junior high school are you from?"

Occasionally, the exchange of remarks took place between the instructor and one student. Sometimes, the student was voicing the discontent of other class members and the group felt relieved because their views were represented. For example, one student stated his discontent with the class, "This class isn't what I thought it was going to be. I thought I was going to learn how to write better themes." This kind of conversation followed:

INSTRUCTOR: In other words, you are disappointed in the class.

STUDENT: Now don't get me wrong. I think it is a good class and it's interesting, but themes are what I get credit for and I don't get any practice in here.

INSTRUCTOR: You feel as if it isn't helping you in the way you want to be helped.

STUDENT: Well, it isn't what I expected. I didn't know what I was getting into.

INSTRUCTOR: You feel you were misled, perhaps cheated. You can't help resenting it.

STUDENT: I guess so. I guess this is one kind of help I need, but it looks like it takes a lot of time away from other important things I've got to do, too.

This student became noticeably more cooperative and more receptive after having an opportunity to discuss his resentment, the pressures he felt, and his ambivalent feelings toward the classwork.

In one class, the boys aggressed vigorously against the girls. No girls appeared on the following class day. After it became apparent that they were not coming, the boys began to be very uneasy.

S. No. 1: Where are the girls?

T: You wonder where they are.

S. No. 1: It sure is funny for all of them to be absent.

S. No. 2: Wonder if it has anything to do with yesterday's discussion.

T: You think you might have been too rough on them.

S. No. 3: Aw, it's just a coincidence. They'll be back tomorrow.

However, the girls continued to stay away and the boys continued to speculate on their absence.

S. No. 4: No girls.

T: This really concerns you.

S. No. 5: Doc, do you think what we said had anything to do with this?

T: You're beginning to think it might.

S. No. 6: I really like girls. We weren't mad at them. Do you think they thought we were?

T: You're a little worried.

S. No. 7: Come to think of it. We were pretty rough.

T: You think you might have been too hard on them.

S: No. 8: We've been pretty browned off at all the girls, and we took it out on these few in here.

S. No. 9: Ever since school started.

S. No. 10: Do you think they'll ever be back?

T: You'd like them to come back.

S. No. 10: Sure. They make the class better.

S. No. 2: Maybe if we want to keep them in the class, we'd better treat 'em better, if they come back.

On the fourth class day, Ernestine returned to class.

S. No. 1: Hi Ernie! (*Chorus echoes the greeting.*)

ERNESTINE: (*A little defensively.*) Hi.

S. No. 2: Don't sit over there by yourself. Sit with us.

T: You're glad she's back. (*Chorus answers, "Sure. Yes."*)

S. No. 3: Are the other girls coming back?

ERNESTINE: I don't know.

S. No. 4: Why did they stay away?

ERNESTINE: Maybe they didn't like the browbeating.

S. No. 4: We weren't mad at them.

ERNESTINE: Sounded like you were.

S. No. 4: Well, maybe we were a little bit mad about the situation here, but not personally at these girls.

ERNESTINE: Maybe they couldn't tell the difference.

S. No. 5: When they come back, things will be different.

T: You have a changed attitude toward the girls.

S. No. 5: I think we all do.

On the next class day, the remaining girls returned, and interpersonal relationships improved steadily.

GROUP PROCEDURES WITH YOUNGER STUDENTS

Some of the subjects which can be discussed by younger students are these: What do we want to accomplish in the reading class this week (or this month or this year)? What do we like best and what do we like least about the reading class? How can we tell that we are doing better? What part of the story do we like best? What makes a good leader?

Questions regarding interpersonal relations arising during class periods or play periods can be discussed. The teacher can inquire, "Is this a problem? Would you like to talk about it? What shall we do about it?" A decision may not be reached in one discussion. If interest flags, the teacher might ask, "Are you tired of talking about this? Would you like to wait and talk about it again sometime?"

A group of children in the primary grades were interested in a discussion which followed an incident described by the teacher.

T: Once upon a time there was a man who was very much interested in chickens. He found that in every flock there is one chicken who can peck all the other chickens and none of the others can peck him. Then there is another chicken who cannot peck the head chicken, but can peck all the rest, and they cannot peck him. Another cannot peck the two ahead of him, but he can peck all the rest, and so on. There is one chicken who gets pecked by everybody and cannot peck anybody. Why do you think this happens?

A: He is the littlest.

B: All the others are bigger.

T: You think all the others peck him because he is the littlest.

A: Yes. That is what happens lots of times. If I would see that little one I would help him.

T: You would like to help him.

A: Yes, because it isn't his fault because he is little. He can't help it. He feels bad.

T: You feel sorry for the little chicken.

A: Yes.

B: I do, too.

T: A. and B. feel sorry for the little chicken.

C: Maybe this one chicken is different from the rest.

T: You think he gets pecked because he is different.

C: If somebody is different, the others don't like him.

T: You feel as if the others don't like him.

C: He'll never have any fun.

T: It's hard to get along because he is different.

D: If I was the one who got pecked, I'd run away and hide and come back when I was grown and kill 'em all.

T: You would be so angry that you would feel like hurting them.

D: Yes, but if I was the head chicken I'd peck all of 'em.

T: You'd like to be the head chicken.

D: Yes, because then I could peck all of 'em.

T: You would get satisfaction out of pecking them.

D: Yes, but what I'd like better is to grow up and show all of them that were bad to me when I was little.

T: You would like to pay them back.

D: Yes.

E: Why should all those chickens peck that other chicken even if he is different or even if he is little?

T: You wonder why.

E: I wouldn't peck him, if I was a chicken. I'd tell the others, "You should not peck this chicken."

C: But maybe they wouldn't pay any attention.

E: Then I'd say, "Can't we talk this over?"

T: You think that might help.

E: Sure it helps to talk things over.

T: What do the rest of you think about this?

F: I think they ought to talk it over and decide what to play that this little chicken could play, too.

After talking longer, the group decided that was what should be done. The first pupil to speak was the smallest boy in the room and the youngest in his family. Pupil C. was ignored by her classmates much of the time because she was not allowed by her parents to learn to square dance or to play baseball. Pupil D. felt resentful toward his parents and his brothers. It seems apparent that these pupils were actually discussing their own problems. The solution, talking it over and including retiring pupils, was one which they used frequently in attacking school and playground problems.

Reflection of feeling can often be used in handling conflicts between pupils. A quarrel was going on between pupils A. and B. and threatened to become violent.

T: A. and B. are angry with each other.

B: He shouldn't have punched me.

A: I didn't punch him. He got in front of me.

B: He punched me in the stomach like he was mad at me. (*Seems on the verge of tears.*)

T: B. is upset, because he thinks A. is mad at him.

A: I didn't really punch him in the stomach. I just wondered what he had in there. He acted like he was mad at me.

T: A. wonders if B. is mad at him.

B: It was only my little green story book I was taking home, to read to my mother.

A: I really don't know what we should do about it.

T: You think something should be done.

A: No. (*Wonderingly.*) I already apologized.

The two boys smiled at each other and went away with their arms around each other.

Some of the most important expressions of feeling among grade-school pupils are related to resentment to older and bigger people. Some of these feelings were expressed in a role-playing session. The roles were: two sisters and the father and mother.

T: The father has come in from the barn to tell his wife that the milk-stool is broken. They wonder if the children might have done it. Pretty soon, the children come in. The father begins talking.

FATHER: When I went out to milk I found out the milk-stool is broken. I can't milk without my milk-stool.

MOTHER: Oh my! I suppose the children did it. What shall we do? Shall we spank them or send them to bed for a week?

F: I think we ought to mend the milk-stool.

(*The two daughters come in.*)

M: Your father says that the milk-stool is broken. Did you do it?

GIRLS: No we didn't.

M: Well how could it have got broken?

ALMA: I think Gordon did it.

HELEN: I know he did.

M: Did you see him?

A: Well . . . yes.

H: I didn't really see him, but I saw him coming out of the barn and run. (*Silence.*)

T: Shall we ask the class what they think about this play? (*Cast agrees.*)

B: Did the brother really do it?

A: No, we just said he did.

C: Why did you say that?

A: Well, we would have got blamed if we hadn't.

T: You didn't want to get blamed.

H: No, because we didn't know what they might do to us.

T: You were afraid.

H: Yes.

B: Were you mad at your brother?

A: No, but he's bigger and he can take the blame better than we can.

H: Besides, he doesn't like girls and he's mean to us.

T: You feel that he doesn't like you.

H: He doesn't. And besides he tells on us, so we have to pay him back.

T: You feel as if he has it coming to him.

H: Yes, he does. He thinks because he is bigger we have to do what he says.

T: You don't like that.

A: Boys are like that . . . to girls, sometimes.

T: You feel that boys are sometimes unfair to girls.

A: Big brothers are . . . but sometimes they're nicer.

H: Maybe we shouldn't have told that.

A: Maybe there would be some other way.

T: Would you like to play the scene over?

They agreed and played it over. Both these girls had older brothers who attempted to dominate them. Apparently, they welcomed an opportunity to express their aggressions in a situation which promised no reprisals.

Cunningham[38] describes a number of uses for group discussion among elementary-school children. One of its functions, she believes, is to help them define good leadership and choose good leaders who can help the group make progress toward group goals. Examples are given of the sensitivity of children to effective leadership. Fourth- and fifth-graders

---

[38] Cunningham, Ruth, et al., *Understanding Group Behavior of Boys and Girls,* Bureau of Publications, Teachers College, Columbia University, New York, 1951, pp. 122ff.

evaluated leaders in these terms: gives everybody a chance; got around to everyone; wanted to do what we wanted to do; gave her suggestions but took ours; got things done. Special abilities were recognized: "He is good at helping us to do so and so." Different leaders were regarded most competent for different projects.

Steps in problem solving were described: defining the problem, gathering evidence, suggesting solutions, testing solutions, evolution in changed behavior. Personal problems were discussed. The children listed things they wanted to improve about themselves. Other subjects were: how can we play ball better; how can I get along better with my sister; how can I get people to like me; how can I get more friends.[39]

Evaluating their group discussions, these children stated they: liked the way all of us were some kind of a leader; liked to know I was an important person as all the rest of the people; liked to be able to give suggestions without everybody laughing at you.[40] When listing experiences regarded as valuable, this group placed emphasis on opportunities to be a leader or representative of people their own age.[41]

Cunningham and her associates recommended proceeding from discussion of home experiences and relationships to problems of the world community.[42] The relation of their own group processes to world affairs was apparently understood by junior-high-school pupils. A representative remark by one pupil was this, "We learned about how to get along together, to work in groups, also about how people in other countries get along together and they get along together and they get along just like we do."[43]

EVALUATION OF LEADERSHIP

The teacher, and later the class, might profit by examining the degree to which the needs of the group are understood and met. Phillips[44] has prepared a list of the needs of the group members: a sense of belonging, of being welcome for one's total self; a share in planning the group goals; a feeling that the goals are within reach and make sense to the individual; a belief that what is being done contributes to human welfare, that its value extends beyond the group itself; a share in making the rules of the group; a knowledge in clear detail of what is expected of the individual; responsibilities that challenge the member within the range of his

[39] *Ibid.*, pp. 275ff.
[40] *Ibid.*, p. 288.
[41] *Ibid.*, p. 265.
[42] *Ibid.*, p. 281.
[43] *Ibid.*, p. 282.
[44] Phillips, Don, "Basic Needs of People in Groups," mimeographed, Hillsdale College, Hillsdale, Michigan.

abilities and that contribute toward reaching the goals of the group; evidence that progress is being made toward the goals which have been set; to be kept informed; confidence in the leader. Speaking for the member, he says, "The situation in which I find myself must make sense to me regardless of how much sense it makes to the leader." He suggests that the leader rate himself, giving a possible 10 points for each need he is conscientiously trying to meet, and asks, "What would be your score now? A month from now? How would your members rate you now? A month from now? How would you rate your own leader?"

Factors preventing self-expression in groups are listed by Phillips.[45] (1) Early training has not encouraged discussion (home, school, church, etc.). (2) Physical environment is not favorable (stuffy, hot, cold, poorly lighted, formal or uncomfortable seating arrangement, distance from speaker, etc.). (3) The group is unprepared for discussion. (4) The leader, expert, or a member tries to dominate. (5) Members are hampered by fear of: ridicule, taking a stand which may be unpopular, deficiency in grammar, stuttering, exhibiting lack of control, appearing stupid, being contradicted, offending others, etc. When discussion time is ineffectively used or when groups fail to arrive at a decision, these possible causes might be reviewed with the group.

Two means of self-evaluation by the leader or teacher are offered here. Items included in each might be used as a basis for discussion by a class or by teachers involved in self-training.

Self-Rating Scale for Leaders

Do you (1) always, (2) frequently, (3) occasionally, (4) seldom, (5) never . . .

1. Ask the class early in the year to help state the goals of the class? 1 __ 2 __ 3 __ 4 __ 5 __

2. Later in the term call for a restatement of goals of the class? 1 __ 2 __ 3 __ 4 __ 5 __

3. Take time to let the students review progress toward goals? 1 __ 2 __ 3 __ 4 __ 5 __

4. Permit digressions from the course outline if they seem to be profitable? 1 __ 2 __ 3 __ 4 __ 5 __

5. Help class members get acquainted with each other and with you? 1 __ 2 __ 3 __ 4 __ 5 __

6. Encourage students to express their own opinions as well as to recite facts? 1 __ 2 __ 3 __ 4 __ 5 __

[45] Phillips, Don, "Factors Preventing Self Expression in Groups," mimeographed, Hillsdale College, Hillsdale, Michigan.

7. Divide the class into small groups for discussion purposes? 1 __
2 __   3 __   4 __   5 __

8. Give students an opportunity to respond to lectures and readings?
1 __   2 __   3 __   4 __   5 __

9. Present more than one point of view? 1 __   2 __   3 __   4 __
5 __

10. See to it that shy or retiring members get to talk? 1 __   2 __
3 __   4 __   5 __

11. Let the class decide what to study next? 1 __   2 __   3 __   4 __
5 __

12. Let the class help plan a project? 1 __   2 __   3 __   4 __   5 __

13. Ask for opinions on methods? 1 __   2 __   3 __   4 __   5 __

14. Ask for opinions on helpfulness of subject matter? 1 __   2 __
3 __   4 __   5 __

15. Ask how the class can be improved before the end of the semester?
1 __   2 __   3 __   4 __   5 __

16. Interview students who are lagging? 1 __   2 __   3 __   4 __
5 __

17. Interview students whether they are in trouble or not? 1 __   2 __
3 __   4 __   5 __

18. Respond to feelings expressed by members. 1 __   2 __   3 __
4 __   5 __

Self-Rating Scale for Leaders

Check any that seem appropriate or write in a description of your practice.

1. If a student offers what appears to be an honest opinion with which you disagree, do you:
   __(a) treat it with respect?
   __(b) ask him if he would be willing to look for more facts?
   __(c) ignore him?
   __(d) disagree with him?
   __(e) ridicule him?
   __(f) _____?

2. When one student tends to dominate class discussion do you
   __(a) permit this?
   __(b) offer your own opinion?
   __(c) ask the class for other contributions?
   __(d) break the class up for small group discussion?
   __(e) ask a classmate to summarize what has been said?
   __(f) _____?

3. When opinions are presented as facts, do you
   —(*a*) point out the error?
   —(*b*) ask if others agree?
   —(*c*) ask where the speaker got his information?
   —(*d*) ask if this contribution agrees with facts available?
   —(*e*) inquire of the class where other information can be found?
   —(*f*) _____?

4. When you see that the class is tired, do you say something like this:
   —(*a*) I think we need a seventh-inning stretch.
   —(*b*) Shall we go on with this or shall we stop a minute to stand up and move about a little?
   —(*c*) I know you are tired, but we must keep at this if we are to accomplish anything.
   —(*d*) "This reminds me of a story . . . ."
   —(*e*) Class is dismissed.
   —(*f*) _____.

5. When some students behave in a high-schoolish manner, do you say something like this:
   —(*a*) If you can't behave in here, you will have to get out.
   —(*b*) X., Y., and Z. will see me after class.
   —(*c*) X., Y., and Z. please sit in the front of the room.
   —(*d*) It seems the class has a problem; is there anything we can do about it?
   —(*e*) Some people in this class are obviously not mature enough for college work.
   —(*f*) Please be quiet.
   —(*g*) _____.

6. When a subject seems exhausted, do you
   —(*a*) ask for more contributions?
   —(*b*) ask if it is time to move on to another subject?
   —(*c*) ask a class member to summarize what has been said?
   —(*d*) summarize yourself and ask for comments?
   —(*e*) contribute neglected items of information?
   —(*f*) _____?

7. When it is apparent that the class agrees on an important point, do you
   —(*a*) recognize and summarize agreement?
   —(*b*) go on to the next point?
   —(*c*) summarize and ask the class if your statement represents their impressions?
   —(*d*) _____?

8. When members are in disagreement, do you
   __(*a*) ignore it?
   __(*b*) summarize points of disagreement?
   __(*c*) try to cover it up?
   __(*d*) recognize, "Mr. A. feels very strongly that so and so is true and Miss B. feels just as strongly that it is not true."?
   __(*e*) settle the disagreement by giving your opinion?
   —(*f*) _____?

SUMMARY

Group procedures are introduced as a means of helping students to solve problems related to reading, to solve general problems, and to create a classroom climate favorable to growth and learning. The reading class is not limited to improving skills, but can contribute to general education and citizenship training.

Excerpts from classroom discussions are given to illustrate setting group goals, leadership training, group decision on academic subjects, exploring personal problems, and evaluating classroom procedures. Four types of leadership are defined. Some advantages of democratic group leadership over other types of leadership are stated, and studies are cited in support of cooperative thinking and group decision. Democratic leadership is said to be superior to other kinds in terms of: productivity, originality, initiative, morale, self-discipline, personal adjustment, objectivity, cooperation with others, quality of performance, and changes in behavior. Communication among members is believed important to the performance of the group. The instructor's role of leadership is gradually relinquished to the members. The leader helps the members get acquainted, states the problem before the group, gives each an opportunity to contribute, shows respect for each member and each contribution, summarizes, clarifies, and states points of agreement and disagreement. Techniques for meeting hostility are given. Reflection of feeling, as used by the leader, is explained and illustrated. The incidental use of group problem-solving is discussed and illustrated. Role-playing is suggested as a means of helping students to meet threatening situations and as a springboard for discussion. Illustrations are given of the use of group procedures with younger students. Self-evaluation by the leader is proposed and instruments which might be used are introduced.

CHAPTER 7

Counseling the Retarded Reader

Both group experience and individual treatment were mentioned in Chapter 1 as important aspects of remediation. Counseling is the individual side of remediation. From test data, conversation, behavior in class, and all available information about the client, the counselor can make a tentative decision as to whether the student is amenable to counseling and how long a period of counseling will be needed to help him overcome handicaps, use his abilities, or secure needed information. One interview is recommended for each student. The counselor and client can decide together whether counseling should be continued.

If the reading instructor is also a counselor, there are many advantages in his doing the counseling. The continuing group contact helps to cement a relationship of mutual respect and trust. The two kinds of contacts supplement each other. The element of personal interest in the student carries over into the classwork and has a motivating effect. In the class, the instructor sees a side of the student's personality which is not so readily apparent in the interview. For example, he sees the student work in the context of a group. If the teacher does not counsel, he should work closely with the counselor.

COUNSELING SITUATIONS

Some of the problems which reading students bring to the counselor will be similar to those treated in any counseling center. In the light of research findings on the characteristics of the high "Q," low "L" student, one can anticipate a number of naïve, indifferent, or constricted students, perhaps than the usual proportion. Such cases require a somewhat different approach from the customary opening question, "How can I help you?"

Among the various interview situations which can be anticipated are these:

1. The student shows symptoms of a physical handicap, little evidence of an emotional problem, and a need for professional diagnosis from outside authorities.

2. There is evidence of an emotional problem which appears to consume the energies of the student and interfere with improvement.

3. Symptoms of serious emotional involvement and physical handicaps are lacking, but the student has no apparent objective, vocational or otherwise, or only vaguely defined objectives.

4. The student shows few symptoms of emotional problems, but he was previously unaware of a reading problem and wishes to talk over his situation.

5. The student is aware of his reading problem, but doubts his ability to improve.

6. The student is aware of his reading problem, believes he is improving, but wants to check his impressions with instructor or counselor.

7. The student does not recognize that he has any problems and makes an appointment merely because it is required.

8. The student vehemently denies that he has any problems.

9. The aggressive, belligerent student is disturbing the class and needs an opportunity to blow off steam in a situation where he will not do damage to group or individual morale.

10. The student has little faith in the class or in counseling.

11. The problem appears to be limited background or inadequate training.

12. The student wishes to pursue some subject discussed in class.

13. Progress is hampered by a temporary problem such as financial need, illness, or family emergency.

14. The student comes principally because he is curious about his test results.

15. The student wants more help with study schedule, vocabulary drill, or other skills than he can get in class.

16. The reading problem is complicated by a combination of several of these factors.

Judging from research findings presented in previous chapters, some students will not know what kind of people they are nor what kind they wish to be. Many will be unwilling to accept responsibility. Some will lack the maturity to do a task thoroughly or completely or to work independently on any problem. Some will have the notion that it is not respectable to talk about personal problems or to recognize that one has a problem. Some problems will be so well concealed from the student himself that he will be unable to verbalize them.

In order to overcome handicaps and to make the necessary changes in behavior, the client must learn, just as he does in the classroom, except that learning about self is often more painful and more difficult than learning subject-matter. The counselor needs to consider how much resistance is present before counseling begins and how the counselor must behave in order to avoid raising the client's resistance. One of the important considerations before the counselor is this, "In what kind of counseling climate will this particular client learn what he needs to know?"

If counseling is to be successful, the counselor and the client must communicate with each other. The client who does not have the necessary self-esteem finds it difficult to communicate with others. He may shut out a part of the world and refuse to see it. The world does not look the same to him as it does to a person with wholesome self-esteem. Words and phrases have different meanings for these different kinds of people. The printed word has different meanings. For example, varying reactions may be found to the simple question, "Do you like to walk in the country?" The constricted, over-conformative person may hesitate while he reviews how the gang would answer. Maybe it would be "corny" to like to walk in the country. Better not take a chance on being labeled a hick. Or he might feel called upon to defend the beauties and virtues of walking or living in the country. The paranoid might think it over, too, "I wonder what he means by that? Why is he asking me a question like that? He must have some hidden motive. Is he suggesting, probing, insinuating anything?" The hypochondriac might feel too ill and weak to walk anywhere or he might dwell on the dangers of poison ivy, sunstroke, or insect bites. A person with hysteria might think of hay fever. The boy who stated he did not like the farm, the sunshine, the hard work, the dark farmhouse might react explosively to this question. If the counselor is to understand his client's talk, he must be able to see into the world of the client. And he must consider how his statements and questions will be interpreted by the client.

GOALS OF COUNSELING

Some of the goals of counseling are implied by the foregoing remarks. Simply stated, they are: to help the client solve problems and to help him get needed information. In individual cases, the goals may be: to help the client see himself more clearly and to see his environment more clearly and realistically; to help him to formulate or clarify goals; to help him recognize problems and make plans to overcome them if possible. In the case of the retarded reader, the counselor hopes that the experience of communicating thoughts and feelings and relief from emotional stress will help the individual to improve his communicative skills and to make progress toward independent thinking, planning, and problem solving.

One of the important goals in counseling is to help the disturbed client to like, accept, and respect himself. Without belief in self, he cannot use his abilities to the fullest and he cannot live harmoniously with other people. This point of view is presented by Gardner Murphy, who asserts that[1] " . . . unlovely self-pictures lead to unlovely views of others . . . " and conversely,[2] " . . . positive attitudes toward what lies within the self go hand in hand with positive attitudes toward all that lies beyond it."

Recent studies of the counseling process suggest, tentatively at least, that when counseling is successful, the client gradually improves his opinions of self and others.[3] Preliminary to describing a research project involving 31 clients, Rogers and his colleagues make this prediction for client-centered therapy,[4] " . . . that the individual will change in the direction of increasingly viewing others as persons of worth." The authors also hypothesize that[5] " . . . following therapy an individual will be more effective in problem-solving." The progress of one client, Mrs. Oak, through therapy is described in detail and judged successful by the counselor's rating, evaluation by retest with the TAT, and other measures. Among evidences of success, according to the rating of the therapist were improvement in personal integration and life adjustment. Also cited was the client's satisfaction with the outcomes of therapy.[6] The authors comment that perhaps the greatest change is in confidence in self.[7] Mrs. Oak was asked to sort 100 descriptive statements, choosing those which best described her; she sorted them a second time, choosing those which described how she would like to be, and a third time, choosing those which best described the ordinary person. This routine was repeated at the conclusion of therapy, seven months later and a year later. Review of changes in her sortings suggest that Mrs. Oak's opinion of herself became more like her ideal. Her opinion of the ordinary person also moved closer to her concept of the ideal person. The changes

---

[1] Murphy, Gardner, *Personality: A Biosocial Approach to Origins and Structures,* Harper & Brothers, New York, 1947, p. 497.

[2] *Ibid.,* pp. 596–597.

[3] Rogers, Carl, et al., *Studies in Client-Centered Psychotherapy,* Psychological Service Center Press, 1275 New Hampshire Ave. N.W., Washington 6, D. C., 1951, pp. 63ff, 97ff, 103ff.

[4] *Ibid.,* p. 24.

[5] *Ibid.,* p. 25.

[6] *Ibid.,* pp. 56–57.

[7] *Ibid.,* pp. 63–65.

reflected in the sortings suggested a change in self-concept toward more security, confidence, emotional maturity, expressiveness, and warmth, and decreasing guilt, resentment, and defensiveness.[8] Test and retest with the TAT suggested that at the close of therapy the client felt less threatened by people, interpreted less implied scorn from others, was increasingly able to accept the idiosyncrasies of others rather than to condemn or fear them.[9] In the opinion of friends, she appeared less dependent, less defensive, less selfish, less ambivalent, less inclined to blame others, and more basically democratic.[10]

Seventeen clients judged improved by counselors (and by TAT test and retest) sorted the 100 descriptive statements, according to self, ideal, and ordinary person. When sortings before and after therapy were compared, the opinion of self had moved closer to the concept of the ideal person.[11] Ratings drawn from test and retest of 23 people with the TAT suggest that these changes took place during therapy: improved attitudes toward mother, father, siblings, mate, self, superiors, peers, work, community, etc.[12] To establish the reliability of interpretation, 12 clinical psychologists gave interpretations on all other scales for five clients. Agreement was high. Agreement on 24 of the 25 ratings was high between the two clinicians who studied all TAT records. These results were in agreement with the impressions of therapists. A group which received no therapy, but which was tested at the same intervals made little change in their TAT records.

CHOOSING METHODS AND TECHNIQUES

As can be seen from the list of situations with which the counselor is confronted, techniques differ according to the needs of the student and according to his receptiveness. Some students need information and others need an opportunity to explore personal problems. Some who need information will not be able to make use of it because of resistances and emotional blocks. If a screening test indicates a visual problem, the student may or may not be able to make use of the information about where he can obtain a professional diagnosis. If a student is interested in choosing a vocation, he may need to know where he can take more tests or learn of opportunities in various occupations. Information about study

[8] *Ibid.*, pp. 66ff.

[9] *Ibid.*, pp. 60–61.

[10] *Ibid.*, pp. 97ff.

[11] Rogers, Carl R., and Rosalind F. Dymond (eds.), *Psychotherapy and Personality Change*, University of Chicago Press, Chicago, 1954, p. 36.

[12] *Ibid.*, Chap. 9.

skills or efficient use of time may or may not be welcome. If the problem is lack of information, the techniques are not the same as in the case of an emotional problem. In each case, the counselor tries to discover whether the client needs information and at what point in counseling he can make the best use of it.

The orientation of the counselor and his philosophy govern his choice of techniques. Writers on this subject agree that counseling is a learning situation. They often disagree on the kind of techniques which can produce learning. In the past 12 or 15 years, two patterns for counseling have been widely discussed. This apparent schism between directive and non-directive (or client-centered) counseling produced various reactions among counselor trainers. Some became committed to one or the other. Others shied away from the subject, expressing, at times, a reluctance to admit acquaintance with either. A feeling of insecurity seems reflected in these responses: "Why get involved in this controversy?" or "There is really no difference between the two." The subject became almost as sensitive as "academic freedom" or "McCarthyism."

Some solved the dilemma by asserting that, "Eclecticism is the answer." We submit that a truly eclectic counselor will be well acquainted with both methods of counseling and with the philosophy and techniques of other methods, as many as possible. Ignoring these contributions produces a superficial eclecticism which is neither directive, non-directive, nor counseling. Counseling is not merely a friendly conversation, with the counselor in the role of a good-tempered and patient godfather.

The effective counselor must have techniques and skills and he must have a philosophy which ties them together. Furthermore, if one becomes committed to a naïve and superficial stand in early stages of training he may resist learning the necessary skills for professional performance.

A graduate student once hurried into the office of his instructor with his textbook in his hand and announced, "*You* are non-directive!" This accusation was expressed in the tone of voice he might have used to declare, "You are a fellow traveler." He offered as proof the fact that the chapter on counseling contained so-and-so more pages on the subject of non-directive counseling than on directive counseling, ignoring a 47-page chapter on measurement and test interpretation which described the tools of the directive counselor. This student had made up his mind about counseling before thoroughly exploring the possibilities and had closed his mind to one of the major contributions to the profession.

Henry Borow[13] described three or four viewpoints which apply here

[13] Borow, Henry, "The Proper Use of Occupational Information," address before the annual convention of the National Vocational Guidance Association, Chicago, April 5, 1955.

as well as to the field of vocational guidance. Analyzing professional literature on counseling, he noted articles which emphasize the giving of information, some of which emphasize the use of standardized tests, and a few which attempt to integrate the two in the general counseling process. In another part of his address, he described the impact of non-directive counseling upon student personnel work as having produced among both the information givers and the psychometrically oriented a temporary state of emotional and philosophical disorder from which they emerged somewhat chastened and improved. A little of each, he said, has rubbed off on the other.

We shall try to introduce both viewpoints and some others (as fairly as one can in a brief chapter) with the strong suggestion that the beginning counselor explore these methods thoroughly before attempting to use any of them. College classes and a more intensive study of books and articles on counseling methods will be required before an intelligent choice can be made. After studying various techniques and using them in supervised practice, the counselor is better prepared to choose than if he becomes committed to a point of view on the basis of rumor and hearsay. Even after years of experience, counselors find themselves modifying their practices. The following is merely an introduction.

SOME VIEWPOINTS ON COUNSELING

Points of agreement can be discerned among the exponents of various methods, but there are some distinguishing characteristics of each. All directive counselors do not use exactly the same methods. Neither is all non-directive counseling exactly the same. The way in which each counselor applies any method reflects his own values, habits, and personal adjustment.

Directive Counseling

Some characteristics usually associated with directive counseling are these:

1. The counselor secures all of the information that he can, before he sees the client, from test results, school records, teachers, high-school principals, parents, etc.

2. He gives the client information about himself, curricula, vocations, tests, recreational opportunities, resources of state and community, human nature, study skills, at a time when the client appears able to make use of it.

3. He may guide the conversation into channels which appear most fruitful.

4. He may ask questions, make suggestions, present alternative courses of action, describe the possible consequences of certain choices or decisions.

5. He may take some responsibility for decision-making, guiding the student into what appears to be a suitable curriculum, vocation, or extra-class activity, etc.

6. He answers questions, responding to the client principally at the verbal or intellectual level.

7. He may refer the student to other specialists, instructors, outside agencies, or suggest materials for the student to read.

The directive counselor believes he has information from sources and experiences not available to the client. Perhaps, he feels that he has no right to withhold it. He may feel that to withhold information shows a lack of respect for the client, and takes away from him the opportunity for an intelligent decision. He knows, however, that learning takes place when the information answers a felt need. Williamson[14] warns against giving advice without first making certain that it is appropriate to the individual student.

The well-known five steps in counseling often followed by directive counselors are presented by Williamson and Darley:[15] (1) analysis and synthesis of all available data about the student; (2) diagnosis; (3) prognosis; (4) counseling; (5) follow-up.

After the client explores his problem, Thorne[16] suggests that: the client and the counselor discuss objectively unrealistic or erroneous attitudes; the client proposes a solution; the counselor presents alternatives; the counselor assigns definite tasks; discussion follows on how to face problems realistically.

Directive counseling appears to have been instrumental in improving retention of students, achievement, liking for school, attendance, persistence in college, decrease in discipline problems, and student-faculty relations. Studies suggesting these and other outcomes are reported in Woolf and Woolf.[17]

In terms of learning theory, the client who is directively counseled possibly experiences the confirming reaction when information offered is meaningful to him. In the case of a report on test results or psychological

---

[14] Williamson, E. G., *Counseling Adolescents,* McGraw-Hill Book Company, Inc., New York, 1950, p. 54.

[15] Williamson, E. G., and J. G. Darley, *Student Personnel Work,* McGraw-Hill Book Company, Inc., New York, 1937, pp. 168ff.

[16] Thorne, Frederick C., "Directive Psychotherapy," *J. Clinical Psychol.,* vol. 1, no. 2, April, 1946, p. 378.

[17] Woolf, Maurice D., and Jeanne A. Woolf, *The Student Personnel Program,* McGraw-Hill Book Company, Inc., New York, 1953, pp. 8–13, 21.

interpretation, he may feel, "This is like me. This fits!" When receptive to information about vocations, study skills, visual training, etc., he may feel, "I can use this." Reinforcement may also be enhanced if the client understands that the counselor is genuinely interested in him. When the client successfully performs tasks assigned by the counselor, he may experience the feeling of reward necessary to success.

Certain trends in directive counseling are suggested by recent writings on this subject:

1. The counselor apparently allows the client a greater proportion of the talking time than formerly.

2. The counselor apparently permits the client more freedom in guiding the conversation.

3. More emphasis is placed on the emotional side of learning.

4. Urging, warning, blaming, moralizing, probing are seldom, if ever, recommended.

5. The client is encouraged to make his own decisions after all available and relevant information is presented.

6. The counselor plays a less authoritarian role than formerly and some might be appropriately labeled non-authoritarian rather than directive.

7. Rather than guiding the client into suitable activities, he offers information and leaves decisions to the client. In other words, the counselor shares more responsibility with the client.

Non-directive Counseling

Some characteristics commonly associated with non-directive counseling (also called client-centered or emergent) are these:

1. The counselor gathers little, if any, information about the client, believing that he can better respond to the client if he approaches the interview without preconceived impressions.

2. He gives little or no information.

3. The client is told that the time is his to use as he wishes, the counselor follows the leads given him by the client, and the client guides the interview.

4. The counselor does not ask questions, give suggestions, offer alternatives, or describe possible consequences.

5. Decisions are left to the client.

6. The counselor tries to see how things look to the client and to respond within these limits, paying close attention to subtle expressions of emotions, emotional tone, facial expressions, gestures, physical tension, and other than verbal expressions.

The foregoing six points are modifications of the views of Carl Rogers.[18] Adequate understanding requires thorough study of his works.

The principal distinguishing characteristic of non-directive counseling, in our opinion, is the technique of reflecting feeling. The counselor tries to show by his responses to the client that he understands how the client sees the situation and the client's feelings toward himself and his situation.[18] When trying to learn to use reflection of feelings, the beginner finds himself searching for just the "right" word, and feeling for the client's real attitude. Sometimes, he fumbles around in his own vocabulary, becoming very conscious of the process, perhaps temporarily losing contact with the client. At some point, he may discover that he has "hit the right feeling" with exactly the term most meaningful to the client. This moment of mutual understanding is a new experience for both. The client may or may not try to verbalize the reaction. One client said explosively, "Now you're talking down my alley!" Others say, "Yes," or nod, smile, or continue to pursue the subject, showing by depth of feeling and candor, recognition of the counselor's understanding, interest, and good faith. A kind of communication takes place beyond the surface level. It is difficult to describe. Sometimes, the counselor notes in the facial expression and posture of the client a visible response to the impact, as if with his whole being the individual says, "This is important. This never happened before. This fits. He knows. We both know. This is how it really is." The client has learned something significant about himself and something about trusting others. He has never felt so thoroughly understood and affirmed before.

The counselor's tone of voice as well as his words can convey meaning to the client.[19] Suppose he says, "You resented that." It may mean, "I am following your story and I understand." It can also be said in a manner that conveys, "How surprising!" or "Shame on you!" or "How shocking!" Reflections of feeling should not be colored with shock, blame, etc.

Sometimes, the counselor may recognize that the client is expressing an emotion or a problem which may be difficult to discuss or which by conventional standards would be considered an inappropriate subject for discussion. The counselor may sense that the approaching revelation is close to a problem of his own, or he may fear that he cannot cope with the situation. In the phraseology of the profession, "the counselor feels threatened." The beginning counselor hesitates to say, "You feel worthless," or "You are beginning to believe that your parents did not love

[18] Rogers, Carl, *Client Centered Therapy*, Houghton Mifflin Company, Boston, 1951, pp. 23, 32, 42, 44.
[19] *Ibid.*, p. 28.

you," or "You feel that everyone is against you." He may discover that the appropriate response is, "You didn't want to come for this interview." If this is what the client means, he needs to say it and have it recognized. Recognition does not mean assent or approval. It merely signifies, "I see what you mean."

When the client feels that the counselor really does understand and accept his feelings and the way he sees the situation, the two, counselor and client, have arrived at a point where they can communicate and work together on the problem. The client cannot see the world as the counselor sees it, so if they are to communicate, the counselor must be able to see through the eyes of the client.

In cases of certain kinds of deep emotional disturbances, this kind of communication appears to be necessary for improvement. After finding that he is understood, the client eventually recognizes that he does not need to defend his actions. Apparently he must relieve himself of aggressions, doubts, fears, etc., before he can begin to function in an effective manner.

Seeing the client's reaction to the correct reflection of feeling is a growth experience for the counselor. His attitude of acceptance, respect, and understanding is not completely achieved until he has tried these responses and has seen them work. The experiences of the counselor and his attitudes are circular in effect. He makes the response because of his attitude of respect and acceptance, but the response modifies the attitude in the direction of more respect, acceptance, understanding, and so on.[20]

After a time, the counselor may find that he no longer must search for the "right" word. He begins to feel, to some degree, with the client. He gets into the client's perceptual field and sees the situation as the client sees it. He checks occasionally with the client to see if his impressions are correct. Describing the process of interview, a counselor with 20 years of experience explained, "I almost forget myself, put myself in the place of the client, and try to see the situation as he does."

Most counselors believe themselves to be permissive and accepting toward their clients. Few wish to find fault with their clients, to make them feel guilty, or to point out where they might have acted differently. Non-directive counselors go further. They believe that if they suggest how a problem might be solved, they imply doubt of the individual's worth and ability to make decisions for himself. Complete acceptance, in their definition, means belief that the individual does have the right and the power to work things out for himself, with such understanding as develops from deep communication between himself and the counselor. We are all aware that having accurate and complete information

[20] *Ibid.*

does not ensure that one will act wisely. Complete acceptance by the counselor is believed to minimize the client's resistance to learning.[21]

Implied in this method is the belief that the most meaningful and permanent learning comes about when the individual discovers for himself the most effective solution. It is aimed at independence for the individual. When the counselor takes more than his share of responsibility, the client may remain dependent.

Among the many aspects of non-directive therapy which might be discussed is the change which usually takes place in the client's responses if progress is made. Rogers[22] describes a rise and decline of negative expression, followed by ambivalent and then positive expressions of feeling. "The more violent and deep the negative expression (provided they are accepted and recognized), the more certain are the positive expressions of love, of social impulses, of fundamental self-respect, of desire to be mature." This development, he says, is one of the most certain and predictable aspects of the whole process.

Some counselors find it difficult to respond to expressions of ambivalence. These are some suggestions, "You feel two ways about this. You feel divided. You want to and you don't want to. You like it, but at the same time, you don't like it, etc."

The counselor may feel somewhat confused after listening to a long involved response in which several feelings are expressed. Curran[23] suggests a "forking response." Here is an example: "You enjoy your work, like your employers, want to please them, and you enjoy the praise they give you, but at the same time you want to do well in your studies, and it is difficult to find time for all of the interesting things you could do here."

Silence is a problem to some counselors. The client may be thinking over what has been said, or struggling to find the words to express himself. He may resent an interruption. On the other hand, he may interpret the counselor's silence as rejection. Some believe that a summary statement at this point helps the interview along. Something like this may be acceptable: "You were talking about . . . . Would you care to tell me more about this?" Or "It might be helpful if we were to review what has been said." Or "During the last three interviews you told me these things . . . . Did I understand you correctly?" Review or summary statements are, of course, used by counselors with other orientations.

[21] *Ibid.,* p. 193.

[22] Rogers, Carl, *Counseling and Psychotherapy,* Houghton Mifflin Company, Boston, 1942, pp. 35–39.

[23] Curran, Charles A., "Structuring the Counseling Relationship, A Case Report," *J. abnorm. and soc. Psychol.,* vol. 39, 1944, pp. 189ff.

Some of the evaluative studies of non-directive counseling are mentioned in this chapter in connection with the discussion of goals. Improved attitudes toward self and others and improved functioning appear to have been among the outcomes. Watt[24] used test and retest with the Minnesota Multiphasic Personality Inventory in studying the results of non-directive counseling in the treatment of delinquents. The evidence suggests that the clients moved toward recognition and acceptance of reality as it is seen by others. Twenty-two subjects were selected and paired as nearly as possible on the basis of age, intelligence, grade placement, and other records. From each pair, one was selected for counseling and the other placed in the control group. The experimental group made more gains toward better adjustment on three scales than did the control group and the differences were significant at the 1 per cent level. Differences on two other scales were significant at the 5 per cent level. Gains shown by remaining scales and two other measures of personality were favorable to the experimental group, but not statistically significant.

Why and how does learning take place in the client in non-directive counseling? It is possible that the client experiences reinforcement or a confirming reaction when ideas fit together, when he senses that he is accepted and understood, when he feels that he has discovered something new about himself or his environment. In his discussion of the law of effect, Stroud[25] points out that the definition of effect is not restricted to pleasurable after-effects, but rather implies a confirming reaction, a sort of biological reinforcement or tension reduction. The larger pattern of goals and strivings of the individual and the degree to which the consequences appear to belong to an act influence which results are experienced as satisfying. When the client no longer needs to defend himself and progresses to the point where he glimpses a little more of his environment, he may feel something like this, "This is how things really are." As he explores himself, he probably experiences reinforcement when he discovers, "Maybe I'm not such a bad fellow after all." Reward can be subtle, as in the experience of acceptance, self-understanding, relief from tensions, seeing a new way out of a dilemma.

Some trends in non-directive counseling are suggested by Rogers'[26] chapter on the training of counselors and therapists. Some of the early

---

[24] Watt, George D., "An Evaluation of Non-directive Counseling in the Treatment of Delinquents," *J. Educ. Res.*, vol. 42, no. 5, January, 1949, pp. 343–352.

[25] Stroud, James B., *Psychology in Education*, Longmans, Green & Co., Inc., New York, 1946, pp. 369–370.

[26] Rogers, Carl, *Client-centered Therapy*, Houghton Mifflin Company, Boston, 1951, pp. 429–478.

non-directivists gave the impression that there was only one right way to counsel. Rogers[27] points out the advantages of helping the counselor-in-training to discover how he might naturally counsel. He also suggests that the instructor avoid producing in the counselor-in-training guilt, rebelliousness, or a feeling of "oughtness" which may result from insistence on a single point of view. These remarks appear to reflect growing flexibility in his views toward counseling.

Although some differences can be seen in the two methods, there are also some apparent similarities. The technique of mental catharsis, allowing the client to talk himself out, often associated with non-directive counseling, is employed by many counselors with different orientations. The importance of attitude of the counselor toward the client is universally recognized.

The question of the amount of responsibility taken by the counselor is often debated. Although the non-directive counselor places responsibility on the client for introducing whatever subjects he wishes to discuss, for guiding the interview, and for decision-making, he actually assumes some responsibility when he accepts the individual as a client. In our opinion all counselors have gradually moved in the direction of sharing responsibility with the client, of regarding the counseling interview as a problem-solving situation with both counselor and client working on the client's problem.

Cottle[28] finds a number of elements common to all systems of counseling. He makes the following points: (1) The counseling relationship is based on mutual trust and respect and the counselor's belief in the client's growing capacity to solve his own problems. (2) Communication involves gestures, posture, voice inflection, and facial expression, as well as counselor understanding and use of the client's vocabulary. (3) All counselors make use of general knowledge about people, attained both from scientific study and from living with others in many walks of life. (4) As the client progresses in therapy, he makes a change in expressed feelings from negative to ambivalent to positive feelings or from confusion and uncertainty to constructive thinking and planning or from the need to hide the real self to being himself, and these changes in attitudes are reflected in his behavior. (5) In one way or another, the counselor conveys to the client the limitations and procedures to be observed in interview.

Similarities were found between directive and non-directive counselors in a study of 230 interviews by 35 counselors from five university coun-

[27] *Ibid.*, p. 459.
[28] Cottle, William C., "Some Common Elements in Counseling," *Personnel and Guidance J.*, vol. 32, no. 1, September 1953, pp. 4–8.

seling centers.[29] The interviews were analyzed by two judges with regard to the degree to which the counselor gets ahead of the client's last remark and the degree of pressure in counselor's remarks. Counselor responses were rated on the amount of "lead" by means of a scale of from 1 to 50. Although only eight of the counselors reported they were non-directive counselors, others who called themselves directive were rated as demonstrating less lead than some of the non-directive counselors. Among the seven counselors rated as showing the least amount of lead, four were directive counselors. It is interesting to note that among 82 clients only 13 were said to have no adjustment problems. Apparently counselors tended to employ less lead in cases of adjustment problems than in other cases. Test interpretation was reported used in only eight cases.

Some of the decisions which must be made by the counselor are discussed by Seward Hiltner.[30] He describes a shy, retiring girl whose mother is trying to get her to take a more active part in church work and social events. He came to believe that it would be wrong for him to manipulate the girl to join an activity, even though, on the surface, it appeared to be a good thing for her. She was resisting the domination of her mother by the only means available to her. If her mother and pastor had been successful in involving her, Hiltner says, Charlotte would have been convinced that her own poor self had no self-starter. The last small bit of resistance to unbearable domination would have been destroyed. "If Charlotte had been able to participate because *she* wanted to and affirmed it for herself, in activities of the group, it would have been immensely helpful to her! But so long as that meaning for Charlotte is one of knuckling down to Mother, and not affirming herself, it will not be useful to her." He suggests counseling.

The charge has been made that non-directive counselors actually maneuver their clients and control the situation by choosing one of several expressions to respond to. It probably is a temptation to many counselors to frame responses with the intention of leading the client to follow a certain line of reasoning or to arrive at a conclusion which appears reasonable and desirable. No truly non-directive counselor would do this.

A combination of several methods will be described in the remainder of this chapter. Requiring each reading student to make an appointment, as we suggested in another chapter, is a violation of the non-directive code, as the client is presumed to have the right to make this decision for himself and to be more receptive to counseling if he takes the step

[29] Danskin, D. G., and Robinson, "Differences in the 'Degree of Lead' Among Experienced Counselors," *J. of Counseling Psychol.*, vol. 1, no. 2, 1954, pp. 78–83.

[30] Hiltner, Seward, *The Counselor in Counseling*, Abingdon Press, Nashville, Tenn., pp. 46–49.

under his own power. Among reading students, we have found many who responded well to non-directive counseling, even though the first interview was required. At the close of each interview, the door was left open for them to return if they wish, and the majority of those with emotional problems take advantage of the opportunity.

A fairly recent book by Pepinsky and Pepinsky[31] presents some interesting ideas about counseling. From the data available about the client, the counselor perhaps with help from colleagues, constructs a hypothetical man. He can then make some predictions about how the client will act during therapy and how long a period of therapy will be needed. If the client fails to behave as predicted, the counselor reviews the data and the processes of counseling to see whether he misinterpreted the data or whether his own behavior in counseling has interfered with progress and possibly revises his hypothesis. To follow this line of reasoning further, one might conclude that the fears, anxieties, needs, ambitions, etc., of the counselor do affect the counseling process. If he is conscientious, he wants the client to improve. The counselor's awareness of his own status and anticipated satisfactions accruing from successful counseling are involved. If he becomes impatient because the client does not behave as predicted or does not make progress as fast as he would like, or does not say what is expected, his effectiveness is greatly impaired. These observations call attention to the dangers of preconceived notions about the client. On the other hand, if the counselor is forewarned and personally secure, he may be able to make use of test results and other case data. It would be a mistake to set a goal of making the Pa score come down or raising the social adjustment score. It is not the function of the counselor to try to force the client to conform to a norm or a standard or to adopt the values of the counselor. The client must be free to develop his own values and standards.

Neither should counseling be regarded as a subtle way of enforcing cultural values. Accepting them may be one of the outcomes of counseling, but it does not come about as a result of manipulation or exhortation. Disregard for the standards of society is not the result of "not knowing," but of being unable to find satisfactions in observing them. The rebel cannot be unaware of the values and standards of the society in which he lives. Concern for the values of others does not come about readily unless the individual can accept himself and believe in his own worth.

Most clients, probably all of them, have been told and told about good and bad behavior. A seven-year-old of our acquaintance has been lectured so many times that he doesn't hear the admonitions any more.

[31] Pepinsky, Harold, and Pauline Pepinsky, *Counseling: Theory and Practice*, The Ronald Press Company, New York, 1954, pp. 206–232.

He doesn't even hear things he really wants to hear. An eight-year-old heard, "Be a good boy," daily from his grandmother, weekly from his Sunday-school teacher, and frequently from his teacher. Certainly when he fought with the younger pupils, mutilated the school furniture, and drew naughty pictures, his behavior was not the result of not knowing. After a year of counseling and being recognized for the good things he did, he was able to use the information which he had accumulated and to apply it to behavior.

Many counselors believe that clients do not work on their problems unless they are under stress. Some believe that unless the client is under stress to some degree, counseling is not indicated since he is not in a state to make use of the service. Some take the responsibility of producing stress by giving information from test results or other sources or by having pressure brought by the high-school principal, instructors, or other outside sources. Others would hesitate to become so manipulative. Some counselors employ psychological interpretation, explaining to the client the reasons behind his behavior or the probable source of his problem.

Some interrupt the process of reflecting feeling to point out that what the client is saying does not agree with previous remarks or even to state that what the client says does not sound reasonable. If rapport is good, the client trusts the counselor, feels that what he says will not be held against him, and feels that the counselor respects him, and the counselor can make hard-hitting statements without damaging the counseling relationship.

SOME CONSIDERATIONS IN COUNSELING

In the case of a visual problem, lack of vocational objective, or any situation where the problem is essentially lack of information, directive counseling is appropriate. If the client needs to express aggression, hostility, feelings of inferiority, self-doubt, anxiety, or other intense emotions, the counselor will often find that reflection of feeling works wonderfully well. Obviously, this kind of client will need a large share of the talking time and will doubtless welcome the opportunity to take the lead in interview. Students with temporary problems, such as failing grades or family emergencies, usually respond well to non-directive techniques, but they often need information, too.

People with deviate Hy and Hs scores often have fears, anxieties, and dilemmas about which they need to talk freely to an understanding listener. In such cases the counselor will doubtless hear a good deal about ailments, medications, and physical symptoms. He will have opportunities to answer, "These symptoms are troublesome, worrisome, annoying . . . ."

Among retarded readers, we commonly find numerous anxiety cases. The counselor can anticipate expressions of indecisiveness, vacillation, and ambivalence. Anxiety clients labor under a sense of impending doom. Some waken in the morning frightened. Some fears are concrete; some are vague. All obstacles are mountains, and they can't tell the mountains from the molehills. They are afraid they can't make it, can't meet the demands, won't pass their classes, won't be able to keep their jobs. Tasks look hopelessly difficult. They can't make up their minds. If they do, they worry about the decision. The counselor can make use of these responses: "You feel two ways about it. It is difficult to make up your mind. You feel as if something terrible might happen. It looks hopeless to you. The job looks too hard."

We have found among retarded readers a considerable number of students who do not produce deviate scores on standardized personality tests, but whose behavior, conversation, and projective test results suggest constriction of personality, exaggerated respect for conventions and authority, over-conformity, stereotypy, loss of spontaneity, etc. Starting a conversation with a client like this is like pulling teeth. The client has little or no awareness he has a problem. He does as he is told. He has been a good, faithful Sunday-school member and a devoted member of the 4-H Club. He got the prize for perfect attendance at school. He doesn't listen to dirty stories; he is always polite to teachers; and now that he has a crew haircut and levi jeans like the other boys, things are all set. He may be dimly aware that he can't read, write, or carry on a conversation well enough to get by in college.

People like this have submitted to the press of environment, and their extreme conformity has been rewarded. To some extent they have a feeling that one just doesn't talk about personal problems; it is not nice to say anything bad about parents, teachers, Sunday-school teachers, etc. They are the very people who need to learn to communicate beyond the surface level, but beginning stages are rough. As one can plainly see, no free manifestations of emotion are going to be forthcoming. A non-directive approach may result in long periods of silence, and the client may terminate counseling after one or two interviews. On the other hand, if the counselor takes too much responsibility in the interview, the client may resist authority or become more dependent on authority. In such cases, we have found that a beginning can be made with directive counseling, with the counselor gradually relinquishing responsibility as the client becomes more aware of his problems and better able to take responsibility. The counselor may begin with test results, questions, explanations, etc., but remains alert to hesitant expressions of emotion and responds to them. In class discussions, the client may hear others express emotion and recognize that such expressions are accepted by the instructor. He may discover that there are others like him in the class. His conformity is caused by insecurity. As he feels increasingly comfortable with classmates and instructor, he may become able to admit into consciousness his underlying needs and emotions and to express them in interview.

The person inclined toward depressive moods needs to express his feelings of hopelessness and worthlessness, but many depressives have such a restricted verbal output that the counselor becomes discouraged with non-directive techniques. A deviate score on the depression scale of the MMPI will lead the counselor to expect expressions of low morale. Responding to the feeling of the moment is one way of handling this kind of case.

Either anxiety or depression can interfere with concentration and attention. In such cases, counseling is indicated.

A person with a deviate Pa score may be highly verbal, respectful of intellectual achievement, given to rationalizing, fond of elaborately logical explanations. He likes to produce evidence to support his statements. When the counselor makes a statement, this kind of client wants it "nailed down" and all the reasons and facts given. He may express aggressions, retaliativeness, sensitivity, suspicion, all of which lend themselves to reflection of feeling. If the Pa client decides to take counseling, he will be likely to stay with the counselor, but he will probably change slowly, if at all. In our experience, some Pa clients responded to reflection of feeling with visible physical reactions, flushing or turning pale, veins standing out on the temples, clenched fists, etc. Then, apparently, between counseling interviews, some sort of recapitulation took place, followed by more release of feeling in the next interview. The Pa client's customary resistance to authority is an argument for non-directive techniques which probably produce the least amount of retaliativeness toward the counselor.

The client with a high score on either the Pd or manic scales tends to have few deep feelings. For this reason, it is difficult to apply non-directive techniques. The manic may become impatient if the interview moves slowly. The counselor can reflect: "You feel impatient," or "You feel nothing is being accomplished," or "You feel you can't stand it unless something happens." On the other hand, some counselors believe that since the manic operates at the verbal level and has little emotion to express, a purely directive approach is more effective. It may be possible to discuss with such a client which of his ideas conform to reality and which do not.

Non-directive counselors commonly stay with the client's feelings, reflecting only what is expressed by the client. In the case of manic clients, we have occasionally deliberately anticipated reactions, "getting ahead" of the feeling expressed at the moment, or interpreting generalized feelings and attitudes. Used in moderation, this type of response appeared to help the client to move forward in counseling.

When counseling the client with a deviate manic score, the counselor should remember that college students in late adolescence often produce this test pattern. At this age, a deviate manic score is not so serious as it might be if the client were older. The manic commonly has respect for authority and expects the counselor to exert authority. If non-directive techniques are employed, the counselor might have opportunities to reflect, "This conversation surprises you," or "You expected something different in the counseling interview." The counselor can expect a good deal of trivial and irrelevant conversation. Possibly the manic relieves tensions through this chatter. The college freshman is in the midst of new and exciting experiences. New horizons are opening; anything might happen; adventures are ahead of him. He wants to do everything worth doing. When counseling the manic, the counselor may have opportunities to respond to these feelings and attitudes.

Sometimes a student obviously needs a long period of counseling and would respond to non-directive techniques, but for lack of time, the counselor employs other techniques. For example, a college freshman with a high hysteria score came in for an interview near the time of semester exams. He was dissatisfied with his themes, performance on test results, reading skills, and himself. He was under stress and needed to blow off steam. After reflecting feeling for a while, the counselor explained, "Your immediate problem has to do with examination week. You could find out some very helpful things for yourself if you had more time, but since the time is very short, I will tell you some things that you could do." Together, they made a study schedule, planned the most efficient use of time, and discussed underlining and other study tricks. Part of the problem was lack of information. The student questioned whether he had sufficient ability to do college work. The counselor explained his test results and told him that thousands of students survive in college with similar abilities. The client returned to say that he had used all of the suggestions and passed his examinations. A digression from the non-directive pattern of counseling helped him over a temporary obstacle, although a longer period of counseling was required to make permanent changes in personal adjustment and behavior. The danger in such a case is that having solved the immediate problem, the student would assume that he no longer needed help, or become dependent on the counselor.

On the other hand, without the kind of help given in this case, the client would probably have failed his examinations. The resulting increase in frustration and decrease in self-esteem would have complicated his problem further. Probably he would have dropped out of college, thus losing his opportunity for counseling.

PROBLEMS OF BEGINNING COUNSELORS

An experienced counselor understands that progress may be slow and hard to recognize. He will not become so frustrated himself if the signs of progress are few and faint. The young counselor, eager to prove his competence, may become impatient if progress is slow. He feels that his status and security depends on showing results. He has not become sensitized to small signs of progress. If the client fails to respond favorably to counseling in early interviews, he may actually develop concealed hostility to the client, thus delaying or halting progress.

One gets the impression from the Pepinskys[32] that if counseling is successful, the client's anxiety will be reduced. The inexperienced counselor may expect this development during the first interview. Depending on the severity of tension and the nature of the client's adjustment, improvement may require many interviews. Tension may mount during early stages of counseling or when the client approaches the discussion of a serious problem. With some clients, tension apparently is reduced during each interview, but rises between interviews.

The young counselor would like to perform miracles and sometimes expects them to occur in two or three interviews. He may put his confidence on superficial measures. A young woman working with delinquent boys became very much interested in one bright boy. She gave him a ring and told him whenever he was tempted to break a law or a rule to look at the ring and it would remind him that she believed in him. When this stratagem failed, she and others were greatly disturbed, feeling that this experience proved the hopelessness of rehabilitation. It is not reasonable to suppose that lifetime habits in response to frustration will be effaced with artifice. Learning does not take place so easily. Even a frustrated eight-year-old after six years of striving to satisfy basic needs, to reduce tensions, and to meet unreasonable demands will do well to demonstrate progress in a year's time.

In our contacts with graduate students, in training to become counselors, we have observed the following tendencies. They readily understand and accept directive techniques, but fail to see the possibilities in non-directive techniques. Many overlook the possibility that regardless

[32] Pepinsky, Harold, and Pauline Pepinsky, *Counseling: Theory and Practice,* The Ronald Press Company, New York, 1954, pp. 206–207, 215, 222, 238.

of the obvious suitability of the information or advice which the counselor might give, some clients will be unable to make use of it. When discussing non-directive techniques, they seldom mention reflections of feeling as a major technique, or the fact that emotions and attitudes are involved in learning. Some completely reject the non-directive method, but it is interesting to note that those most vehemently opposed to it respond defensively to authoritarian counselors when they themselves play the role of the client.

Trainees usually describe non-directive counseling as "letting the student talk himself out." They usually neglect to mention ways in which the counselor can show understanding, the value of feeling with the client, of trying to see the world as it is seen by the client. Many criticize the method because they say the counselor is so little involved. Actually, the non-directive counselor is deeply involved when he is feeling with the client and co-experiencing with the client a painful and frustrating failure, or the reward of a long-delayed success.

Non-directive counselors do not commonly use praise. Directive counselors use praise and reassurance when they feel that it will help. People with social-welfare interests often like the idea of praising people. We believe that the judicious use of praise and reward is occasionally appropriate, but praising the student can make him dependent on the counselor. When the counselor says, "This is the way I like to see you do it," he is placing himself in a position of authority and the student in an inferior position. Actually, the client experiences a profound feeling of reassurance when he recognizes that he is thoroughly accepted by the counselor.

Possibly one reason that trainees find directive counseling more acceptable is that it fits the usual pattern of school, church, and home experience, which in our society tends to be authoritarian. Directive counseling flatters the counselor and places him in the enjoyable position of the expert. While many skillful directive counselors do not behave in an authoritarian manner, the beginning counselor with public-school experience often interprets the process of directive counseling from an authoritarian orientation.

When the counselor insists on offering information to a client who does not recognize his need for it or who resists it, he may be demonstrating a need to prop up his own self-esteem. Hiltner[33] calls attention to the dangers involved in assuming that the counselor should have all the answers. If we defend our ignorance or attack with our knowledge, he says we ignore the first essential, concentration on understanding the client.

Inexperienced counselors, attempting to use the non-directive method, appear to be more sensitized to negative than to positive expressions of

[33] Hiltner, *op. cit.*, p. 60.

feeling. They should be able to recognize and respond to feelings of glee, satisfaction, pride, etc., "You feel good today. You like this. This pleases you. You feel proud of yourself."

One of the pitfalls of counseling is that the counselor may try to satisfy his own needs through his clients. To some degree, this is possible, of course. There are many satisfactions associated with helping students and watching them grow. However, if the counselor is insecure and unsure of himself, if he lacks normal social satisfactions, he may feel the need to display his superiority, to accelerate the client's progress, or to manipulate the client's personal life. The counselor needs to see his own needs clearly, to understand which of them can be met through his work and which satisfactions must be sought elsewhere.

It is always a temptation to rely heavily on test data. One needs to remind himself frequently that a high Pd score on the Multiphasic does not necessarily indicate that the client will be in trouble with the law. It may reflect resistance to conventions, rebellion against strict, puritanical behavior standards, a questioning attitude toward the church, dissatisfaction with college rules. A strong manic score may indicate the normal exuberance of a college student. The controlled manic may be a very productive person. A deviate Pa score may be the result of sensitivity and persistence, but not retaliativeness. A woman with a deviate Mf score may like sports, adventure, science, and professional status without abnormality. A perfect home adjustment score may be produced by a person who is covering up his problem. Tendencies suggested by a deviate score may be modified by tendencies measured by other scales or not measured by the available instruments.

When reviewing with a client the progress in counseling, the counselor may be inclined to dwell on remaining problems. Signs of progress should not be overlooked. We are reminded of a client who had noticeably reduced signs of rigidity, but who had made little progress in understanding boy-girl relationships. She was inclined to inject irrelevant talk into the interview. In his haste to get on with the "real" issues, the counselor reviewed only such developments in interviews which pointed up the remaining problems. The interview closed in tears and expressions of confusion by the client. However, in subsequent interviews, following a more thorough appraisal of developments, the relationship was restored and further progress was made.

FIRST INTERVIEW

It is customary in the first interview to explain the counseling relationship, state how much responsibility the counselor is willing to take, describe the role of the counselor and the role of the student, state how much time is available, etc. If the reading class is conducted as described, a part of the usual orientation has already taken place. The student may have already decided how he wants to use the counseling situation, what information he needs, or what problems he wishes to introduce. Not many feel apprehensive. Most students feel that a friendly relationship has already been established. If the reading instructor is also the counselor, they need not feel they are coming to a stranger.

Some are quick to indicate the basis on which they want to do business, to ask for test results, to discuss progress charts, or to introduce study problems. Those who are doing well may come to have their opinions confirmed.

Some will over-react to the new demands of college. Stress produced by academic demands may make them feel the need for counseling. The counselor then has an opportunity early in the first interview to respond to tensions and anxieties. Some will be defensive. The counselor responds, "You are not sure you want to talk about this," or "You feel reluctant to talk."

If the interview moves slowly in the beginning, he can say something like this: "Many reading students have questions which they prefer to discuss alone with the instructor or the counselor or which might not be of interest to other members of the class. The time is yours to use as you wish. We can go over your progress chart or test results, or we can spend the time discussing personal matters or questions raised in class. You are welcome to come back as often as you wish." Bordin[34] calls attention to the confusion and anxiety which may arise in the mind of the client from an unplanned relationship.

If the student has checked a problem on a problem checklist or the individual record form or autobiographical questionnaire, the counselor might remark, "I notice that you checked on our record forms that you would like to discuss. . . . Would you like to talk about that now?"

Themes, autobiographies, and records offer possibilities for opening remarks, "How did you develop an interest in chemical engineering?" Or, "Your experiences as a ranch hand must have been interesting but rugged. Would you like to tell me more about them?"

If an emotional problem is suspected, sometimes the student will lead into it from responses to the House-Tree-Person Test or the TAT. The counselor gives him the opportunity by appropriate remarks, "Your drawing of the human figure is small, and his back is turned. Can you tell me more about this?" Or "Would you care to tell me what you were think-

[34] Bordin, E. S., "Student Personnel Work and Personality Development," *Personnel and Guidance J.*, vol. 33, no. 4, December, 1954, pp. 196–197.

ing as you drew this?" Or "Sometimes these figures suggest how one feels about himself. Could you tell me something about your feelings about yourself?"

The attitudes and behavior of reading students sometimes produce a situation which might be called the Boy Scout approach. The instructor is the scoutmaster. The client wants to be a good scout and pass his tests and get his merit badges. Learning to read, from his point of view, is something like learning to make a fire with flint and steel, but he will do his best for his country and his troop. He remembers to address the scoutmaster as, "Sir," and never questions his authority.

Another type of client reminds one of a fraternity relationship in which the client is well-behaved and respectful, going through the proper motions, never permitting himself to be less than perfect in his behavior.

In each case, the counselor tries to sense how the client sees the situation and to respond appropriately.

A REALISTIC VIEW OF ANTICIPATED OUTCOMES

No counselor can expect to be 100 per cent successful in counseling. Some clients in each class will probably fail to show improvement. In some cases, progress will not become apparent until some time after counseling is terminated. In some, the counselor may never know the results. In many cases, the results will not be startling or dramatic.

CASE STUDIES

Condensed versions of several case studies with typical responses to illustrate various aspects of counseling follow. Some responses which would be repetitious or seemingly irrelevant have been deleted. Most of the interviews with reading students were 20 to 30 minutes duration. Some were shorter. The average gains of classes will be reported in the chapter on evaluation.

Case of Daniel Longwell, College Freshman

Entrance test results were available as shown in Table 7-1.

The total reading rank falls 28 percentile points below his rank on the American Council on Education Psychological Examination. Tested linguistic ability is appreciably lower than quantitative ability. Test results strongly indicate a reading problem and a potential for improvement.

Before entering reading class, Dan was given the Minnesota Multiphasic Personality Inventory, and the following behavior pattern was

TABLE 7-1
SEPTEMBER TEST RESULTS OF DANIEL LONGWELL

Test	Raw score	Percentile	Norms
ACE			1954 local
Q	52	85	
L	63	54	
Total	115	69	
Coop reading			1954 local
Vocabulary	20	40	
Speed	19	48	
Comprehension	11	39	
Total	50	41	

suggested by the results: depressed, sensitive, shy, probably tender-hearted, may feel persecuted, may have some physical symptoms, short memory span, probably ill at ease with others, may feel inferior, probably does not accept the masculine role, probably has difficulty in concentrating, undoubtedly feels insecure. Emotional involvement appears probable. MMPI scores are charted in figure 1.

EXCERPTS FROM INTERVIEW, FEBRUARY 2

COUNSELOR: Sometimes reading students find that talking things over privately helps them to make progress. I would be glad to help you in any way that I can. I'll not give you advice and will make no decisions for you, but if you agree, I'll try to help you think through your situation.

CLIENT: I'm passing all my classes. (*Seems a little on the defensive.*) Sometimes I get pretty tense. (*Pause.*) I guess it would be all right for me to talk things over with you.

Co: Would you like to start by telling me something about yourself?

CL: I seem to be slow in warming up, in getting started in reading and study. I want to get started, but something holds me back. I have to make myself go ahead.

Co: This bothers you.

CL: I am slowed down when others are going ahead.

Co: Makes you feel as if you are left behind right at the start.

CL: It's a real handicap on a true-false test. Seems like I ought to get started faster.

Co: You are not satisfied with this situation.

CL: I just don't feel any confidence in my ability to take hold and get going quickly. In grade school we seemed to have time there to get everything done. We didn't have to hurry so fast.

Co: You feel the pressure of the test situation and you are not sure you can cope with it.

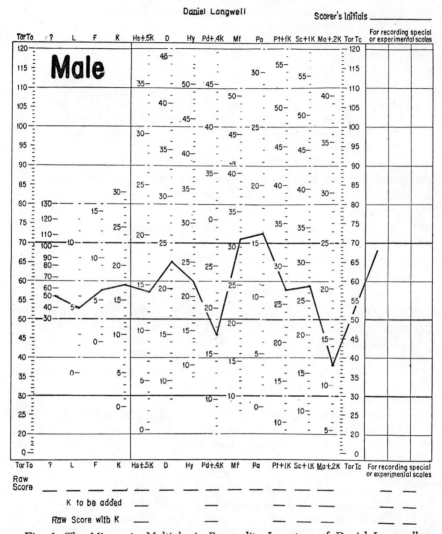

Fig. 1. The Minnesota Multiphasic Personality Inventory of Daniel Longwell.

CL: I know I'm smart enough, but somehow I can't get my bearings. It kind of unnerves me.

Co: It scares you.

CL: It's not the grades. I make grades O.K. I always have. It's just that I'm afraid that eventually I might not.

Co: You are afraid that being slow to get started would eventually count against you.

CL: Yes. I seem to fret and stew about how I'm going to come out. I have to make myself read and re-read everything, and I have to make myself concentrate. I have to examine things too long before I can make up my mind.

Co: This worries and puzzles you, and you are not satisfied with yourself.

CL: And another thing! Any little thing will distract me, even a dog walking by, or somebody talking.

Co: You feel as if this is a handicap.

CL: I'd like to be able to concentrate so that nothing would disturb me.

Co: You wish this were possible.

CL: (*Pause.*) You know in grade school I had a rough time. I'm undersized and it was easy for kids to run over me. I didn't like the heavy sports and they would make fun of me and I was the last to be chosen for games and teams and sports events. Some thought I was a sissy. . . .

Co: Their attitude was pretty hard to take.

CL: I didn't like it, but they were so much bigger. What could I do? I'd like to. . . .

Co: You resented what they did to you.

CL: Wouldn't anyone? I could never do anything.

Co: You wanted to do something and couldn't.

CL: Yes. (*Tears came to his eyes.*) Almost every night on the way home, somebody was waiting to trip me or fight, or call names or sneer. . . .

Co: These were painful experiences.

CL: Yes. I just never knew where I stood. I guess I really didn't belong. Part of it was my father. I think the neighbors didn't like him very well. When they were angry with him, their kids would take it out on me. It wasn't really a feud, but they didn't get along.

EXCERPTS FROM INTERVIEW, MARCH 16

Co: What's on your mind today?

CL: I am embarrassed because of the way I behaved last time.

Co: I understand.

CL: I feel embarrassed about the whole thing . . . sounds as if I had a terrible time and feel sorry for myself and I broke down. . . .

Co: You feel ashamed.

CL: Well, a person should have more control, and then the things I said. I just got started and didn't stop.

Co: You feel you revealed too much.

CL: Well it doesn't seem that bad to me today. It probably seemed to you that I got beat up every day.

Co: You want to be sure that I understand how it really was and you don't want to present it as worse than it was, but actually it still seems pretty rough to you.

CL: Yes, but it doesn't seem as bad as I acted. I mean, I shouldn't have got that upset.

Co: You are disturbed because you feel you should have shown more control.

CL: (*Long pause.*) I've been sick a lot in my life, not really sick . . . but I have had an upset stomach. I don't like being light and thin and half sick and low on energy. I don't understand why I get sick at my stomach. I've been to all kinds of doctors. Maybe they helped a little. My folks say it's nervousness. I think so, too, but what causes the nervousness?

Co: Tell me more.

CL: In high school when I had to go to any social event, it would upset me. I wanted to go, in a way, but I was afraid they wouldn't like me.

Co: I see. You wanted to go, but you dreaded it, too.

CL: Yes. Sometimes I couldn't eat before a party.

Co: Our time is up. Shall I see you next week?

CL: Yes.

CASE NOTES, MARCH 16

Dan brought his progress chart in for me to see. He is greatly pleased to see that his speed has risen steadily from 250 per minute to between 500 and 600 words per minute. Comprehension ranges between 80 and 100 per cent.

EXCERPTS FROM INTERVIEW, MARCH 23

Dan began to speak as soon as he was inside the door.

CL: These false-true tests and multiple choice are just guessing games. You can know things perfectly well and still foul up just because you are trying to see what particular shading of meaning the instructor wants. Sometimes none of choices are really right. We are supposed to see which one is the nearest correct. (*Gives illustration.*)

Co: It sort of burns you up when you know the answer but can't make this knowledge count.

CL: Yes, it makes me mad . . . and _____'s tests! You wonder if he knows the first principle about making a test. The items, the organization, they look like something he had cooked up in about 30 minutes.

Co: You just don't like any part of his tests.

CL: I guess I don't. Suppose he has to use them, but really there are more stupid questions in his tests. You know the dumber you are the better you could do on his tests. (*Gives example.*) See! A moron could answer O.K., and a better student would think, "A prof would never put a simple question like that in a test."

Co: It seems to you like an unfair test.

CL: It sure does. When I know I could write out answers perfectly and make good grades, I have to stumble around with his stupid questions.

Co: It is very irritating to you.

Cl: You take calculus. I like the kind of exam you get in there. It makes sense. If you can think, it counts on your grade.

Co: You feel it's fair and you get justice.

Cl: Yes. (*Pause.*) You know I was sick for a half day and well I just felt exhausted, just run out of energy. I don't know why. Seems like I use up a lot of energy whether I'm working or not. And if there is something extra to do, I just don't have enough.

Co: You feel apprehensive about running out, feel you have to be careful to conserve it.

Cl: Seems that I don't have as much as other people. And yet I'm healthy. The doctor's can't find anything wrong.

Co: This is kind of confusing to you. You wonder why.

FOURTH INTERVIEW, MARCH 30

Co: How are you today?

Cl: Tired. I wonder if I'm not studying too hard.

Co: Tell me more.

Cl: I seem to have my goals set high and good grades are very important to me. I seem to feel I've just got to stay in there and work all the time . . . too much.

Co: You feel you have to do it. Is that the way it is?

Cl: And I also think it takes too much effort to accomplish what there is to do. Seems like I have to pour a lot of effort into everything I do.

Co: Like you have to overcome something in yourself at the same time you are giving energy to the task.

Cl: Yes. And even after I have my lesson pretty well, I keep right on studying past the point that it does any good.

Co: You're wondering if you are driving yourself to the point of diminishing returns and if it is paying off.

Cl: I certainly am, and I find life a little dull studying all the time—no real fun any time.

Co: You find yourself on the verge of being bored, studying so much.

Cl: I see others going around doing a lot of things and having a good time. I wonder how they do it. I would like that but I don't know how.

Co: You wish you could but you wonder how they do it.

Cl: I know I couldn't. I don't feel secure with people . . . conversation gets artificial too fast and I get embarrassed too easily.

Co: You just don't feel comfortable with people.

Cl: I seem to do fairly well if things are casual and accidental, like talking to my neighbor in the next chair about a test, but being really social is beyond me.

Co: Looks pretty formidable to you.

Cl: It does. I just feel that people don't want to hear what I have to say and . . . especially, well, girls . . . or boys, I guess either, my own age.

Older people, I can talk to, but I know I need to mix with students my own age. I always wonder what they think of me when I'm around.

Co: You are wondering what you can do to enjoy social relationships with people your own age.

Co: How would you like to use the time today?

CL: There is something about my performance that is not good. I have to prime myself, beat myself into it when I start work, put forth all kinds of effort in order to perform well, and if people are looking on, I know they wonder.

Co: You are aware of some kind of resistance in yourself and that you use energy to overcome it. You are not sure it is wholesome and you wonder if other people notice it. Is this the way it is?

CL: To complicate things, I feel that, when I'm in a box, a situation in which I've got to deliver or be embarrassed, I feel like regurgitating.

Co: I see. You already have a lot of your own motivation in the situation, almost too much. Then when the pressure is on, it almost makes you sick.

CL: It's a funny thing; it only happens when I think there is no escape.

Co: It is when you feel trapped that this feeling comes on.

CL: (*Long silence.*) There is one more thing that may be related to my nervousness. My mother . . . I don't mean to be critical but it seems to me that my mother works too hard . . . sometimes unnecessarily. Then she gets sick. We worry about her, both my father and I, and take care of her and get her on her feet again.

Co: Yes, this worries you.

CL: It does. She gets well and then she will repeat the situation to the point that makes me wonder.

Co: You wonder why. You worry about it and you perhaps are a little tired of it, too.

CL: Yes, but I really don't understand it.

Co: You are puzzled by her self-sacrificing ways.

CL: I'm ashamed to say it, but it looks almost as if she did it on purpose. But she probably isn't aware that she does.

Co: You feel a deep concern about your mother, but you also feel some doubt about her motives.

CL: We offered to move to a smaller house and to get help, but she refused because she said it was impractical. She insists on doing it even when she knows it makes her sick.

Co: You feel there is a solution, but she won't accept it; that perhaps she doesn't want a solution. She won't let you find a solution.

CL: It's like she wants to over-work and make herself sick.

Co: You're beginning to wonder whether or not she enjoys being a martyr.

CL: (*Tries to speak, but can't get anything out . . . looks pale.*)

Co: It almost makes you sick to think about it.

CASE NOTES

During this time, Dan appeared to gain confidence in himself in class discussion. He had always recited in class, even though he had to drive himself to do it. Gradually, a change could be seen in the nature of his contributions. He had learned that his classmates resented an outstanding performance from him, so he began to ask clever questions, giving others opportunities to shine. Instead of a stellar performance, he was able to participate genuinely with others. He was noticed chatting easily and cheerfully with classmates between periods. Less tension was apparent in his manner and facial expressions. Late in the semester, he mentioned that he had become able to get started on tests early in the period in all classes except one. He complained less and less of fatigue and other physical symptoms. Continued counseling was recommended.

A comparison of test with retest results suggests much less blocking, less resistance, and greater ease of performance. The following percentile ranks reported in table 7-2 indicate gains in vocabulary, reading speed, and comprehension according to retest with the Cooperative Reading Test.

TABLE 7-2
TEST AND RETEST RESULTS OF DANIEL LONGWELL

Test	First test		Final test		Norms
	Raw score	Percentile	Raw score	Percentile	
Coop reading					
Vocabulary	20	40	30	69	
Speed	19	48	31	77	
Comprehension	11	39	15	58	
Total	50	41	76	70	1954 local

The final percentile rank in total reading ability is now consistent with his total ACE rank at the 69th percentile. Gains in comprehension suggest improvement in attention and concentration.

His rank on the linguistic scale of the ACE climbed from the 54th to the 70th percentile. His progress chart indicates that his gains in speed have been maintained. In contrast to his early record of 250 to 300 words per minute, his speed the last two weeks of the semester ranged between 520 and 650 words per minute, with comprehension scores of 90 to 100 per cent.

Remarks included in his final critique of the class were favorable, "Group discussions and evaluation of articles helped me in understanding and evaluating other reading material. . . . This course in developmental reading has improved my reading skill in every phase of the class objectives. . . . The discussion groups have helped me to better express myself to others."

He was not retested with the MMPI but will take it again in the fall. Observations of his behavior and interview records suggest improved personal adjustment.

Case of Pearl Miller, College Freshman

Pearl was referred to the reading clinic by her English instructor who reported that she appeared unable to make full use of her abilities. Her classroom performance was uneven, sometimes quite satisfactory and sometimes inferior. The same was true of themes. She reported that while she usually read well under pressure, she felt that lesson preparation required more time than it should. She found herself going over and over her assignments without actually getting the full meaning. Her instructor asked her to read aloud and she gave a poor performance. He believed her to be a conscientious student, perhaps handicapped by an emotional block or possibly by limited academic background. Although total reading scores are consistent with tested abilities, her classroom performance and reports of study time suggest that she is required to spend more time and energy in reading than should be necessary. Her September test results are given in table 7-3.

TABLE 7-3
SEPTEMBER TEST RESULTS OF PEARL MILLER

Test	Raw scores	Percentiles	Norms
ACE			Local, 1954
Quantitative	37	38	
Linguistic	66	62	
Total	103	51	
Coop reading			Local, 1954
Vocabulary	25	55	
Speed	27	69	
Comprehension	19	74	
Total	71	66	

As these scores do not show the usual discrepancy between linguistic and quantitative ability or the required difference between total ACE and reading scores, this student was not enrolled in the reading class. On the basis of her instructor's referral, she was accepted for counseling.

When the student was retested with a reading test in December after three months of college work, but before counseling, her reading scores were lower than in September, ranking at the 55th and 73d percentiles in speed and comprehension, according to the same norms.

The case is included here because it illustrates the process of counseling, the use of test results in counseling, and the progress of an atypical case.

During early interviews, Pearl chattered constantly about her activities, classes, instructors, roommates, the dormitory, her part-time work in the bookstore, church, the new tennis court, the student newspaper, etc. In spite of the volume, her conversation could not be said to be very revealing. Little information was offered about her family, childhood, or her own feelings. She mentioned her beautiful older sister who was said to be very much at ease on social occasions, very talented, much loved and admired by everybody, including Pearl. Fragments about home and family were left incomplete while she hurried on to interject some irrelevant bit of information about the weather or a new skirt.

According to Pearl, one should always think well of other people, think good thoughts, support the church actively, fulfill promises, tell the truth. One should not gossip or criticize others or hurt their feelings.

Considerable time was spent in describing her fiancé, a paragon of virtue with very high behavior standards and saintly habits. His activities, aside from philosophizing, studying, and good works, included only the cleanest and manliest of sports. He would have liked immediate marriage, but Pearl explained that she had asked for a couple of years in which to "grow up." They had known each other since grade-school days when they played ball and ran foot races with each other.

INTERVIEW NOTES, NOVEMBER 15

Pearl reports that her eyes hurt; bright lights and sunshine hurt them; she has headaches and backaches; is often very much fatigued; likes to read, but it is hard work; says she reads one word at a time; grades in high school were good; grades here are satisfactory; works 11 hours per week.

INTERVIEW NOTES, DECEMBER 3

Sister makes top grades; Pearl says she feels inferior to her sister and classmates. Says she has a great curiosity about everything, says teachers don't have enough time to answer her questions; says she is trying to form a philosophy of life; says her feelings go "flat"; has headaches when things don't go right, when she is supposed to measure up to something, when expected to excel.

INTERVIEW NOTES, DECEMBER 10

Father is strict; parents not affectionate or demonstrative; never praise; necessities are provided, but very little fun. Says she is always doing things for people, substituting for them in their jobs or helping with lessons; doesn't know why she does these things as they take time from her own work and lessons. Feels she is not growing fast enough. There are so many things to learn.

INTERVIEW NOTES, DECEMBER 16

Likes for things to get moving, impatient, also feels need for more time; schedule is crowded; feels pressure when there is too much to do; gets fatigued; apparently keeps her head when under stress. Does not like too many controls imposed on her. Wants to know more about people, is curious about people. Says she has had no headaches lately. Sometimes works so many hours that she has to study late at night or get up early.

INTERVIEW NOTES, JANUARY 13

Administered MMPI. Scores suggest: (1) fixed ideas and systems of fixed ideas, rigidity, suspicion, hypersensitivity, persistence, resistance to authority, much attention to logic; (2) anxiety, ambivalence, possibly some vacillation; (3) liking for activities of men; possibly drive for dominance; (4) defensiveness; (5) shyness. Probably will be slow to respond, slow to trust the counselor, will expect intellectual analysis, probably will feel the counselor is holding out on her if he fails to report test results, probably has a preconceived idea of a counselor and the proper way for him to behave and will be suspicious of any deviation.

Some significant responses to MMPI questions are these: likes mechanics magazines, newspaper articles on crime, horseback riding, science, conversations about sex, newspaper editorials, tall women, mannish women, history, adventure stories; does not mind spiders, snakes, mice, dirty stories, sexy movies; likes to work with men; attracted to members of own sex; not attracted to members of opposite sex; has been sorry she is a girl; would like reporting sports news; would not like work of a dressmaker, secretary; does not like love stories or movie love scenes; believes in Biblical prophecies, second coming of Christ, miracles performed by Christ, Hell and the Devil in afterlife; is very religious; reads the Bible frequently; family does not like vocational choice; person to whom most attached was not a woman; man who had most to do with client was very strict; parents often object to her friends; relatives not in sympathy with her; has been jealous of relatives; parents required strict obedience; feelings are easily hurt; believes anyone who works hard has a good chance of succeeding; seldom puts off tasks; frequently finds it necessary to stand up for what she thinks is right; knows who is responsible for most of her troubles; is hurt by criticism or scolding; cries easily; resents being taken in by clever person; has often felt strangers are looking at her critically; worries because she might have hurt the feelings of others; corrects people who express an ignorant belief; good intentions are often misunderstood. Several answers suggest inability to express aggressions or criticisms of others.

These items are not significant out of context, except as they help the counselor prepare to respond to the client.

ANALYSIS OF MMPI SCORES

Are the characteristics suggested by the MMPI supported by the client's behavior?

RETALIATIVENESS. Very little apparent, except for excessive sweetness toward people who have hurt her feelings, perhaps with the idea of making them ashamed of themselves, although this may be only an attempt to make herself secure.

HYPERSENSITIVITY. This characteristic is suggested by many of her remarks, "I can't bear to hurt anybody's feelings. I never criticize anybody because I know how criticism hurts. I can never refuse to do a favor for anybody, because I can't bear to hurt their feelings." She often asks for advice, but when it is given, she gives resistance to it. Early in counseling, the counselor indicated that she was welcome to return for another interview if she wished. She interpreted this as rejection, saying that she would have preferred an invitation to return. Visible reactions to pleasure or distress are noted. Feelings of persecution or superiority, suspiciousness. Hints that her sister was favored by parents. Wonders if her housemates are exploiting her. Wonders why the counselor says so-and-so, or why he asks certain questions; wonders what he means by some statements; checks herself when she is approaching an intimate subject; frequently breaks off in the middle of a confidence; casts inquiring looks at counselor.

The counselor should try to avoid reading anything into a client's behavior because it fits a hypothesis. However, he should not ignore intuitive insights about a client either.

FIXED IDEAS AND SYSTEMS OF FIXED IDEAS. This symptom is apparent in her rigid observance of her own protocols: never criticize anybody, always finish what you start; anything worth doing is worth doing well; always be on time; make a time schedule and stick to it; people can do almost anything if they put their minds to it; set a goal and then reach it; don't let anything get in the way. Any decision to make a certain amount of money, read a certain number of pages, complete a certain assignment, wash her hair before bedtime, or to do any other task is law, and she is disturbed if she can not follow her own plans. The inability to express aggressions is a part of this rigid pattern of behavior. Going to church, clean living, and perfection in behavior (as she interpreted it) are consistent with this mode of adjustment. Other people are expected to mean what they say, do what they promise, appear right on time, and behave according to stereotyped expectations.

RATIONALIZING AND LOGIC. Her beliefs are neatly documented and she expects any information given by others to be supported by evidence. She is not satisfied until her questions are answered fully and completely, down to the last period. She analyzes her own behavior and experiences and explains it logically.

ANXIETY. Although some anxiety and vacillation are apparent, they are tempered by persistence and rigidity. Some symptoms are blocking in reading and study and uncertainty about being accepted by others. Headaches, fatigue, eyestrain may be related to anxiety, as they decrease with counseling. Vacillation is seen between getting married and not getting married, helping others and getting her own work done, seeking approval and defensiveness, desire to talk over problems versus preserving independence. She often interrupts her study schedule to do favors for others, wash her hair, baby-sit, etc., and then studies very late. She is not sure what curriculum is best for her and is trying to make a vocational choice. She vacillates on these questions, but, of course, she is only 18 years old.

MASCULINITY. A tendency to like masculine activities is reflected in her remarks, "I like men to pal around with . . . like swimming, hiking, tennis, baseball. It's all so much fun until someone wants to marry you. I'm not sure I want to be a wife. I like to meet all the kids where I work and make friends with them. I like the comradeship and fellowship. It's all fun until some of the boys ask to walk me home. Then it's kind of spoiled. It kind of helps to be engaged, so I can refuse without hurting their feelings." This tendency is suggested by a deviation on the Mf scale of the MMPI, and supported by behavior, but the significance of the score is not known. It may reflect only immaturity in identification with the same-sex parent.

NOTES ON HOUSE-TREE-PERSON TEST

Bilateral symmetry is seen in the three drawings, said by Machover to denote emotional control, usually associated with repression, emotional distance, and over-intellectualization.[35] Ambivalence and conflict are suggested. Barriers to communication are suggested by the lack of paths and windows in the house picture and the lack of hands in the drawing of the human figure. Only the face of the house is presented, suggesting a defensive façade shown to the world while the real self is concealed. The drawing of the house suggests a complicated personality, many facets. The pencil stroke in all pictures is light with many retracings, suggesting feelings of insignificance and insecurity. Only the head and shoulders of the human figure are shown; emphasis is on the intellect; the sexual area is cut off; perhaps the subject is taboo. The picture is a male figure, suggesting confusion in identification. A small neck restrains impulses from the body from reaching the intellect, and is said to indicate excessive control. Eyes and ears are open to learning. Arms close to sides suggest rigidity; they cannot reach out for social contact. Rigidity, ambivalence, barriers to communication, and confusion in identification as suggested by the H-T-P appear to agree with the results of the MMPI.

NOTES ON THE SZONDI

The Szondi was administered only once, and thus the interpretation reflects only temporary adjustment. (Reactions following an experience of need satisfaction are said to be momentarily different from those given during the process of building up tensions resulting from lack of satisfaction.)

Results of the Szondi suggest that the client meets problems on an intellectual plane. Strong control is apparently exerted over emotions. Idealism is strongly indicated. Repeatedly, responses given are of a type said to be found among people of above-average ability and those engaged in intellectual pursuits or the arts. Some conflicts and tensions are suggested, but are handled in such a way as not to interfere appreciably with productivity. Inability to

[35] Anderson, Harold H., and Gladys L. Anderson, *Introduction to Projective Techniques*, Prentice-Hall, Inc., Englewood Cliffs, N. J., 1951, p. 359.

express aggression may be a handicap to this person in achieving recognition. The pattern is seldom pathologic and seldom if ever found among violators of rules or laws.

The responses suggest a conflict between the need to communicate with others and the need to preserve the inner integrity of personality. The stronger need is to preserve the barrier between self and others. This person is apparently trying to understand self and to solve psychologic problems at the conscious level. Intellectual objectivity prevents her from losing herself in an emotional reaction. Love is probably not defined as a physical relationship, but more nearly as clinging to the idea of a person. Almost as much satisfaction and enjoyment is found in the thought of the love-object, idea, or person as in possession. The limitations of the person in forming close ties may not be a problem, because she will probably find a socially acceptable outlet, is capable of intense appreciation of beauty and ideas, may feel that ideas are safer than depending on people for satisfactions, and is probably able to explain her conflicts at the conscious level. Responses suggest a strong need for tender love, a necessary component of every mature sexual drive, either male or female, but the pattern indicates that the need is denied. The drive is toward femininity as defined in western society, toward being the passive recipient of tenderness, love, and care, but apparently the need is not accepted or recognized. The pattern suggests a tendency toward efficient use of time, high productivity, tendency to keep busy, a pattern often offered by people who sublimate their aggressiveness by active pursuit of scientific or intellectual interests. Tensions produced by the need to master environment are discharged by continuous activity, usually at the abstract, conceptual level. The need is to manipulate concepts rather than people or objects. Young people with this pattern often give the effect of "trying too hard," being "too good," exerting too much self-control. Also suggested are the following: frustration of oral needs which is relieved by talkativeness or other oral activity; over-active conscience; and the search for companionship on the intellectual level.

Likenesses can be seen between the results of the MMPI, the H-T-P, and the Szondi in suggested rigidity, conflict, barriers to communication, and confusion in identification (resistance to accepting the feminine role).

How should the counselor respond to this client? He will try to avoid any statement or term which might be interpreted as criticism. He will be prepared to reflect: "You feel hurt. Your feelings were hurt." Instead of using terms such as critical or suspicious, he will substitute, "You wonder what he had in mind." Or "You are not sure you are ready to trust me." Or "You sometimes think they are trying to get something out of you." Or "You wonder if there is some underlying meaning to this remark." When the client tells about her rigid schedule or her use of time or the drive to finish a self-imposed task, the counselor may respond, "You feel you have to do it." He may have opportunities to say, "You feel a need to be as good as you can be." Or "You like to have things

nailed down, like to see the evidence before you make up your mind."
Or "You like for instructors to answer your questions fully and completely." When responding to ambivalence, he might say, "You are not
sure you want to get married, but you hate to hurt his feelings." Or "You
want to do favors for others, but you feel the drive to get your own work
done." Or "You want the boys to like you, but you really don't enjoy
dating."

INTERVIEW NOTES, JANUARY 17

Says she cannot reach her ideals, feels inferior. Repeated that she doesn't
like to hear criticisms of others, doesn't like to be criticized herself, doesn't
like gossip or poor sportsmanship.

INTERVIEW NOTES, JANUARY 24

Still searching for a philosophy, impatient for it to jell, thinks people are
the most important, wants to know how they act and why, says her feelings are
easily hurt, says she expects to get satisfaction from relations with other people.
She says when she has to speak in public, she always has a coughing spell even
though she has no cold.

INTERVIEW NOTES, JANUARY 27

Family not demonstrative or affectionate. Says her mother likes her and
doesn't criticize her. Says she has decided the reason she can't criticize people
or do anything to hurt them is that she is afraid of alienating them, wants
them to like her. Described nervous behavior of her sister. Says she feels nervous or tense herself when she goes home. Neither has been home much this
year.

INTERVIEW NOTES, FEBRUARY 17

Likes courses but gets bored when she feels nothing is going on. Thinks
some instructors do a good deal of bluffing and come unprepared. Thinks they
spin their wheels. Has felt depressed. Has decided to work hard, even if she
takes a beating. Must control herself and use time wisely. Feels she must force
herself to be happy. Depressed mood has lasted for several days. Feels de-
feated when she does not live up to her own expectations. Wonders why she
thinks she must work so hard. Says she likes to be independent. Says her boy
friend is depressed after he visits her. "Usually when something bad happens,
I can go back to my room and pretend it didn't happen, and the next morning
things are just like they were before, all straightened out."

INTERVIEW NOTES, FEBRUARY 22

"I never let my feelings show if I can help it. Often I don't say what I really
think. I don't want to hurt people." Says she doesn't understand why she feels
negative at times and not at other times, why she feels tolerant of people at
some times and not at other times. Says she bottles up her feelings. Still feels

inferior, can't stand gossip. Says she has forgotten most of her childhood experiences. Still trying to shape ideals, trying to find out what is important.

INTERVIEW NOTES, MARCH 5

Mentioned her outdoor interests. Has decided not to study so hard. Wonders why she feels she must study so hard and work all of the time. Wonders about the natures of men and women. Feels sort of mixed up about woman's role. Is looking for something to tie experiences together and make them mean something.

"People will like me for what I am and not because I do favors for them. I got real mad yesterday at my roommate and said what I thought for the first time . . . . I like men. They are nicer than girls, but I just can't stand to let them hold my hand or kiss me. I can even tell when they are going to try it. . . . I want to keep on counseling until after I go home Easter."

EXCERPTS FROM INTERVIEW

CL: My boy friend is nice, but you know, some of these other boys are nice. One of them asked to walk me home. When it gets personal I don't like it so well. I like to work alongside, but . . . .

Co: As long as you're a pal, it's all right.

CL: That's what I want to be, a pal. (*Silence.*) . . . Oh, it's a wonderful day. I'd just love to be outdoors.

Co: You would like to play hooky.

CL: (*Fishy stare, as if to say, "Wonder what he means by that!"*)

Co: You wonder whether I'm kidding or not.

CL: Well I don't always understand what people mean. My roommates are always explaining jokes to me.

Co: You were telling me about your boy friend. Would you care to talk more about him?

CL: I wrote him a letter and told him I'm not worthy of him. I'm not mature enough to be married. I'm not sure I'd make a good wife.

EXCERPTS FROM INTERVIEW, MARCH 15

CL: I thought of something I want to tell you. Once my sister sang a beautiful solo at church. Our father told her that she did a wonderful job. The next Sunday I sang. It wasn't wonderful, but it wasn't bad. He didn't say a thing.

Co: This still hurts.

CL: I did a lot of things pretty well but he never did say anything.

Co: You hungered for your father's approval.

CL: (*Veins stood out on temples; client flushed.*)

INTERVIEW NOTES

The first half of the interview is usually spent in trivial conversation. The last half usually goes better. Pearl was humming a tune today as she left the office.

INTERVIEW NOTES, MARCH 30

Mentioned jealousy between her and her sister. Gets along with younger brother. Can still beat him in tennis and foot races. Says she doesn't know as much as she should about sex. Mother never mentions the subject. Says she couldn't understand the jokes in a recent movie. Her roommates explained them to her. Says her mother is submissive. Neither parent is affectionate.

EXCERPTS FROM INTERVIEW, MARCH 30

CL: I like to talk with men. Their talk makes more sense to me. I like their games and outdoor activities. Otherwise, though . . . .

Co: You don't like it when they get personal.

CL: No, I don't. A boy tried to kiss me last week and I haven't got over it yet. I don't like to be touched. I can tell when they are thinking about it. It upsets me when I know they're thinking about it.

Co: You don't want men to make love to you.

CL: That's right, but I'll get over that some day, don't you think?

Co: You feel you are making some progress in this direction.

CL: Yes, but I want to be counseled again. When I go home, I'll have a date with my boy friend. I'm not engaged to him any longer, but I'll give him a date. I've had some other dates here, a few. I want to tell you something else. Sometimes, I permit myself to criticize other people now. I believe it is more normal.

EXCERPTS FROM INTERVIEW, APRIL 7

Pearl chattered a while about classes, clothes, etc.

Co: Last time you were telling me some of your attitudes toward men.

CL: I was just leading up to talking about my mother. She was supposed to have authority, but now we all know she really didn't. Dad was the boss. She wasn't a very warm person.

Co: Maybe that is why it is hard for you to play the role of a woman. Perhaps you didn't want to be like her, and at the same time you could not get the approval of your Dad. Perhaps you are not sure you want to be a woman.

CL: What can I do about it?

Co: We can talk about it again and see if we can work out something.

INTERVIEW NOTES

A switch from non-directive response to interpretation is often accepted by the client, and sometimes she progresses in subsequent interviews as if it were her own idea. She was quiet and thoughtful, but apparently not depressed.

INTERVIEW NOTES, APRIL 13

Boy friend threatened her. Says she can't go with him unless she stays engaged. He says if she marries him, she must give up her own wishes and live for him alone. She says she is thinking it over.

MAY 26 REVIEW OF DEVELOPMENTS IN THE CASE OF PEARL MILLER

A retest with the MMPI shows that several scores moved appreciably toward the mean. Results are reported in table 7-4. Lowered percentile ranks suggest improvement.

TABLE 7-4
MMPI TEST AND RETEST RESULTS OF PEARL MILLER

	First testing	Second testing
Lie score	70	56
Pa	67	56
Anxiety (Pt)	63	50
Social introversion	62	42

These test results suggest that the client is more straightforward (noted also in interview), less rigid, less anxious, and not so shy. She now shows some willingness to alter her schedule to suit the convenience of others or when it appears sensible for her own welfare. She seldom expresses suspicions of other people, is somewhat more able to express aggressions when appropriate, is beginning to believe her standards for behavior somewhat unrealistic, interprets less criticism from the remarks and behavior of others, and takes time for some social life. Some symptoms of ambivalence and anxiety remain, but headaches and other physical symptoms seldom appear. Growing self-confidence and wholesome aggressiveness are indicated both by the change in social introversion score and in behavior. She says she feels more sure of herself, more at ease with people, more accepted by people. She spends about the same amount of time in study as before, but apparently accomplishes more. She has been completing extra assignments in all classes. Her grade average for the semester

TABLE 7-5
TEST AND RETEST RESULTS OF PEARL MILLER

Test	First testing		Final testing		Norms
	Raw scores	Percentile	Raw scores	Percentile	
ACE					1954 local
Quantitative	37	38	51	80	
Linguistic	66	62	75	82	
Total	103	51	126	83	
Coop reading					1954 local
Vocabulary	25	55	30	69	
Speed	27	69	33	95	
Comprehension	19	74	21	89	
Total	71	66	84	78	

is better than B. She has found a new and more suitable part-time job and has cut down on the number of hours of work. Her employers are favorably impressed with her work. She has made arrangements to live in a cooperative house for the coming year and decided to attend summer school.

She reports that she is able to make better use of study time and can read more rapidly. Final test results (table 7-5) indicate gains in all areas and suggest that she has become increasingly able to make effective use of her abilities.

A part of the increment in reading may be due simply to classwork and study. However, in view of the amount of gain and the fact that she apparently lost skills between September and December before beginning counseling, a part of the gain can presumably be attributed to counseling.

Case of Norbert Shore, College Freshman

This case is included to illustrate the kind of interview which one often experiences with retarded readers. Unlike the conversations described in foregoing pages, the client offers little information about himself. Few items of importance are discussed, and yet the client appears to benefit from the personal contact and makes improvement. An inexperienced counselor might be inclined to assume that nothing is happening and to give up after the first interview.

The following test data were available about the client early in the semester: scores from ACE, Cooperative Reading Examination, Diagnostic Reading Tests, and MMPI. Results are presented in tables 7-6 and 7-7. MMPI results are in terms of standard scores.

TABLE 7-6
SEPTEMBER TEST RESULTS OF NORBERT SHORE

Test	Raw score	Percentile rank	Norms
ACE			1954 local
Quantitative	50	78	
Linguistic	51	27	
Total	101	47	
Coop reading			
Vocabulary	9	9	
Speed	12	28	
Comprehension	9	26	
Total	30	17	
Diagnostic reading			Denver
Speed	235 w.p.m.	13	
Comprehension (story)	16	49	
Vocabulary	36	23	
Comprehension (study)	30	45	
Total comprehension	66	30	

TABLE 7-7

MMPI Scores of Norbert Shore

K (defensiveness)	68
Hypochondriasis	62
Depression	68
Hysteria	64
Psychopathic deviate	64
Pt (anxiety)	75
Social introversion	78

There is a marked discrepancy between his "Q" and "L" scores and a marked difference between total ACE rank and total reading rank, suggesting a reading problem and a potential for improvement. Judging from his MMPI results, he can be expected to have a very small verbal output, feelings of worthlessness and insecurity, fears, anxieties, tension, concern over physical health, and a tendency toward physical symptoms such as headaches, nausea, upset stomach, etc. He may show indifference for rules and conventions. He will probably be very shy. His visual examination showed good eye coordination and visual acuity.

Excerpts from Interview, October 4

Co: As you know, I ask for an appointment with each of my students. Many of them like to spend the time talking over personal matters. Sometimes talking things over here helps students to improve their reading skills. Could you tell me a little about yourself?

Cl: What do you mean?

Co: Perhaps you would like to tell me about your classes, your past schooling, work experience, or about your reading.

Cl: I'm taking agriculture. I live on a farm. That's about all there is to it. (*Pause. Client squirms, twists, gets embarrassed and red in the face.*)

Co: It's hard to talk about yourself.

Cl: (*Long silence; visible discomfort.*)

Co: Can you tell me about your choice of vocation? Are you satisfied with it?

Cl: Yes.

Co: What do you plan to do?

Cl: Suppose I'll run the farm someday.

Co: Can you tell me about your reading?

Cl: I can't read very well, and English has always been very hard for me.

Co: Anything with words in it is hard.

Cl: (*Silence.*)

Co: Can you say any more about your reading?

Cl: No. (*Looks sheepish.*)

Co: You'd like to talk more but it's hard to do.

Cl: Yes. (*Pause.*) About the reading, I don't concentrate very well. I can't go fast.

Co: You are a little discouraged about this.

CL: Yes. (*Silence. Looks at counselor, squirms, twists, opens his mouth, but does not speak.*)

Co: It's hard to talk . . . to express yourself.

CL: I don't know what to say. Guess I haven't learned much.

Co: Tell me more.

CL: (*Silence.*)

Co: It just seems that there is nothing to say.

CL: First three years in high school, I just went to school. The last year I worked.

Co: You became more interested the last year.

CL: Yes, but I didn't know much. I'd missed a lot.

Co: Yes.

CL: Math was the only thing that was easy . . . everything else hard.

Co: Our time is nearly up. Would you care to work on this again?

CL: I don't know. I don't know what to say or if I can. I don't know.

Co: You are in a difficult position when you have to talk . . . almost afraid of getting in such a position.

CL: Yes.

Co: Shall we agree that this is one of your problems?

CL: Yes, but I don't know what I can do about it.

Co: Suppose we try once more, next week.

CL: O.K. I'll try.

EXCERPTS FROM INTERVIEW, OCTOBER 11

Co: What shall we talk about this morning?

CL: (*Looks panicky.*)

Co: Still pretty hard to talk.

CL: (*Flushes, looks embarrassed.*)

Co: It's quite an ordeal to talk to anyone.

CL: Yes. (*Pause.*) Sometimes I want to talk in class, but I get scared.

Co: I understand.

CL: When I'm introduced to another fellow I can't talk . . . can't think of anything to say.

Co: Perhaps it's the fear of not being able to say something.

CL: That's it; I am afraid to talk. I think what I might say would be the wrong thing, that nobody would be interested in what I have to say.

Co: You're afraid they won't accept what you say or that they may be critical of what you say.

CL: Something like that. You know I'm just not sure they will like me. I don't feel important or anything . . . just the opposite . . . like why should they like me. (*Said with great effort.*)

Co: You are afraid they won't like you and you feel sort of unworthy . . . unimportant.

CL: Yes. (*Long pause.*) That article in class this morning, I just couldn't get any meaning out of it. I don't know. I just couldn't.

Co: You feel pretty discouraged about it.

CL: I should be able to get something. I missed a lot of questions on the test over it.

Co: It seemed very difficult and you wonder if you are getting anywhere.

CL: I just wonder if I can improve . . . seems like I try and get nowhere.

Co: You feel almost hopeless about it.

CL: I don't know if I can make it in there and in English.

Co: It looks almost impossible to you. . . . Our time is up. Shall I see you again?

CL: Yes.

COUNSELOR'S NOTE, OCTOBER 18

It was so difficult for Norbert to express himself that he finally gave up and decided to try again next week.

EXCERPTS FROM INTERVIEW, OCTOBER 25

Co: What's on your mind today?

CL: I've just decided that I've been having word trouble ever since I was in the second grade. I mean I couldn't learn them or use them. I have ideas all right but I can't get them into words. I just bog down. Then I get afraid that I can't get the words and then I don't.

Co: It's as if the fear shuts off the words.

CL: Yes. I'm afraid the words won't come . . . that I can't get my idea out and that it won't be clear.

Co: I understand.

CL: Not knowing many words or having trouble with them makes me shy of people . . . almost keeps me from talking to anybody.

Co: Almost makes you afraid of people.

CL: And you know I have a younger sister that's the same way.

Co: Yes?

CL: I don't know why I feel this way about words.

Co: You wonder why.

CL: I guess it's because I never got started in the second grade.

Co: Anyway you feel greatly handicapped speaking and reading.

CL: (*Silence. Squirms, gets red in the face.*)

Co: It's hard to talk. . . . You run out of words and feel afraid no more will come. You feel embarrassed and tense.

CL: Yes. I sort of dread coming to interview because I know I can't talk for a whole 20 minutes. It's just not there and I can't.

Co: I know how you feel. You begin to feel like you can't cope with the situation. It scares you to think of talking very long.

CL: Yes. (*Long silence.*)

Co: (*Recapitulates.*) These are some of the things we have talked about in here. Since you were in the second grade, you have felt greatly handicapped in the use of words. During the first three years of high school, you felt that not much went on. During the last year, you worked hard, but you felt that you had missed a lot. You feel more confident about mathematics. Talking is an ordeal. You dread a situation where you will be required to talk so much that it almost makes you afraid of people. You are not sure people will like you and you are afraid they will not be interested in anything you might say. You feel unimportant and embarrassed. You are not sure you can improve. Is this the way it seems to you?

Cl: Uh huh. (*Silence.*)

Co: Do you feel like giving up today?

Cl: (*With obvious relief.*) Yes.

Co: Shall I see you again?

Cl: Yes.

EXCERPTS FROM INTERVIEW, NOVEMBER 8

Co: How are things going for you?

Cl: Not very good.

Co: Tell me more.

Cl: It's still words. I still feel tied up, like there is something that binds me.

Co: Like words are hard to take in or give out?

Cl: Yes. And it's funny, but I feel this way more about some kinds of words than about others.

Co: Yes?

Cl: Well, for example, I can get science words better than English words.

Co: This is a bit puzzling to you.

Cl: Yes, in a way . . . . Math is easy for me and science is not too bad.

Co: You have felt successful in math and you feel better able to cope with things related to it.

Cl: Maybe. (*Silence.*)

Co: Anything else on your mind today?

Cl: I'd like to talk, but when I get here I can't think of anything to say.

Co: You like to come, but you run out of ammunition. Maybe you feel sort of constricted . . . tied up.

Cl: It's not only with you. It's with anybody. I have four sisters and I don't talk much with them, and I don't talk much with my parents.

Co: It's just hard to communicate with anybody. You have never talked much with anybody. You want to, but you feel you can't.

Cl: Yes, I really want to get so I can talk, and read and write themes. By the way, I got a "C" on a theme the other day.

Co: This is encouraging to you.

Cl: I never thought I could make a grade like that.

Co: You're surprised and you are pleased, too.

Cl: Yes, it doesn't seem so, and I'm sure I couldn't write another as good.

Co: When something good happens to you, you can hardly believe it is true, and you are not sure it could ever happen again.

Cl: Yes . . . like it won't go on or last.

Co: Our time is about up. How do you feel about working further on your problem?

CL: I understand it better now. I think counseling has helped some. Sometimes I didn't make very good use of it. I guess I'll just try on my own for a while. My classwork will carry me along, I think.

Co: You feel you'd like to see how you get along without it for a while. Feel free to come back any time if I can help you.

CL: O.K.

COUNSELOR'S NOTE

About this time, Norbert began to participate in class discussion occasionally. His contributions were ordinary, but he managed to contribute a few statements. He began to make brief comments in the buzz groups, and took his turn at reporting the opinions of the small group. Some of the members of the class were quite relaxed and informal in their reports, including jokes and personal references in their reports. Some members took delight in teasing one of the girls about her boy friend and included some of this in a report on group decisions. Norbert was much embarrassed. He was never able to join in the good-natured chatter, but he gradually appeared more comfortable in the class.

COUNSELOR'S NOTE, JUNE 26

Met Norbert today at the swimming pool. He hurried over to greet me with genuine warmth and held out his hand. We carried on a long conversation (for him) and he did his share of the talking with apparent ease. Said he was working hard on the farm this summer. He explained that he had been invited to a rush party and seemed pleased to have this attention.

Gains in reading skills are shown in table 7-8.

TABLE 7-8
TEST AND RETEST RESULTS OF NORBERT SHORE

Test	First testing		Second testing		Norms
	Raw score	Percentile	Raw score	Percentile	
Coop reading					1954 local
Vocabulary	9	9	14	21	
Speed	12	28	26	68	
Comprehension	9	26	13	49	
Total	30	17	53	45	
Diagnostic reading					Denver
Speed (w.p.m.)	235	13	355	85	
Comprehension (story)	16	49	17	62	
Vocabulary	36	23	40	38	
Comprehension (study)	30	45	31	52	
Total comprehension	66	30	71	45	

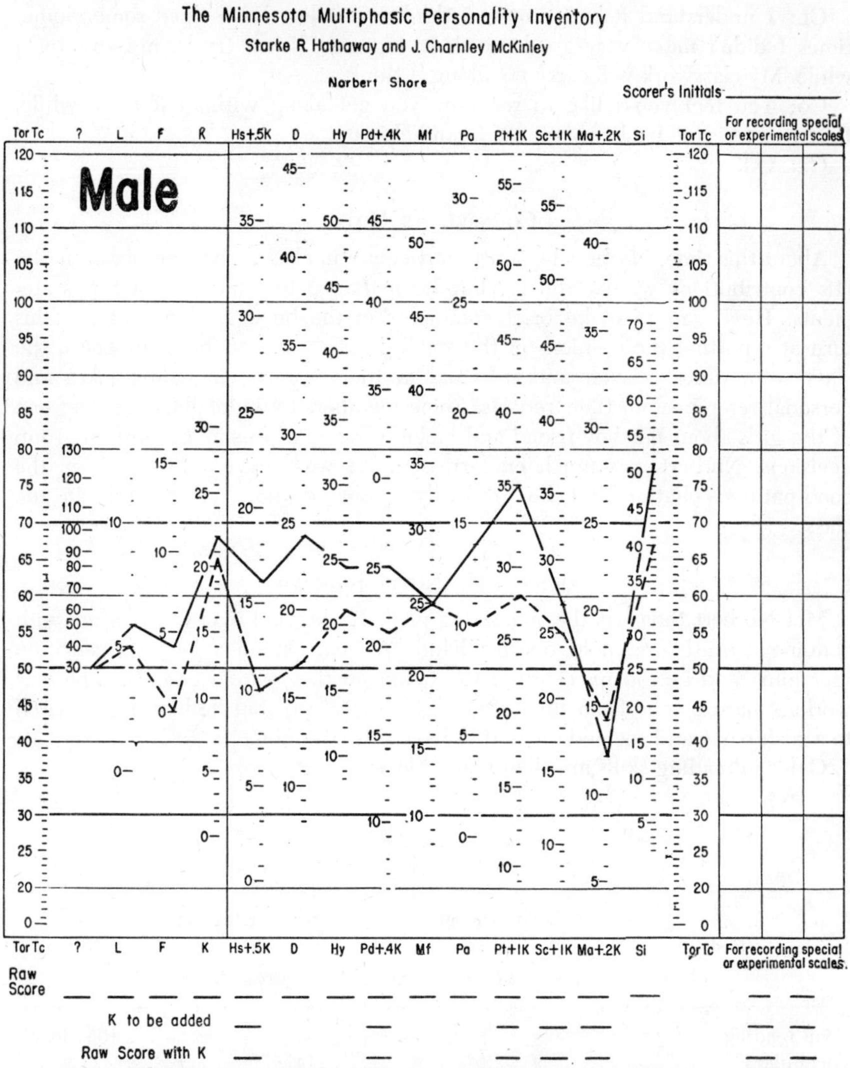

The Minnesota Multiphasic Personality Inventory

Starke R. Hathaway and J. Charnley McKinley

Norbert Shore

Scorer's Initials

Male

Fig. 2. The Minnesota Multiphasic Personality Inventory of Norbert Shore.

Improvement is indicated by both tests in all areas. Daily progress records also indicated gains in speed and comprehension. While early comprehension scores hovered around 80, with some as low as 50 per cent, seven of his last nine scores in comprehension were 90 per cent. His first speed scores ranged between 210 and 300 words per minute. The last six scores ranged between 230 and 390 words per minute. Improvement in personal adjustment is suggested by test and retest with the MMPI recorded in figure 2. The first scores are graphed in solid lines and final scores in broken lines. Retest with the ACE showed an increment in tested quantitative ability and total score, but none in linguistic ability.

If these changes in MMPI scores represent true gains, the client is presumed to have reduced defensiveness (K), depression, physical symptoms of emotional stress, anxiety, and shyness. He might be expected to be less concerned over his physical health, somewhat more accepting of rules and conventions, more aggressive and self-confident, more at ease in social situations, possibly more in touch with reality as it is viewed by his contemporaries. Probably he feels a higher level of energy and a greater sense of personal worth, is better able to make constructive use of his energies and abilities, meets with fewer frustrations, and is better able to cope with problems and the demands of his environment. A slight increment in manic score suggests that he is becoming more like other college students in his interest in a variety of activities. Probably the most significant changes are in the depression and anxiety scores which suggest gains in morale, self-esteem, constructive use of energies, hope for the future, and fewer fears and anxieties.

Gains are also suggested by test and retest with the Bender Visual Motor Gestalt. Retracings and frames surrounding the first drawings suggested insecurity. The second series of drawings were without frames, pencil strokes were firmer, and fewer retracings were apparent. Improvements were made in accuracy of reproduction. These changes suggest growing confidence, self-esteem, and willingness to do a task thoroughly and completely.

Case of Elaine Garth, College Freshman

The following information was available in the early part of the semester: scores from ACE, Cooperative Reading Examination, Diagnostic Reading Tests, and MMPI. They are shown in tables 7-9 and 7-10.

TABLE 7-9
SEPTEMBER TEST RESULTS OF ELAINE GARTH

	Raw score	Percentile	Norms
ACE			1954 local
Quantitative	46	66	
Linguistic	56	38	
Total	102	49	
Coop reading			
Vocabulary	−9	0	1954 local
Speed	11	25	
Comprehension	0	1	
Total	2	1	
Diagnostic reading			Denver
Speed (w.p.m.)	224	8	
Comprehension (story)	15	40	
Vocabulary	37	27	
Comprehension (study)	24	16	
Total comprehension	61	19	

TABLE 7-10

MMPI SCORES OF ELAINE GARTH

Depression	72
Pd	66
Masculinity	65
Pa	58
Pt (anxiety)	68
Social introversion	63

The Keystone visual skills test showed normal vision with the exception of fusion at the near point. She could maintain fusion, but had a tendency to over-converge.

From these data, one can assume a reading problem, emotional involvement, and a potential for improvement. Counseling is indicated in addition to regular work in the developmental reading class.

If she can be relieved of depression and anxiety, her reading skills may improve. Deviate scores on the depression, psychasthenia, and social introversion scales suggest tendencies toward low morale, low self-esteem, feelings of inferiority and insecurity, self-doubt, little hope for the future, fears, anxieties, worries, distractibility, inability to concentrate, lack of social skills, and lack of confidence in social situations. She might be expected to have a low verbal output, be confused about identification with women, and perhaps to show a lack of respect for rules and conventions. Possibly her daily performance will be uneven. She may be sensitive to criticism and manifest suspiciousness, rigidity, and resistance to change.

Probably the first administration of the Cooperative Reading Examination did not represent her true reading ability, as she was given a different test again a few days later and produced a percentile rank of 19. We can speculate that emotional disturbance, possibly fear of the test situation, depressed her first scores, or that the test with a greater range permitted a more accurate picture of her skills.

EXCERPTS FROM INTERVIEW, OCTOBER 4

Co: Elaine, as you know, I gather a considerable amount of data about each of my students, thinking that it will help us to name or identify reading problems and other conditions that interfere with improvement. After this is done, we talk things over and try to decide what might be done. Can you tell me a little about yourself.

CL: After graduating from high school, I worked for a summer as a secretary in a hospital. I liked that because . . . well . . . I guess they liked me. Here, I miss that. You know, I hated to leave the job and come to school.

Co: Yes . . . tell me more.

CL: Well I am taking home ec, but I'm not sure I'm suited for it. Maybe I ought to find out about other opportunities.

Co: You feel uncertain about your choice.

CL: Yes, but don't have to make up my mind right away I guess. We can talk about that later. You know, I have to work 20 to 24 hours a week. I have seven sisters and brothers, and you see, I have to help myself. I signed up for 15 hours and I'm worried if I can make it . . . I mean make good enough grades to stay in college.

Co: You are beginning to wonder if you have too much of a load. You don't feel sure of yourself. You worry about it.

CL: Well, you see, if I work from one to five every day and study from seven to twelve at night, well, I'm wondering if that is enough time to study.

Co: It seems to you like a pretty complicated situation.

CL: Yes, I'm afraid I can't make it. You know, I can tell already that this place is hard, I mean classwork. I feel so different here. I was salutatorian in grade school.

Co: It looks like a hard row to hoe.

CL: And I read so slowly and it's hard to cover all the reading and my assignments are so long.

Co: This worries you.

CL: This reading business is just an added handicap . . . enough to keep me down.

Co: You are wondering if you can win . . . I know you feel discouraged. Our time is up. Perhaps you would like to continue counseling sometime next week.

CL: Yes.

EXCERPTS FROM INTERVIEW, OCTOBER 14

Co: What's on your mind today?

CL: Seems like all I do is work. By the time I'm through with going to class all morning, working all afternoon, I'm tired and my study at night isn't doing me much good.

Co: You feel as if the time you invest doesn't yield enough profit.

CL: Yes, I work at it, but I don't accomplish enough. I seem to be interested, but I just can't concentrate. It seems the stuff just won't go in my head.

Co: You spin your wheels a good deal of the time.

CL: Yes and I know that I've just got to get the stuff or fail.

Co: It's as if calamity isn't far off, and time is passing.

CL: I didn't know it would be like this. I knew it would be harder than high school. It's spending all that time and not getting much of it that bothers me. Makes me feel like I'm not very bright.

Co: You are beginning to doubt whether you are smart enough to make it.

CL: Oh I don't like to think that. (*Silence, looks hurt.*)

Co: Your feelings are easily hurt.

CL: Yes . . . I guess I'm no good anyway and I'm just trying to cover up.

Co: You're feeling pretty low . . . pretty depressed.

CL: I don't seem to have enough ideas or have them fast enough.

Co: You feel dissatisfied with yourself. Our time is up for today. Shall we make another appointment?

CL: Yes.

EXCERPTS FROM INTERVIEW, OCTOBER 21

Co: How are you today?

CL: Oh! I'm tired all of the time.

Co: Generally fatigued.

CL: Yes, it's a load to carry, but I've got to keep going. I studied last night, and about 12 o'clock I tried to rethink what I had read during the last hour, and I'm beginning to think those last hours don't pay off.

Co: Not enough yield for the time invested.

CL: That's right, especially when the time is late at night. I really don't know the stuff and so next day I feel awkward and embarrassed in class. I'm afraid to recite. I see others reciting that don't know. I don't respect them. They are just trying to get by easy. I sometimes feel like talking, asking some of the better students before or after class what some of the answers are, but I feel embarrased to do it. Anyway, I'm shy and I want to be independent.

Co: You feel the need for help, but you also want to be independent and you don't like to embarrass yourself by asking.

CL: I don't want to be obligated to others.

Co: Tell me more.

CL: It's funny. I'm working most of my way with my earnings last summer and my 70 dollars a month here. But even if my folks would give me that money, I would still feel like paying my own way.

Co: You just don't like being obligated to others.

CL: I guess so.

Co: You are willing to pay a price to be independent.

CL: I guess so, but I seem to get hurt in the process.

Co: Do you feel that it's better for you even if you have to pay a price?

CL: Yes.

Co: Our time is up. Shall I see you again?

CL: Yes.

EXCERPTS FROM INTERVIEW, NOVEMBER 2

Co: How are you today?

CL: I'm pretty discouraged. I'm just low in "L" as you call it and I don't see how I can make up 18 years of low "L."

Co: You feel as if you were cheated in "L" and you feel hopeless about improving it.

CL: I go to reading class three times a week. This takes three perfectly good hours and I'm not improving.

Co: Makes you feel as if you are wasting this time in reading class.

CL: And by the time I add an interview once a week, it really takes a lot of time . . . enough to prepare another lesson.

Co: You are wondering if the time you invest in reading and counseling is worthwhile.

CL: This sounds pretty awful, but I really don't feel that I'm getting anywhere. I go over and over the words, but I don't like it and they are hard, and I can't remember them. Why are words so hard for me?

Co: You are embarrassed to say so, but you feel it isn't doing you any good and you feel discouraged and perhaps resentful.

CL: I guess I do. I've just got to make 15 hours or more a semester, but I don't know. . . .

Co: You feel you must do it, but you are not sure you can. Our time is up. Do you want to continue next week?

CL: Yes.

EXCERPTS FROM INTERVIEW, NOVEMBER 9

CL: I got a letter from my brother.

Co: Yes?

CL: He has always been a good student.

Co: Yes.

CL: My folks have been proud of him.

Co: I see.

CL: (*Pause.*) He asked me about grades. I guess he is in a position to ask since he has always made good grades, but . . . .

Co: You are not sure you like his inquiring.

CL: I'm sure he doesn't understand my situation. He expects me to make good grades. (*Pause.*) You know what . . . I'd just as soon quit school.

Co: It looks like one way to get out from under the pressure.

CL: You know my folks expect me to make just as good grades as my brother and they don't know if I can.

Co: You feel it's a bit unfair.

CL: I suppose they have the right to expect it, but I don't think I'm good enough to do what they expect.

Co: You would like to please them and you don't want to criticize them, but you are not sure that they know enough about the situation to judge.

CL: Yes, and they don't seem to understand I'm doing the best I can and how hard it is.

Co: You are a little resentful and unhappy about their attitude.

CL: (*Pause.*) I think I'll stay in school one year, that is, one semester longer, just for the folks. They expect it.

Co: You have about made up your mind you can stick it out for one year. Our time is up. Do you want to continue counseling?

CL: I don't know. It seems that I can read a little better at times and since I don't plan to go four years . . . I can sort of last one more semester under my own power . . . I guess I'll just continue the classwork, but not counseling. Thanks for helping me.

Co: Now that you have made a decision, things seems a little better.

CL: Yes.

CASE NOTES

This student made use of the counseling situation and improved her skills. Reading scores are now fairly consistent with tested scholastic aptitude. Results of reading tests and retests are given in table 7-11.

TABLE 7-11
TEST AND RETEST RESULTS OF ELAINE GARTH

Test	First testing		Second testing		Norms
	Raw score	Percentile	Raw score	Percentile	
Coop reading					1954 Local
Vocabulary	−9	0	19	38	
Speed	11	25	19	48	
Comprehension	0	1	14	52	
Total	2	1	52	43	
Diagnostic reading					Denver
Speed (w.p.m.)	224	8	238	15	
Comprehension (story)	15	40	17	62	
Vocabulary	37	27	44	56	
Comprehension (study)	24	16	33	66	
Total comprehension	61	19	77	64	

Her daily progress chart indicated an average gain in speed of 105 words per minute.

The second MMPI suggests that modest gains were made in personal adjustment with the exception of social introversion, but because of the high lie score, the scores are not entirely reliable. The high lie score suggests that the client deliberately chose answers most favorable to her. Allowing for some distortion, however, we might assume that some progress has been made in the direction of acceptance of reality as it is seen by her contemporaries and in acceptance of laws, behavior standards, and conventions of society. Apparently rigidity, hypersensitivity, and suspiciousness have been lessened. Defensiveness has apparently been reduced. Judging from the client's behavior and the amount of her improvement in reading skills, it is also reasonable to suppose that her anxiety, depression, and distractibility have been somewhat lessened and that self-esteem and self-confidence have increased. Without relief from anxiety and depression, it seems unlikely that her reading skills would have improved so markedly. Test and retest scores are charted in figure 3. First scores are shown by a solid line and retest by a broken line.

Improved personal adjustment is suggested by retest with the Bender Visual Motor Gestalt. The first figures, drawn in September, were very small. Retracings were apparent, and some of the figures were drawn as many as three times. Figures drawn at the close of the semester were larger and distributed over the page. There was less retracing and less duplication. These changes are

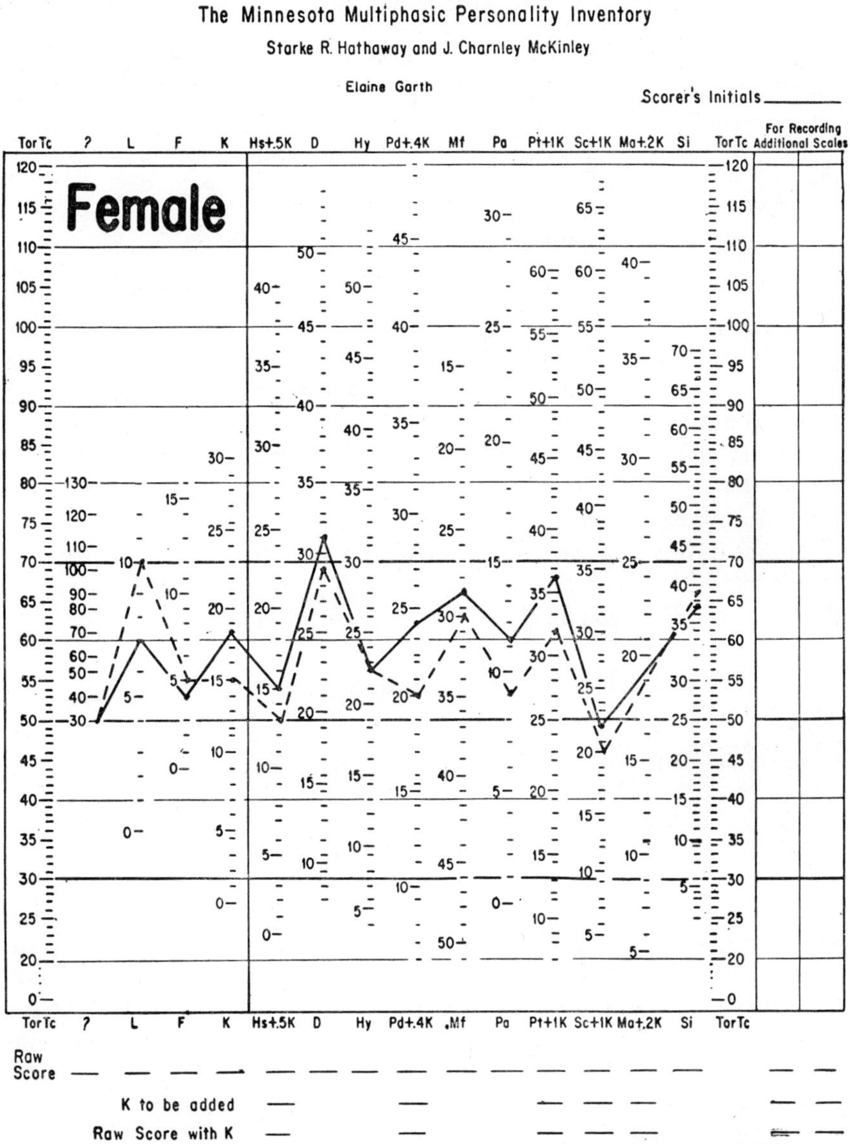

The Minnesota Multiphasic Personality Inventory
Starke R. Hathaway and J. Charnley McKinley

Fig. 3. The Minnesota Multiphasic Personality Inventory of Elaine Garth.

presumed to indicate progress toward feelings of adequacy, security, and self-confidence.

September drawings, offered in response to the House-Tree-Person test, included four trees, two houses, and a male figure. January drawings included only one of each, and the human figure was a female. Such changes are believed to represent improved security and progress toward appropriate acceptance of the female role.

Perseveration (repetition of figures) is believed to indicate rigidity in emotional organization and obsessive-compulsive tendencies. Reduction of perseveration, as seen in the final drawings, suggests that these tendencies declined. The lack of paths in her final house picture and the lack of hands in the drawing of the human figure suggest that communication is still difficult. Shading suggests that depression is still a problem. The absence of shrubs and ornamentations on the house is said to indicate a barren existence.

During the semester, Elaine showed increasing interest in the classwork and took an increasingly active part in the discussions. She apparently became integrated into the group, lost some of her shyness, and manifested growing self-confidence. Her remarks early in the semester reflected indifference toward the reading class and lack of understanding. Later, her contributions demonstrated that she was reading with interest and understanding. She was increasingly able to relate her remarks to the central ideas of the reading selections and to pay sustained attention. At times, it was apparent from her alert facial expression that she had something to say. The instructor responded, "I believe Elaine has something to say. Can you help us here, Elaine?" Eventually, she began to volunteer.

Her work in English class also improved. She made an average grade on her final theme and an average grade for the semester in English. A number of outside factors probably interfered with progress toward personal adjustment. The combination of a full class load and heavy work schedule left only evening hours for study. With her limited reading skills, she felt herself in a situation with which she could not cope. Financial worries and the pressure from home created additional stress. It is probable that the nature of her part-time job was also a handicap to wholesome personal development. Her employer was a highly nervous, hard-driving, dissatisfied woman with a defensive and resentful attitude toward the college, toward men, and toward authority in general. In the counseling interview, Elaine reflected many of the attitudes of her employer. It seemed that she absorbed some of her employer's attitudes and values and identified with her to some degree. Continued counseling was recommended.

Case of Shila Morton, College Freshman

Shila was assigned to developmental reading class on the basis of high "Q" and low "L" scores, as measured by the American Council on Education Psychological Examination, and her rank on the Cooperative Reading Examination. They are shown in table 7-12.

TABLE 7-12
SEPTEMBER TEST RESULTS OF SHILA MORTON

Test	Raw score	Percentile	Norms
ACE			1954 local
Quantitative	50	78	
Linguistic	58	42	
Total	108	59	
Coop reading			1954 local
Vocabulary	26	58	
Speed	23	60	
Comprehension	6	15	
Total	55	49	

The test pattern suggested underdeveloped linguistic ability, since her "Q" score ranked her in the upper 22 per cent of her class and her "L" score was 36 percentile points lower. Her rank in vocabulary and speed were satisfactory, though lower than rank in quantitative ability, but her tested comprehension score ranked in the lower 15 per cent of her class. Her total reading score was 10 percentile points lower than her total score on the scholastic-aptitude test. Thus, she was judged to have a reading problem and a potential for improvement.

The results of the Minnesota Multiphasic Personality Inventory suggested no serious problems, with the exception of shyness and social introversion. The Si score was 1.3 standard deviations above the mean. Shyness was also manifested in class and in interview.

Her scores on eight of the MMPI scales fell below the mean. Few studies are reported on the meaning of low MMPI scores. In this case, the low scores accentuate the relative importance of the Si score. Scores which deviate below the mean suggest that the client's responses are dissimilar from those of the majority of her contemporaries and that possibly her view of reality does not coincide with the popular concept. (It would be interesting to investigate whether or not low scores are symptomatic of repression.)

Her Keystone Ophthalmic Telebinocular Visual Skills Test revealed extreme nearsightedness and poor fusion at the near point. She wore glasses which corrected the refractive error, to some extent, but which were not intended to correct the defect in fusion.

Her total rank on the Diagnostic Reading Test was about the same as total rank on the Cooperative Reading Test. Tested speed, story comprehension, and vocabulary, according to the Diagnostic, were below average by Denver norms.

Interview Notes, October 28

Shila came in and asked to have her test results explained. Reported the ACE, Coop, and Diagnostic. She asked about the other test (MMPI), and I explained that the results suggested shyness. She agreed.

Excerpts from Interview, November 5

Cl: I was surprised about my test scores. I don't feel quite right about making a low score on the reading test. I thought I read all right.

Co: It was a shock and perhaps you feel that the test score doesn't represent your true ability to read.

Cl: I really don't know. I've always read a lot and I seem to get meaning. I really don't understand why I would go down on the test.

Co: You are puzzled about it.

Cl: I've read so much and I've always made good grades in English and other subjects like math and science, too.

Co: You are wondering whether or not if it is a fair evaluation.

Cl: Yes, because I've always done well in school. I just don't feel right about it.

Co: You feel upset . . . almost as if you were accused of something.

Cl: Well, if it's really so, I guess I should know about it, only I didn't expect . . . .

Co: It's hard to understand.

Cl: Perhaps it really is so, only it's funny I've always felt just as good in reading as other people. I suppose it's possible to be this way and not know it. Is there anything else about the test results?

Co: You already know about your nearsightedness, but perhaps you don't know that your eyes do not work well together at the near point, that is at reading distance.

Cl: Is there anything I could do about it? Should I see a doctor?

Co: Sometimes it is possible to improve eye coordination with visual training.

Cl: Who could I see to find out about this?

Co: (*Gives suggestions.*)

Cl: I'll think about this.

Co: Do you want to come back next week and talk about this again?

Cl: Yes.

Excerpts from Interview, November 12

Cl: I found out that I should take some visual training.

Co: Yes.

Cl: But I don't think I will. I'm so busy now with so much studying and everything . . . . Maybe I can next summer when I'm at home.

Co: You'll think about it later.

Cl: (*Silence.*)

Co: Last time you were telling me how you felt about being assigned to the reading class.

Cl: Oh, it's O.K. now. I've found out other girls with good high-school records are in there, too.

Co: You had thought there would be some embarrassment connected with it.

Cl: Yes, and I didn't like being assigned to a kind of lower level class . . . where poor students would be.

Co: You were afraid of the reputation you might get.

Cl: (*Smiles.*)

Co: You don't mind so much now . . . being obliged to take it.

Cl: No. (*Silence.*)

Co: Last time we talked about shyness. While it probably seems to you that it has little to do with reading, it is involved in communication with other people. Would you care to talk more about this?

Cl: I know I'm shy, but I don't know how to get over it. How would I?

Co: Sometimes it helps to talk about it.

Cl: Talking about it would help me get over it?

Co: You are surprised and skeptical.

Cl: I don't see how it would help.

Co: It sounds pretty farfetched to you.

Cl: Yes and I don't see what it has to do with reading.

Co: You feel doubtful.

Cl: Well it might help some people, but I'm so busy and I don't think . . . .

Co: You're inclined to think that it would not help you.

Cl: Maybe by attending class, I can improve in reading and in talking with other people. I think that would be enough.

Co: You would rather not make another appointment for counseling.

Cl: That's right.

EXCERPT FROM INTERVIEW, DECEMBER 1

Cl: (*Appears disturbed.*)

Co: You're feeling upset today.

Cl: I'm not doing so well.

Co: Do you want to talk about it?

Cl: I'm making low grades in two classes . . . almost failing one. I work hard, too. I don't know what to do.

Co: You are getting frightened.

Cl: Yes, but I'm more disgusted with myself. I've never made grades like that. My folks would be concerned . . . but they wouldn't be mad at me. I would hate for anybody to know.

Co: You feel embarrassed.

Cl: I'm beginning to wonder if I can make it. It's December and I have less than two months to catch up.

Co: The time is so short that you are beginning to feel panicky.

CL: (*Silence, then tears.*)

Co: It's a big problem . . . you feel helpless . . . you've tried hard but it hasn't paid off and you can't help crying.

CL: (*Weeps . . . silence.*)

Co: You're not sure you can handle the situation and you're very much upset.

CL: (*More tears.*) I guess I'll just have to work harder.

Co: You're beginning to think there may be some hope.

CL: My time is up and I'll have to go.

Co: Would you care to talk about this again?

CL: No. Nobody can do this for me. I have to do it myself.

Co: You feel as if you may be able to handle the situation.

CASE NOTES

Shila's final test scores are compared with early scores in table 7-13. MMPI test and retest results are charted in figure 4. The first scores are indicated by the continuous line. Final scores are shown by dotted lines.

TABLE 7-13
TEST AND RETEST RESULTS OF SHILA MORTON

Test	First testing		Second testing		Norms
	Raw score	Percentile	Raw score	Percentile	
Coop reading					1954 local
Vocabulary	26	58	33	76	
Speed	23	60	24	62	
Comprehension	6	15	11	39	
Total	55	49	68	62	
Diagnostic reading					Denver
Speed	247	21	355	86	
Comprehension (story)	14	30	15	40	
Vocabulary	40	38	51	83	
Comprehension (study)	32	59	31	52	
Total comprehension	72	48	82	80	

Reading test scores are now fairly consistent with tested scholastic aptitude. Uneven performance was suggested by her daily progress chart, but scores during the last six sessions of class ranged from 200 to 440 words per minute, as compared with a range during the first six sessions of 180 to 320 words per minute. She improved in all classes, and her semester grades in all courses were passing or better.

As can be seen from the two MMPI profiles, the Si score remained the same, suggesting that the client still suffers from shyness. The Mf score moved above the mean and now deviates very little from the average score for women. The D and Hs scores moved closer to the mean, suggesting that her concept of

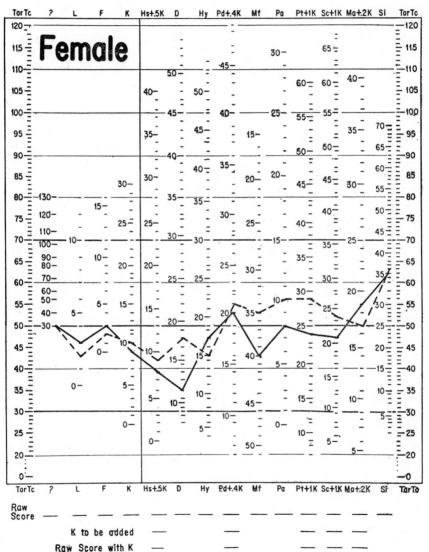

Fig. 4. The Minnesota Multiphasic Personality Inventory of Shila Morton.

reality is more nearly like that of her contemporaries. The second Pt score does not deviate markedly from the mean, but anxiety appeared to mount in interview.

The first drawings of the Bender were surrounded by frames, suggesting insecurity. Inconsistency of stroke suggested ambivalence and vacillation between submission and aggression. In the final reproduction of the Bender figures, frames were omitted and retracings were fewer, changes said to represent improved personal security and sense of personal worth and less need for external props. The pencil strokes were more consistent, a change which suggests less ambivalence.

The House-Tree-Person drawings were more heavily drawn the second time, a development believed to mean an increase in aggressiveness and self-confidence. The door and path to the second house are more accessible, and may mean that communication is a little easier. Portraits of a female head and face, offered both times, are believed to reveal great respect for intellectual accomplishment. Less femininity, as suggested by the MMPI retest, is also indicated by changes in the drawing of the second portrait which shows stronger features and a boyish haircut.

Improvement in reading skills is indicated by all measures except the study comprehension subtest of the Diagnostic Reading Test. Gratifying gains in vocabulary were indicated by both tests.

During the latter part of the semester, she began to participate in classroom discussion with increasing interest and self-confidence.

This case study illustrates the kind of everyday counseling frequently required of the reading clinician. The client elected to discontinue counseling and to delay investigation of her visual problem, but she made reasonable use of the classroom situation and demonstrated improvement in reading skills.

The Case of Delbert Pepper, Second-grader

The scores of this eight-year-old on the Coordinated Scales of Attainment ranked him at grade 2.2 in vocabulary recognition and 1.7 in reading comprehension. His rank of .4 in picture-word association brought his total rank down to considerably below average by national norms. Since he was the oldest member of his grade, these scores suggested a reading problem. When tested informally with a second-grade reader at the first semester level, he made 23 errors for every 100 running words, or more than twice as many as average. The first three grades are in the same room. His sister is in the first grade.

HOUSE-TREE-PERSON TEST

The outside boundaries of all pictures were heavily reinforced (awareness of controls or need for outside controls); the house lacks windows, doors, and paths (communication is difficult); house is very complicated (self and environment are complicated and hard to understand); guns shoot through the house and lethal rays radiate from it (hostility). The human figure is a male (identification with same sex); face is profile (evasiveness); there is no eye (may wish not to see some portion of environment or self); head and body face different directions (conflict). Other characteristics were: thin neck (shuts off body impulses from the intellect); bilateral symmetry in body (repression, social distance, intellectualization); pencil strokes cut the paper (aggressions); prominent nose and hat (infantile preoccupation with sex). A female figure, added voluntarily, showed the following features: long hair (curiosity about sex at the infantile level); long skirt (concealed curiosity about sex); feet are turned in (guilt). Another picture shows genitals (challenge to social decorum).

FAMILY HISTORY AND OTHER NOTES

Lives with an aunt and uncle who provide necessities, but display some resentment at being obliged to take care of the boy, criticizes him publicly, are suspected of punishing him severely. Younger sister is also cared for by aunt and greatly favored, apparently. The boy has been shifted around among several relatives and was apparently less than welcome. Parents of other pupils criticize him in his presence and seem reluctant to have their children play with him. Pupils also remark openly that he is a bad boy. His Sunday-school teacher called at the school and related that she has been telling him to be a good boy at school. The school children report that he is rough with his little sister and the younger pupils. He hits and cuts the school furniture with his knife, pencil, and toys, says he likes to fight, invites the older boys to fight with him.

In his stories and remarks, he expresses more dislikes than likes, more hostility than warmth, more negative than positive feelings. He wishes for many things, to be elsewhere, to be somebody else, to have more toys, to have more friends. Violence is often expressed. He tells stories in which he describes hurting animals and people.

The primary problem appears to be an emotional one with reading disability as a secondary problem. Obviously, this situation places him under stress. He is unable to satisfy his deepest needs for self-esteem and security. He apparently expends a great deal of energy in aggression, but also exerts a great deal in self-control.

This case history includes few interviews, but there were a number of occasions when counseling techniques were used with Delbert in the presence of his classmates.

CASE NOTES, SEPTEMBER 15

Several pupils came running in from the playground to report that Delbert hit his little sister.

TEACHER: Do you want to tell me about this?

CL: She was throwing clods at other kids. I just wanted to keep her from hurting them.

T: You wanted to protect the other children.

CL: Yes. I didn't mean to hurt her.

T: It was an accident.

CL: Yes.

CASE NOTES, SEPTEMBER 18

Quarreled with playmates. Restless, squirmed in his seat, put his head down on desk. Jabbed his paper and the desk with his pencil.

T: Delbert feels bad today.

CL: (*Nodded.*)

T: Doesn't feel like working.

CL: (*Did not answer, but presently began to study.*)

The group took a hike. Delbert ran into another child . . . might have been an accident. The other children scolded. One of them asked, "Why didn't you leave Delbert at the schoolhouse? He always makes trouble." He turned around at once to go back, stomping his feet.

T: This makes you mad.

CL: Aw. They're always picking on me.

T: You feel as if they're against you.

CL: They are. If they don't want me I won't go.

T: You don't like to be where you feel you are not wanted.

CL: Yes. (*Starts in the direction of the other children.*)

T: You'd really like to go.

CL: Yes. (*He went on with the rest of the children and was very well behaved.*)

CASE NOTES, SEPTEMBER 24

Delbert disturbed the singing so much this morning that we gave up trying. Later in the day, the other pupils sent a committee to ask to sing in the afternoon.

T: Shall we ask all of the class?

COMMITTEE: Yes. (*All pupils agreed except Delbert.*)

T: Delbert doesn't want to sing.

(*D. whispered to children sitting near him. One of them reported that he said he really wanted to sing. No trouble the rest of the day.*)

CASE NOTES, SEPTEMBER 26

CL: This work is too hard and too long and too silly.

T: You don't like the work.

CL: (*Nods and jabs at paper.*)

T: You wish you didn't have to do it.

CL: (*Starts to work.*)

During art period, D. refused to share his supplies with his sister and she cried.

T: Delbert wants the paints and his sister wants them, too. (*Both nod.*)

T: Sister wants them so much that she has to cry.

CL: She's just a cry-baby . . . always gettin' me in trouble.

T: You feel a little bit mad at her.

CL: She does things, but she never gets caught.

T: You feel this isn't quite fair.

CL: No.

SISTER: He hits people and then he gets in trouble. (*Smiles.*)

T: Sometimes you like to see him get into trouble.

SISTER: (*Nods and gets out her own art supplies.*)

CASE NOTES, SEPTEMBER 29

Delbert hit Jim with his toy gun. Both stomped in as school started, looking very angry.

T: Do you want to talk about this?

J: He hit me.

T: That makes you very angry.

D: But he called me a bad name.

T: Delbert is angry and Jim is angry, too.

D: We want to fight outdoors.

T: You want to fight. (*Both nodded.*)

D: Call all the others to watch us.

T: You would like to have the others watch the fight.

D: Yes.

T: You may fight outside near the window, but you may not take the gun. The other pupils have work to do. They will stay in here. (*They went outside, talked things over, and returned with their arms around each other.*)

CASE NOTES, OCTOBER 31

D. took part in a program. His aunt says she is pleased . . . thinks he did his part well . . . says he is a good worker. This is the first time she has expressed approval of him.

NOVEMBER TESTS

Grade rank in reading, Coordinated Scales of Attainment, 2.07; comprehension, 2.0; *Weekly Reader* test, 2.1.

CASE NOTES, NOVEMBER 10

Delbert wrote a story, "I like A., because she is a good girl. I like C., because he is a good boy and treats me nice. I like P., because she is a good girl. I like O., because he is a friendly boy." (This is the first time he has ever said he likes anyone. He expresses increasingly positive feelings.)

CASE NOTES, NOVEMBER 13

Read well today, and finished his exercises. Classmates commented favorably on his work. Delbert smiled.

T: You feel proud of yourself.
Cʟ: (*Nods.*)

Case Notes, November 20

Told about sticking a pitchfork in a cat.
T: You felt like hurting something.
Cʟ: (*Nods.*) I stuck it in and its guts came out. (*Looks around to see how others are taking it.*)
T: You like to say things to surprise people and make them listen to you. You like to have people pay attention to you.
Cʟ: (*Nods.*)

Case Notes, November 25

Delbert had a cocker spaniel puppy in his desk.
T: You would like to keep him with you today.
Cʟ: (*Nods.*)
T: You understand that there is a rule against this. (*Explains about lunch-room regulations.*)
Cʟ: (*Nods.*)
T: Shall we ask the other pupils what to do?
Cʟ: O.K.
(*They suggested that he be permitted to keep the puppy a few minutes before putting the puppy out. Presently, he took him to the door and let him go.*)

Case Notes, November 24

Delbert finished his work promptly and was excused to help the cook.
T: You like to do this.
Cʟ: (*Nods.*)
Gave him a note to take to his aunt. He asked to have it read to him.
T: You are afraid it might have something bad in it.
Cʟ: Yes.
After hearing it read, he said it was all right and took it home.

January Weekly Reader Test

Grade rank, 2.4.

Case Notes, February 2

Cʟ: Couldn't we turn our chairs around and face the other way? We just sit this way and look at the same old blackboard all of the time. Let's do something different.
T: You get tired of the same old thing.
Cʟ: Yes.
T: Shall we ask the other pupils?
Cʟ: Yes.
(*They agreed and we turned the chairs around.*)

CASE NOTES, FEBRUARY 15

Showed colored slides of Japanese scenes. Delbert wrote, "We saw some slides at school. They were pretty. I liked all of them. We saw Japanese people dressed up." (Expresses more positive feeling, more likes.)

CASE NOTES, FEBRUARY 18

Delbert played house with the girls. Seemed to be having a good time.
T: You are having fun today.
CL: (*Nods.*)
OPAL: He's acting real nice.
T: You like to have him around. (*Children agreed.*)

CASE NOTES, MARCH 4

Katy missed two words in spelling.
CL: Did she miss two? (*Katy cried.*)
T: Katy feels sad because she missed two words.
CL: I didn't make her cry, did I? I didn't mean to. Everybody misses words sometimes.
T: You don't like to think that you made her cry.

CASE NOTES, MARCH 30

Delbert wrote, "I want to learn to protect other people."

CASE NOTES, APRIL 1

Delbert and Katy asked to work together on an exercise. They worked very faithfully and finished it together, talking in low tones. Delbert asked if he could work ahead in his workbook. Finished his writing book and started a new one.

APRIL HOUSE-TREE-PERSON TEST

Portrait is full-face with eyes and broad smile (happier and less evasive, more open to social communication). Arms are out for social communication. Houses have gone through several stages during the year, gradually losing their hostile symbols. In an intermediate stage, they were shown with many rooms attached to each other or a series of houses attached to each, an arrangement suggesting compartmentalization of feelings and facts. These pictures gave the impression of perspective which may mean that some parts of personality require less concealment than others. Windows and doors began to appear in the drawings of houses, suggesting avenues to communication. The final house is a simple, straightforward drawing, more nearly like those usually offered by children of his age. The addition of trees and a sun suggest that life is more interesting. These changes suggest that his view of reality is now close to that of his classmates. Now reads Third Reader, easy book, unfamiliar materials, with 14 errors for every 100 running words . . . not quite average for beginning third grade.

Coordinated Scales of Attainment, reading grade rank, 2.9, shows gains since November of .9 of a grade in total rank; spelling gain from grade 2 to 2.9; arithmetic average from grade 2.8 to 4.5, by national norms. (An adult in the community volunteers the statement that he has made more progress than any child in school, notes change in behavior.)

STORY: "I like to come to school. My friends are (names 10 pupils). People are good to me. It is fun to play."

LETTER TO TEACHER AFTER CLOSE OF SCHOOL. "I hope you are feeling well and I hope your folks are feeling well."

SUMMARY: Some of the conversations reported were actually repeated many times. For example, there were many occasions when he expressed the wish to leave the school, the feeling that he was not wanted there or that people were against him. The response was, "You feel as if you must get away. You don't like to be where you feel people don't like you. You feel that people are against you. You feel that others do same things that you do, but do not get punished."

Many times he expressed aggressions against the school, the teacher, and classmates. She responded, "Right now, you feel as if you don't like it here. You are angry with me and with the boys and girls." When he seemed to feel that the situation was unbearable, she reflected, "You feel as if you can't stand it any longer."

During the year, his expressions of hostility and aggression gave way gradually to expressions of cheerfulness, satisfaction, and warmth. He had fewer fights and became more sensitive to the feelings of other children. In the classroom, lunchroom, and on the playground, he became more cooperative with his schoolmates and more interested in group activities. These changes in attitudes were reflected in his drawings. A gradual change could be seen in the attitudes of foster parents, school children, and community toward him.

Samples of work throughout the year indicated much improvement in writing, spelling, and language. He voluntarily made the change from manuscript to cursive writing. Test results indicated gains in reading skills of more than one grade (1.2) in eight months of school.

SUMMARY

Counseling the retarded reader requires sensitivity to the client's needs, his expectations regarding counseling, and the way in which he sees his situation. Depending on the needs of the client, the counselor hopes to help him solve problems, get needed information, understand himself and his environment, formulate or clarify goals, improve in communicative skills, and move toward independent thinking and problem-solving. Progress in counseling may result in increasing self-acceptance and acceptance of others.

The counselor should be well acquainted with a variety of methods and techniques. Some characteristics of directive and non-directive counseling are briefly described, and illustrations are given of their uses with retarded readers. Similarities in methods are cited. Directive techniques are discussed in connection with visual problems, vocational choice, study skills, test interpretation, temporary emergencies, and all problems which are essentially lack of information. Reflecting feeling is discussed as it might be applied to counseling depressives, anxiety cases, and others with deep emotional involvement. The behavior of defensive, constricted, and uncommunicative clients in interview is described. Characteristic responses of manic and paranoid personalities to counseling are suggested. Attention is called to the learning process during counseling.

Impatience, unrealistic expectations, status needs of the counselor can interfere with progress. The counselor can satisfy some of his own needs through his work, but not all. Caution in the use of test scores is advised. A deviate score on a personality test may reflect some of the characteristic tendencies, but not others. If recapitulation is used as a counseling technique, the counselor should not permit his interest in the client's problems to overshadow strengths and signs of progress.

Orientation to counseling is begun in the reading class. Some students are prepared to make active use of the first interview. Others need priming. Some examples of opening counselor statements are given.

Five case studies illustrate the processes of counseling, the use of test results, a variety of student problems, and the evaluation of progress.

CHAPTER 8

Evaluating Developmental Reading

Any school program can be improved by careful and objective evaluation. Among the benefits are these: (1) teachers learn which objectives have been reached and where they need to improve; (2) evidences of improvement serve as a reward for teachers; (3) results can be used for informing the public and staff; (4) interest in the program is stimulated; (5) results of evaluation can be used in defending the program and justifying expenditures. Evaluation in terms of objectives may lead to revising them or to stating them more clearly. Materials and methods can be reviewed and assessed in the light of evaluation.

Some sort of evaluation goes on anyway. In the absence of a planned appraisal, the program will likely be assessed on the basis of vague impressions, rumors, and splinters of knowledge. Critics of a program are often more vocal than its supporters.

Books and magazine articles attacking the schools during the past few years consistently reported misinformation and conclusions based on insufficient evidence. A program of continuous evaluation and reports to the public can forestall such attacks and render them relatively harmless.

Industry and the professions commonly assume responsibility for evaluating and publicizing their own achievements, setting standards, and disciplining their own members. In contrast, any member of the community feels perfectly competent to judge the effectiveness of the public schools, regardless of his training, experience, or information. Rewards in the form of rank, pay, and recognition could be more fairly awarded if members of the teaching profession assume responsibility for assessing their own achievements. Evaluative instruments are not infallible but they are better than guessing, speculating, and drawing conclusions from bits of evidence. As they are more universally used, they will doubtless improve.

Evaluation of teachers by other teachers is not usually practical. One teacher seldom knows very much about what goes on in another classroom. Even administrators with an occasional visit to each teacher get only a glimpse of the year's work. One disgruntled student or one parent can raise an uproar that obscures the gains of the class as a whole. The teacher's unsupported estimate of his own work is open to question. Comprehensive and objective evaluation is a protection to the teacher.

Means of evaluation should be thoroughly explored by those who are doing the work. The plan should not be imposed upon the teachers by the administration or personnel staff. All staff members concerned should share in the planning. Information about funds, ordering, and scheduling can come from administrative officers. Counselors, psychometrists, and other specialists can furnish information about the value and uses of tests and other instruments and methods of treating data. The teachers can consider which they can use to the best advantage and share in making the final decisions.

The instruments used in evaluation should fit the stated objectives. Unless the objectives are clear to the teacher and the students, meaningful appraisal is virtually impossible. Obviously, the final results must also be comparable with the items of information gathered about the students at the beginning of the school term. Thus, plans for evaluation cannot be left until late in the year, but should be considered in early stages of planning the course.

Objectives agreed upon by one class and teacher were to improve: speed, comprehension, concentration, spelling, interest, vocabulary, study habits, self-confidence, social skills, and the ability to analyze and appraise reading selections. They also agreed to try to identify and correct ocular defects and to explore feelings that might relate to efficiency in reading. One can notice that these objectives go beyond reading speed and comprehension. A thorough evaluation of gains would then include the measurement of total growth, rather than gains in reading skills alone.

Items such as speed, vocabulary, and comprehension can be measured by standardized tests. Spelling can be measured by test and retest with the Pollock and Baker[1] word lists or the list given in Appendix B of this book. Some standardized personality tests are also available. Concentration, interest, morale, discussion skills, self-confidence, skill in analyzing reading materials are less amenable to quantitative measurement. We suggest that standardized testing be supplemented by other data, such as student opinion, and observations of the teacher. Behavior in class, spread of participation, quality of response, length and quality of written compositions are worth noting in evaluation.

In addition to the standardized test and retest, the progress record is an aid to evaluation, as it gives a day to day estimate of performance. A composite record of the class can be constructed.

[1] Pollock, T. C., and W. D. Baker, *The University Spelling Book,* Prentice-Hall, Inc., Englewood Cliffs, N. J., 1955, pp. 6–12.

Improvement in concentration is related to reduction of anxiety. If test and retest with a personality inventory or a projective technique indicates reduction of anxiety, this finding is one indication that concentration may be improved. Reports of the students and observations of instructors are sources of information on this subject. Improvement in comprehension scores suggests that concentration is improved.

Increased interest in reading is shown by mounting interest in discussions, volume of voluntary reading, statements of students, quality of response, and the like. A rise in the interest-maturity score on the Strong Vocational Interest Blank might also be related to improvement in interest, since some items scored on this key relate to reading and verbal interests. Generally broadened interests and likes are reflected in a rise in the IM score. Retest with the interest-maturity scale of the SVIB is of value in view of the study by Woolf and Woolf[2] suggesting a relationship between linguistic ability and interest-maturity. Changes in SVIB scores on any scale should be noted. If the student moves toward a primary interest pattern, the change might be considered evidence of maturity.

Changes in study habits might be reflected in a comparison of test with retest results, using the Wrenn-Larsen Study Habits Inventory which appears in their book, *Studying Effectively*.[3] Comments of students on their own progress in this area would also be of value.

Illustrations are given in Chapters 1, 3, 4, and 6 of the use of reading and personality tests in evaluation. Instead of repeating these materials, we shall offer excerpts from annual reports to show what kind of information might be included. Some of the basic items to be included in the annual report of the developmental reading program are the following: (1) average gains of the class or classes as measured by standardized test and retest; (2) average gains of the class or classes as indicated by progress reports; (3) results of test and retest with a personality inventory or projective techniques; (4) results of a questionnaire or critique measuring student opinion of the class; (5) evidence from other instructors showing progress in study skills, classroom performance, attitudes, etc.; (6) illustrative case records showing individual progress; (7) comments of the reading instructor. Other data which might be included are the results of test and retest with the American Council on Education Psychological Examination, samples of students' work, ratings of discussion and leadership sessions, tachistoscope records, SVIB studies, students who were treated for visual problems, and any research done by the

[2] Woolf, Maurice D., and Jeanne A. Woolf, "Is Linguistic Ability Related to Maturity?" *J. appl. Psychol.*, vol. 39, no. 6, 1955, pp. 413–415.
[3] Wrenn, C. Gilbert, and Robert P. Larsen, *Studying Effectively*, Stanford University Press, Stanford, Calif., 1949.

reading instructor. The reports on evaluation should be preceded by a brief explanation of the organization of the program, criteria for selecting students, the objectives of the program, and techniques employed.

REPORTING STANDARDIZED TEST RESULTS

Table 8-1 reports the differences between initial raw scores and final raw scores of a group of college freshmen tested before and after one semester of developmental reading with the American Council on Education Psychological Examination and the Cooperative Reading Examination. The data were treated statistically to determine whether or not the differences were true differences or a result of chance.

TABLE 8-1

GAINS OF READING STUDENTS IN ACE SCORES AND READING SCORES, SPRING SEMESTER, 1955

	Degrees freedom	Mean increase	Range of increase	t-Score	Confidence interval
Linguistic	58	4.03	1.8 to 6.2	3.66	95
Quantitative	58	3.05	1.3 to 4.8	3.54	95
Reading speed	65	7.38	5.6 to 9.1	8.39	95
Comprehension	65	10.85	9.3 to 12.4	13.61	95

SOURCE: Woolf, Maurice D., Annual Report on Developmental Reading, Kansas State College, Manhattan, Kans., 1955.

A t-score of more than 3 represents a true difference between the two means. All of the increases reported here are significant beyond the 1 per cent level of confidence. The increases in reading speed and comprehension are particularly outstanding.

Some college freshmen show improvement in reading skills whether they are enrolled in reading classes or not. In order to determine whether or not the increment of students enrolled in developmental reading is the result of treatment and training, the gains of reading students might be compared with the gains of students of similar abilities and problems who are not given reading. Such a study is reported here. The 1955 spring semester reading class will be called the experimental group, and the students who were not enrolled in reading will be called the control group. Both the experimental group and the control group were composed of college freshmen from the entering class of 1954. All produced the high "Q," low "L," and low reading test pattern. All ranked above the 35th percentile, according to their total ACE scores. The experimental group was given developmental reading for one semester. The control group was enrolled for a traditional English class. Both groups were tested and retested with the Cooperative Reading Examination.

When initial scores of the control group were compared with their retest scores at the close of the semester, the mean score in reading speed had dropped slightly, but not significantly. The difference between the mean score in comprehension was represented by a t-score of 2.07, indicating that the control group made a mean gain in comprehension which approaches significance. The differences between test and retest results of the control group are reported in table 8-2.

TABLE 8-2

A COMPARISON OF READING TEST AND RETEST SCORES OF COLLEGE
FRESHMEN NOT ENROLLED IN DEVELOPMENTAL READING CLASSES

	Degrees freedom	Mean difference	t-Score	Significance
Speed	96	−0.618	0.82	none
Comprehension	96	1.40	2.07	.05*

A comparison of the mean differences of the two groups shows that the experimental group had gained significantly more than the control group in reading speed and comprehension in one semester's time. The differences are compared in tables 8-3 and 8-4.

TABLE 8-3

A COMPARISON OF THE MEAN GAINS OF AN EXPERIMENTAL GROUP
AND A CONTROL GROUP IN READING SPEED

	Mean gain	Difference	$S_{\bar{d}}$	t-Score	Degrees freedom	Significance
Experimental	7.38					
Control	−0.618	8.00	1.17	6.84	161	.001***

TABLE 8-4

A COMPARISON OF THE MEAN GAINS OF AN EXPERIMENTAL GROUP
AND A CONTROL GROUP IN READING COMPREHENSION

	Mean gain	Difference	$S_{\bar{d}}$	t-Score	Degrees freedom	Significance
Experimental	10.85					
Control	1.40	9.45	1.11	8.51	161	.001***

Thus it appears that the developmental reading students made true gains in reading speed and comprehension and that they made greater gains by statistically significant margins than a matched group of students who were not enrolled in developmental reading. The amount of gain made by the experimental group above that of the control group appears to be a result of their participation in developmental reading.

In order to determine whether or not successive classes of reading students would consistently make greater gains than matched students who were not given reading instruction, a study of this kind should be repeated. Similar results were obtained when the scores of another group of reading students were compared with those of another matched control group in the spring of 1954. The control group apparently lost in tested comprehension and gained little in speed, while the experimental group gained in both skills. The t-scores calculated on the test and retest results of both groups are shown in table 8.5.

TABLE 8-5

A COMPARISON OF t-SCORES CALCULATED FROM THE RESULTS OF TEST AND RETEST OF THE EXPERIMENTAL GROUP AND A CONTROL GROUP WITH THE COOPERATIVE READING EXAMINATION, SPRING, 1954

	Speed t-Score	Significance	Comprehension t-Score	Significance
Experimental	5.79	.001***	4.16	.001***
Control	1.71	.10	−2.04	.05*

When the first mean raw score of the control group was compared with the final mean raw score in reading speed, very little gain was shown, as represented by a t-score of 1.71. The first mean raw scope of the control group in reading comprehension when compared with the final mean raw score indicated a significant loss in comprehension as represented by a t-score of −2.04. The gain of the experimental group in reading speed was represented by a t-score of 5.79, significant beyond the 1 per cent level of confidence. The gain in comprehension of the experimental group was represented by a t-score of 4.16, significant beyond the 1 per cent level of confidence. Thus, it appears that the 1954 students who did not have reading instruction did not make a significant gain in reading speed and lost significantly in comprehension, while the students in developmental reading classes made gains in both skills by statistically reliable margins. The data from the test results of the two groups were then treated to determine whether or not the difference in test and retest results of the experimental group were statistically greater than the difference in the test and retest results of the control group. The findings are reported in table 8-6.

When the mean gain of the experimental group in reading was compared with the mean gain of the control group, the true difference as represented by a *t*-score of 5.09 favored the experimental group. When the mean gain of the experimental group in reading comprehension was compared with the mean gain of the control group, the true difference as represented by a *t*-score of 4.39 favored the experimental group. Both *t*-scores are statistically significant beyond the 1 per cent level of confidence. Thus it appears that the gains of the experimental group are a result of participation in reading instruction. Judging from the data

TABLE 8-6

A COMPARISON OF THE MEAN GAINS OF AN EXPERIMENTAL GROUP AND A
CONTROL GROUP OF COLLEGE FRESHMEN IN READING
SPEED AND COMPREHENSION, 1954

	Differences in mean gains	*t*-Score	Degrees freedom	Significance
Speed	3.20	5.09	71	.001***
Comprehension	5.00	4.39	71	.001***

SOURCE: Woolf, Maurice D., Annual Report on Developmental Reading, Kansas State College, Manhattan, Kans., 1954.

presented in tables 8-1 through 8-6, reading students consistently made significantly greater gains in reading skills than did students of similar abilities and handicaps who did not have reading instruction.

Teachers, administrators, members of the board of education, or groups of parents who read the report might like also to know the amount of gain in terms of percentile points. Hence it is well to include a statement something like this: "Average gains of the 35 students in developmental reading class, by standardized retest, amounted to 30 percentile points in speed and 16 percentile points in comprehension."[4] An explanation of percentile rank should be given for the benefit of readers not acquainted with the term.

REPORTING PROGRESS RECORDS

The average daily comprehension and speed scores of the class can be calculated and charted on a progress record blank, as shown in figure 5.[5]

[4] Woolf, Maurice D., Annual Report of Developmental Reading Program, Kansas State College, Manhattan, Kans., 1954.

[5] Woolf, Maurice D., Annual Report on Developmental Reading, Kansas State College, Manhattan, Kans., 1953.

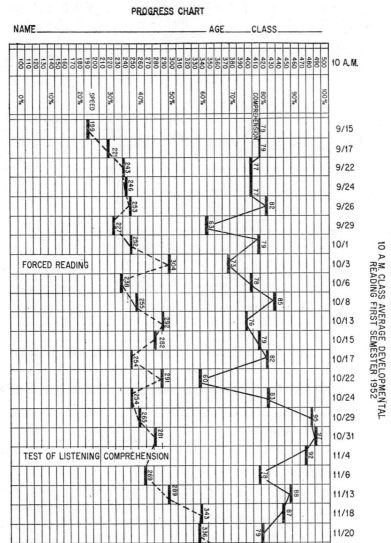

Fig. 5. Progress Chart showing group gains in Reading Speed and Reading Comprehension during 25 sessions of 1 semester of Developmental Reading, 1st semester, 1952.

Although the scores fluctuated, when the average of the first six scores is compared with the average of the last six, a gain is shown. The students whose gains are reported in figure 5 ranked in the lower 35 per cent of the freshman class in scholastic aptitude, as well as in reading ability. Thus, their gains are not as pronounced as those of some of the higher ability groups.

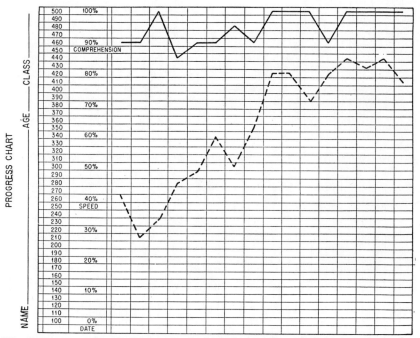

Fig. 6. Progress Record of an Individual Student in Developmental Reading Class. Second Semester, 1955.

An example of an individual progress record might also be given in the annual report. The gains of a college freshman enrolled in developmental reading class in the spring of 1955 are shown in figure 6.

REPORTING GAINS IN PERSONAL ADJUSTMENT

Chapter 7 included several test profiles showing students' gains, according to scores on the Minnesota Multiphasic Personality Inventory. The scores of the class can be averaged and charted in the same way, or they can be reported in table form or in an explanatory paragraph.

The results of testing and retesting 25 reading students with the Minnesota Personality Scale are shown in table 8-7. Although a trend is seen

TABLE 8-7

A COMPARISON OF TEST AND RETEST SCORES OF 25 READING STUDENTS,
USING THE MINNESOTA PERSONALITY INVENTORY

Scale	Mean raw scores	Percentile	Retest mean raw scores	Percentile	Critical ratio
Morale	171.00	60	173.50	70	.633
Social adj.	198.30	21	221.10	41	2.62
Family adj.	140.30	55	142.30	57	.373
Emotional	163.50	60	161.10	55	368

SOURCE: West, William E., "The Effectiveness of Certain Remedial Procedures As They Influence Reading Performance and Personality Adjustment," master's thesis, Kansas State College, Manhattan, Kans., 1947.

toward a better adjustment, the only significant gain was on the social adjustment scale. These students met four times a week for six weeks.

Students whose Minnesota Personality Inventory Scores were reported in table 8-7 differed from the usual developmental reading group in a number of respects. They came to the class voluntarily. Their IQ's ranged from 98 to 139, as measured by the Wechsler-Bellevue. The period of time spent in class was very short.

Group gains in personal adjustment might be reported something like this:[6]

A significant change among a group of 43 developmental reading students, as measured by the MMPI was a tendency toward more definite identification with an appropriate sex role. A comparison of initial Mf scores with final scores showed that this group moved toward the mean on the Mf scale during one semester of developmental reading instruction. The difference between the pre-test and retest scores was represented by a *t*-score of 2.11, significant at the 5 per cent level of confidence.

It is interesting to note that 23 of these students who showed improvement in personal adjustment, as measured by the MMPI, also showed progress in reading skills as measured by standardized tests. Twenty showed improvement on the MMPI, projective techniques, and standardized reading tests. In individual cases, progress was indicated by retest with six instruments, the MMPI, House-Tree-Person, Bender Visual Motor Gestalt, ACE, and two reading tests, as well as the progress chart.

The relationship between improvement in personal adjustment and gains in reading speed can be illustrated by the records of nine of these

[6] Woolf, Maurice D., unpublished study, Kansas State College, Manhattan, Kans., 1955.

students who reduced their anxiety scores on the MMPI. The reduction of anxiety scores and corresponding gains in speed are reported in table 8-8.

TABLE 8-8
REDUCTION OF ANXIETY (Pt) SCORES AND CORRESPONDING GAINS IN
READING SPEED OF NINE STUDENTS, AS MEASURED BY RETEST
WITH THE MMPI AND THE DIAGNOSTIC READING TESTS AFTER
ONE SEMESTER OF DEVELOPMENTAL READING

Student no.	Reduction of Pt standard score	Percentile points gain in speed
1	9	39
2	15	72
3	9	4
4	14	44
5	15	7
6	8	48
7	18	72
8	8	36
9	17	91
Average	12.5	45.8

Five students who moved toward the mean on the Si scale from 8 to 13 percentile points made an average gain in speed of 72 percentile points and an average gain in comprehension of 17 points. One of these leaped from the 9th to the 95th percentile in speed, from the 11th to the 66th in vocabulary, and doubled his percentile rank in comprehension. Six students from the same group who lowered their Hs scores by 8 to 16 standard score points made an average gain in reading speed of 48.3 percentile points. Five students who lowered their manic scores by 7 to 33 standard score points made an average gain in tested reading speed of 38.2 percentile points. One who reduced his manic score 28 points gained 51 percentile points in comprehension. Four students who reduced their depression scores by 7 to 28 standard score points averaged a gain in speed of 67.7 percentile points. Four who reduced Pa scores by 11 to 17 standard score points averaged a gain in speed of 64 percentile points. Five males who moved toward a masculine identification made an average gain of 56.8 percentile points in speed.

Interest in the reading program is almost always stimulated by reports which include sample drawings from the House-Tree-Person Test and the Bender Visual Motor Gestalt. They should be accompanied by explanations, interpretations, and supporting data. Comparing the first Bender drawings of student, D. B., with those submitted at the close of the semester, these remarks would be helpful:

The first figures were very small, crowded into the upper one-third of the page, and surrounded with heavy frames which were shaded. The size of the figures suggests that he felt insignificant and insecure. The frames suggest the need for external controls. The shading is believed to be associated with anxiety and since it gives the effect of rotation may reflect the feeling that events and environment are spinning around and perhaps he feels in danger of spinning. Possibly, he feels the need of something stable to "hang on to." The second drawings, made three months later at the close of the semester, used a full page and were noticeably larger. The stroke was more even and stronger. Frames were omitted, and erasures were fewer. The accuracy of the drawings was greatly improved and there was no shading or rotation. These changes suggest that he is more confident, secure, relaxed, expansive, self-reliant, and stable, and less rigid, ambivalent, constricted, dependent, and anxious. The improvement in accuracy, especially noted in five of the nine drawings, is said to reflect maturity or improvement in willingness to do a task thoroughly and completely. In January, he expressed anxiety about grades which were then below a "C" average and are now passing. His progress chart records a gain of 90 words per minute in the first nine weeks with comprehension remaining at about 80 per cent. At the same time, retests indicate gains in reading speed, comprehension, and scholastic-aptitude scores, as presented in table 8-9.

TABLE 8-9
GAINS OF READING STUDENT, D. B., AS
MEASURED BY STANDARDIZED TESTS

	February percentile	April percentile
ACE		
Quantitative	38	57
Linguistic	27	40
Total	30	46
Coop reading		
Speed	10	40
Comprehension	8	33

SOURCE: Woolf, Maurice D., Annual Report on Developmental Reading, Kansas State College, Manhattan, Kans., 1954.

Teachers are very much interested in drawings of the human figure, especially those which suggest changes from identification with the opposite sex to same-sex identification. Examples of these drawings with appropriate explanations stimulate interest in the developmental reading classes.

REPORTING INDIVIDUAL GAINS

While it is important to know the mean gain for a class, the spectacular progress of some individual members is often concealed in reports of class averages. Including in the annual report some brief case histories makes it more readable and more real to the people who receive the report. For example, a male student in the fall of 1954 gained 86 percentile points in reading speed, 55 percentile points in vocabulary, and doubled his percentile rank in comprehension, according to test and retest with the Diagnostic Reading Tests. At the same time, he reduced his Social Introversion score on the MMPI by 12 standard score points and made a change toward a more masculine identification by 8 standard score points.

Serious problems suggested by the MMPI scores of another male student were depression, rigidity, hypochondriasis, anxiety, hysteria, social introversion, defensiveness, and lack of identification with the appropriate sex role. During the semester, all of these scores moved toward the mean and his lie score came down. His drawings also indicated progress toward social receptivity, self-confidence, understanding of self, and a more interesting and satisfying life and less need for external props and support. He gained 91 percentile points in reading speed and 19 percentile points in comprehension, according to the Diagnostic Reading Tests.[7]

REPORTING THE RESULTS OF COUNSELING

Although it is difficult to determine to what extent counseling influences progress, one can include in the report some examples of cases who failed to show progress until counseling was in progress. A female student in the fall semester class of 1954 showed little change on her daily progress record until she was counseled. During extensive counseling, she moved from the 21st and the 5th percentiles in reading skills to the 93d and 75th percentiles in speed and comprehension, respectively, according to test and retest with the Diagnostic Reading Tests. She reduced her anxiety score from 73 to 55, her hysteria score from 61 to 47, and made changes toward the mean in four other areas measured by the MMPI. Many erasures, helping lines, and small figures in her first drawings suggested feelings of insecurity and insignificance. Improvements in pictures presented at the close of the semester suggested gains in confidence, personal security, self-esteem, and social expansiveness.[8]

[7] Woolf, Maurice D., Annual Report on Developmental Reading, Kansas State College, Manhattan, Kans., 1955.

[8] Woolf, Maurice D., *op. cit.*

Five counseling interviews with a college freshman in the spring semester of 1954 appeared to facilitate his progress. He raised his speed score 14 percentile points and his comprehension score 43 percentile points. ACE rank changed from 87th to 99th percentile in "Q," from the 52d to the 83d percentile in "L," and from the 69th to the 94th percentile in total score. Gains in adjustment appeared to be toward maturity, decisiveness, and self-understanding. He wrote in his final critique of the class,[9] "My concentration ability increased to the extent that now while I study I can get more done in the same length of time it used to take me to get half as much done. . . . If a student looks at the course from the standpoint of what he can gain, this course can and will be fun to him." Other examples of individual gains are given in Chapter 5.

REPORTING STUDENT OPINION

Student opinion can be sampled by means of a questionnaire or critique, as well as by noting verbal responses, offered informally or in class discussion. Either a questionnaire with a scale of five points, ranging from "Most agreement" to "Least agreement," or multiple-choice items give the student more latitude in his responses than does a true-false questionnaire. A critique gives the student more freedom to express opinion than any other device, but results are difficult to assess and tabulate. A structured critique provides a brief outline for the student to follow, giving him the main points which might be appraised and perhaps reminding him of features which he might otherwise overlook. Although not all students follow the outline, this device makes tabulating the results easier. A questionnaire administered to reading classes invited student opinion on methods of teaching, materials, quality of instruction, objectives, progress, and other aspects of the class. It was answered by 62 students. The items, together with the number of responses given on a scale of from 1 to 5, are shown in table 8-10.

Instructions were as follows:

Your answers to the following questions will help us evaluate our work in reading. Read each statement carefully and indicate your answer to each by drawing a circle around one of the numbers in the series, 1 to 5. A circle around number 1 means *no;* a circle around number 5 means *yes.* Answers in between tend towards yes or no. In other words, a circle around number 1 indicates the lowest rating you can give, while a circle around number 5 indicates the highest rating of agreement that you can give. In the example below, if you greatly resent having to take remedial reading, you would answer by drawing a circle around number 5. Example: I resent having to take remedial reading. 1 2 3 4 ⑤.

[9] Woolf, Maurice D., Annual Report, Kansas State College, Manhattan, Kans., 1954.

TABLE 8-10

RESULTS OF STUDENT EVALUATION OF THE WORK OF
THREE EXPERIMENTAL SECTIONS IN DEVELOPMENTAL READING

	Number of Responses				
	Not agree				Agree
	1	2	3	4	5
1. The remedial work is dull and uninteresting.	39	8	3	6	6
2. The discussions are a waste of time.	42	8	5	2	5
3. My speed of reading has improved.	2	6	7	7	40
4. I could read with more interest when I knew there was going to be a panel discussion.	15	7	12	13	15
5. The topics we read were interesting to me.	1	2	9	17	33
6. I feel that I made educational growth in the reading class.	1	1	7	18	35
7. My reading comprehension has improved.	0	3	10	21	28
8. My attitude toward members of this class is more friendly now than in the beginning.	4	1	6	9	42
9. It seems to me that the teaching method centered attention on the class.	0	1	14	17	29
10. It seems to me that the teaching method centered attention on the teacher.	22	10	19	3	9
11. I feel less important as a person after taking remedial reading.	37	6	12	6	1
12. I feel that my reading problems were not taken care of as well as they should have been.	26	19	5	8	9
13. The methods used seemed interesting.	5	1	4	9	45
14. I consider time spent in reading class worthwhile.	5	1	1	10	44
15. The aims of this class were never made clear to me.	33	4	4	7	13
16. There should have been more group discussion.	5	5	23	10	18
17. There was not enough variety of activity.	22	8	15	7	11
18. I was bored all the time during reading sessions.	43	7	3	3	5
19. We made progress toward our objectives.	1	1	5	12	42
20. I think the reading program should be in addition to the regular 5-hour, 1-A course in Eng.	22	4	3	8	22
21. I can concentrate better now.	3	5	5	18	28
22. My ability to pay attention has improved.	1	4	6	20	29
23. My dislike for reading is still with me.	27	10	8	5	11
24. Reading is still as difficult as ever.	27	9	12	9	5
25. Morale in this class is low.	30	9	6	12	5
26. I would like to have known some of my classmates better.	5	2	11	15	27
27. Outside distractions still bother me while I am reading.	18	5	11	14	15
28. I think there is something about my eyes that keeps me from reading fast.	34	1	5	8	12
29. I can get details now when I read.	3	6	18	15	19
30. I always did get the details.	18	13	14	8	6
31. I am satisfied with progress I made in reading.	7	7	6	16	25

SOURCE: Woolf, Maurice D., Annual Report on Developmental Reading, Kansas State College, Manhattan, Kans., 1953.

TABLE 8-10 (*Continued*)

	Number of Responses				
	Not agree				Agree
	1	2	3	4	5
32. I like the idea of panel discussion.	6	1	8	11	34
33. There is no carry-over from reading to preparation for my other subjects.	18	6	8	7	21
34. I feel better able to cope with the reading situations with which I am faced.	2	3	5	20	30
35. Reading is a grade school subject and should not be required of college students.	37	7	3	3	11
36. I am more interested in getting a grade in Written Com. than in learning to read better.	30	9	15	2	2
37. I prefer that the same teacher do all the work for the class.	26	5	18	5	5
38. I prefer more drill on the fundamentals of English instead of remedial reading.	21	10	17	5	7
39. There is a relation between my ability to read and my grades in college subjects.	4	7	6	11	33
40. My reasoning has not been improved by remedial reading.	24	7	9	10	14
41. I liked the articles in the *Reader's Digest*. They are more like articles I'll read in later life.	3	1	3	14	42
42. I liked the articles in *Reading for Opinion*. They gave both sides of the question.	3	4	10	20	24
43. I learned how to judge an article, that is, whether or not the author is prejudiced.	3	4	11	18	29
44. I have improved my ability to skim.	2	8	4	16	33
45. My eye span has improved.	3	2	9	16	29
46. We should have more panel discussions.	7	7	8	19	21
47. Panel discussions should be carried on in such a manner that we really reach a decision.	5	5	11	13	27
48. I think I can learn more through lectures than I can through reading.	23	5	12	6	12
49. I think other people learn more through reading than they do through lectures.	6	4	23	8	20
50. I think the printed word is my best source of information.	10	5	12	11	23
51. Lack of vocabulary is one of my problems in reading.	10	3	4	12	35
52. My eyes fatigue easily.	22	6	6	15	11
53. I seem to get sleepy when I read.	11	15	9	16	10
54. I feel tired and sleepy most of the time.	33	8	11	6	3
55. Reading interests me more now than when we started our remedial work.	3	4	8	17	30
56. I feel embarrassed to be in this class.	46	4	4	4	2
57. We should have worked more on vocabulary.	9	6	17	13	16
58. I get the general ideas but miss the details when I read.	8	8	12	20	13
59. I have other problems that I think interfere with my ability to read.	17	7	11	14	11

TABLE 8-10 (*Continued*)

	Number of Responses				
	Not agree				Agree
	1	2	3	4	5
60. I am having academic difficulty in one or more of my courses.	10	4	9	10	29
61. We have worked on the right problems in class.	0	4	7	24	25
62. I believe tachistoscope training helped me.	4	4	10	9	34
63. The tachistoscope training frustrates me.	36	10	7	6	3
64. In general I liked the methods used in reading class.	4	2	0	16	40
65. The reading clinic increased my writing skill.	6	8	18	10	17
66. I prefer to have two separate teachers for remedial reading and for Written Communications.	3	2	7	5	42

The trend of student opinion was favorable to the developmental reading class. The number of most favorable and least favorable answers relating to progress during the semester are presented in table 8-11. Items were rated according to a five-point scale, but figures in the table are not weighted and represented only the number of most favorable and least favorable responses.

TABLE 8-11
STUDENTS' ESTIMATES OF PROGRESS IN DEVELOPMENTAL READING CLASS

	No. most favorable	No. least favorable
Increased speed	40	2
Educational growth	35	1
Improved comprehension	28	0
Progress toward objectives	42	1
Increased ability to concentrate	28	3
Increased ability to pay attention	29	1
Increased ease in reading	27	5
Satisfaction with progress	25	7
Improved judgment with regard to authors' prejudices	29	3
Improved ability to skim	33	2
Improved eye span	29	3
Increased interest in reading	30	3
Increased ability to cope with reading situations	30	2

SOURCE: Woolf, Maurice D., Annual Report on Developmental Reading, Kansas State College, Manhattan, Kans., 1953.

The number of most favorable and least favorable responses to items relating to attitudes toward the class are compared in table 8-12. Figures in the table were not weighted and represented only the number of students giving most favorable or least favorable responses to the items.

TABLE 8-12

STUDENTS' OPINIONS ON METHODOLOGY, MATERIALS, AND MORALE IN
DEVELOPMENTAL READING CLASSES, FALL SEMESTER, 1952

	No. most favorable	No. least favorable
Work is interesting (by implication, Item 1)	39	6
Not a waste of time	42	5
Topics interesting	33	1
Increased friendliness toward class members	42	4
Interesting methods	45	5
Time spent worthwhile	44	5
Aims of class were clear	33	13
Enough variety of activity	22	11
Not bored	43	5
Morale in class	30	5
Like panel discussion	34	6
Like *Reader's Digest*	42	3
Like *Reading for Opinion*	24	3
Would like more panel discussion	21	7
Learning through reading versus lectures	20	6
Not embarrassed to be in this class	46	2
Tachistoscope helped	34	4
Liked methods	40	4

SOURCE: Woolf, Maurice D., Annual Report on Developmental Reading, Kansas State College, Manhattan, Kans., 1953.

Those who believed that the teaching method centered on the class were: most favorable—29; least favorable—0. Those who believed that teaching method centered attention on the teacher were 9 as compared with 22 who believed that the method did not center attention on the teacher, according to extremes of ratings. One person indicated that he felt less important as a person after taking remedial reading as compared with 22 who indicated they did not feel less important, according to extremes of ratings. Answers to item 12 were favorable to the way in which reading problems were handled in a ratio of 26 to 9, according to extremes of ratings. Answers to items 37 and 71 appear favorable to the present cooperative arrangement between English teachers and the reading clinician.[10]

Tables 8-10, 8-11, and 8-12 report the responses of students in a low ability group. When classes of students with higher tested scholastic aptitude were given a similar questionnaire, they indicated that they observed a carry-over to other classes and improved discrimination in judging content and the frequency of favorable responses to these items

[10] Woolf, Maurice D., Annual Report on Developmental Reading, Kansas State College, Manhattan, Kans., 1953.

was greater than among the low ability group. Counseling was introduced as a regular part of the program following the administration of this questionnaire.

A report on critiques might include the number of students commenting favorably or unfavorably on the various classroom procedures: speeded reading, comprehension testing, daily progress records, discussion, analysis of propaganda, tachistoscope drill, etc. Suggestions for improving the class often reflect the students' satisfaction or dissatisfaction with the class. If the critique can be compared with a paper written early in the semester by the same student, improvement can often be noted in spelling, effectiveness of expression, organization, style, and length. The students' remarks as to their own improvement might be tabulated. The report is enhanced by remarks such as this from a student's critique of the class, "I have completed a course that will help me much in days to come. We did many things, such as discussing our problems as a group. This taught me leadership, as I led the group at some meetings." His critique mentions improvement in speed, vocabulary, and comprehension. He particularly enjoyed the tachistoscopic drill and suggested that more time be spent on spelling.[11]

REPORTING ATTENTION TO VISUAL PROBLEMS

Since visual problems handicap some retarded readers, some attention should be paid in the annual report to diagnosis, referrals, and treatment of conditions associated with reading disability. In three classes totaling 80 students, 61 indicated on entrance forms that they were concerned about visual problems in one way or another.

The following is an excerpt from a report which deals with visual handicaps.[12]

Among 65 students enrolled in second semester classes or who came for individual help with reading problems, 39 either wore glasses or were diagnosed as having visual problems. Of this number, 24 were diagnosed as having difficulty with convergence, fusion or suppression of vision. Esophoria (one or both eyes tend to turn in) was diagnosed in four cases, three of whom showed no tested gains in either speed or comprehension. The fourth made a tested gain of 12 percentile points in speed, or considerably less than the average gain of the group. Three were fitted with lenses by physicians during the semester, but none of the students received visual training. These numbers are too small to be statistically significant, but these observations suggest that

[11] Woolf, Maurice D., Annual Report on Developmental Reading, Kansas State College, Manhattan, Kans., 1954.
    [12] *Ibid.*

committee of faculty members to assist in planning and evaluation, when meeting at the close of a school year, approved the organization, methods, and materials employed and recommended that the classes be continued in the same fashion for the following year. Studies of attendance, grade averages, drop-outs, and disciplinary problems might be useful in evaluating the outcomes of the reading program and related services.

EVALUATING PROGRESS IN THE ELEMENTARY SCHOOL

The foregoing paragraphs report evaluation of a college program. Most of the techniques described could be applied or adapted to high-school classes in developmental reading. Instruments described in Chapters 3 and 4 might be substituted for the ACE and Cooperative tests.

Elementary-school teachers will find evidences of progress in anecdotal records, work samples of pupils, observations on personal development, incomplete sentence tests, and counseling interview notes, as well as standardized test results. They usually have more opportunity than other teachers to judge whether or not reading instruction has a carry-over value for the pupil in his other classwork.

An analysis of errors from the tests and retests would indicate whether or not the number of errors had declined and in what particular areas errors were corrected during the time between test and retest. An examination of subtest scores would allow for an analysis of gains in particular areas such as vocabulary, comprehension, word attack, etc. Individual gains and average class gains might be reported in terms of grade rank or months instead of percentile ranks. A reduction of the number of errors for every 100 running words at the appropriate grade level might be noted in reports of individual pupils. This has been described in Chapter 3.

Although speed tests would not be used either for evaluation or diagnosis among children in the primary grades or the severely retarded, they could be used for the moderately retarded at the junior-high-school levels. Many of the questions in the questionnaire to measure student opinion would not be suitable for use in the grades, but a shorter and simpler questionnaire could be employed.

Grade-school children can write critiques, and usually enjoy doing it. Even primary pupils like to state what they want to accomplish in reading class and to review their gains. Their comments can be recorded by the teacher if necessary.

Excerpts from case histories, work samples, and writings of pupils, given in Chapter 4, illustrate changes in modes of expression, quantity of output, spontaneity, skills, vocabulary, attitudes, and behavior. Descriptions of paintings and drawings produced at various times reflect progress in personal development.

SUMMARY

Evaluation rewards teachers by presenting their achievements in tangible form. It acquaints the teachers with their achievements of problems yet to be solved and suggests the effectiveness of their methods. Its results can be used in defending the program, informing the public, and planning improvements in the school. In the absence of a planned appraisal, the program may be assessed on the basis of insufficient or inaccurate evidence. The planning and operation of evaluation should involve the reading teachers and should be done in terms of stated objectives. Reports should include the appraisal of total growth.

This chapter includes tables from annual reports presenting test and retest results with standardized instruments and comparing gains of reading students with students of similar abilities who did not receive reading instruction. Examples are given of individual and group progress charts, reports of personality tests and projective techniques, and samples of student opinion. Excerpts from annual reports include mention of the results of counseling, visual problems, number of individual interviews, services to the public, tachistoscopic records, grades, attendance, dropouts, disciplinary problems, and reports of other teachers. The techniques described can be adapted and modified for use in the elementary and secondary schools.

CHAPTER 9

In-Service Education

In-service education of teachers in the teaching of developmental reading and related student personnel techniques will aid and supplement training received in college classes. Its advantages are: (1) teachers can study problems in their own schools; (2) topics of greatest interest to the greatest number can be explored; (3) techniques can be applied immediately and reviewed in the light of actual experience; (4) team spirit and group morale can be generated among the participants; (5) all interested staff members can participate.

THE LONG-TERM PROGRAM

The initiative for promoting the training program might come from the administrators, the reading teacher, student personnel staff, or any teacher who is interested. All staff members might be asked to participate in discussing and deciding whether the program is needed and acceptable. If all do not care to participate, it could be offered for those teachers who collaborate in the teaching of reading. Some of the subjects which might be studied, such as group leadership and counseling, would be helpful to any teacher.

Some reward, extra remuneration, a lighter class load, or college credit should be arranged if possible. Faculty members who participated in a counselor-training program at the University of Illinois received extra remuneration and were excused from part of their regular duties.[1] They spent 32 hours in class, meeting twice a week for two hours each time.

Groups meeting once or twice a week have, in our experience, been more successful than those which meet less often. Apparently interest and enthusiasm begin to lag in a two weeks lapse between meetings, and time is wasted in review and reorientation to the subject.

[1] Gilbert, William M., "Training Faculty Counselors at the University of Illinois," in Williamson, E. G., *Trends in Student Personnel Work*, University of Minnesota Press, Minneapolis, 1949, p. 304.

Some groups continue to meet after the training period is completed. The post-training meetings can be well spent in case conferences, exchange of information, reviewing professional literature, and discussion of mutual problems.

The final decision on the subjects to be studied should be left to the participants. The possible subjects might be reviewed and briefly described by a counselor, the reading teacher, a visiting expert, or administrator. Suggestions from the faculty could be added, and the list of subjects submitted for the consideration of the group. A study of reading problems among local students could be used to stimulate interest and as a basis for making the study agenda. Decisions by the participants increase the possibility of success. The time, place, and order of business should be their decisions.

HOW TO BEGIN

For those who like a blueprint for initiating a program, we have prepared a schedule of events leading to an in-service training program. It need not be followed precisely. For example, the study of school needs might precede other steps.

1. Call a meeting.
2. Introduce the subject.
3. Invite comments, questions, and suggestions and give them consideration.
4. Be prepared for resistance.
5. Call for volunteers to investigate possibilities and report at a later meeting.
6. Survey local school needs, possibilities, and existing services.
7. Investigate the programs of other schools.
8. Provide information and cite other sources of information.
9. Review problems which might be solved.
10. Seek the help of specialists in universities, state department of education, and other schools.
11. Discuss how much responsibility the faculty would want to take in carrying out the program.
12. Permit the faculty to decide.

LEADERSHIP

The choice of a leader is very important, as his attitudes and behavior will be reflected in the morale of the group and in their application of principles and practices in the classroom. The leader of the group might be the school counselor, a reading specialist, or a visiting expert, if available, or a leader might be chosen by the group from among their own ranks. Experts might be brought in from colleges, state departments of education, or other school systems to serve as resource consultants.

SOME PRINCIPLES OF FACULTY LEADERSHIP

Suggestions for leadership given in Chapter 4 are applicable to leadership among the faculty. Among those which help to ensure harmony and achievement in training sessions are the following:

1. Abide by group decision.
2. Show respect for all contributions and questions.
3. Ensure availability of essential information.
4. Provide time for consideration and study preceding decision.
5. Provide opportunities for thorough participation.
6. Encourage retiring members to participate.
7. Encourage attention and adaptation to local needs.
8. Anticipate that progress may be slow.
9. Recognize small signs of progress.
10. Wait on faculty decision if necessary.
11. Recognize the value of existing services.
12. Recognize faculty contributions to personnel services when possible by

a. Financial recognition
b. Professional advancement
c. Publicity
d. Personal recognition
e. Reduced academic duties
f. College credit.

13. Encourage self-evaluation.
14. Permit digressions if all or most of the members are interested.

Teachers, like other groups, sometimes wander from the subject. If the digression is on a subject of interest to all members, the most effective use of time may be to pursue it at the time when it is introduced. Some in-service-training groups have discussed with interest such items as philosophy of education, disciplinary problems, student-teacher relationships, academic freedom, and others.

Attention might be called to some of the errors in leadership. Don't: try to cover everything important in one session or one day; force a program of in-service education on teachers; ignore their major interests; insist that they study what the leaders consider important; be threatened by disagreement; overlook the need of teachers for satisfaction and security in their work.

INTERPERSONAL RELATIONS

Some of the factors which may hamper progress among any group are discussed by Corey.[2] "Hurt feelings" were discovered by one group to interfere with productivity. Among the situations believed to contribute to hurt feelings were these: a person's convictions are rejected by other members; any situation with which he is identified and for which he feels responsible is disparaged; a situation he believes to be important and serious is not accepted as important and serious by others; he feels he is being blamed; he feels anxious, insecure or unsafe, either in the immediate situation or even other situations not brought into the discussion; someone else has just been hurt by him or by others. Frank discussion of these problems and of the feelings of members apparently brought about improved harmony and reduction of tensions in this group. A flexible program of study would allow for the exploration of factors such as these which might restrict the output of the faculty or interfere with harmonious teamwork in this and other aspects of their work. In his discussion of in-service training, Thelen[3] points out the advantages of participation in a group where one can express his feelings of doubt, hostility, excitement, etc.

POSSIBLE SUBJECTS

The following list of subjects might be considered by teachers planning in-service training in reading: (1) causes of reading problems; (2) applying psychological principles to the teaching of developmental reading; (3) emotions and reading; (4) diagnosis and sectioning; (5) methods and techniques; (6) group leadership; (7) counseling the retarded reader; (8) materials; (9) evaluating the reading program. The teachers' suggestions might be given first, or they might be added to the above list before the final decisions are made. More than one class period could be spent on each subject. Some references which could be used are included in a brief bibliography at the close of this chapter.

Demonstrations of group leadership and counseling would be valuable. At least one session might be spent on the demonstration of the tachistoscope and various other instruments. When studying diagnosis, the teach-

[2] Corey, Stephen M., *Action Research*, Bureau of Publications, Teachers College, Columbia University, New York, 1953, pp. 109–118.

[3] Thelen, Herbert A., *Dynamics of Groups at Work*, University of Chicago Press, Chicago, 1954, p. 77.

ers would find it a valuable experience to take the tests themselves and make their own case folders. The study of case records, including test data, would aid them in understanding the process of diagnosis and test interpretation. Case analysis and pseudocounseling are valuable experiences for the teacher in training. Recorded interviews, if available, are also useful. After studying a particular case, the teachers might enjoy playing out a case conference.

PSEUDOCOUNSELING

Pseudocounseling ordinarily follows the study and discussion of counseling and demonstrations of two or three methods. Two teachers are asked to volunteer to play the roles of the client and the counselor. The school counselor or reading teacher or the group leader chooses a suitable case record on which to base the interview. The case data are mimeographed and made available to all class members. Additional data are given the member who is to play the role of the client. Role-playing is followed by group discussion, dividing into small groups, and using recorders if the group is large. The following materials have been used in training sessions with teachers.

Pseudocounseling: Case of C. W., Materials for Role of the Client

High school junior, female, age 16, farm girl rooming in town; has part-time job.

HEALTH: Has asthma; wheezes and puffs when she talks.

REMARKS: Feels pressure to do well in school, on the job, in music; sometimes feels very tired; worries about English; says she sometimes plays the piano very well, but can't depend on it; always afraid this will not be a good day, that she will find herself unable to perform. Feels her English teacher doesn't believe in her; feels rejected; blocked when trying to answer questions in class; often cries without knowing why; says her music teacher keeps hammering away at her. Her roommate leaves the cleaning of the room to her; feels imposed upon; thinks she shouldn't mind this, but she does. One sister is a tomboy and helps in the fields. C. W. cannot do this because of her asthma, but she takes water out to the farm hands during the harvest season; worries because she cannot be more help at home. She says her family is "just wonderful," talks a good deal about her sisters and how capable they are, but never mentions her mother. Thinks maybe she ought to get a job during the summer and stay in town. Likes men, "You can depend on them." Doesn't like to compete with girls in piano or schoolwork. Isn't sure that women like her; feels girls and women pick on her and run her down. Sometimes has a different opinion from teachers and classmates, but hesitates to say so. Wants to be liked. Feels insecure in the affections of her family, but shies away from talking about it.

Pseudocounseling: Case of C. W., Materials for Role of the Counselor and for All Members of Training Group

High school junior, female, age 16.

INTELLIGENCE: ACE percentile is "Q," 78; "L," 38; reading, 35; English, 50; Science, 60; and Math, 65.

GRADES: Mostly B except English. B plus in math and science.

ACTIVITIES: Won first place in piano in state contest; accompanies for school choir; has a part-time job; cheer leader; spectator sports.

STATED INTERESTS: Don't know; maybe music.

HEALTH: Serious attacks of asthma; allergic to grain dust.

FAMILY: Very strict, hard workers, reserved in manner; father is successful farmer; 3 sisters and one brother.

TEACHERS SAY: Conscientious student.

A simple form for evaluating a meeting provides for rating it: no good, mediocre, all right, good, or excellent. Space is provided to answer these questions: What part of the meeting was most valuable to you? What is your best suggestion for making another such meeting more valuable to *you?*

USING THE SERVICES OF THE EXPERT

The traditional way of learning from an authority is to ask him to speak to the group. The study of the psychology of learning suggests that people learn more and their learning is more permanent when members of the group participate actively in discussion, giving their impressions of readings, responding to the remarks of speakers, relating their own experiences, and asking questions. Audience participation allows less time for the speaker, but his suggestions are more often followed by action.

In discussing the values of involving the membership in the planning and the work of a meeting, Kelley quotes William H. Kilpatrick, "A lecturer is one who talks in someone else's sleep." Outcomes of in-service teacher-training by the workshop technique are described by Kelley, "We have had enormous success in bringing about changes in people . . . so that they behave differently." He discusses two factors in a successful workshop situation: (1) the learner is cast in an active rather than a passive role; (2) it helps to satisfy the need of the members for working and communicating with others and being accepted by others. Interest in group meetings was enhanced, as Kelley[4] suggests, when it finally oc-

[4] Kelley, Earl C., "Human Values in the Workshop Technique," *Adult Leadership,* vol. 3, no. 2, June, 1954, pp. 4ff.

curred to someone " . . . to ask the learners what their concerns were, and to hold meetings on these concerns."

It may be difficult for a group to accept this method of study. They may feel that it gives their guest too small a part in the program. However, authorities in many fields who have participated as members in group discussions found their efforts more effective than when they lectured to the group.

Some specialists can suggest references, provide case studies, or tell where to get them, provide sample tests or tell where to get them, administer tests, suggest other authorities whose help might be available for planning or discussion, draw on their own professional experiences to illustrate the use of methods and techniques, demonstrate techniques, help to plan the series of meetings, provide reading lists, suggest suitable college classes for further training.

Although many teachers feel the sessions are intrinsically valuable, some would prefer to get college credit for their work. If this is the case, the group might want to investigate whether or not a class of this kind might be sponsored by the extension department of some college or university. A course entitled, "In-service-course in Education," is sometimes given. Credits can sometimes be arranged in "Special Investigations" or "Special Problems in Education." A group of teachers in one school who asked for a course of this kind secured the help of three college professors and a member of the state department of education staff. Two of the guest consultants were from the state university and one was from a state college. Boards of education of some schools have provided funds for such a series.

THE WORKSHOP

The workshop, like the long-term program, will be more acceptable to participants if they have helped to decide that it should be given and to choose the subject. Advance preparation contributes to its success. If a visiting expert is employed, he might provide advance information on the subjects to be discussed, the schedule of events, opportunities for participation, and his own qualifications. Plans for the workshop should be discussed by the local planning committee with the leader or visiting expert.

The amount of subject matter covered would, of course, depend on the length of time available. Whether it is a one-day program or a week, some time should be reserved for audience participation.

In a one-day meeting, an over-view of the program can be presented. In a week, some techniques can be explored.

In the fall of 1954, teachers in a large Kansas high school agreed to make the teaching of reading the subject for study during the annual teachers' workshop, preceding the opening of the school year. Plans were made by a teachers committee working with the school principal and the speaker from one of the state colleges. Publicity was given the workshop by the local newspapers and the school paper. Arrangements were made for the school to mimeograph materials and for a supply company to provide machines and instruments for demonstration purposes. Electrical outlets were checked and room arrangements made. The meeting was subsidized by the board of education, and teachers' salaries were paid for the week's work. The program is given here.

MONDAY

8:00 A.M. Opening meeting: Greeting, superintendent. Overview of the workshop, principal.

9:45 A.M. Coffee break.

10:15 A.M. Discussion of local problems by teachers in small groups; reconvene to hear reports from small groups; summary of small group reports and remarks by visiting speaker on "The Nature and Scope of Reading Problems."

1:30 P.M. Demonstrations of four types of leadership with teachers as leaders; discussion in small groups of types of leadership; reconvene for reports from small groups; summary by speaker; group decision on the kind of leadership to be used in the workshop; distribution of leadership materials. Committees organize.

TUESDAY

8:00 A.M. Address by speaker: Causes, gathering information, diagnosis and sectioning. Questions from audience.

9:00 A.M. Discussion in small groups, with teachers as leaders and recorders.

10:00 A.M. Coke break.

10:15 A.M. Reconvene for recorders' reports, summary, questions; tentative decisions on tests and testing procedures.

11:00 A.M. Demonstration of Telebinocular, View-Lex, films, tachistoscope.

1:30 P.M. Display of reading materials: book-lists, tests, test profiles, case folders, exercises, professional literature; distribution of bibliography of reading materials suitable for use in high-school reading classes.

WEDNESDAY

8:00 A.M. Demonstration of classroom routine, skimming, speeded reading, comprehension testing, progress record; discussion with teachers in the roles of students; discussion in small groups, "Can we use these techniques?"

10:00 A.M. Coke break.

10:15 A.M. Reconvene for small group reports; questions.

11:00 A.M. Summary by speaker; group decision; distribution of handbook on the Teaching of Developmental Reading.

1:30 P.M. Address by speaker: Analysis of Propaganda; demonstration; selections read by teachers; small group discussion; reports by recorders; summary by speaker; group decision, "Can we use this technique?"

6:00 P.M. Dinner for all participants with the Board of Education.

THURSDAY

8:00 A.M. Demonstration: Classroom routine, skimming, speeded reading, comprehension testing, progress record, discussion with teachers in the roles of students; discussion in small groups; reconvene for recorders' reports; summary by speaker; teachers check their own progress.

10:00 A.M. Counseling demonstration with a teacher playing the role of the client (test data distributed to all); discussion in small groups; reconvene for recorders' reports; questions; summary by speaker; tentative group decision, "Can we use this?"

1:30 P.M. Address by speaker: Techniques for evaluating the reading program; small group discussion; reconvene for recorders' reports; questions; tentative group decision; distribution of sample evaluation forms and reports.

FRIDAY

8:00 A.M. Summary of the week's work; small group discussion; recorders' reports; committee reports and recommendations; forms distributed for evaluating the workshop; speaker's summary; group decision and plans for the future.

11:00 A.M. Report on the evaluation of the workshop.

The majority of the teachers showed small gains in reading speed when retested on Thursday. They became involved in the group discussions and appeared greatly interested in using the leadership techniques and analysis of propaganda. Leadership skills appeared to improve, recorders' reports became more concise and more meaningful, and interest mounted during the week. The speaker used a Vu-Style reflector during the Tuesday morning lecture to project samples of student responses to the House-Tree-Person and Bender Visual Motor Gestalt tests. Examples were shown of the students' drawings before and after a semester's work in developmental reading. The degree to which the teachers were able to absorb and make use of new ideas presented is reflected in the committee reports which were mimeographed and distributed to all staff members.

GROUP REPORTS ON THE TWELFTH ANNUAL TEACHERS' WORKSHOP, 1954,
BLANK HIGH SCHOOL

The conclusions and recommendations presented here are the products of the faculty of Blank High School in their Twelfth Annual Workshop. The theme of the workshop was "Reading Problems." These final reports were developed by five (5) faculty groups, each having studied one special area of the reading problem.

The faculty as a whole agreed upon the following definition of "The Problem":

In Blank High School there are students who get no satisfaction from reading. There are those whose memories lapse sometime between the beginning and end of a paragraph. There are those who are not interested in reading and those who have a poor vocabulary, comprehension, and speed, but who have a good potential to improve. There are many who have difficulty in concentrating, in a sustained way, and those who read one word at a time, and others who have visual troubles, especially interference with binocular vision.

Part of the problem is how can we identify these students and give remediation, correction, or stimulation to them and how can we motivate them to develop to their potential.

The five topics of the problem explored by separate groups were these:

Group I   Philosophy of the Reading Program
Group II   Reading Objectives
Group III   Techniques of Diagnosis and Procedures for Improvement
Group IV   Organization and Administration of the Program
Group V   Evaluation.

GROUP I REPORT
PHILOSOPHY OF THE READING PROGRAM

We should provide a reading program to enable our students to achieve to their potentialities. To help a child who has reading difficulties, we must consider the whole child, including emotion as well as intellect. Every reading problem has multiple causes which must be discovered before reading can be improved.

We must provide a student-centered program that will enable our students to solve general problems that interfere with specific problems in reading, and discharge their communicative responsibilities in a democratic society.

GROUP II REPORT
READING OBJECTIVES

We would identify and help solve individual and general problems and attempt to create a democratic atmosphere.

These should be our specific objectives:
1. To increase eyespan;
2. To increase comprehension;
3. To increase reading speed;

4. To build vocabulary;
5. To increase concentration ability or attention span;
6. To develop good study habits;
7. To increase social maturity;
8. To develop interest in a better quality of reading material;
9. To develop a desire to read for enjoyment as well as for information;
10. To develop critical thinking.

All of these would help to create happier, more responsible and more efficient citizens.

GROUP III REPORT
TECHNIQUES OF DIAGNOSIS AND PROCEDURES FOR IMPROVEMENT

In the effort to screen out the poor readers and those who have some difficulties, certain diagnostic methods are available. The following methods are suggested as helpful in identifying those who need assistance in reading.

1. Achievement tests
2. Personal data
3. Anecdotal records
4. Autobiographical sketches
5. Intelligence tests
6. Personality tests
7. Counselor interpretation of interviews
8. Summary of reading ability from elementary school
9. Health reports
10. Progress report or chart on each student
11. Preparation of profile cards showing results of several tests
12. Grade level conferences of teachers.

Specific tests recommended for use are: American Council on Education Psychological Examination; California Personality Scale, with particular attention to those sections of personal and social adjustment; Diagnostic Reading Test (this test measures rate, vocabulary, and textbook comprehension).

In identifying a person who has a reading problem it is suggested that one who shows a discrepancy of 20 or more percentile points between the Q and L scores on the ACE test (if Q is higher) and whose personal and social adjustment ranks comparatively low on the personality test could be tentatively classified as a reading problem.

Procedures for building reading skills through daily classroom practice are illustrated in the following seven steps:

1. Warm-up period
2. Orientation to article to be read
3. Timed reading period, recorded by minutes and tenths
4. Test for comprehension
5. Record speed and comprehension rates on graph
6. Analysis of article for main issue, purpose, assumptions, support of premise by data or facts
7. Group discussion.

The final recommendation with regard to testing is that such a program be initiated at a time during the school year when the students are following a normal routine and results might have greater validity.

Group IV Report
Organization and Administration

1. Acquire a full-time person who is qualified to test students, score results, correlate and integrate materials and give recommendations to the teacher and for office records.

2. The testing program should include all students from the 7th grade basic course to English classes in high school. Evaluation tests should be given at the end of the school year to show progress of students in the reading program.

3. The tachistiscope should be available for the use of any teacher in the classroom. A schedule could be established for checking out the machine through the office.

A schedule such as this might be developed for the use of the T-scope. Use in 7, 8, and 9th grade rooms for five minute periods, during first and fourth hours three days a week—Monday, Wednesday and Friday.

4. Profile card for each student, if obtainable, or make one for use in Blank School.

5. Sectioning according to degree of retardation and abilities.

Group V Report
Evaluation

One can only evaluate in terms of objectives. In evaluating, we are trying to measure changes in the behavior of children. These procedures are suggested for that purpose:

1. Reading and English tests
2. Pacer, T-scope and other mechanical devices
3. Comprehension tests
4. Socio-gram for social compatibility
5. Personality tests (House-tree-person, Minnesota Personality)
6. Progress Charts
7. Reading Charts and Library records
8. Guidance records
9. Personal teacher-pupil interviews
10. Personal interest survey
11. Teacher observation
12. Grades on grade cards
13. Self-appraisal
14. Autobiography
15. Cumulative records
16. Periodic report from all instructors of pupils.

The speaker sent a follow-up report of his impressions of the workshop and gave further information on diagnosis and sectioning. The participants' responses to the 23 items in the evaluation form were averaged and reported to the 40 participants. Each item was rated on a five-point scale ranging from most favorable to least favorable. Additional comments on the workshop were tabulated and reported. Reading classes, based on the committee reports, were begun in this school. The school counselor made plans to do the research for his master's thesis on the problems and progress of reading students.

Most of these subjects were introduced in condensed form in a workshop of a day and a half for the English teachers of another high school. Materials distributed were similar to those used in the week's workshop, but they were left with the group for study following the workshop. The order of events was a little different. Techniques were introduced in the first session, because the speaker felt that these teachers would expect to get something practical from the first meeting and would become involved more rapidly. The schedule of events is given here.

WEEK-END WORKSHOP
FRIDAY

1:30 P.M. Introduction to methods and techniques for developmental reading classes.

2:00 P.M. Demonstration of class with teachers acting as students, tachistoscopic drill, skimming, speeded reading, vocabulary study, comprehension testing, progress record, discussion of selection, questions, discussion of techniques, tentative group decision, "Can we use these techniques?"

3:00 P.M. Break.

3:15 P.M. Leadership demonstration: four types of leadership with teachers as leaders, discussions, questions, tentative decision, "Can we use this?"

7:15 P.M. Address by speaker: Personality and Reading, followed by discussion, tentative decision, "Can we apply these principles to understanding and teaching our students?"

SATURDAY

8:00 A.M. Address by speaker: Analysis of Propaganda

8:45 A.M. Demonstration of class with teachers as students, speeded reading, comprehension testing, progress record, discussion of selection, "Can you identify the propaganda techniques used by this author?" discussion of techniques, tentative group decision, "Can we use these techniques in high-school classes?"

10:30 A.M. Break.

10:45 A.M. Address by speaker: Diagnosis of Reading Problems, followed by discussion, tentative decision, "Can we use these instruments in high-school classes?"

1:30 P.M. Demonstration by speaker: Counseling Students with Reading Problems, with a teacher as the client; discussion, tentative group decision, "Can we use these techniques with our students?"

3:00 P.M. Summary, plans, evaluation of workshop.

The workshop was rated on 14 items by means of a five-point scale with five the most favorable rating. The rating sheet included space for comments by the participants and their suggestions for improvement. The average ratings and comments of the participants were mimeographed and distributed to participants, administrators, and members of the board of education. The workshop was financed by the board of education. The report on evaluation is reproduced here.

REPORT TO BOARD OF EDUCATION, ADMINISTRATION, AND FACULTY
MEMBERS OF BLANK PUBLIC SCHOOLS ON READING WORKSHOP

COMMENTS BY SPEAKER: This is one of the most able workshop groups in my experience. Participants in the leadership and counseling demonstrations and in general discussion showed interest and growing understanding of the problems involved in the teaching of reading and in the learning process.

EVALUATION BY PARTICIPANTS: (The following tabulation is the average of participants' rating of the sessions. Maximum rating is 5.)

1. Leader was acquainted with his subject.	4.88
2. Audience was encouraged to participate.	4.77
3. Time spent was worthwhole.	4.66
4. Workshop methods stimulating.	4.66
5. New ideas presented.	4.44
6. Application of democracy to teaching.	4.44
7. I feel favorable toward a reading program here.	4.44
8. Gained insight into behavior of poor readers.	4.44
9. Time in workshop efficiently used.	4.33
10. I can use these ideas and techniques.	4.33
11. Information presented appropriate to subject.	4.22
12. My interest mounted during workshop.	4.22
13. I made educational growth during workshop.	4.11
14. Participation by audience was general.	4.00

RATINGS OF SESSIONS:

Propaganda techniques	4.87	Discussion techniques	4.66
Personality and reading	4.87	Reading techniques	4.50
Diagnosis	4.66	Counseling	4.22

Four participants showed strong interest in a class on this subject.

MENTIONED SPECIFICALLY AS MOST HELPFUL: Counseling demonstration; study of personal problems involved; diagnostic techniques; discussion periods; actual working committees; critical reading; leadership demonstration.

IMPROVEMENTS SUGGESTED: More time; more aids such as films, slides, etc.; more about treatment; more specifics on use of tachistoscope and other equipment; not distribute reading materials until immediately before timed reading; leader should speak more distinctly.

OTHER COMMENTS: Would feel favorable to reading program here if present teaching load and other duties would permit; all teachers should have heard counseling demonstration.

It is rather surprising to us to find school boards so interested in the subject of developmental reading. The school board of a small school financed a three-day visit for their reading teacher to a college reading clinic and paid a substitute to teach her classes in her absence. After her return, in cooperation with the county superintendent of schools and city school administrators, she promoted a one-day workshop for high-school and elementary-school teachers in the county. Two resource consultants were secured to help plan and lead the discussions. Each school contributed toward financing the meeting. Questions and suggestions were submitted by teachers in advance of the workshop. Representatives from the county teachers organization met with the consultants to plan the meeting.

ONE-DAY WORKSHOP

This schedule might be used for a one-day meeting.

8:00 A.M. Demonstration of classroom techniques with teachers playing the roles of students: Tachistoscopic drill, skimming, speeded reading, comprehension testing, progress records, discussion of selection, small group discussions, reports of recorders, summary by consultant, tentative group decision, "How can we use these techniques?"

9:30 A.M. Address by consultant no. 1: How can we locate the retarded reader?

10:15 A.M. Teachers of grades 7 through 12 meet with consultant no. 1; elementary school teachers meet with consultant no. 2; divide into small groups with recorders and leaders chosen from among the teachers; discussion on choice and use of tests in diagnosis; reports from recorders; general discussion; questions; summary.

12:00 Lunch; materials on display.

1:00 P.M. Brief address: Analysis of Propaganda, followed by speeded reading, comprehension testing, progress records, comparison of teachers speed scores with morning scores; analysis of selection (for use of propaganda techniques) using small groups, leaders and recorders from among the teachers; discussion, summary by consultant, tentative group decision, "Can we apply this procedure in the reading class?"

2:30 P.M. Demonstration of four types of leadership, using teachers as leaders; small group discussion; recorders' reports, general discussion, summary by consultant, tentative decision.

3:30 P.M. General meeting, summary of the day's work, plans, evaluation, committees formed for follow-up.

The following is a report of the evaluation of such a meeting. Items were rated on a scale of 1 to 5, with 5 as the most favorable score. Averages are reported.

AVERAGES OF THE EVALUATION OF COUNTY TEACHERS' WORKSHOP ON READING

Effectiveness of Planning, Leadership and Presentation

1. Planning 4
2. Lectures 4
3. Discussions 4
4. Use of time 3
5. Morale of group 4
6. Interest shown 4

7. Organization 3
8. Decisions reached 4
9. Objectives of this workshop stated clearly 4
10. Problems were defined 4
11. Participants able to communicate with each other 3
12. Professional growth made 4
13. Attitudes of members 3
14. Choice of topics covered 4
15. Effectiveness of speaker's presentation 4
16. Creative ideas stimulated among members 3
17. Opportunities for participation by members 4
18. Extent of participation by members 3
19. Quality of participation by members 4
20. Speaker's understanding of public school needs 4
21. Speaker's acquaintance with subject 5
22. Effort put out by speaker 4
23. New ideas and information introduced 4
24. Quality of group leaders' reports 4

Methods, Materials and Information Presented Today

1. Usefulness to me 4
2. Psychol. background 4
3. Diagnostic techniques 4
4. Teaching hints 4
5. Discussion methods 4
6. Standardized tests 4
7. Speeding reading 4
8. Comprehension tests 4
9. Follow-up plans **pending**
10. Drills 4
11. Exercises 4
12. Book list 4
13. Materials 4
14. Equipment 4
15. Displays 4
16. Counseling 4
17. Machines 4
18. T-scope 4
19. Demonstration of types of leadership 5
20. Analysis of propaganda techniques 5

Positive comments **16**
Negative comments **4**

Teachers' opinions of the outstanding points of one meeting were summarized by a follow-up committee in this report.

SUMMARIZATION OF READING WORKSHOP, HIGH-SCHOOL LEVEL

Teachers named these as usable ideas:

1. Incidentally counseling students through which we learn to better understand their problems and in turn to help them more effectively.

2. Use of T-scope in teaching reading, vocabulary, and spelling.

3. Method of effectively presenting controversial subjects.

4. Mimeographed list of material sources. (Would like to have a list of books for retarded readers.)

5. Knowledge of various kinds of reading problems and their relation to the emotional life, stressing that teachers need to know the student as a "whole" person.

6. Demonstration of the "daily grind" in use of the various tools of presenting lessons. (T-scope, tests, materials, vocabulary drill, speed reading, and follow-up procedures.)

7. How methods and tools used in reading workshop may easily and effectively carry over in other areas of learning (science, etc.).

8. Breaking up in groups for variety. Students would like this chance to view their ideas before a small group especially if they are shy.

9. Demonstrations of various types of leaders was especially effective in putting across a necessary point.

SUMMARIZATION OF READING WORKSHOP, ELEMENTARY-SCHOOL LEVEL

The elementary teachers summarized the day's activities by listing the following as ideas they had gained:

I. Testing
   A. Standardized tests
   B. Teacher-made tests
II. Techniques
   A. Completion exercises
   B. Themes and stories
      1. Things I like_____
      2. Things I don't like_____
   C. Interpreting pictures
III. Ideas
   A. Use of a teacher-made substitute for the T-scope
   B. Every teacher is a counselor
   C. Pupil-teacher planning
   D. Use vocabulary study
   E. Democratic leadership in the classroom

In these various types of training sessions, opportunity was provided whenever possible for the participants not only to state problems and respond to speeches, but actually to experience the reading class as it might be experienced by students. By their comments during the meetings and the plans and programs which followed them, the teachers demonstrated that learning was taking place. Two demonstrations of the "daily grind" in a one-day meeting crowds the schedule somewhat, but the members are usually surprised to find a small gain in reading speed when they record their words per minute the second time. Interest always mounts with this discovery. Having gone through the routine, most of them feel fairly confident in attempting it themselves.

The remarks of participants following the leadership demonstration are often revealing. One teacher mused with chagrin, "They all looked at me and said I'd do for a hard-boiled dictator." Another said, thoughtfully, "I'm afraid I'm more the benevolent autocrat type." These and other remarks suggest that a process of re-evaluation of teaching methods had begun among the participating teachers.

In the schedule of events for the one-day meeting, the leadership demonstration was purposely left until near the close of the program. It was a strenuous day, and by mid-afternoon, the members needed something to revive interest. Role-playing of the four types of leaders has been repeatedly effective in performing this function.

Whenever time permits a counseling demonstration, the interest of the group is almost always captured. Those who play the roles of the clients report that it is one of the most helpful experiences in their professional lives. Some teachers from each workshop or in-service training group are stimulated to enroll for summer-school classes in guidance, counseling, and the teaching of reading.

SUMMARY

Decisions regarding in-service education should be made by the teachers. Opportunities for active participation should be offered. Participants should be rewarded, if possible, by extra pay, lighter load, or other recognition. Certain leadership principles and techniques are applicable to both students and teachers. Interpersonal relations among staff members cannot be ignored. A flexible in-service education program would allow for the exploration of such relations.

A long-term program of training and three workshops are described. Illustrations from actual experience include the daily schedules, evaluative reports of each, and accounts of action which followed meetings. Participants were involved, not only in planning, discussing, deciding, and evaluation, but also in experiencing classroom procedures as they might be experienced by students. Each program described included leadership training and experience in group procedures.

BIBLIOGRAPHY FOR IN-SERVICE TRAINING

General

Bond, Eva: "Reading and Ninth Grade Achievement," Bureau of Publications, Teachers College, Columbia University, New York, 1938.

Dolch, E. W.: *The Psychology and Teaching of Reading*, Ginn & Company, Boston, 1931.

Harris, Albert J.: *How to Increase Reading Ability*, Longmans, Green & Co., Inc., New York, 1940.

National Society for the Study of Education: *Reading in the High School and College*, Forty-seventh Yearbook, 1948.

Strang, R., and F. C. Rose: *Problems in the Improvement of Reading in High School and College*, Science Press, Lancaster, Pa., 1940.

Witty, Paul, and K. Kopel: *Reading and the Educative Process*, Ginn & Company, Boston, 1939.

Woolf, Maurice D., and Jeanne A. Woolf: *The Student Personnel Program*, McGraw-Hill Book Company, Inc., New York, 1953.

Emotions and Reading

Bennett, C. C.: *An Inquiry into the Genesis of Poor Readers*, Bureau of Publications, Teachers College, Columbia University, New York. Contributions to Education, no. 755, 1935.

Ephron, B. C.: *Emotional Difficulties in Reading*, Julian Press, New York, 1953.

Gates, A. I.: "Failure in Reading and Social Maladjustment," *J. National Educ. Ass.*, vol. 25, 1936.

Korchin, Sheldon J., Jerome L. Singer, and Robert O. Ballard: "The Influence of Frustration on the Reproduction of Visually Perceived Forms," *Personality*, vol. 1, no. 1, January, 1951, pp. 54ff.

McKillop, Anne Seely: "The Relationship Between the Reader's Attitude and Certain Types of Reading Responses," doctoral dissertation, publication no. 2543, University of Michigan microfilm, Ann Arbor, Mich., 1951.

Postman, L., J. S. Bruner, and E. McGinnies: "Personal Values as Selective Factors in Perception," *J. abnorm. and soc. Psychol.*, vol. 43, 1948, pp. 142–154.

Robinson, Helen M.: *Why Pupils Fail in Reading*, University of Chicago Press, Chicago, 1946.

Sherman, Mandel, and Elizabeth Bell: "An Experiment in Group Frustration," *Personality*, vol. 1, no. 1, January, 1951.

Strang, Ruth: "Reading and Personality Formation," *Personality*, vol. 1, no. 2, April, 1951.

Tulchin, S. H.: "Emotional Factors in Reading Disability," *J. Educ. Psychol.*, vol. 26, 1935, pp. 444ff.

Vorhaus, P. G.: "Non-Reading as an Expression of Resistance," *Rorschach Res. Exchange*, vol. 10, 1946, pp. 60ff.

Visual Problems and Reading

Bear, Robert M.: "The Dartmouth Program for Diagnostic and Remedial Reading with Special Reference to Visual Factors," *Educational Rec. Suppl.*, vol. 20, supplement 12, January, 1939, p. 76ff.

Carmichael, Leonard, and W. F. Dearborn: *Reading and Visual Fatigue,* Houghton Mifflin Company, Boston, 1947.

Clark, B.: "Binocular Anomalies and Reading Ability," *Amer. J. Ophthalmology,* vol. 23, 1950, pp. 885ff.

Eames, T. H.: "The Ocular Conditions of 350 Poor Readers," *J. Educ. Res.*, vol. 32, September, 1938, pp. 10ff.

English, Horace B.: *Child Psychology,* Henry Holt and Company, Inc., New York, 1951, pp. 270ff and 481ff (short treatment only).

Gray, et al.: "Reading," *Rev. Educ. Res.,* vol. 7, December, 1937, pp. 505ff.

Joslin, Ethel S.: "Physical Factors in Reading," *Columbia Optometrist,* vol. 22, December, 1949, pp. 6ff; February, 1950, pp. 5ff.

Robinson, Helen: *Clinical Studies in Reading,* Chicago University Press, Chicago, Bulletin no. 2.

Robinson, Helen M.: "Factors Related to Monocular and Binocular Reading Efficiency," *Amer. J. Optometry,* vol. 28, 1951, pp. 337ff.

Romaine, Hunter: "Reading Difficulties and Eye Defects," *Sight Saving Rev.,* vol. 19, no. 2, pp. 98ff.

Sullivan, R. R. Commander (MSC) U. S. N.: "The Navy Eye Protection—Eye Correction Program," *Sight Saving Rev.,* vol. 19, no. 1, Spring, 1949, pp. 25ff.

Classroom Climate and Group Leadership

Cunningham, Ruth: *Understanding Group Behavior of Boys and Girls,* Bureau of Publications, Teachers College, Columbia University, New York, 1951.

Horrocks, Winifred B.: "A Sociometric and Psychometric Analysis of Results of Optimalizing Classroom Interpersonal Relationships," dissertation, Ohio State University, 1949 (found that using socialized recitation and group-centered procedures over a two-quarter period, students improved in personal adjustment and tended toward better grades when compared with other classes traditionally taught).

Journal of Educational Research, October, 1951, vol. 45, entire issue, particularly articles by Herbert A. Thelen and Hugh V. Perkins.

Kreitlow, B. W.: "Group Dynamics: It Can Work for Teachers Too?" *Wisconsin J. of Educ.,* vol. 84, September, 1951, pp. 18ff (characteristics of a successful group discussion; advantages of new group procedures).

Lifton, Walter M.: "Group Therapy in Educational Institutions," *Rev. Educ. Res.,* vol. 24, no. 2, April, 1954, pp. 156–165.

———: "The Teacher's Role in Mental Hygiene, Therapy and Social Reconstruction," *Progress. Educ.,* May, 1955, pp. 65ff.

McKeachie, W. J.: "Group Decision Makes Democracy Work," *Religious Educ.,* vol. 46, March, 1951, pp. 90ff.

McNally, Harold J.: "Group Process in Education—Foundation for Democratic Living," Thirty-seventh Annual Schoolmen's Week Proceedings, University of Pennsylvania, April, 1950, pp. 141ff (importance of the process by which children learn, role of the teacher in the group, need for teacher training in the group process).

Parker, J. C., and W. P. Golden, Jr.: "In-Service Education of Elementary and Secondary School Teachers," *Rev. Educ. Res.*, vol. 22, June, 1952, pp. 193ff.

Powell, John Walker: *Education for Maturity*, Hermitage House, Inc., New York, 1949 (illustrates uses of group participation and power of small group in learning and action).

Stainer, M. B.: "Experiment in Group Instruction," *Wisconsin J. Educ.*, vol. 84, October, 1951, pp. 9ff (group decision in the classroom, gains are described).

Thelen, Herbert: *Dynamics of Groups at Work*, University of Chicago Press, Chicago, 1954.

Reading Lists for Classroom Use

Carter, Homer J. L., and Dorothy J. McGinnis: *Learning to Read: A Handbook for Teachers*, McGraw-Hill Book Company, Inc., New York, 1953, Chap. 6.

Giles, R., and D. E. Cook: *Children's Catalogue*, The H. W. Wilson Company, New York, 1951.

Harris, Albert J.: *How to Increase Reading Ability*, Longmans, Green & Co., Inc., New York, 1950, appendix.

Rue, E.: *Subject Index to Books for Intermediate Grades*, American Library Association, Chicago, 1940, grades 3 to 9.

Spache, George D.: *Good Books for Poor Readers*, Reading Laboratory and Clinic, University of Florida, Gainesville, Fla.

Testing

Froelich, C., and J. G. Darley: *Studying Students*, Science Research Associates, Chicago, 1952 (includes names and descriptions of tests suitable for high-school use and explanations of simple research and statistical methods).

Counseling and Play Therapy

Axline, Virginia M.: "Nondirective Therapy for Poor Readers," *J. consult. Psychol.*, vol. 11, 1947, pp. 61–69.

Baruch, Dorothy: "Description of a Project in Group Therapy," *J. consult. Psychol.*, vol. 9, 1945, pp. 271–281.

———: "Therapeutic Procedures as Part of the Educative Process," *J. consult. Psychol.*, vol. 4, 1940, pp. 165–172.

Bills, Robert E.: "Nondirective Play Therapy with Retarded Readers," *J. consult. Psychol.*, vol. 14, 1950, pp. 140–149.

———: "Play Therapy with Well Adjusted Retarded Readers," *J. consult. Psychol.*, 1951.

Bixler, R. H.: "Treatment of a Reading Problem through Nondirective Play Therapy," *J. consult. Psychol.*, vol. 9, 1945, pp. 105–118.

Lundvall, Ruth M.: "Play Therapy," *Teacher Educ.*, Illinois State Normal University, vol. 15, 1952, pp. 24–31.

Muench, G.: "The Implications of Play Therapy for Educational Practice," *Educational Administration and Supervision*, 1949.

Porter, E. H., Jr.: *An Introduction to Therapeutic Counseling*, Houghton Mifflin Company, Boston, 1950.

Rogers, C. R.: *Client-Centered Therapy*, Houghton Mifflin Company, Boston, 1951.

Rogers, C. R.: *Counseling and Psychotherapy*, Houghton Mifflin Company, Boston, 1942.

Williamson, E. G.: *Counseling Adolescents*, McGraw-Hill Book Company, Inc., New York, 1950.

APPENDIX A

Easy Books Which Have Interested Retarded Readers and Non-readers

Most of these books are very easy. Some teachers will doubt whether or not they should be given to older pupils. Some are intended to be read to preschool children. However, most of them have been used successfully with seriously retarded readers of junior-high-school age. Older pupils accept them when they discover that even adults find them amusing, providing they are presented in such a way as not to embarrass the pupil. Sometimes, the teacher can ask the pupil to look over the book and "give me your opinion." Sensitive pupils prefer to read them in private. Some of these are essentially picture books with very little reading. However, they are useful to teach words and arouse interest. Furthermore, the retarded reader gets satisfaction from finishing a book and feels as if there is some hope to finish if the book is not too long. Some teachers object to this list because most of the selections are not classics. After building up a vocabulary and a reading habit, pupils are inclined to follow these with good books at more nearly their own level. Most book-list books are too difficult and too long for retarded readers. Choices should be made from the list in terms of the individual's interests and needs. Prices are approximate. The most popular selections are starred.

*Anderson, *Billy and Blaze*. A simple story of a boy and a horse, easy vocabulary, black and white illustrations; used successfully with ages 7 to 14, Macmillan—$2.00.
*Anderson, *Blaze Finds the Trail*. Illustrated, Macmillan—$2.00.
*Anderson, *Blaze and the Gypsies*. Boy recovers horse stolen by gypsies, easy vocabulary, illustrated, liked by retarded readers, ages 7 to 14, Macmillan—$2.00.
Anderson, *A Pony for Linda*. Macmillan—$2.00.
*Anderson, *Blaze and the Forest Fire*. Horse and boy save a community from disaster, illustrated, liked by retarded readers, ages 8 to 14, Macmillan—$1.00.
Anderson, *Linda and the Indians*. For girls third grade and up, Macmillan—$2.00.
*Austin, *Lutie*. Mountain boy does not want to go to school, funny; helps pupil to express aggression vicariously; ages 7 to 14, Dutton—$1.00.
Bartman, *Yank in Africa*. Dog joins army, about fourth-grade level; can be used for retarded readers through high-school age, Whitman—$1.25.
Bartman, *Yank in Sicily*. Dog in battle, fourth through twelfth grades, Whitman—$1.25.
Beim, *Lucky Pierre*. Boy finds treasures, Harcourt, Brace—$1.75.

385

Beim, *The Little Igloo.* Boy and dog in storm; ages 7 to 10, Harcourt, Brace—$2.50.

Bright, *Georgie.* Useful little ghost; ages 7 to 10, Doubleday—$1.25.

Bronson, *Hooker's Holiday.* Monkey in trouble, black and white illustrations; ages 8 to 14, Harcourt, Brace—$1.75.

Bronson, *Cats.* Harcourt, Brace—$2.00.

Buff, *Dash and Dart.* Twin deers; for ages 8 to 14, Viking—$2.50.

*Burton, *Katy and the Big Snow.* Snow plow saves city, illustrated; ages 8 to 14, Houghton Mifflin—$2.00.

Burton, *Calico, the Wonder Horse.* Horse catches bandits, cartoon illustrations; ages 9 to 14, Houghton Mifflin—$1.00.

Burton, *Mike Mulligan and His Steam Shovel.* Man and shovel find home and job, illustrated; ages 8 to 14, Houghton Mifflin—$1.50.

Cavanah and Weir, *Private Pepper of Dogs for Defense.* Life among the WAGS; ages 9 to 14, Whitman—$1.25.

Chandler, *Cowboy Sam.* First grade and up, Beckley—$1.28.

*Conger, *American War Planes.* Facts and stories, interesting to all ages, fairly simple vocabulary, Holt—$2.00.

*Daugherty, *Andy and the Lion.* Patterned after the story of Androcles and the lion, illustrated, interesting to all, funny, simple vocabulary; ages 8 to 14, Viking—$2.50.

D'Aulaire, *Don't Count Your Chicks.* Old folktale, perhaps too childish for older pupils, illustrated, Doubleday—$2.50.

*D'Aulaire, *Leif the Lucky.* Leif Ericson finds America, interesting, colored illustrations; ages 9 to 14, Doubleday—$2.50.

*DeAngeli, *Yonie Wondernose.* Dutch boy saves farm animals from fire; ages 8 to 14, illustrated, Doubleday—$2.75.

Dennis, *The Pup Himself.* Pup joins show troup, humor, illustrated; third grade through sixth, Viking—$1.00.

Dennis, *Burlap.* Dog catches bear, illustrated, third grade through sixth, Viking—$1.00.

*Dennis, *Flip and the Morning.* A colt's day, good pictures; ages 7 to 14, Viking—$2.00.

Dennis, *Flip.* Colt has a dream about flying, good pictures; ages 8 to 14, Viking—$2.00.

Dennis, *Flip and the Cows.* Colt gets acquainted with cows, illustrated; ages 7 to 14, Viking—$2.00.

Ditmars, *Twenty Little Pets.* Unusual animals of 20 countries, illustrated, vocabulary is too difficult for seriously retarded, Messner—$2.50.

Edmunds, *Matchlock Gun.* About fourth-grade level, Dodd, Mead—$2.50.

*Edmunds, *Two Logs Crossing.* Boy trapper, about fifth-grade reading level, but interesting to older boys and girls, Dodd, Mead—$2.00.

Elliott, *Timothy Titus.* Boy gets lost, easy, verse, Doubleday—$.50.

Flack, *Angus Lost.* Scotty dog story, illustrated; ages 8 to 12, Doubleday—$1.00.

*Flack, *Angus and the Cat.* Scotty dog's adventures with cat, illustrated, some pupils find this very funny; ages 8 to 12, Doubleday—$1.00.

Flack, *Angus and the Ducks.* Illustrated; ages 8 to 10, Doubleday—$1.25.

Flack, *Humphrey.* One hundred years along the wayside with a box turtle, more reading in this than in some listed here, about fourth-grade level, Doubleday—$2.00.

Flack, *The New Pet*. Two young children meet their new baby brother, illustrated; ages 7 to 9, Doubleday—$1.50.

*Flack, *Walter, the Lazy Mouse*. Walter is late to school, late to lunch, gets lost, and has adventures. Even older pupils like this, more reading than most easy books; ages 9 to 14, illustrated, Doubleday—$2.00.

Flack, *What to Do About Molly*. Baby-sitting problem; ages 7 to 10, Houghton Mifflin—$1.25.

*Friskey, *A Goat Afloat*. Children make a boat, goat takes a ride, illustrated, manuscript print, very simple, but sometimes appeals to older pupils, third-grade level, Whitman—$1.50.

Friskey, *Potluck with Lobsters*. Whitman—$1.00.

Friskey, *Seven Diving Ducks*. Whitman—$1.00.

*Friskey, *Surprise on Wheels*. Children make a train and ride down hill in it, illustrated, manuscript print; ages 7 to 10, Whitman—$1.50.

Friskey, *Randy and the Crimson Rocket*. Boy flags train, illustrated, manuscript print; ages 7 to 10, Whitman—$1.50.

*Friskey, *Today We Fly*. Children take a plane ride, illustrated, manuscript print, have used with older pupils, very simple vocabulary; ages 7 to 12, Whitman—$1.50.

*Friskey, *The House that Ran Away*. Goat in playhouse, illustrated, manuscript print, ages 7 to 9, Whitman—$1.50.

*Friskey, *Wings over the Woodshed,* Children make a plane, illustrated, manuscript print; ages 7 to 13, some severely retarded 14-year-olds have liked this, Whitman —$1.50.

*Friskey, *Scuttlebutt and the Carrier Kitten*. Dog and cat take a plane ride, illustrated; ages 8 to 14, Wilcox and Follett—$1.25.

*Friskey, *Scuttlebutt Goes to War*. A little dog on a transport ship, illustrated, usually liked even by adults, third-grade level, Wilcox and Follett—$1.25.

Gág, *Nothing at All*. Invisible dog gets a home, fantasy; ages 8 to 10, Coward-McCann—$1.50.

*Garbut, *Michael the Colt*. Colt learns about the world; ages 8 to 10, Houghton Mifflin—$.85.

Gates, et al., *Bruce and Barbara*, Primer level, Macmillan—$.20.

Gates, et al., *In Came Pinky*. Primer level, Macmillan—$.20.

Gates, et al., *Painted Calf*. Primer level, Macmillan—$.20.

Gates, et al., *Surprise Box*. Primer level, Macmillan—$.20.

Gates, et al., *Animal Parade*. First-reader level, Macmillan—$.20.

Gates, et al., *Elsie the Elephant*. First-reader level, Macmillan—$.20.

Gates, et al., *Mr. Joey and the Pig*. Circus story, first-reader level, Macmillan—$.20.

Gates, et al., *Polly the Kid*. First-reader level, Macmillan—$.20.

Gates, et al., *Sing Canary Sing*. First-reader level, Macmillan—$.20.

Gates, et al., *Tip*. Stray dog finds lost girl, first-reader level, Macmillan—$.20.

*Gates, et al., *Always Ready*. Two boys and a boat in a storm; some junior-high boys like this, second-reader level, Macmillan—$.20.

Gates, et al., *Animals Are Fun*. Second-reader level, Macmillan—$.20.

Gates, et al., *Animals Work Too*. Second-reader level, Macmillan—$.20.

Gates, et al., *Pueblo Indian Stories*. Second-reader level, Macmillan—$.20.

Gates, et al., *We Go Away*. Second-reader level, Macmillan—$.20.

Gates, et al., *Fifty Winters Ago*. Third-grade level, Macmillan—$.20.

Gates, et al., *Little Bear, the Indian Boy*. Third-grade level, Macmillan—$.20.

Gates, et al., *Tony and Jo-Jo*. Third-reader level, Macmillan—$.20.

Gates, et al., *Trails in the Woods*. Third-grade level, Macmillan—$.20.

Gay, *Pancho and His Burro*. Mexican family go to market; ages 7 to 10, Morrow—$2.00.

Gramatky, *Little Toot*. Tugboat story, interesting to most, third grade and up, Putnam—$1.75.

Gramatky, *Loopy*. Airplane story, interesting to most, fourth grade and up, Putnam—$2.75.

Hader, *Pancho*. Good pictures, Macmillan—$2.50.

*Hader, *The Mighty Hunter*. Indian boy plays hooky from school to hunt, colored pictures; ages 7 to 12, Macmillan—$2.75.

*Harris, *The Big Lonely Dog*. Dog finds a home, illustrated, repetition is helpful and amusing; ages 7 to 10, Houghton Mifflin—$1.00.

*Hawkins, *A Puppy for Keeps*. Illustrated by Kurt Wiese; ages 8 to 11, Holiday—$1.00.

Hawkins, *Who Wants an Apple*. Apple is a girl, primary vocabulary, Holiday—$1.00.

Hawkins, *Don't Run Apple*. Ages 7 to 9, Holiday—$1.00.

Henry, *Born to Trot, Justin Morgan Had a Horse, King of the Wind, Brighty of the Grand Canyon, Sea Star, Misty of Chincoteague,* About fourth-grade level, interesting to all ages, illustrated, Rand, McNally—$2.75.

Heward, *Twins and Tabiffa*. Cat saves house from fire, Macrae-Smith—$1.50.

Hobson, *A Dog of His Own*. Viking—$1.00.

*Hogan, *Nicodemus and the New Shoes*. Baby sister drops new shoes in mud, Dutton—$1.50.

Hogan, *Twin Deer*. Dutton—$1.50.

Hogan, *Bear Twins*. Dutton—$1.50.

*Huber, *Ranch Book*. Very easy; Ages 7 up, Macmillan—$1.68.

James, *Smokey*. Appeals to some and not to others; a little difficult for slow readers to get started but after they do some like it, illustrated by author, grade 6 up, Scribner—$2.00.

Johnson, *Carlo, The Hound Who Thought He Was a Calf*. Appeals to some and not to others; a little difficult for slow readers to get started but after they do some like it, third grade and up, Harcourt, Brace—$1.75.

Johnson, *Runaway Puppy*. Appeals to some and not to others; a little difficult for slow readers to get started but after they do some like it, third grade and up, Harcourt, Brace—$2.25.

Johnson, *Smallest Puppy*. This appeals to some and not to others; a little difficult for slow readers to get started but after they do some like it; third grade and up, Harcourt, Brace—$2.00.

Kingman, *Pierre Pidgeon*. Boy builds ship in a bottle, grade 3 and up, Houghton Mifflin—$2.00.

Martin, *Brave Little Indian*. Intended for small children but interesting to fourth- or fifth-graders, illustrated, Winston—$1.00 and $2.23.

Mason, *Caroline and Her Kettle Named Maud*. Macmillan—$2.00.

Mason, *Matilda and Her Family*. Illustrated, Macmillan—$1.50.

Mason, *Susannah, the Pioneer Cow*. Illustrated by Petersham, grade 2 and up, Macmillan—$1.25.

Mason, *Timothy Has Ideas*. Second grade and up, Macmillan—$1.50.

*Mason, *Young Mr. Meeker*. Oregon trail, about fourth-grade level, interesting to older pupils, Bobbs-Merrill—$2.00.

McClosky, *Homer Price*. Boy and pet skunk catch robbers, funny, about fourth-grade level; interesting to ages 11 to 17, Viking—$2.00.

McGinley, *The Horse that Had His Picture in the Paper*, Illustrated, Lippincott—$2.00.

McGinley, *The Horse that Lived Upstairs*. Grade 2 and up, Lippincott—$1.25.

Miller, *Miss Lizzie*. Dog plays cupid, primary, Viking—$1.50.

Newberry, *April's Kittens*. A little girl and her cats, appeals to almost all girls and some boys, illustrated, fourth grade and up, Harper—$2.50.

*Newberry, *Marshmallow*. Black cat and white rabbit, whimsical, good illustrations, appeals to almost all girls and some boys, fourth grade and up, Harper—$1.75.

Newberry, *Mittens*. Cat story, illustrated, appeals to almost all girls and some boys, fourth grade and up, Harper—$1.50.

Seuss, *And to Think that I Saw it on Mulberry Street*. Upper primary vocabulary, second grade and up, Vanguard—$1.50.

*Stong, *Honk, the Moose*. Moose invades town, is adopted by boys, illustrated, about third or fourth-grade level, interesting to all ages, Dodd, Mead—$2.75.

*Wells, *Mr. Tootwhistle's Invention*. Railroad history cleverly told, cartoon illustrations, humor; ages 7 to 11, Winston—$1.00.

*Wells, *The Pirates' Apprentice*. Boy is kidnapped and makes life miserable for pirates, very easy and interesting, funny, cartoon illustrations; ages 8 to 14, Winston—$1.25.

Wilder, *Little House on the Prairie*. (And all her books). Interesting to all ages, fourth-grade level and up, Harper—$2.00.

Williamson, *The Little Elephant*. Ages 7 to 9, Doubleday—$1.00.

Williamson, *Baby Bear*. Second grade and up, Doubleday—$1.00.

*Williamson, *Lion Cub*. Lion cub gets lost, has adventures, illustrated; ages 7 to 11, Doubleday—$1.00.

*Williams, *Timid Timothy*. Clever cat story, good pictures, repetition is helpful and not tiresome, Scott—$1.25.

Books for Retarded Readers of Upper Grades, High-school and College Age

Allen, *Wilderness Way*. French lad follows La Salle through the wilderness to the mouth of the Mississippi, illustrations by Larry Toschik; ages 12 to 16, Longmans —$2.75.

American Boy Action Stories. Selections from Barbour, Kelland, etc., Doubleday—$1.50.

Annabel, *Alaskan Tales*. Autobiography and adventure story of a 16-year-old who hunts bear and moose, trades for furs, learns to be a guide, A. S. Barnes—$2.50.

Baker and Bridges, *Wild Animals of the World*. Recommended by American Museum of Natural History, Garden City—$3.95.

Baker, *Venture of the Thunderbird*. Voyage of two young brothers around Cape Horn to the Pacific Northwest in the early days of the fur trade; ages 12 up, McKay—$3.00.

Baumann, *Caves of the Great Hunters*. True story of French children's discovery of a cave which led to a new light on ancient man, illustrations in 2 colors, honor book for older boys and girls, *New York Herald Tribune*. Children's Spring Book Festival, Pantheon—$3.00.

Bell, *Midnight Creek*. Said to be an exceptionally well-written new western novel, Crowell—$2.75.

Best, *Garram the Hunter*. Son of African chief and his dog, high-school age, Doubleday—$1.50.

Brooks, *Blazing Alaska's Trails*. Published by University of Alaska and Arctic Institute of North America, illustrated, 528 pages, published first in 1922 and reissued in 1954,—$4.00.

Burford, *North to Danger*. True adventures of a young American who sought work and excitement in Alaska, John Day—$3.75.

Burns, *Horses and their Ancestors*. Recommended by American Museum of Natural History, color illustrations by Paula Hutchinson, McGraw-Hill—$2.50.

Burt, *Young Jed Smith*. Childhood of Famous Americans Series, boy in early nineteenth century becomes a famous mountain man, Bobbs-Merrill—$1.75.

Cavanaugh, *We Came to America*. Stories of immigrants; for ages 14 and up, Macrae Smith Co.—$3.50.

Cecil, *Kata, Son of Red Fang*. Dog of the north, part wolf; ages 12 and up, Winston —$2.50.

Chapin, *Heavy Water*. Adventure story with authentic historical background, teen-ager explores Minnesota border chain of lakes, junior and senior high school. Chapin has lived all of his life in Minnesota, was editor of a country newspaper, is author of *Long Wednesdays;* illustrated by Nils Hogner, Abelard-Schuman—$2.50.

Clark, *The Rivers Ran East*. Rediscovery of the seven cities of Eldorado in Peru, true adventure, Funk—$5.00.

Clymer, *Those Wonderful Old Automobiles*. New and interesting stories of early autos, illustrated, McGraw-Hill–$5.95.

Conibear, *Devil Dog*. Story is about a dog in the northwest country, part wolf; Conibear is co-author of *The Wise One;* illustrations by John Scott, Sloane—$3.50.

Cooke, *The Narrow Ledge of Fear*. Story of skiing, mountain-climbing, plane wreck, Nelson—$2.50.

Cooke, *Fighting Indians of the West*. Brief interesting biography of Cochise, Geronimo, Sitting Bull, Crazy Horse, etc., full of facts; author is sympathetic with Indians; juvenile, Dodd, Mead—$2.95.

Cooper, *Great Horse Stories*. Eighty-two drawings by Paul Brown, 21 stories, true and fictional, Doubleday—$3.75.

Day, *Gene Rhodes, Cowboy*. Story of a real cowboy who rode the range in New Mexico for 30 years, illustrations by Lorence F. Bjorklund; ages 12 and up, Rhodes is a writer, Messner—$2.75.

Darling, *Luck of the Trail*. Young Moderns, dog story of north; ages 12 to 17, Doubleday—$1.50.

Diole, *The Gates of the Sea*. Translated from the French by Ross, illustrated, amphibious journey around the coasts of Sicily, much of it under water, *Science News Letter* Book of the Week, April 30, 1955, Messner—$4.50.

Dorian, *Trails West and the Men Who Made Them*. Location of famous trails, their history, and stories of men who made them and used them, line drawings; ages 10 and up, McGraw-Hill—$2.50.

Douglas, William O., *Strange Lands and Friendly People*. Douglas' trip with his 12-year-old son from the tip of Persia through Arabia and Palestine, high school and college age, Harper—$5.00.

Earle, *Paws, Hoofs, and Flippers*. Story of mammals by an authority on nature and art, illustrated by author; ages 12 and up, Morrow—$3.50.

Farnsworth, *Winged Moccasins*. Story of Shoshone Indian girl who crossed the Rockies as interpreter and guide for Lewis and Clark, illustrations by Bjorklund; age 12 and up, Messner—$2.75.

Farnsworth, *Guests of the Tetons*. Trip through canyons, glaciers and wild flowers with bears as guides, illustrated by Griffity, younger readers, but good for any age, University of New Mexico, $2.00.

Fletcher, *The American Indian*. Customs, environmental adaptations, excellent chapters on the great cultures and brief biographies of well-known Indians, Grosset—$2.95.

Ford, *Audobon's Animals*. Reproductions of Audobon's paintings in color with his notes on wildlife, Natural History Club, upper elementary and high school, Crowell—$7.75.

Frankel, *Shortcut to Photography*. About cameras—how to use, composition, exposure, developing, printing, pictures, illustrated with photos by author and by high-school students; for ages 12 and up, Sterling—$2.50.

Freuchen, *Ice Floes and Flaming Water*. Rescue of stranded whalers in Northern Greenland told by a noted Arctic explorer, author of *Vagrant Viking* and *Arctic Adventure,* high school and college, Messner—$3.95.

Fulton, *Moccasin Trail*. Boy takes trail with Kit Carson; ages 12 to 17, Young Moderns Edition, Doubleday—$1.50.

Garst, *Joe Meek*. Biography of Joe Meek, trapper, explorer, U. S. Marshal in territorial Oregon; ages 12 and up, Messner—$2.75.

Grange, *Those of the Forest*. About the life of wild creatures, line drawings by Olaus Murie, favorable reviews in *Christian Science Monitor, New York World Telegram, Los Angeles Examiner, Washington Post,* Flambeau—$4.75.

Guthrie, *The Big Sky* and *The Way West*. Sloane—$3.75.

*Halliburton, *Book of Marvels*. Selections from his adventure tales, seventh grade and up, Bobbs-Merrill—$2.50.

Handel, *Canoe Camping*. Illustrated, how to do it, A. S. Barnes—$3.00.

Harrer, *Seven Years in Tibet*. Young German escapes to Tibet and makes friends with Dalai Lama, illustrated, non-fiction, Dutton—$5.00.

Hayes, *Land Divided*. Canada in 1755, British clash with French, story of a 15-year-old boy; literary award in Canada; ages 10–15, Westminster—$2.50.

Herbert, *Mr. Wizard's Science Secrets*. Experiments that look like magic, Popular Mechanics—$3.00.

Hoffman and Sim, *Mammals: A Guide to Familiar American Species*. Pocket size, to help identify wild animals, illustrations in color, Simon and Schuster—$1.95.

Hughes, *Famous American Negroes*. Careers of 18 American negroes, illustrated with photos; ages 12 and up, Dodd, Mead—$2.75.

Hunter, *African Hunter*. Story of a famous African hunter, jungle experiences, elephants, tigers, lions, illustrated with photos and diagrams, Young Readers' Edition; ages 12 to 16, Harper—$2.50.

Hyde, *Driving Today and Tomorrow*. Illustrated driving manners and safety, a section on hot-rods, McGraw-Hill—$2.50.

Ingstad, *Nunamuit*. Norwegian explorer describes life among primitive people in Northern Alaska, illustrated, Norton—$3.95.

Johnson, **Indian Country**. Stories of American frontier, Ballantine—$2.00.

Knight, *Brave Companions*. Heroism of two dogs and a boy; ages 12 to 17, Doubleday—$2.25.

Krumgold, *And Now Miguel*. Mexican boy, younger readers, but good for any age, illustrated, Newbery winner, Crowell—$2.75.

Kraus, *Square Dances of Today*. How to teach and call, illustrated, musical arrangements, A. S. Barnes—$3.00.

Lampman, *Tax-Mah-Na-Wus*. Caught by a hostile tribesman and sold as a slave, Tom made friends with Lt. Phil Sheridan, illustrations by Bennett; ages 12 and up, Doubleday—$2.75.

Lampman, *Witch Doctor's Son*. Rogue River and Yamhill Indians, customs and beliefs are background for well-written adventure story of Northwest, Doubleday—$2.75.

Lane, *Greatest Adventure*. Story of Jack London, school days, oyster pirating, riding the rails, whaling in Pacific, gold mining in Alaska, color illustrations by Quinn, Aladdin—$1.75.

Lauritzen, *The Ordeal of the Young Hunter*. Navajo boy wishes to be a hunter, must be a sheepherder, halftone illustrations by Hoke Denetsosie; ages 9 to 11, Little, Brown—$2.75.

Lewisohn, *Animals, Men and Myths*. Harper—$5.00.

Le Sueur, *The River Road*. Abe Lincoln's trip down the Mississippi River to New Orleans while he was still in his teens, illustrated by Watson; ages 10 to 14, Knopf —$2.50.

Leopold and Darling, *Wildlife in Alaska*. About caribou, reindeer, and other animals, recommended by *Journal of Forestry*, authors are conservationists, Ronald—$2.75.

Lippincott, *The Phantom Deer*. Rescue of a fawn, illustrated by Paul Bramson; ages 12 to 16, Lippincott—$3.00.

Liers, *An Otter's Story*. True story of two otters and their family in Michigan and Wisconsin, illustrated by Plazzo, a famous painter of animals, Viking—$2.50.

MacArthur, *Desert Watches*. Hazardous crossing of Sahara, expected to appeal to those who liked *Kon-Tiki*, Bobbs-Merrill—$3.50.

Machetans, *Where Else but Alaska*. Honeymoon in an Eskimo village, seal hunt, dog team, illustrated by photos; ages 12 and up, Scribner—$3.00.

Mackenzie, *Men Without Guns*. United States Medical Corps in World War II, illustrated with Abbott collection of paintings, Doubleday—$5.00.

Mannix, *Adventure Happy*. Travels in jungle with two small children, visits to wild animals, bringing some home, trials of feeding baby vampires, illustrated with photos, Simon & Schuster—$3.95.

McNeer, *War Chief of the Seminoles*. About Osceola, chief of Seminoles who opposed loss of Indian land to white men in Florida; ages 10 to 15, line drawings in two colors, Random House—$1.50.

McNickle, *Runner in the Sun*. Land of Free Series, about Indian search for corn, irrigation, and reclaiming soil before the coming of the white man, line drawings by Alan Houser, Winston—$2.75.

McSpadden, *Pioneer Heroes*. Stories of 10 men, illustrations by Hallock; ages 12 and up, Crowell—$3.00.

Means, *The Rains Will Come*. Story of Hopi Indians, traditions and customs described in accurate detail, black and white drawings by Hopi artist, Fred Kabotie, Houghton Mifflin—$2.50.

Medary, *Each One Teach One*. Story of a Congregational missionary who taught 60 million people to read in 239 languages and dialects, illustrated with photos and charts; ages 12 and up, *Science News Letter* Book of the Week, March 6, 1954, Longmans—$3.00.

Megargie, *The Dog Dictionary.* 130 sepia portraits of dogs, highly recommended, World—$3.95.

Menninger, *How to Be a Successful Teen Ager.* Dating, getting along with others, illustrated; ages 18 and up, Sterling—$2.95.

Michener, *Tales of the South Pacific.* Macmillan—$3.75.

Michener, *Sayonara Means Good-bye.* Random House—$3.50.

Morenus, *Northland Adventure.* Mystery, danger, adventure; ages 12 and up, Dodd, Mead—$2.50.

Motor's *Auto Repair Manual.* How to make repairs on 21 autos: brakes, carburetors, generators, fuel pumps, etc., Motor, 250 West 55th Street, New York—about $7.50.

Neider, *Man Against Nature.* True adventure: Peary, Orville Wright, Lindbergh, Richard Henry Dana, William Beebe, Byrd, Schweitzer, also accounts of such events as Chicago fire, Lisbon earthquake, and eruption of Vesuvius, Harper—$5.00.

Newsom, *Wagons to Tucson.* Post-Civil War travel through Apache country, pioneer scout, love story, Little, Brown—$3.50.

Nolan, *George Rogers Clark.* Illustrations by Lee Ames; ages 12 and up, Messner—$2.75.

O'Hara, *My Friend Flicka, Thunderhead, Green Grass of Wyoming.* Lippincott—$3.00.

O'Rourke, *Ride West.* Ballantine—$2.50.

Patterson, *Dangerous River.* About the wild beauty of the Canadian Northwest, adventure, illustrated with photos, maps, drawings, Sloane—$5.00.

Pease, *Heart of Danger.* Tale of Tod Moran as a spy in occupied France, winner of 1946 award of Child Study Association and 1948 award of Boys' Club of America, Doubleday—$2.50.

Penfield, *Lost Treasure Trails.* Documented stories of 807 treasures, lost mines, etc., where to look for them, plus stories about people who found treasure, illustrations by Glaubke, Grosset—$2.50.

Powers, *True Adventures on Westward Trails.* Stories of De Soto, Kit Carson, Lewis and Clark, line drawings by Bjorklund; ages 12 to 16, Little, Brown—$2.75.

Pringle, *Danger Mountain.* Author has tested and authenticated setting and plot, photos; ages 10 to 14, Roy—$2.50.

Quimby, *Indians of the Western Frontier.* Reproductions of paintings of George Catlin, paperbound, *Science News Letter* Book of the Week, Chicago Natural History Museum—$.60.

Renick and Tyler, *Buckskin Scout and Other Frontier Stories.* World—$2.50.

Richter, *Light in the Forest.* About a white boy captured by Indians and reclaimed in adolescence by white parents, his Indian education and problems of adjustment, now available in 25-cent edition, Knopf; also *The Trees, The Fields, The Town, Sea of Grass,* Knopf—$2.50–$4.00; *Sea of Grass,* Bantam—25¢.

Robinson, *Spindleshanks.* Young boy involved in American Revolution, illustrated by Peter Burchard; ages 10 to 14, Oxford—$3.00.

Rose, *Gentle House.* A young displaced person and an American school teacher, Houghton Mifflin—$2.75.

Sandoz, *Buffalo Hunters.* Hastings—$4.50.

Schaefer, *Shane,* Condensed from novel, illustrated by John McCormack; ages 12 and up, Houghton Mifflin—$2.75.

Schwarzkopf, *Fur, Fin, and Feathers.* Eight nature stories about wildlife drama, illustrations by Dimitri Alexandroff; ages 12 and up, Crowell—$2.75.

Schmidt, *Homes and Habits of Wild Animals.* Facts about animal life, contains some accounts of caribou, deer, beaver, and others, colored illustrations, Donohue— $2.00.

Scoggin, *The Lure of Danger.* True adventure in dangerous jobs, Knopf—$3.00.

Scott, *Hudson of Hudson's Bay.* "Uncommonly interesting," says *The New York Times Book Review;* ages 10 to 15, Abelard—$2.50.

Small, *Dangerous Duty.* Young John Craig, ship's boy with Commodore Perry in Japan, illustrations by Rus Anderson, Oxford—$3.00.

Steele, *Story of Leif Ericson.* Addition to the Signature Book Series under supervision of Enid LaMonte Meadowcroft, illustrated by Lape, Grosset—$1.50.

Strong, *Snow King.* Story of herd dog of Lapland who came to U. S. and rescued two American fliers; ages 12 and up, Dodd, Mead—$2.50.

Stuart, *A Seal's World.* Adventure story, first three years in life of a seal, illustrated, *Science News Letter* Book of the Week, McGraw-Hill—$4.00.

Thompson, *Sierra Ranger,* Life of ranger, fire fighting, wild life, etc., ages 12 and up, Dodd, Mead—$2.50.

Trefflich, *They Never Talk Back.* Adventures with animals in captivity; you may recognize this as the book which includes the incident of the 100 monkeys which got out and visited firemen and a wholesale grocery, Appleton-Century-Crofts— $3.50.

Tunis, *Wheels.* A pictorial history, story of wheels from the ancient Egyptian sledge on rollers to the latest transcontinental bus, drawings by author, *Science News Letter* Book of the Week, World—$3.95.

Ullman, *Age of Mountaineering.* Illustrated history of mountain climbing by author of *The White Tower,* Lippincott—$7.50.

Ullman, *Banner in the Sky.* About a 16-year-old boy and a mountain, by the author of *The White Tower;* ages 15 to 18, Lippincott—$2.75.

Vangouny, *Greenland Waters.* Life in the north, first seal catch, adventures at an ice cap, line drawings by Creekmore; ages 10 to 14, Macmillan—$2.00.

Walker, *Around a Rusty God.* Story of a Chinese boy with two goats to raise and a war to worry about, gives the peasants' perspective on war, illustrated by Pitz, ages teens and adults, fairly easy reading, Dial Press—$3.00.

Werner, *Walt Disney's Living Desert.* Based on film, color photos and drawings, Simon and Schuster—$2.00.

Wibberley, *The Epics of Everest.* Illustrated by Vaughn-Jackson, *Science News Letter* Book of the Week; ages 12 to 16, Farrar, Strauss—$3.25.

Williams, *Bandoola.* Sequel to *Elephant Bill,* illustrated by Fitz, elephant and his Burmese trainer during World War II, Doubleday—$3.50.

Wood, *Wild Winter.* Sixteen-year-old boy wants to write, spends winter in unheated cabin in Alberta, Canada; ages 11 and up, Houghton Mifflin—$2.25.

Worth, *They Loved to Laugh.* Five boys and an orphan girl, illustrations by de Angeli, ages 12 to 16, Doubleday—$2.25.

Other Materials
(Always use an unfamiliar reader.)

American Education Press, Little Wonder Series, paperbound books, grades 1 to 8.

Ginn & Company third reader, second semester, often interesting to retarded readers in upper grades, accompanied by a good workbook.

Lyons publishers, *Little Road, Wide Road, Open Road, Broad Road,* grade 1 and up.

Macmillan, Aviation Readers.

Row, Peterson, Unitext, easy reading for sixth- and seventh-graders.

Scott, Foresman, separate reader series.

Wheeler Publishing Co., American Adventure Series, graded adventure stories, very interesting, subjects are Indians, history, adventure, biography; Betts is editor, teacher's guide book and general manual are available, D. H. Kay, 224 Maiden Lane, Kansas City, Mo.

My Weekly Reader, use lower levels for retarded readers, 400 S. Front St., Columbus 15, Ohio.

Popular Mechanics Magazine, 200 E. Ontario St., Chicago 11, Ill.

Popular Science Monthly, 353 Fourth Avenue, New York 10, N. Y.

Science News Letter, for high-school and college students, Science Service, 1718 N. Street, N. W., Washington 6, D. C.

Reading Games, Remedial Education Center, Washington, D. C.

Films for beginners, inquire of Mrs. Esther Burr, Box 493, Upland, California.

Film series for high school, manual, tests, and supplementary materials, prepared under direction of Dr. J. B. Stroud, Bureau of Audio-Visual Instruction, Extension Division, State University of Iowa, Iowa City, Iowa.

Matthews and Perdue, graded book list for reluctant readers, *Library Journal,* December 15, 1953.

APPENDIX B

Spelling Words

their
receive
too
writer
writing
written
all right
separate
until
privilege
definite
there
believe
its
it's
occur
occurred
occurrence
occurring
describe
description
tragedy
decide
decision
occasion
sense
familiar
your
you're
appearance
conscious
conscience
pleasant
stop
stopped
stopping
surprise

occasionally
succeed
success
successful
interest
beginning
immediate
immediately
coming
embarrass
grammar
humor
humorous
exist
existence
lose
during
woman
certain
commit
committed
committing
criticism
disappear
villain
marry
marries
marriage
character
complete
friend
truly
accidentally
doesn't
foreign
foreigners
performance

losing
disappoint
rhythm
study
studies
studied
studying
convenience
convenient
difference
different
than
athletic
to
business
equipped
equipment
principal
principle
prophecy
prophesy
benefit
beneficial
benefited
benefiting
belief
write
precede
succession
personal
personnel
choose
chose
choice
similar
profession
unnecessary

develop
environment
recommend
fascinate
finally
necessary
necessity
probably
speech
argument
image
imagine
imaginary
imagination
quiet
then
forty
exaggerate
familiar
escape
meant
where
chief
hero
prejudice
affective
weather
whether
fourth
criticize
varies
various
category
excellence
grammatically
repetition
prevalent

excite
excited
excitement
exciting
experience
government
laboratory
tried
acquaint
acquaintance
affect
accept
accommodate
excellent
opportunity
probably
disastrous
passed
past
acquire
busy
business
Negro
Negroes
among
height
origin
original
prominent
pursue
shining
practical
effect
governor
prepare
appear
mere
possible
ridicule
desirability
desire
knowledge
excitable
favorite
interrupt
persistent
reminisce
weird
friendliness
fulfil

together
descend
descendent
heroes
heroine
lonely
opinion
parliament
possess
professor
restaurant
they're
two
definition
define
ninety
summary
summed
attended
attendant
attendance
heroic
paid
quiet
accept
acceptance
acceptable
accepting
dominant
predominant
optimism
relieve
religion
independent
independence
particular
technique
transferred
discipline
disciple
humor
humorist
happiness
response
further
oppose
opponent
propaganda
propagate
therefore

began
begin
beginner
control
controlled
controlling
arguing
proceed
achieve
achievement
possession
psychoanalysis
psychopathic
psychosomatic
analyze
humorous
quantity
accident
characteristic
characterized
hypocrisy
hypocrite
operate
planned
suppress
whose
author
authority
authoritative
athlete
challenge
liveliest
livelihood
liveliness
lives
philosophy
sponsor
across
aggressive
article
suppose
basis
acknowledgment
adequate
adjourned
affectionate
affectionately
affidavit
agencies
all right

intelligence
intelligent
realize
really
led
loneliness
prefer
explanation
interpretation
interpret
useful
useless
using
noticeable
noticing
basically
before
conceive
conceivable
consider
considerably
continuous
dependent
extremely
satire
careless
careful
conform
maintenance
parallel
permit
exercise
involve
leisure
leisurely
sergeant
subtle
Britain
Britannica
completely
dealt
divide
attaching
attorneys
auditorium
bankruptcy
basketball
beneficial
bored
bulletin

piece
temperament
carrying
carried
carries
carrier
suspense
amount
curriculum
disease
especially
fallacy
financier
politician
political
relative
scene
sophomore
huge
conceive
conception
confirmation
congratulations
congress
conscience
conscientious
conscious
consistent
continent
continuous
controversy
conveniently
cooperate
correspondence
counsel
countenance
coupe
courtesies
courtesy
criticism
curiosity
curious
customer's
damage
damaged
debit
mortgage
mustn't
mutual

hindrance
indispensable
laid
length
lengthening
remember
several
substantial
tendency
whole
accompanying
absurd
acceptable
accommodate
accommodation
accompanying
accrued
accustomed
acknowledging
decidedly
deem
definitely
delegates
delinquent
deny
despair
determined
dining
disappoint
disappointment
discretion
divine
documents
dormitory
dropped
duty
dying
economic
economical
economics
edition
efficiency
elementary
eliminate
employees
enemies
prior
privilege
procedure

alumni
amiable
analysis
anniversary
annoyance
annum
anticipate
anticipating
anticipation
anxiety
apology
apparent
apparently
appetite
appropriate
approximate
approximately
arrangements
ascertain
enemy
enthusiasm
enthusiastic
entrance
epistle
equipped
ere
esteemed
eventually
existence
exists
expenditure
exquisite
extraordinary
facilities
fascinating
financially
folk
folks
folly
fundamental
galvanized
genius
geometry
gorgeous
grateful
grippe
satisfactorily
scandal
scheduled

bungalow
buried
canceled
canceling
cancellation
canvass
catalogues
cease
ceased
Chautauqua
chemistry
collateral
committed
committee
communicate
comparatively
competent
completing
completion
guarantee
guaranteed
guardian
imitation
immediately
immensely
incidentally
inconvenience
inconvenienced
indefinite
indefinitely
infinite
initiation
innocent
intellectual
itemized
judgment
kindergarten
laboratory
literally
magnificent
materially
mathematics
melancholy
memorandum
minimum
miscellaneous
tragedy
transformed
triumph

mysterious
mystery
necessarily
negotiations
occasionally
opportunities
ordinarily
originally
pamphlet
pamphlets
partial
perceive
permanently
phase
philosophy
physician
picturesque
pneumonia
possess
preferred
prejudice
president's
principles
advise
entertain
influential
influence
significance
moral
morale
morally
playwright
source
capital
capitalism
counselor
fictitious
primitive
regard
roommate
story
stories
strength
forward
pertain
safety
satisfy
satisfied
sentence

psychology
questionnaire
rating
receiver
reckon
recognition
recommend
recommendation
recommendations
recommended
recommending
referred
referring
refrigerator
regretted
remembrance
representatives
requisition
restaurant
rheumatism
ridiculous
role
romantic
theory
theories
tremendous
vacuum
view
accomplish
arouse
arousing
guidance
guiding
ignorance
ignorant
magnificent
magnificence
narrative
obstacle
shepherd
simply
simple
straight
synonymous
themselves
them
amateur
attack
attitude

seized
so-called
solemn
sorority
specific
specifically
specimen
specimens
spiritual
statistics
strenuous
sufficiently
supplement
suspicion
sympathetic
technical
temporarily
temporary
thorough
thoroughly
today's
tonnage
tournament
boundary
clothes
expense
fantasy
fantasies
irrelevant
laborer
laboriously
labor
later
license
medieval
naturally
noble
peace
sacrifice
strict
symbol
actually
actuality
actual
adolescence
adolescent
against
appreciate
appreciation

unanimous
unfortunate
unfortunately
unusually
vacancies
vacancy
violence
virtue
virtues
visible
voucher
vulgar
week's
accompanies
accompanied
accompaniment
hear
here
luxury
approach
approaches
physical
advice
experiment
field
hungry
hungrily
hunger
interfere
interference
likeness
likely
likelihood
magazine
maneuver
mechanics
medicine
medical
miniature
mischief
omit
persuade
those
thought
tragedy
yield

APPENDIX C

Individual Record Form

Name_____ Date_____ Age___ Sex___

Present address_____ Home address_____

Please check or double-check any of the following items which seem to apply to you. I would like to improve in:

_____ reading speed
_____ reading comprehension
_____ attention span
_____ study habits
_____ concentration
_____ theme writing
_____ study schedule
_____ outlining
_____ taking lecture notes
_____ leadership
_____ people's opinions of me
_____ vocabulary

_____ ability to make friends
_____ conversation
_____ manners
_____ interest in studies
_____ interest in reading
_____ health
_____ personal appearance
_____ getting along with brothers and sisters

_____ self-confidence
_____ public speaking
_____ other _____

Father's name_____ Occupation_____
Mother's name_____ Occupation_____
Parents—still living together_____ separated_____ divorced_____ remarried_____.
Name of guardian, if any _____
Number of brothers _____ Number of sisters _____

Complete these items:

Subjects I like: _____
Subjects I dislike: _____
In my leisure time I do these things: _____
Books I have read lately: _____
Kind of work I think I would like best: _____
If I could be doing what I want to 15 years from now, I would _____

I plan to finish college. _____ yes _____ no
If you have had any of the following common afflictions, please give the age when they were discovered, when treated, and present condition.

400

	Age	Treated	Present condition
Hearing defects	___	___	___
Speech defects	___	___	___
Eye defects	___	___	___
Nervousness	___	___	___
Sleeplessness	___	___	___
Frequent or persistent headaches	___	___	___
Car-sickness	___	___	___
Asthma, hay fever, etc.	___	___	___
Other ___	___	___	___

Answer the following, true or false:

___ 1. I feel that my reading vocabulary is limited.

___ 2. It is hard for me to concentrate when I read.

___ 3. It is hard for me to pay attention when I read.

___ 4. I do not read unless I feel it is absolutely necessary.

___ 5. I look at the words but I often feel that I am not getting meaning.

___ 6. I feel that I need to improve my reading skills.

___ 7. My eyes get tired when I read.

___ 8. I worry about things I should or should not have done.

___ 9. Reading is hard work.

___10. Lights hurt my eyes.

___11. Words blur sometimes.

___12. I am troubled when I think about the future.

___13. I believe that I fail to see some of the words when reading.

___14. I have to stop and reread some of the passages when I am studying.

___15. I often feel unhappy because other people might not like me.

___16. I do not have enough to talk about in company.

___17. I get tired and sleepy when I read.

___18. I have trouble making myself study.

___19. I worry for fear other people might make fun of me.

___20. I would like more chances to have fun with people of my own age.

___21. I do not like to recite out loud.

___22. I am often embarrassed in front of other people.

___23. I am unable to decide what work I would like.

___24. I do not know how much time I should spend in study.

___25. It troubles me to think I might not be able to measure up to what others expect of me.

___26. I spend more time alone than other people of my own age.

___27. I often have a feeling that other people are criticizing me.

___28. I often wonder if the things I have to do are worth doing.

___29. It is hard for me to get acquainted with people.

___30. I often wonder if I am as good as other people.

___31. A person has to be very careful when talking to others or they might find out something he doesn't want them to know.

___32. I seem to need someone around that I can depend on.

___33. I lack self-confidence.

___34. I need to broaden my interests.

___35. I sometimes get car-sick when riding.

___36. I usually do not enjoy being with members of the opposite sex.

___37. Something seems lacking in my relationship with my parents.

BIBLIOGRAPHY

Abbott, E. Carleton: "Relationship between Variation in Silent Reading Ability and Mental Ability," dissertation, University of Pennsylvania, Philadelphia.

Adams, Fay, et al.: *Teaching Children to Read*, The Ronald Press Company, New York, 1949.

Adelman, H. M., and G. Rosenbaum: "Extinction of Instrumental Behavior as a Function of Frustration at Various Distances from the Goal," *J. exp. Psychol.*, vol. 47, 1954, pp. 429ff.

Adorno, T. W., E. Frenkel-Brunswick, D. J. Levinson, and R. N. Sanford: *The Authoritarian Personality*, Harper & Brothers, New York, 1950.

Anderson, Harold: "Domination and Social Integration in the Behavior of Kindergarten Children and Teachers," *Gen. Psychol. Monogr.*, vol. 21, 1939, pp. 287ff.

————, and Gladys Anderson (eds.): *Introduction to Projective Techniques*, Prentice-Hall, Inc., Englewood Cliffs, N. J., 1951.

Anderson, John P.: "Study of Relationship between Certain Aspects of Parental Behavior of Junior High School Pupils," Bureau of Publications, Teachers College, Columbia University, New York, 1940.

Annis, A., and N. C. Meier: "The Induction of Opinion through Suggestion by Means of 'Planted Content'," *J. soc. Psychol.*, vol. 5, 1934, pp. 65ff.

Arps, G. F.: "A Preliminary Report on Work with Knowledge Versus Work without Knowledge of Results," *Psychol. Rev.*, vol. 24, 1917, pp. 449ff.

Axline, V. M.: "Non-Directive Therapy for Poor Readers," *J. consult. Psychol.*, vol. 2, 1947, pp. 61ff.

Ayer, Mary E., and R. G. Bernreuther: "Study of the Relationships between Discipline and Personality Traits in Little Children," *J. gen. Psychol.*, vol. 50, 1937, pp. 165ff.

Barker, R. G., T. Dembo, and K. Lewin: "Frustration and Regression, an Experiment with Young Children," *University of Iowa Studies: Studies of Child Welfare*, vol. 18, no. 1, 1941.

Bartlett, E. R., and Dale B. Harris: "Personality Factors in Delinquency," *School and Society*, vol. 43, May 9, 1936, pp. 653ff.

Bartlett, Frederick: "The Transfer of Training," *Bull. Ass. Int. Psychotech.*, vol. 3, 1954, pp. 20ff.

Beams, H. L.: "Affectivity as a Factor in the Apparent Size of Pictured Food Objects," *J. exp. Psychol.*, vol. 47, 1954, pp. 197ff.

Bear, Robert M.: "The Dartmouth Program for Diagnosis and Remedial Reading with Special Reference to Visual Factors," *Educ. Rec. Suppl.*, vol. 20, supplement 12, January, 1939, pp. 76ff.

Beier, E. B.: "The Effect of Induced Anxiety upon Some Aspects of Intellectual Functioning," thesis, Columbia University, New York, 1949.

Bell, J. E.: *Projective Techniques*, Longmans, Green & Co., Inc., New York, 1948.

Bennett, C. C.: "An Inquiry into the Genesis of Poor Readers," Teachers College Contributions to Education, no. 755, Columbia University, New York, 1935.

Benton, A. L.: "The Minnesota Multiphasic Inventory in Clinical Practice, *J. Nerv. Mental Dis.*, vol. 102, 1945, pp. 416ff.

Berens, C., and M. Enos: "Ocular Factors in Reading Disabilities," *Amer. J. Ortho-psychiat.*, vol. 17, July, 1947, pp. 397ff.

Betts, A.: *The Prevention and Correction of Reading Difficulties,* Row, Peterson & Company, Evanston, Ill., 1936.

————: Paper reported in *Science News Letter,* March 6, 1954, p. 152.

Bevelas, A., and K. Lewin: "Training in Democratic Leadership," *J. abnorm. soc. Psychol.,* vol. 37, no. 1, January, 1942, pp. 115ff.

Bills, R. E.: "Non-Directive Play Therapy with Retarded Readers," *J. consult. Psychol.,* vol. 2, 1950, pp. 140ff.

Birge, H. L.: "Psychosomatic Ophthalmology," *Sight Saving Rev.,* vol. 19, no. 4, Winter, 1949, pp. 202ff.

Bixler, Ray H.: "Treatment of a Reading Problem through Non-Directive Play Therapy," *J. consult. Psychol.,* vol. 9, no. 2, March–April, 1945, pp. 105ff.

Bloom, D. S.: "The 1955 Normative Study of the Tests of General Educational Development," *School Rev.,* March, 1956, pp. 110–124.

Bond, Eva: "Reading and Ninth Grade Achievement," Bureau of Publications Teachers College, Columbia University, New York, 1938.

Boney, C. D.: "Reading—Go Slow," *School Exec.,* vol. 65, September, 1945, pp. 561ff.

Book, W. F., and L. Norvel: "The Will to Learn: an Experimental Study of Incentives in Learning," *Pedagogical Seminary,* vol. 29, 1922, pp. 305ff.

Bordin, E. S.: "Student Personnel Work and Personality Development," *Personnel and Guidance J.,* vol. 33, no. 4, December, 1954, pp. 196ff.

Borow, Henry: The Proper Use of Vocational Information, address before the Annual Convention of NVGA, Chicago, April 5, 1955.

Brown, J. I.: *Efficient Reading,* D. C. Heath and Company, Boston, 1952.

Bruner, J., and L. Postman: "Perception, Cognition and Behavior," *J. Personality,* vol. 18, no. 1, September, 1949, pp. 20ff.

————: "Symbolic Values as an Organizing Factor in Perception," *J. soc. Psychol.,* vol. 27, second half, May, 1948, pp. 203ff.

Capwell, D. F.: "Personality Patterns of Adolescent Girls: I, II," *J. appl. Psychol.,* vol. 29, 1945, pp. 212ff, 289ff.

Carmichael, Leonard, and Walter Dearborn, *Reading and Visual Fatigue,* Houghton Mifflin Company, Boston, 1947.

Carr, H. A.: *Psychology,* Longmans, Green & Co., Inc., New York, 1926.

Cassel, R. N.: "Primary Principles of Learning," *Peabody J. Educ.,* vol. 31, 1954.

Cavanaugh, Lyman A.: "Reading Behavior with Regard for Thyroid Imbalance," *Claremont College Reading Conference Thirteenth Yearbook,* 1948, pp. 98ff.

Champney, Horace: "Parent Behavior as Related to Child Development," paper read to American Association for Advancement of Science, December, 1939.

Clark, B.: "Binocular Anomalies and Reading Ability," *Amer. J. Ophthalmology,* vol. 23, 1950, pp. 885ff.

Corey, S. M.: *Action Research,* Bureau of Publications, Teachers College, Columbia University, New York, 1953.

Cottle, W. C.: "Some Common Elements in Counseling," *Personnel and Guidance J.,* vol. 32, no. 1, September, 1953, pp. 4ff.

Cowen, E. L., and E. G. Beier: "Threat-Expectancy, Word Frequencies, and Perceptual Pre-Recognition Hypothesis," *J. abnorm. and soc. psychol.* vol. 49, 1954, pp. 178ff.

Cunningham, Ruth, et al.: *Understanding Group Behavior of Boys and Girls,* Bureau of Publications, Teachers College, Columbia University, New York, 1951.

Curran, C. A.: "Structuring the Counseling Relationship: A Case Report," *J. abnorm. and soc. Psychol.*, vol. 39, 1944, pp. 189ff.

Danskin, D. G., and F. P. Robinson: "Differences in the 'Degree of Lead' Among Experienced Counselors," *J. Counseling Psychol.*, vol. 1, no. 2, 1954, pp. 78ff.

Darley, J. G.: *Clinical Aspects and Interpretation of the Strong Vocational Interest Blank*, Psychological Corporation, New York, 1941.

Dawe, Helen C.: "Environmental Influences on Language Growth," in Ramond G. Kuhlen and George G. Thompson (eds.) *Psychological Studies of Human Development*, Century Psychol. Series, Appleton-Century-Crofts, Inc., New York, 1952.

Dellone, A.: "Individualized Instruction in Reading," *Baltimore Bull.*, vol. 25, October–November, 1947, pp. 94ff.

Deri, S.: *Introduction to the Szondi Test*, Grune & Stratton, Inc., New York, 1949.

de Weerdt, E. H.: "A Study of Improvability of Fifth Grade School Children in Certain Mental Functions," *J. Educ. Psychol.*, vol. 18, 1947, pp. 547ff.

Deutsch, Morton: "An Experimental Study of the Effects of Cooperation and Competition upon Group Process," *Human Relations*, vol. 2, no. 3, July, 1949, pp. 199ff.

Diven, K.: "Certain Determinants in the Conditioning of Anxiety Reactions," *J. Psychol.*, vol. 3, 1937, pp. 291ff.

Dolch, E. W.: *The Psychology and Teaching of Reading*, Ginn & Company, Boston, 1931.

Dollard, J., and N. E. Miller: *Personality and Psychotherapy*, McGraw-Hill Book Company, Inc., New York, 1950.

Drake, L. E., and W. B. Thierde: "Further Validation of the Social I. E. Scale for the MMPI," *J. Educ. Res.*, vol. 41, 1948, pp. 551ff.

Eames, Thomas H.: "A Frequency Study of Physical Handicaps in Reading Disability and Unselected Groups," *J. Educ. Res.*, vol. 4, April, 1930, pp. 98ff.

———: "The Effect of Glasses for the Correction of Hypermetropia and Myopia on the Speed of Visual Perception of Objects and Words," *J. Educ. Res.*, vol. 42, no. 7, March, 1949, pp. 534ff.

Edmiston, R. W., and C. E. Hollahan: "Measures Predictive of First Grade Achievement," *School and Society*, April 13, 1946, pp. 268ff.

———, M. E. Henlon, and Floyd Raser: "Special Emphasis to Improve Attendance," *J. Educ. Res.*, vol. 41, no. 1, September, 1947, pp. 35ff.

Eels, Kenneth, et al.: *Intelligence and Cultural Differences*, University of Chicago Press, Chicago, 1951.

Ellis, Albert: "Questionnaire versus Interview Methods in the Study of Human Love Relationships," *Amer. Sociolog. Rev.*, vol. 12, 1947, pp. 541ff.

English, Horace B.: *Child Psychology*, Henry Holt and Company, New York, 1951.

Ephron, B. C.: *Emotional Difficulties in Learning*, Julian Press, New York, 1953.

Eriksen, C. W.: "The Case for Perceptual Defense," *Psychol. Rev.*, vol. 61, 1954, pp. 175ff.

Ewers, Dorothea W. F.: "Relations between Auditory Abilities and Reading Abilities: A Problem in Psychometrics," *J. exp. Educ.*, vol. 18, March, 1950, pp. 239ff.

Fey, W. F.: "Acceptance of Self and Others, and Its Relation to Therapy-Readiness," *J. Clin. Psychol.*, vol. 10, 1954, pp. 269ff.

Findley, W. G.: Review in O. K. Buros (ed.), *Mental Measurements Yearbook*, Gryphon Press, Highland Park, N. J., 1953.

Fireman, Peter: *Perceptualistic Theory of Knowledge,* Philosophical Library, Inc., New York, 1954.

Fisher, Bernard: "Group Therapy with Retarded Readers," *J. Educ. Psychol.,* vol. 44, no. 6, October, 1953, pp. 354ff.

Fleming, Louise, and W. W. Snyder: "Social and Personal Changes Following Non-Directive Play Therapy," *Amer. J. Orthopsychiat.,* vol. 17, 1947, pp. 101ff.

Flory, C. D.: "Classroom Teachers Improve the Personality Adjustment of Their Pupils," *J. Educ. Res.,* September, 1944, pp. 1ff.

Fox, J. B., and J. F. Scott: "Absenteeism: Management's Problem," *Bus. Res. Studies,* Harvard University, Cambridge, Mass., no. 29, 1943.

Frank, L. K.: *Feelings and Emotions,* Doubleday Papers in Psychology, Garden City, N. Y., 1954.

Frenkel-Brunswick, Else: "Intolerance of Ambiguity as an Emotional and Perceptual Personality Variable, *J. Personality,* vol. 18, no. 1, September, 1949, pp. 109, 130ff.

Froelich, C., and J. G. Darley: *Studying Students,* Science Research Associates, Chicago, 1952.

Gates, A. I.: "Failure in Reading and Social Maladjustment," *J. National Educ. Ass.,* vol. 25, 1936.

————, and G. A. Taylor: "The Acquisition of Motor Control in Writing by Preschool Children," *Teachers' College Rec.,* vol. 24, 1923, pp. 459ff.

Gibson, J. J.: *The Perception of the Visual World,* Houghton Mifflin Company, Boston, 1950.

Gilbert, G. M.: "The New Status of Experimental Studies on the Relationship of Feeling to Memory," *Psychol. Bull.,* vol. 35, 1938, pp. 124ff.

Gilbert, W. M.: "Training Faculty Counselors at the University of Illinois," in E. G. Williamson (ed.), *Trends in Student Personnel Work,* University of Minnesota Press, Minneapolis, 1949.

Glock, Marvin D.: *The Improvement of College Reading,* Houghton Mifflin Company, Boston, 1954.

Graham, A. B., and J. L. Hill: Report to American Academy of General Practice, *Science News Letter,* April, 16, 1955, p. 249.

Gray, William S., *On Their Own in Reading,* Scott, Foresman and Company, Chicago, 1948.

————, et al.: "Reading," *Rev. Educ. Res.,* vol. 7, December, 1937, pp. 505ff.

Greenberg, P. J.: "Competition in Children: An Experimental Study," *Amer. J. Psychol.,* vol. 44, 1932, pp. 221–248.

Greenspoon, J.: "The Effect of Verbal and Mechanical Stimuli on Verbal Behavior," quoted in Ruch, Floyd, *Psychology and Life,* Scott, Foresman and Company, Chicago, 1948.

Haire, M.: "Some Problems of Industrial Training," *J. Soc. Issues,* vol. 4, 1948, pp. 41ff.

Halbower, Charles: "A Study of Differences in Personality, Intelligence, and Scholastic Achievement between Sorority and Unaffiliated Women," thesis, Kansas State College, Manhattan, Kans., 1949.

Hamrin, Shirley: *Chats with Teachers about Counseling,* McKnight & McKnight Publishing Company, Bloomington, Ill., 1950.

Hanawalt, N. G.: Comment in O. K. Buros (ed.), *Fourth Mental Measurements Yearbook,* Gryphon Press, Highland Park, N. J., 1953, p. 29.

Hanlon, T. E., et al.: "Congruence of Self and Ideal Self in Relation to Personality Adjustment," *J. consult. Psychol.,* vol. 18, 1954, pp. 215ff.

Hardwick, R. S.: "Types of Reading Disability," *Childhood Educ.*, vol. 8, 1932, pp. 425ff.

Harris, A. J.: *How to Increase Reading Ability*, Longmans, Green & Co., Inc., New York, 1940.

————: "Motivating the Poor Reader," *Educ.*, vol. 73, May, 1953, pp. 566ff.

Harris, R. M.: "How Well Do You Read?" in James I. Brown, *Efficient Reading*, D. C. Heath and Company, Boston, 1952.

Hathaway, S. R., and J. C. McKinley: Manual, Minnesota Multiphasic Personality Inventory, Psychological Corporation, New York, 1951.

Hathaway, S. R., and P. E. Meehl: *An Atlas for the Clinical Use of the MMPI*, University of Minnesota Press, Minneapolis, 1951.

Havens, Virginia: "A Prediction of Law School Achievement from High School Rank, Reading Test Scores, Psychological Test Scores, and Average Grades in Pre-Law Courses," *J. Educ. Psychol.*, vol. 34, April, 1948, pp. 237ff.

Hendry, C. E.: *A Decade of Group Work*, Association Press, New York, 1948.

Hildreth, Gertrude: "Interrelationships among the Language Arts," *Elem. Sch. J.*, vol. 47, June, 1948, pp. 538ff.

Hiltner, Seward: *The Counselor in Counseling*, Abingdon Press, Nashville, Tenn., pp. 46ff.

Hoffman, R. E.: "How Motivation Influences Student Learning," *USAF ATC Instructors J.*, vol. 5, 1954, pp. 64ff.

Horrocks, W. B.: "A Sociometric and Psychometric Analysis of Results of Optimalizing Classroom Interpersonal Relationships," dissertation, Ohio State University, Columbus, 1949.

Hoyt, Donald: "Measurement and Prediction of Permanence of Interests," pending publication in W. L. Layton (ed.), *Counseling Use of the Strong Vocational Interest Blank*, University of Minnesota Press, Minneapolis, 1954.

Hoyt, D. P., and Warren T. Norman: "Adjustment and Academic Predictability," *J. Couns. Psychol.*, vol. 1, no. 2, 1954, pp. 96ff.

Hutchins, Robert: "Are Our Teachers Afraid to Teach?" *Look Magazine*, March 9, 1954.

Jackson, Joseph: "The Relative Effectiveness of Paper and Pencil Test, Interview, and Rating as Techniques for Personality Evaluation," *J. soc. Psychol.*, vol. 23, 1946, pp. 35ff.

Jenkins, D. H.: "Research in Group Dynamics," *Soc. Educ.*, vol. 12, no. 8, December, 1948, pp. 347ff.

Jensen, M. B.: "Reading Deficiency as Related to Cerebral Injury and to Neurotic Behavior," *J. appl. Psychol.*, vol. 27, December, 1943, pp. 535ff.

Johanson, A. M.: "The Influence of Incentives and Punishment upon Reaction Time," *Arch. Psychol.*, vol. 8, 1922, whole no. 54.

Johnson, M. W.: *Verbal Influences on Children's Behavior*, University of Michigan Monograph in Education, University of Michigan Press, Ann Arbor, Mich., 1939.

Johnson, W.: *People in Quandaries*, Harper & Brothers, New York, 1946.

Jones, Daisy M.: "An Experiment in Adaptation to Individual Differences," *J. Educ. Psychol.*, vol. 34, May, 1948, pp. 257ff.

Jones, E. L.: *An Approach to College Reading*, Henry Holt and Company, Inc., New York, 1953.

Jones, L.: "Frustration and Stereotyped Behavior in Human Subjects," *Quart. J. exp. Psychol.*, vol. 6, 1954, pp. 12ff.

Joslin, Ethel S.: "Physical Factors in Reading," *Columbia Optometrist,* vol. 22, December, 1949, pp. 6ff; February, 1950, pp. 5ff.

Kaplan, Louis: "The Annoyances of Elementary School Teachers," *J. Educ. Res.,* May, 1952, pp. 649ff.

Keister, M. E.: "The Behavior of Young Children in Failure," *University of Iowa Studies in Child Welfare,* vol. 14, 1938, pp. 27–83.

———, and R. Updegraf: "A Study of Children's Reactions to Failure and Experimental Attempt to Modify Them," *Child Development Monograph,* vol. 8, 1937, pp. 241–248.

Kelley, E. C.: "Human Values in the Workshop Technique," *Adult Leadership,* vol. 3, no. 2, June, 1954, pp. 4ff.

Klein, M.: "A Contribution to the Theory of Intellectual Inhibition," *Intern. J. Psychoanal.,* vol. 12, 1931.

Korchin, S. J., J. L. Singer, and R. G. Ballard: "The Influence of Frustration on the Reproduction of Visually Perceived Forms," *Personality,* vol. 1, no. 1, January, 1951, pp. 54ff.

Kottmeyer, William: "Readiness for Reading," *Elem. Engl.,* vol. 24, October, 1947, pp. 355ff.

Lecky, P.: *Self-Consistency, A Theory of Personality,* Island Press Co-operative, Inc., New York, 1945.

Leichty, Dr. M.: Report to Midwestern Psychological Association, reported in *Science News Letter,* May 8, 1954, p. 292.

Leuba, C. J.: "An Experimental Study of Rivalry in Young Children," *J. comp. Psychol.,* vol. 16, 1933, pp. 367ff.

Leuba, C. J.: "An Evaluation of the Bell Adjustment Inventory at Antioch," unpublished, Antioch College, Yellow Springs, Ohio.

Levy, D. M.: "Primary Affect Hunger," *Amer. J. Psychiat.,* vol. 94, 1937, pp. 643ff.

Lewin, K.: *A Dynamic Theory of Personality,* McGraw-Hill Book Company, Inc., New York, 1935.

———: "Group Decision and Social Change," in Newcomb and Hartley (eds.), *Readings in Social Psychology,* Henry Holt and Company, Inc., New York, 1947, pp. 330ff.

———, R. Lippitt, and R. K. White: "Patterns of Aggressive Behavior in Experimentally Created Social Climates," *J. soc. Psychol.,* vol. 10, 1939, pp. 298ff.

Lewis, Norman: *How to Read Better and Faster,* Thomas Y. Crowell Company, New York, 1951.

Lifton, W. M.: "The Teacher's Role in Mental Hygiene, Therapy, and Social Reconstruction," *Prog. Educ.,* May, 1955, pp. 67ff.

Lorge, I., and E. L. Thorndike: "The Influence of Delay in the After-Effect of a Connection," *J. exp. Psychol.,* vol. 13, 1935, pp. 186ff.

Lough, O. M.: "Teachers College Students and the Minnesota Multiphasic Personality Inventory," *J. appl. Psychol.,* vol. 30, 1946, pp. 241ff.

———: "Women Students in Liberal Arts, Nursing and Teaching Training Curricula and the Minnesota Multiphasic Personality Inventory," *J. appl. Psychol.,* vol. 31, 1947, pp. 437ff.

Lown, Wilfred: "The Relationship between Claimed Problems of College Freshmen and Problems as Indicated by Objective Tests," unpublished thesis, Kansas State College, Manhattan, Kans. 1948.

Lyons, C. F., and E. B. Lyons: "The Power of Visual Training," *J. Amer. Optometric Ass.,* December, 1954, pp. 256ff.

Lysak, W.: "The Effects of Punishment upon Syllable Recognition Thresholds," *J. Exp. Psychol.*, vol. 47, 1954, pp. 343ff.

McClelland, D. C., and A. M. Liberman: "The Effect of Need for Achievement on Recognition of Need Related Words," *J. Personality*, vol. 18, no. 2, December, 1949, pp. 236ff.

McClelland, F. M., and J. A. Ratliff: "The Use of Sociometry as an Aid in Promoting Social Adjustment in a Ninth Grade Home Room," *Sociometry*, vol. 10, no. 2, May, 1947.

McGinnies, E., and W. Bowles: "Personal Values as Determinants of Perceptual Fixation," *J. Personality*, vol. 18, no. 2, December, 1949, pp. 224ff.

Machover, K.: "Drawing of the Human Figure: A Method of Personality Investigation," in H. Anderson and G. Anderson (eds.), *An Introduction to Projective Techniques*, Prentice-Hall, Inc., Englewood Cliffs, N. J., 1951.

McKillop, A. S.: "The Relationship between the Reader's Attitudes and Certain Types of Reading Response," dissertation, University of Michigan Microfilm, Publication no. 2543, Ann Arbor, Mich., 1951.

McKinley, J. C., and S. R. Hathaway: "A Multiphasic Personality Schedule: II. A Differential Study of Hypochondriasis," *J. Psychol.*, vol. 10, 1940, pp. 255ff.

McKinney, F.: "Personality Adjustment of Students as Related to Factors in Personal History," *J. appl. Psychol.*, vol. 23, 1939, pp. 660ff.

MacLean, Malcolm: "A Multi-Sensory Approach to Reading," *Claremont College Reading Conference Yearbook*, 1948, pp. 103ff.

Maier, N. R. F.: "The Quality of Group Decision as Influenced by the Discussion Leader," *Human Relat.*, vol. 3, 1950, pp. 155ff.

————: *Frustration*, McGraw-Hill Book Company, Inc., New York, 1949.

Marsh, Charles J.: "The Diagnostic Value of the Bell Adjustment Inventory for College Women," *J. soc. Psychol.*, vol. 17, February, 1943, pp. 103ff.

Maslow, A. H.: *Motivation and Personality*, Harper & Brothers, New York, 1954.

Meek, L. H.: "Behavior Problems in the School," *Teachers Coll. Rec.*, vol. 37, January, 1936, pp. 300ff.

Merrill, M. A.: *Problems of Child Delinquency*, Houghton Mifflin Company, Boston, 1947.

Meyers, C. E.: "The Effects of Conflicting Authority on the Child," in Lewin, et al., *Authority and Frustration*, Department of Publications, State University of Iowa, Iowa City, Iowa, 1944.

Morris, W. W.: "Other Projective Methods," in H. Anderson and G. Anderson (eds.), *Introduction to Projective Techniques*, Prentice-Hall Inc., Englewood Cliffs, N. J., 1951.

Morrison, Donald: "Visual Skills and Visual Training," *Claremont College Reading Conference Thirteenth Yearbook*, 1948, pp. 62ff.

Muller-Eckhard, Hans: "Contribution to the Pheno-Analysis of the Obsessive-Compulsive Neurosis," *Psyche. Heidel.*, vol. 8, 1954, pp. 143ff.

Murphy, Gardner: *Personality: A Biosocial Approach to Origins and Structures*, Harper & Brothers, New York, 1947.

Myers, C. R.: *Toward Mental Health in School*, University of Toronto Press, Toronto, Canada, 1939.

National Committee on Reading, *Twenty-Fourth Yearbook of the National Society for the Study of Education*, Public School Publishing Company, Bloomington, Ill., 1925, pp. 4ff.

Neidt, C. O., and L. D. Edmison: "Qualification Responses Used with Paired Statements to Measure Attitudes toward Education," *J. Educ. Psychol.*, vol. 44, no. 5, May, 1953, pp. 305ff.

Nelson, Patricia: "Changes in Attitudes, Values, and Personality Adjustment after Two Years of College Experience," unpublished study, Kansas State College, Manhattan, Kans., 1951.

Park, George E.: "Reading Difficulty (Dyslexia) from the Ophthalmic Point of View," *Amer. J. Ophthmal.*, vol. 31, January, 1948, pp. 28ff.

Patrick, J. K.: "Studies in Rational Behavior and Emotional Excitement: II, The Effect of Emotional Excitement on Rational Behavior and Human Subjects," *J. comp. Psychol.*, 1934, vol. 18, pp. 153ff.

Pederson, R. A.: "Validity of the Bell Adjustment Inventory When Applied to College Women," *J. Psychol.*, vol. 9, 1940, pp. 227ff.

Pepinsky, H., and P. Pepinsky: *Counseling: Theory and Practice*, The Ronald Press Company, New York, 1954.

Percival, W. P.: "A Study of the Courses and Subjects of School Failure," doctoral dissertation, Teachers College, Columbia University, New York, 1926.

Perkins, H. V.: "Climate Influences Group Learning," *J. Educ. Res.*, vol. 45, no. 2, October, 1951, pp. 117ff.

Pflieger, E. F.: "A Study of Reading Grade Levels," *J. Educ. Res.*, vol. 42, no. 7, pp. 541ff.

Phillips, Don: "Basic Needs of People in Groups," mimeographed, Hillsdale College, Hillsdale, Michigan.

Pollack, T. C., and W. D. Baker: *The University Spelling Book*, Prentice-Hall, Inc., Englewood Cliffs, N. J., 1955.

Rapaport, David: *Diagnostic Psychological Testing*, Year Book Publishers, Inc., Chicago, 1948.

Redl, F.: "Resistance in Therapy Groups," *Human Relat.*, vol. 1, no. 3, 1948, pp. 307ff.

Remmers, H. H., and N. L. Gage: *Educational Measurements and Evaluation*, Harper & Brothers, New York, 1943, 1955.

Ribble, Margaret: *The Rights of Infants*, Columbia University Press, New York, 1934.

Rich, G. J.: "Childhood as Preparation for Delinquency," *J. Educ. Sociol.*, vol. 27, 1954, pp. 404ff.

Robinson, Helen M.: *Why Pupils Fail in Reading*, University of Chicago Press, Chicago, 1946.

Roethlisberger, F. J., and W. J. Dickson: *Management and the Worker*, Harvard University Press, Cambridge, Mass., 1939.

Rogers, Carl: *Client-Centered Therapy*, Houghton Mifflin Company, Boston, 1951.

————: *Counseling and Psychotherapy*, Houghton Mifflin Company, Boston, 1942.

————, and Rosalind F. Dymond (eds.): *Psychotherapy and Personality Change*, University of Chicago Press, Chicago, 1954.

————, et al.: *Studies in Client-Centered Psychotherapy*, Psychological Service Center Press, 1275 New Hampshire Ave., N. W., Washington 6, D. C., 1951.

Romaine, Hunter: "Reading Difficulties and Eye Defects," *Sight Saving Rev.*, vol. 19, no. 2, pp. 98ff.

Ruch, F. L.: *Psychology and Life*, Scott, Foresman and Company, New York, 1948.

Russell, D. H.: "Unsolved Problems in Reading, A Symposium," *Elem. Engl.*, vol. 31, October-November, 1954, pp. 325ff, 416ff.

Sanchez-Hidalgo, Efrain: "Youth the School, and the Contemporary World," *Pedagogia*, vol. 1, 1953, pp. 7ff.

Schwidder, Werner: "Symptom Picture, Basic Structure and Therapy of the Obsessive-Compulsive Neurosis," *Psyche. Heidel.*, vol. 8, 1954, pp. 126ff.

Schafer, Roy: *Clinical Application of Psychological Tests,* International Universities Press, New York, 1948.

Schlessor, G. E., and C. W. Younge: "Study and Work Habits," *Sch. Rev.*, vol. 53, February, 1945, pp. 85ff.

Schrupp, M. H., and C. M. Gjerde: "Teachers Growth in Attitudes toward Behavior Problems of Children," *J. Educ. Psychol.*, November, 1953, pp. 203ff.

Scott, Carrie M.: "An Evaluation of Training in Readiness Classes," *Elem. Sch. J.*, vol. 48, September, 1947, pp. 26ff.

Sears, P. S.: "Levels of Aspiration in Academically Successful and Unsuccessful Children," *J. abnorm. and soc. Psychol.*, vol. 35, 1940, pp. 498ff.

Shaffer, L. F.: *Psychology of Adjustment,* Houghton Mifflin Company, Boston, 1948.

Shaffer, R. H.: "English Deficiency and Social Adjustment," *J. Higher Educ.*, vol. 20, October, 1949, pp. 373ff.

Shaw, P. B.: *Effective Reading and Learning,* Thomas Y. Crowell Company, New York, 1955.

Siegel, M. G.: "The Diagnostic and Prognostic Validity of the Rorschach Test in a Child Guidance Clinic," *Amer. J. Orthopsychiat.*, vol. 18, 1948, pp. 119ff.

Siegel, S.: "Certain Determinants and Correlates of Authoritarianism," *Genet. Psychol. Monogr.*, vol. 49, 1954, pp. 187ff.

Sloan, W., and W. H. Guertin: "A Comparison of H-T-P and Wechsler-Bellevue IQ's in Mental Defectives," *J. Clin. Psychol.*, vol. 4, 1948, pp. 424ff.

Smith, H. P., and T. R. Tate: "Improvement in Reading Rate and Comprehension of Subjects Training with the Tachistoscope," *J. Educ. Psychol.*, vol. 44, no. 3, March, 1943.

Smith, J. G.: "Influence of Failure, Expressed Hostility and Stimulus Characteristics on Verbal Learning and Recognition," *J. Personality*, vol. 22, 1954, pp. 475ff.

Snygg, Donald, and A. W. Combs: *Individual Behavior,* Harper & Brothers, New York, 1949.

Stordahl, K. E.: "Permanence of Interest and Interest Maturity," *J. appl. Psychol.*, vol. 38, 1954, pp. 339ff., 423ff.

Strachey, J.: "Some Unconscious Factors in Reading," *Intern. J. Psychoan.*, vol. 11, 1930.

Strong, E. K.: *Vocational Interests of Men and Women,* Stanford University Press, Stanford, Calif., 1953.

Stroud, J. B.: *Psychology in Education,* Longmans, Green, & Co., Inc., New York, 1946.

Super, Donald: *Appraising Vocational Fitness,* Harper & Brothers, New York, 1949.

Super, D. E., and H. P. Moser: "Relationships between Interest Maturity in Ninth Grade and Other Indices," Bureau of Publications Teachers College, Columbia University, New York.

Thelen, H. A.: *Dynamics of Groups at Work,* University of Chicago Press, Chicago, 1954.

Thorndike, E. L.: *Human Learning,* Appleton-Century-Crofts, Inc., 1931.

Thorne, F. C.: "Directive Psychotherapy," *J. Clin. Psychol.*, vol. 1, no. 2, April, 1946, pp. 378ff.

Thurstone, L. L.: *A Factorial Study of Perception,* University of Chicago Press, Chicago, 1944.

Tiegs, E. W.: Diagnosis in the Reading Program, Bulletin no. 10, California Test Bureau, 1951.

————: Educational Diagnosis, California Test Bureau, 1951.

————: *Tests and Measurements in the Improvement of Learning,* Houghton Mifflin Company, Boston, 1939.

Torrance, E. P.: "Methods of Conducting Critiques of Group Problem-Solving Performance," *J. appl. Psychol,* vol. 37, no. 5, 1953, pp. 394ff.

————: "Perception of Group Functioning as a Predictor of Group Performance," *Research Studies of the State of Washington,* vol. 21, no. 3, September, 1953, pp. 262ff.

————: "The Phenomenon of Resistance in Learning," *J. abnorm. and soc. Psychol.,* vol. 45, no. 4, October, 1950.

————: "The Behavior of Small Groups under Conditions of Survival," *Amer. Sociolog. Rev.,* vol. 19, no. 6, December, 1954, pp. 752ff.

————: Summary Counseling Bureau Studies Completed between September, 1950, and June 1, 1951, Kansas State College, Manhattan, Kans, 1951.

————: Summary Research, Counseling Bureau, 1945–1950, Kansas State College, Manhattan, Kans., 1950.

Traxler, Arthur E.: "Research in Reading in the United States," *J. Educ. Res.,* vol. 42, no. 7, March, 1949, pp. 496ff.

Tulchin, S. H.: "Emotional Factors in Reading Disabilities in School Children," *J. Educ. Psychol.,* vol. 26, 1935, pp. 444ff.

Tyler, H. T.: "Evaluating the Bell Adjustment Inventory," *Junior Coll. J.,* vol. 6, 1936, pp. 353ff.

Ullman, Shirley: "A Comparative Study of Reading Rate Controllers Technique Versus the Speeded Book Reading Technique for Reading Improvement on the College Level, dissertation, New York University, New York Publication no. 2515, 1950.

Vanderplan, J. M., and R. R. Blake: "Selective Sensitization in Auditory Perception," *J. Personality,* vol. 18, no. 2, 1949, pp. 252ff.

Van Steenberg, Neil: Review in O. K. Buros (ed.), *Fourth Mental Measurements Yearbook,* Gryphon Press, Highland Park, N. J., 1953, p. 50.

Vorhaus, P. G.: "Non-Reading as an Expression of Resistance," *Rorschach Res. Exch.,* vol. 10, 1946, pp. 60ff.

————: "Rorschach Configurations Associated with Reading Disability," *J. Proj. Tech.,* vol. 16, 1952, pp. 3ff.

Waters, R. H.: "The Influence of Large Amounts of Manual Guidance upon Human Maze Learning," *J. gen. Psychol.,* vol. 4, 1930, pp. 213ff.

Watson, G. B.: "Comparison of the Effects of Lax versus Strict Home Training," *J. soc. Psychol.,* vol. 5, 1934, pp. 102ff.

Watson, J. B.: "Do Groups Think More Efficiently than Individuals?" *J. abnorm. and soc. Psychol.,* vol. 23, 1928, pp. 328ff.

Watt, G. D.: "An Evaluation of Non-Directive Counseling in the Treatment of Delinquents," *J. Educ. Res.,* vol. 42, no. 5, January, 1949, pp. 343ff.

Watts, Phyllis: "Application of Clinical Diagnostic Techniques in the Classroom Situation for the Improvement of Reading at the College Level," *J. Educ. Res.,* vol. 42, no. 7, March, 1949, pp. 513ff.

West, W. E.: The Effectiveness of Certain Remedial Procedures as They Influence Reading Performance and Personality Adjustment, thesis, Kansas State College, Manhattan, Kans., 1947.

Wheeler, L. R., and V. D. Wheeler: "A Study of the Relationship of Auditory Discrimination to Silent Reading Abilities," *J. Educ. Res.*, vol. 47, no. 2, October, 1954, pp. 103ff.

Wheeler, R. H.: *The Science of Psychology*, Thomas Y. Crowell Company, New York, 1929.

Whittemore, I. C.: "The Influence of Competition on Performance," *J. abnorm. and soc. Psychol.*, vol. 23, 1924, pp. 236ff.

Williamson, E. G.: *Counseling Adolescents*, McGraw-Hill Book Company, Inc., New York, 1950.

——, and J. G. Darley: *Student Personnel Work*, McGraw-Hill Book Company, Inc., New York, 1937.

Wise, J. H., J. E. Congleton, and A. C. Morris: *The Meaning in Reading*, Harcourt, Brace and Company, Inc., New York, 1953.

Witty, P., and D. Kopel: *Reading the Educative Process*, Ginn & Company, Boston, 1939.

Wolf, T.: "The Effect of Praise and Competition on the Persisting Behavior of Kindergarten Children," University of Minnesota Child Welfare Monograph, Minneapolis, no. 15, 1938.

Woolf, M. D.: Annual Reports, Kansas State College, Manhattan, Kans., 1952–1955.

——: "A Study of Some Relationships between Home Adjustment and the Behavior of Junior College Students," *J. soc. Psychol.*, vol. 17, 1943, pp. 275ff.

——, and J. A. Woolf: "Is Interest Maturity Related to Linguistic Development?" *J. appl. Psychol.*, vol. 39, no. 6, December, 1955, pp. 413–415.

——: *The Student Personnel Program*, McGraw-Hill Book Company, Inc., New York, 1953.

——: "The Case of the Tired Readers," *Personnel and Guidance J.*, vol. 33, January, 1955, pp. 294ff.

Wren, C. G., and R. P. Larsen: *Studying Effectively*, Stanford University Press, Stanford Calif., 1949.

Name Index

Subject Index